BODIES ON THE VERGE

SEMEIA STUDIES

Steed V. Davidson, General Editor

Number 93

BODIES ON THE VERGE

Queering Pauline Epistles

Edited by

Joseph A. Marchal

SBL PRESS

 **PRESS**

Atlanta

Copyright © 2019 by Society of Biblical Literature

Library of Congress Cataloging-in-Publication Data

Names: Marchal, Joseph A., editor.
Title: Bodies on the verge : queering Pauline Epistles / edited by Joseph A. Marchal.
Description: Atlanta : SBL Press, 2019. | Series: Semeia studies ; number 93 | Includes bibliographical references and index.
Identifiers: LCCN 2019000477 (print) | LCCN 2019005544 (ebook) | ISBN 9780884143352 (ebk.) | ISBN 9781628372250 (pbk. : alk. paper) | ISBN 9780884143345 (hbk. : alk. paper)
Subjects: LCSH: Bible. Epistles of Paul—Criticism, interpretation, etc.. | Sex in the Bible. | Queer theology.
Classification: LCC BS2655.S49 (ebook) | LCC BS2655.S49 B63 2019 (print) | DDC 227/.06—dc23
LC record available at https://lccn.loc.gov/2019000477

Printed on acid-free paper.

Contents

Responses

Acknowledgments

The inspirations for this collection, of multiple kinds of bodies, are frankly too many to name. The contents to follow often acknowledge their intellectual, ethical, and spiritual debts, but here I endeavor foolishly to name at least some of the forces that helped us to deliver this book to you.

One of the theses of this collection is that queer forms of interpretation, analysis, expression, or simply use are reaching a tipping point, even a critical mass in biblical studies, and specifically within the study of Pauline epistles and interpretations. You can increasingly see this reflected in conferences, seminars, and symposia. Indeed, a majority of the fabulous essays to follow originated as conference papers at the Annual Meeting of the Society of the Biblical Literature, particularly in special themed sessions of the Paul and Politics and the LGBTI/Queer Hermeneutics units. Therefore, we owe a special note of thanks to the steering committees of both units and to the chairs in particular—Lynn Huber, David Tabb Stewart, and Diana Swancutt—who coorganized these sessions with me and then graciously allowed me to take the lead on editing this collection. Of course, such work is only possible when scholars are willing to innovate, to push and experiment, to extend themselves and the work that still predominantly disciplines approaches to Pauline epistles and interpretations. This is an understated description of the fabulous collection of colleagues whose work is represented in this book. As always, it is humbling to have colleagues trust you with their work, and I remain forever in your debt that each of you agreed to work with me on this collection and graciously accepted me as your editor and collaborator (often in multiple senses).

To be a little less than humble for a moment, though, I would venture to say that the best programs and sites of study in our fields are precisely those that make this work possible. The contributors to this volume come out of such programs and communities, and students and scholars would do well to pay attention to where cutting edge work is happening if they want to make such contributions to our world. The samples of scholarship gathered here are theoretically informed, ethically accountable, and politically reflexive for a reason. Beyond the circles of support and engagement that we have managed to carve out at otherwise disorienting and often dehumanizing meetings, it is important to note that a few of these essays began as papers in graduate seminars run by colleagues at Drew University, particularly Melanie Johnson-DeBaufre and Stephen D. Moore. Indeed, there are places where this work is not marginalized. Still, it is fair to say that several of us have experienced forms of marginalization— we have been pushed around, but not exactly out. Given the conditions of academic labor in the early twenty-first century, I cannot help but think of colleagues who have stepped away, often because they have been pushed out. Many of them showed kindness, provided support, or simply inspired my work and the work of the contributors to this collection. At the moment, I am thinking of Holly Hearon, David Hester, Todd Penner, Lori Rowlett, and Holly Toensing, but because professionalization ostensibly forces a kind of forgetfulness, I know even these acknowledgments of debts are incomplete and inadequate. For now I call these up as one woeful gesture to point us toward all those bodies who have been marginalized, pushed around and down and out, within and beyond our guilds, and to articulate why interpretation should focus more on stigmatization, minoritization, exclusion, and normalization.

Semeia Studies has historically done its part in publishing scholarship in these directions; its catalogue remains an indispensible reading list for what biblical studies at its best is and still might be. It is an honor to add our voices to this series, and we cannot wait to see where else Semeia Studies might go. Many of the essays in this collection went in much better and clearer directions because of the constructive feedback provided by the series board. In that vein we owe an especially strong note of thanks to Denise Kimber Buell and the series editor Steed Davidson for their tireless yet incisive attention to these essays and the collection as a whole. This would not have happened without you, and you made my job as editor easier, minimizing any remaining faults or infelicities within the pages to follow. As always, it remains a pleasure to work with the entire team at SBL Press. Bob Buller, Heather McMurray, Nicole Tilford, Kathie Klein, and their team have once again capably shepherded this project through its final stages and into production.

But in closing I return to specifically acknowledging two groups of people to whom this collection is dedicated. First, this volume is dedicated to those committed scholars who contributed to this collection. It is easier to promote, celebrate, and sing the praises of a project when it involves such wonderful people and perspectives in creating these fabulous bodies. Second, this volume is dedicated to those bodies that are on the line in the use of these texts and traditions. It is no secret that people have done some of the worst things to each other while claiming to be following scriptural mandates, precedents, and examples, most especially (though not only) from Pauline epistles. It is my genuine hope that the kind of work done here and in other, interconnected settings show that we are more than on the verge, past the tipping point, and reaching a critical mass for transforming the conditions for such bodies, and learning how to name, resist, undo, and create alternatives to these dynamics.

Joseph A. Marchal

Abbreviations

Primary Sources

Abr.	Philo, *De Abrahamo*
Acts Paul	Acts of Paul
Aff. dig.	Galen, *De propriorum animi cuiuslibet affectuum dignotione et curatione*
Ann.	Tacitus, *Annales*
Ant. rom.	Dionysius of Halicarnassus, *Antiquitates romanae*
Carm.	Horace, *Carmina*
Clem.	Seneca, *De clementia*
Conf.	Philo, *De confusion linguarum*
Cyr.	Xenophon, *Cyropaedia*
Dig.	Digesta seu Pandectae
Geogr.	Strabo, *Geographica*
Gos. Thom.	Gospel of Thomas
Her.	Philo, *Quis rerum divinarum heres sit*
Hist. Rom.	Cassius Dio, *Historia Romana*; Livy, *Historia Romanorum*
Inst.	Gaius, *Institutiones*; Quintillian, *Institutio oratoria*
Jdt	Judith
Leg.	Plato, *Leges*
2 Macc	2 Maccabees
3 Macc	3 Maccabees
Od.	Homer, *Odyssey*
Pass. Perp.	Passion of Perpetua
Pol.	Aristotle, *Politicus*
Prot. Jas.	Protevangelium of James
QE	Philo, *Quaestiones et solutions in Exodum*
Quaest. conv.	Plutarch, *Quaestionum convivialum libri IX*
Res. gest. divi Aug.	Res Gestae Divi Augusti

Saec.	Horace, *Carmen saeculare*
Vit. Ant.	Plutarch, *Vita Antonius*

Secondary Sources

AB	Anchor Bible
AcBib	Academia Biblica
AGSU	Arbeiten zur Geschichte des Spätjudentums und Urchristentums
AJP	*American Journal of Philology*
AJSR	*Association for Jewish Studies Review*
ANIMA	ANIMA: Critical Race Studies Otherwise
ANTC	Abingdon New Testament Commentary
ASN	American Studies Now: Critical Histories of the Present
BASOR	*Bulletin of the American Schools of Oriental Research*
BCS	Bible and Cultural Studies
BCT	*Bible and Critical Theory*
BibInt	*Biblical Interpretation*
BibInt	Biblical Interpretation Series
BibLim	Biblical Limits
BICS	*Bulletin of the Institute of Classical Studies*
BMW	Bible in the Modern World
BP	Bible and Postcolonialism
BRPBI	*Brill Research Perspectives in Biblical Interpretation*
BR/WT/SJ	Black Religion/Womanist Thought/Social Justice
CAS	Critical American Studies
CBH	Collection Bibliothèque des Histoires
CBQ	*Catholic Biblical Quarterly*
CCT	Controversies in Contextual Theology
CF	Cultural Front
CI	*Critical Inquiry*
CJ	*Classical Journal*
CM/MI	Classical Memories/Modern Identities
CMP	Cultural Memory in the Present
Colloq	*Colloquium*
Contraversions	Contraversions: Critical Studies in Jewish Literature, Culture, and Society
CR	*CR: The New Centennial Review*

CRR	*Critical Research on Religion*
CSA	Cultural Studies of the Americas
CSSHS	Chicago Series on Sexuality, History, and Society
CultAnth	*Cultural Anthropology*
CultRel	*Culture and Religion*
dif	*differences: A Journal of Feminist Cultural Studies*
Div	Divinations: Rereading Late Ancient Religion
ECL	Early Christianity and Its Literature
EvT	*Evangelische Theologie*
GPBS	Global Perspectives on Biblical Scholarship
GLQ	*GLQ: A Journal of Lesbian and Gay Studies*
GTR	Gender, Theory, and Religion
HCS	Hellenistic Culture and Society
HistTh	*History and Theory*
HTR	*Harvard Theological Review*
HTS	Harvard Theological Studies
HUT	Hermeneutische Untersuchungen zur Theologie
IBC	Interpretation: A Bible Commentary for Teaching and Preaching
IG	*Inscriptiones graecae: Editio minor* Berlin: de Gruyter, 1924–
Int	Interpretation
Int	*Interpretation*
Intersections	Intersections: Asian and Pacific American Transcultural Studies
JAAR	*Journal of the American Academy of Religion*
JBL	*Journal of Biblical Literature*
JECH	*Journal of Early Christian History*
JESWTR	*Journal of the European Society of Women in Theological Research*
JFSR	*Journal of Feminist Studies in Religion*
JH	*Journal of Homosexuality*
JHFCB	A John Hope Franklin Center Book
JRS	*Journal of Roman Studies*
JSB	Jewish Study Bible
JSH	*Journal of Social History*
JSNT	*Journal for the Study of the New Testament*
JSNTSup	Journal for the Study of the New Testament Supplement Series

KJV	King James Version
LAO	Latin America Otherwise: Languages, Empires, Nations
Lat	*Latomus*
LCBI	Literary Currents in Biblical Interpretation
LCL	Loeb Classical Library
LD	*Lectio Difficilior*
LNTS	Library of New Testament Studies
LSJ	Liddell, H. G., R. Scott, H. S. Jones, *A Greek-English Lexicon*. 9th ed. With revised supplement. Oxford, 1996.
LXX	Septuagint
MCA	Meridian: Crossing Aesthetics
NAW	New Ancient World
NBf	*New Blackfriars*
Neot	*Neotestamentica*
NIGTC	New International Greek Testament Commentary
NIV	New International Version
NovTSup	Novum Testamentum Supplement Series
NRSV	New Revised Standard Version
NTS	*New Testament Studies*
NW	Next Wave: New Directions in Women's Studies
OB	October Books
OBT	Overtures to Biblical Theology
PCC	Paul in Critical Contexts
PCHMA	Print Culture History in Modern America
PCI	Post-Contemporary Interventions
PGNT	Phoenix Guides to the New Testament
PKNT 2	Papyrologische Kommentare zum Neuen Testament Band 2
PM	Perverse Modernities
PMLA	*Proceedings of the Modern Language Association*
PP	*Past and Present*
PSMA	Politics and Society in Modern America
RA	Rewriting Antiquity
RAC	Race and American Culture
RCRFA	*Rei Cretariae Romanae Fautorum Acta*
RelAmer	*Religion and American Culture: A Journal of Interpretation*

RelArts	*Religion and the Arts*
RelGen	*Religion and Gender*
RSV	Revised Standard Version
RT	Radical Theologies
RTHC	Romans through History and Cultures
SAQ	*South Atlantic Quarterly*
SBLDS	Society of Biblical Literature Dissertation Series
SemeiaSt	Semeia Studies
SerQ	Series Q
Signs	*Signs: Journal of Women in Culture and Society*
SNTSMS	Society for New Testament Studies Monograph Series
SNTW	Studies of the New Testament and Its World
SocAn	*Society and Animals*
SocT	*Social Text*
Syn	*Synkrisis: Comparative Approaches to Early Christianity in Greco-Roman Culture*
TG	Thinking Gender
ThQ	Theory Q
ThS	*Theology and Sexuality*
ThTo	*Theology Today*
TSAJ	Texte und Studien zum antiken Judentum
TTC	Transdisciplinary Theological Colloquia
UCLF	*University of Chicago Legal Forum*
USQR	*Union Seminary Quarterly Review*
VLR	*Virginia Law Review*
WBC	Word Biblical Commentary
WL	Wellek Lectures
WUNT	Wissenschaftliche Untersuchungen zum Neuen Testament
WW	*Word and World*
YJC	*Yale Journal of Criticism*
Yod	*Yod: Revue des études hébraïques et juives*
ZNW	*Zeitschrift für die neutestamentliche Wissenschaft und die Kunde der älteren Kirche*
ZPE	*Zeitschrift für Papyrologie und Epigraphik*

On the Verge of an Introduction

Joseph A. Marchal

Here we begin on the verge, but on the verge of ... what, exactly? Perhaps, we are on the verge of a nervous breakdown, in a not so distant echo of Pedro Almodóvar's 1988 film *Women on the Verge of a Nervous Breakdown*. Certainly, the study of Paul's letters can reduce one to tears, if not always to the edge of a nervous disorder, perhaps especially because these letters have been used to declare certain people and practices as disordered—no longer on the verge, but having crossed over and into the territory of the pathological, the abnormal, the stigmatized, even the condemned. But Almodóvar's movies lovingly, often raucously, embrace the women—and the other gender and sexual minorities—that populate both the centers and the peripheries of their narrative and visual frames. The affairs that drive these characters (sometimes crazily so) are often over the top and out of bounds from respectable society, veering and careening from the sentimental to the violent, mixing high drama and low comedy.[1]

One would be hard pressed to describe Pauline epistles and interpretations as acts of madcap melodrama, and yet, to me at least, Pedro and Pablo share some similar tastes and thus elicit similar attentions and ambivalences. Both are at their most prolific when they work with women. (After all, the present volume's title echoes *Women on the Verge of a Nervous Breakdown*.) Indeed, both relish deploying women and other feminized figures for their own affective aims, often casting women as particularly prone to hysterical behavior. In some of their more disturbing moments, their works depict acts of sexual violence that are hard to

---

1. In case it is not yet obvious, I am far from an authority on either film or music, but I also believe that more amateurish attachments can be helpful entrées into exciting—if conflicting—domains such as queer studies. For one, more scholarly companion to the work of Almodóvar, see D'Lugo and Vernon 2013.

shake.[2] In terms of genre and period, they could not be more different—
Almodóvar's movies are vibrant and twisty—even screwy—affairs, while
Paul's letters often try their best to show precisely how much they are *not*
messing around in the midst of a crooked and perverse generation. Yet
both are simply overstuffed, even bursting, with figures that deserve our
attention, offense, and occasional affection. Almodóvar's breakout farce
Women on the Verge turns around the alternately composed and crazed
lead, Pepa (played by the incomparable Carmen Maura), whose plight
assembles an assortment of audacious, dramatic, and often wronged
women. Their persistence, however, is on display in a range of predicaments with men. One brings along an obnoxiously ardent male lover
played by a younger Antonio Banderas, the only cast member to cross
over into mainstream movie success (likely because there is no justice in
the persistently patriarchal environs of modern movies). Unfurling in an
almost entirely Spanish setting, the movie plays the specter of religious
and racial difference for laughs as another character flees her passionate
boyfriend, whom she discovers is a Shiite terrorist on the verge of hijacking an airplane. Paul's letters, too, feature a capacious cast of coworkers,
including women, slaves, and gentiles. The world of these assembly
communities also include named and unnamed women, prominently
positioned as apostles and prophets, leaders and teachers, more than occasionally in precarious positions. Yet the letters often seek to connect them
in particular ways to male figures. Though Junia was outstanding among
the apostles and the incomparable Prisca takes the lead in more than one
of these audiences, only two other male protégées get their own canonized
sequels, in the pastoral letters to Timothy and Titus. Furthermore, Paul
also plays with notions of the gentiles as racially and religiously different
because of their sexual and gender trouble.

The tendencies on display in Almodóvar's films are recognizable
today as a fairly common gay male identification with divas—fabulous,
if marginalized, suffering yet surviving women. The plight of a diva and
her negotiated performance of exaggerated forms and norms of femininity provide a shiver of recognition, a shot at identification, even a strategy
of thriving for many (proto)queer people. But divas are not for everyone,
nor are the movies of Almodóvar, for that matter. Some viewers find his

---

2. For two recent examples of work on Paul's letters and sexualized violence, see
Matthews 2017; Shaner 2017.

camp aesthetic thrilling, even enabling, others off-putting. Some recognize themselves in the chaos or breakdowns that his female characters recurrently suffer; still others experience a vicarious relief that life is perhaps never as gonzo. Others appreciate these kinds of theatrical techniques but treasure different objects of ambivalent affection. Similar observations can be made about the techniques of Paul's epistles and the reception of them in interpretation. Indeed, as Will Stockton's response can attest, Paul's letters can themselves be objects of intense, even excessive, attachment—though not for everyone! Like many other figures and artifacts, those clambering in and around the epistles invite both serious critiques and campy disidentifications.

So if the early works of neither Pedro nor Pablo are quite your taste, consider "On the Verge" instead, the opening salvo of *This Island* (2004), the final album created by the queer feminist punk dance trio Le Tigre.[3] Alternately stomping, swaying, and demanding a response, its chorus repeats the line "We're on the verge of" four times, without ever completing the clause, leaving the more impatient listener to plead … of what? Of what?! The song simultaneously propels and suspends, its beats skittering together, then cutting herky-jerky in time, evoking a strange temporality and affectivity. For the more textually inclined among us, the lyrics of the verses might provide some comfort, or at least greater clarity. The opening verse warns against keeping to well-worn paths: "Play it so safe to stay on top / Shake it, imitate it, but it still sounds old." As Kathleen Hanna's vocals often operate, the delivery punctuates a sharp—even bratty—indictment and incitement, to herself and her peers. Furthermore, and especially for someone who cannot quite quit historical pursuits from a place of isolation or alienation, the second verse exhorts: "When you're shipwrecked on your mattress I'll come in and show you how / To hijack the past and wind up in the right now." As Almodóvar does in *Women on the Verge*, Le Tigre's "On the Verge" calls up hijacking but reconfigures it as something we can and should do together, suggesting that the past might be a foreign object, but one to which we might do more than campily attach. To be newly present to the present, one can force elements of the past to move in other directions, including ones that address our vulnerably intimate spaces.

---

3. Cvetkovich (2003) opens with reflections on the relation of queer trauma, pleasure, and persistence to another Le Tigre song, "Keep on Livin'" (see also Kotrosits 2018).

Thus Le Tigre figures here less as forms for admittedly audacious juxtapositions with Pauline epistles than as unexplored possibilities for how people interpret and use images and ideas, figures and feelings, from past epistles and the communities that received them. Like many biblical and queer scholars—and those really exciting places where those groups overlap!—"On the Verge" anticipates an alternate future by performing now a specific reworking of the past. To my mind, the many projects of Le Tigre's lead singer and songwriter Kathleen Hanna manage to parallel the multiple—even conflicted—styles and starting points of queer studies. Hanna's best known early band was Bikini Kill, an explicitly feminist punk group known for its confrontational and politically charged ethos and often retrospectively lumped with a large, unwieldy, and inconsistent list of performers under the term riot grrrl (see Darms 2013). One way to narrate the emergence of queer studies is to trace a similarly insurgent, confrontational impulse that sought to trouble both academic and activist work, as in the efforts of groups like ACT UP and Queer Nation (see Berlant and Freeman 1993; as well as Jagose 1996, 107–9; and Turner 2000, 106–7, 145–46). The work of canonizing certain sets of scholars or strategies as queer (or especially so) is also a vexed retrospective process, often bringing together disparate theories, processes, and accountabilities under one—and thus inevitably disputed—banner (see more below).

After Bikini Kill, Hanna recorded a more intimate, lo-fi solo album as Julie Ruin. She remained committed as ever to feminist politics and a DIY approach, but this album had a more refined, stripped-down—if sampler-oriented—sound. Much of the best work in queer studies involves close consideration of form, the craft of the literary and cultural objects queerly reconsidered as well as the craft of the interpretation itself. Indeed, both the deconstructive and the psychoanalytic sorts of queer studies attend to specific details and smaller scenes—of shame and stigma, nonconscious desires and drives, fleeting pleasures and possibilities—within structuring absences, internal incoherences, loose ends, and unthought remainders.

At first blush, Hanna's later collaboration with filmmaking and DJ colleagues in Le Tigre looks like a new wave departure from her previous work into danceable electroclash music. Their albums certainly charted higher than any of her other albums, reaching wider audiences than ever, but the techniques and materials reflect her persistent commitments to feminist and queer politics and lingering interests in sampling from her Julie Ruin project. Indeed, Hanna never entirely left that solo project "behind," recording and performing twice more with others as Julie

Ruin. Queer studies has continued to develop in a range of unanticipated directions, reflecting its vibrant energies and enthusiastic interventions. At times it has enjoyed some crossover successes, reaching more people than ever before, but queer work often does so by simultaneously reaching backward and forward.

By the time we have arrived at Le Tigre, where I began this brief musical tour, we find performers collaborating in a more hybrid, mash-up style—their work is as much about forms and politics that long predate this group. Their synth-beat music gleans elements from hip-hop, while Hanna's own sing-songy but mostly spoken delivery has long reflected clear debts to rap. Their name is even a (conscious?) play upon Lady Tigra, half of the late 80s hip-hop duo L'Trimm. More specifically, then, their work is ambivalently inspired by and borrowed from genres and styles especially created and developed within black communities. Perhaps this is why I (and others) experience this hybrid mash-up as a less-than-happy mixture—danceable but dissonant, as enlivening as enraging (perhaps intentionally so). Likewise, the variety of aims, approaches, objects, and affects assembling under the banner of queer studies might be a creative composite, but this assemblage is also riven by tensions and dissonances, not the least around racialized dynamics.

On the one hand, the persistent DIY ethos of queer studies has meant it can operate as a broad zone within which, or into which, a series of interventions can be made around which figures, forms, or techniques have been prioritized or even institutionalized. On the other hand, many of these interventions were necessary because of the way the field is frequently described through the centering—even the canonization—of white voices or priorities. Thus queer of color critique demonstrates that one can sample different materials, reflect different debts, and reach for different communities. Queer scholars and advocates highlight that questions of approach, or strategy, are also questions about queer archives.[4] In trying to explain what queer is or does, then, one necessarily reflects upon what is in one's queer archive. You may notice, for instance, that this initial narrative clearly follows upon my own pale male privileges and socialization: so far my centering examples are white, producing a northern, nonblack Atlantic (with apologies to Paul Gilroy [1995]). To be sure, I

---

4. For useful reflections on archives as processes and resources, see Muñoz 1999; Cvetkovich 2003; Halperin 2012.

have noted some of the racialized aspects of the objects of my quirky queer attention—the works of Le Tigre, Pedro Almodóvar, and Paul of Tarsus. But to treat race adequately and queerly, one must do more than just "add one more difference" to critiques of marginalization, stigmatization, and normalization.[5] Different archives should be created and used, but interaction with more queer archives should also alter our queer approaches, so that we are not just listing racialized "supplements," thereby reinforcing the (often unmarked) centrality of whiteness and other naturalizing and normalizing vectors of oppression.

On the Verge of ... Queer?

This is in part why I am at least trying to begin on the verge. Like queer, verge is a word with a few meanings and functions.[6] As a noun, it connotes margins, boundaries, and edges. If queer work is on the verge, then it is linked to other voices from the margin(s) (see Sugirtharajah 1991), approaches developed by people from marginalized and minoritized communities. Where scholars are increasingly moving toward minority biblical criticism (Bailey, Liew, and Segovia 2009), then queer could signify the place of sexual (and gender) minorities as critics. Indeed, this type of approach may be what the editors of *The Queer Bible Commentary* have in mind when they describe how the commentary's contents "take seriously both how reading from lesbian, gay, bisexual, and/or transgender perspectives affect the reading and interpretation of biblical texts and how biblical texts have and do affect lesbian, gay, bisexual, and/or transgender communities" (Guest et al. 2006, xiii). A queer reading strategy, then, is one that either comes from or addresses people with a particular attribute, attributes often listed in the expanding acronym LGBTIQ (lesbian, gay, bisexual, trans, intersex, and queer). This kind of strategy may be justified and valued by appealing to scholars from within a frame of contextual hermeneutics; it includes another in a sequence of groups of people who read from this, this, or now this place (with apologies to Segovia and Tolbert [1995]). From this standpoint, a queer strategy of interpretation is

---

5. See, for instance, the critique of this additive, rather than interactive, factoring in intersectional feminist and queer analysis in Puar 2007, 23–24, 204–22.

6. For previous attempts at contextualizing queer studies for religious, theological, and then biblical studies, see Schippert 1999, 2011; Cornwall 2011; Brintnall 2013; Stone 2001; Moore 2001, 7–18; Marchal 2012; Moore, Brintnall, and Marchal 2018.

analogous to and an extension of twentieth-century calls for interpretations by or for women, racial or ethnic minorities, the poor, and colonial subjects (among others). From within such a model, then, queer critics claim a seat by putting sexuality on the table, where previous groups stressed gender, race/ethnicity, class, or imperialism. This is, at least, what Stephen D. Moore (2001, 12–13) initially argues about the introduction and utility of queer studies for biblical studies.

Here and elsewhere, developments within queer approaches to biblical studies repeat or at least reflect discussions and ideas in queer studies at large (beyond religious or theological studies). Key thinkers for queer studies like Gayle Rubin and Eve Kosofsky Sedgwick, for instance, have argued for the importance of treating sexuality as a separate subject of study, involving its own axis of power and structures of oppression (Rubin 1984; Sedgwick 1990, 27–35). In part, then, queer studies did grow out of lesbian and gay studies, with its focus on sexuality and the experience of sexual minorities. But if queer refers to LGBTIQ people and practices only by addressing sexuality, or speaking to or from the experience of sexual minorities, then this appears to cover only half of those represented: the L, G, and B. If gendered practices are foregrounded and the community addressed includes sexual and gender minorities, then trans and intersex people could have some common cause with lesbian, gay, and bisexual groups.

Thus the centrality of sexuality to queer is hotly contested, with scholars such as Judith Butler (1994) insisting that sexuality is interrelated with gender (among other dynamics) and that there should be no proper object for queer theories. This potential dissonance is one reason why the verge remains so evocative to me as I try to explain what makes queer approaches queer. Every declaration of a center remains contested, even as by necessity narrating, or tracing, begins to center certain habits or attentions, inspirations or interlocutors. But, an honest, if troubling introduction to queer studies, within and beyond biblical studies, should aim to explain and elicit that there is no center for queer studies, only some sets of quirky composites, ones that could be assembled in a variety of overlapping, but also competing—even conflicting—ways. This is also one reason I argue for attending to who and what emerges in various queer archives—and not only because Pauline epistles and interpretations sometimes show up. These give us multiple points of entry or departure, additional objects for devotion or repulsion (or both), and competing terminologies and techniques to help each other do things queerly. I can only hope that something here—a flash, an angle, a juxtaposition, even just a hook—can help you as you are (on the verge of) interpreting queerly, but my quirky archiving will hardly be exhaustive (if still exhausting to some). Indeed, even my musical touchstones can be rapidly expanded by attending to other queer biblical critics: Ken Stone's (2005) appeal to safer practices of textual intercourse for food and sex opens with a delicious Suzanne Vega epigram, Madonna rises from the sea in Lynn Huber's (2011) ambivalent gaze at the Whore of Babylon, and Teresa Hornsby (2016) appeals to her own local punk outfit C-Rex in her introduction to transgender biblical interpretation. But to what are you listening?

Returning to the acronym LGBTIQ, we are still left with its nagging, even slippery, closing appendage: the Q (for queer, rather than *Quelle*, the hypothesized sayings source for Matthew and Luke)! Despite disputes in activist and academic circles (and their overlaps), for many, queer is just a synonym for what precedes it in the above acronym. Queer functions as an attribute, a kind of person, even an identity term. Queer works as a convenient one-word catch-all, much easier to spit out in conversation than the list of letters that were gathered around the L and G of lesbian and gay (in often contested fashion within and among those they purported to describe and ally). Abbreviations moved to LGB, LGBT, LGBTQ2, LGBTIQ, or even LGBTIQA—forms alternately signaling the inclusion of bisexual, trans, two-spirit, intersex, queer or questioning, and/or ally (though asexual is also peeking through in some contexts and communities). It would seem that using queer just makes everything easier.

But there is something troubling about being on the verge and about the word queer. These terms have an edge to them; they are not for everyone. The term queer has often been deployed less to figure out whom to include and more to trace and negotiate how exclusion, stigmatization, marginalization, or normalization have operated. As I note above, one of the main reasons the term queer was reclaimed is the defiant and disruptive tone it strikes. Historically, queer has been (and often still is) used in a pejorative, derogatory, and disciplinary way, characterizing its targets as odd, abnormal, or perverse. Indeed, it has been deployed as a (negative) term of identification, as a slang word for homosexuals, but also as an insult to police everyone's behavior, particularly effective among children and young adults (or other infantilized populations). Those groups who have repurposed this word acknowledge these practices and do not dispute that queer connotes abnormality or nonconformity to prevailing points of view, but they do dispute that such a contrary relation to *the normal* and often *the natural* is a negative thing. Queer, then, can indicate a challenge to regimes of the normal, a desire to resist and contest such a worldview. Far from making things easier, it reflects upon hardship and difficulty in the past and the present. Queer reflects histories of insult and injury, embodied experiences of bad feelings and embedded memories of conflicted attachments (see Butler 1993, 223–27). In the face of these, queer advocates for persistence in being difficult and troublesome, not leaving well enough alone, and doing complicated and fraught analytic work.

This second sense of queer, then, reminds me also of a second sense of verge, both functioning less like nouns than verbs. When we are verging on something, we are approaching something closely, or only just approximately, perhaps without touching. To verge on something is to indicate the risk or peril of the activity. When I think about queer approaches to Pauline epistles and interpretations, I cannot help but think of how close we come to controversy, offense, conflict, or contention. If queering involves contesting processes of normalization and naturalization, it also requires moving closer to examples of these processes. Perhaps, then, the act of attending closely to the details of these texts and traditions is something subversive and risky. Queer readers have been drawn—even felt forced— to attend closely to Paul's letters because of significant histories of injury and oppression. The trick is to get close enough to perform this queering without being touched or burned by them anymore. To queer Pauline epistles and interpretations is to trouble them, but efforts to do so stem from the troubles they have already generated and, in turn, have the potential to put the reader or user in other sorts of trouble. As a result, this volume is more than a petition for belonging. Rather, it signals that queer studies, and even Pauline studies (if it comes along for the ride), are on the verge of something subversive, surprising, and spectacular. Queering can do much more than simply provide a new perspective, or even a radical new perspective (with apologies, at least to the latter set of colleagues, like Eisenbaum [2009]).

Because queer is meant to invoke strategies that resist or trouble modes of respectability, normalcy, or inclusion, its troubling disposition inevitably extends to the aforementioned notion of queer as attribute or identity or perspective, new or otherwise! Thus queer can contradictorily connote both a synonym for what precedes it in the acronym LGBTIQ and an interrogation of the identity politics of those terms. Queer gets its energy or force from the way it stands in contradistinction to norms, even those norms generated within minoritized or marginalized communities.

In this second sense, then, queer is less an identity and more a disposition, a mode of examining the processes that cast certain people and practices into categories of normal and abnormal and then of interrogating the various effects of such processes. Not that a person or a text possesses a quality marked queer but rather that one can queer an arrangement of power and privilege or interpret queerly by attending to certain dynamics. Within biblical studies, Moore picks up on this slippery second sense of the term when he describes queer as "a supple cipher both for what *stands over against* the normal and the natural to oppose, and thereby define, them, and what *inheres within* the normal and the natural to subvert, and indeed pervert, them" (2001, 18). This sense of queer shapes the bulk of this collection, which is why it is described as queering Pauline epistles, rather than dispensing a queer perspective on Paul.

On the Verge of … a Queer Canon?

One of this volume's most distinctive and generative features, then, is its sustained interaction with a wide range of queer theories and materials from outside of traditional biblical studies. The chapters that follow suggest, or simply perform, some of the many ways one could relate work on Pauline epistles and interpretations to queer studies. They help us reconsider which resources, questions, concepts, or interlocutors should be engaged for rethinking what one can do with these texts and traditions. They indicate different, if often still overlapping, archives—from each other and from previous attempts to grapple with biblical images, ideas, and arguments.

Because history remains the pink elephant in the big, busy, bookish room of biblical studies, the books of "queer theory" most frequently taken up thus far by biblical scholars are Michel Foucault's three-volume *History of Sexuality* (1988a, 1988b, 1990; notice, for instance, their central place in Moore 2001). I have thrown these works' initial relationship to queer theory in scare quotes, however, for two reasons. First, Foucault was only retrospectively canonized as one in a kinky trinity of founders for queer theory, with Butler and Sedgwick, as queer studies began consciously defining itself in the early 1990s. Indeed, most interpreters hold that the terms queer and theory were first conjoined in a 1991 essay by Teresa de Lauretis, seven years after Foucault died of complications from AIDS.

The first of these volumes appeared in French in 1976, the latter two in the year of his death in 1984. The postmortem release of his work still rivals that of 2Pac, as various collected works, interviews, and lectures have continued to drop, including even a (mostly unauthorized?) fourth volume of the *History of Sexuality* (2018)!

My second contextualizing hesitation around the queer use of Foucault centers around which works, ideas, and techniques have been engaged in biblical studies. Foucault has found the greatest purchase in the interpretation of these texts and traditions, perhaps because, perversely enough, he pursued his questions into some of the most traditional subject areas: Greco-Roman classics. One need not venture much beyond the creaturely comforts of historical criticism and their traditional contexts if one grapples with the two volumes in which he backtracks, albeit selectively and idiosyncratically, to Greek and then Roman texts. When biblical interpreters have turned to the first volume, they have come less for his method for grappling with biopower than some of his more outsized historical proclamations. For instance, he echoed and specified a social constructionist approach to homosexuality by arguing that

> sodomy was a category of forbidden acts; their perpetrator was nothing more than the juridical subject of them. The nineteenth-century homosexual became a personage, a past, a case history, and a childhood, in addition to being a type of life, a life form, and a morphology.... The sodomite had been a temporary aberration; the homosexual was now a species. (Foucault 1990, 43)

In this oft-cited contrast, Foucault aimed to differentiate the homosexual, as a kind of *identity*, from perverse sexual practices (like sodomy), as *acts*. I admit to quoting this audacious formulation too many times to count, especially as it helps to reinforce the increasing historicizing tendency in classical studies, particularly around gender and sexuality. It is likely lurking in the background of my essay puzzling over our relationships to receptivity, but it appears again in Heather R. White's essay as she provides crucial historical contextualization for how we were ever convinced that the Bible was straight. In fairness, a number of biblical scholars have done creative work drawing upon different emphases within Foucault's massive oeuvre. Even in the present volume, Valérie Nicolet employs his disciplinary, discursive notions of power in relation to knowledge, albeit to different, queerly monstrous ends within Galatians than she or others previously have (see Nicolet-Anderson 2012; as well as Castelli 1991a; 1991b; Moore 1994, 95–112; Moxnes 2003; and Fuggle 2013). No wonder, then, that Foucault has been so often resurrected, even sanctified as a queer saint (Halperin 1995)!

Returning to my admittedly sketchy introduction, when scholars were willing a new subdiscipline, alternately called queer theory or queer studies, into existence, Foucault's first volume of *History of Sexuality*, Butler's *Gender Trouble* (1990), and Sedgwick's *Epistemology of the Closet* (1990) were elevated onto an alternative, antifoundationalist altar. As these works reached almost totemic status, Butler and Sedgwick had the distinct advantage of *not* being saints—alive to comment and, where necessary, critique how queer was becoming institutionalized. In some ways they were experiencing what frank assessors of scriptural canons have long known—that such processes of selection and elevation are always retrospective, idiosyncratic, interpellative projections. Indeed, both of them fretted about this queer moment, even as they stressed the lingering, twisting, and troubling potential of queer.

These concerns and stresses can help us as we continue sussing out what queer is or does. Like a good literary scholar (and many others, even biblical language nerds), Sedgwick meditates on the origins of the term:

> Queer is a continuing moment, movement, motive—recurrent, eddying, *troublant*. The word "queer" itself means across—it comes from the Indo-European root -*twerkw*, which also yields the German *quer* (transverse), Latin *torquere* (to twist), English *athwart*. (1993, xii)

In this reflection, the continuing, recurrent temporality of queer sounds like it is always verging on another iteration of twisting and turning. Queer does not belong to any one place or time, and one twist includes Sedgwick's (likely unwitting) evocation of a form of dance already popular in the '90s bounce music scene of New Orleans—twerking. Here we are again, taking a turn with another southern black hip-hop practice, this time popularized by performers like Big Freedia, but ostensibly only crossing over when the white pop star Miley Cyrus performed it (in 2013). Unlike verge, queer connotes crossing—like twerking, queering may even "cross the line" into what some might consider the obscene. Or for those less scandalized by what people do with their bodies, queering may only, if recurrently, approach what troubles.

Queering continues counterintuitively, then, troubling the kinds of problems around category or classification that Foucault also tried to examine. Sedgwick (1990, 24–27; 1993, 6–8) persistently aimed to unravel all of the embedded assumptions within modern notions of sexuality, even as the most common concept of orientation reflects a prevailing poverty of imagination by winnowing it down to ostensibly only one factor: the (perceived) gender of our sexual object choice. In tracing and resisting such presumptions, she shows how the significance of queer cannot be boiled down to the sexual identity *homosexual*. This categorizing cannot entirely capture or discipline what it purports to describe. And to Sedgwick,

> that's one of the things that "queer" can refer to: the open mesh of possibilities, gaps, overlaps, dissonances and resonances, lapses and excesses of meaning when the constituent elements of anyone's gender, or anyone's sexuality aren't made (or *can't be* made) to signify monolithically. (1993, 8)

Sedgwick's elegant prose captures, if only partially (the above is just *one* of the things to which queer can refer), what refuses or unsettles conformity to being captured and classified. This definition helps Stockton to link several of the reflections in his response, but I also think it evokes how the contents of this collection propose a set of possibilities and dissonances for gender and sexuality. These underscore queer's pesky refusal of easy definition, and its accompanying, untidy promiscuity around the cultural objects to which we attach. In the hands of the scholars in this collection, queer approaches demonstrate that there is room for other possibilities—in this instance, for Pauline epistles and interpretations. Like Sedgwick, these other possibilities can be glimpsed, if initially, in the moments of slippage and incoherence (look for such moments in the essays by Tyler M. Schwaller and Benjamin H. Dunning, among others).

If queer so often refuses definition, scholars like Sedgwick and Butler do still wonder about its force, which is to say, its history of vilification and prohibition. As a term of insult and injury, degradation and abjection, queer interpellates its targets (see Butler 1993, 223–26). Butler puzzles over how queer can operate as an act of affiliation and even reparation, in resistance to this history, with others who fail to conform to monolithic signification or disciplinary stigmatization. This act repeats the derogatory identification, but "let us remember that reiterations are never simply replicas of the same" (226). Here, as Dunning describes in his essay, Butler is expanding upon Jacques Derrida (1988) and her own previous work on performative speech in relation to gendered embodiment (Butler 1990).

Repetition and citationality figure prominently in Butler's conceptualization, influential for both feminist and queer studies, of performativity.

Butler (1990, 33) famously asserted, "Gender is the repeated stylization of the body, a set of repeated acts within a highly rigid regulatory frame that congeals over time to produce the appearance of substance, of a natural sort of being." Gender, like many other qualities about bodies, is performative because it is only recognizable through both the practice of certain actions and the wider reception of what these actions mean. In Butler's conceptualization, it is only when one "does" gender "properly" that others identify one as belonging to and "being" a gender. Thus Butler reverses some of the common sense of what bodies are and mean by stressing this doing aspect of embodiment. It is not an innate sense of being that causes us to do gendered things; rather, it is the repeated doing that creates a sense of stably being a particular kind of gender, body, or sexuality (among other things).

Further than this, performativity also helps one see how such orders of stylization and substantiation can be resisted and subverted. By denaturalizing the qualities that people attribute to bodies (like gender), performativity works to undermine the basis of these regulatory frames. Gender (or any other ostensibly existential quality) only appears natural, only seems to be based on the substance of the body, and this appearance occurs only when one's gender is read as normal within the regulatory frame (for Butler, a heterosexual matrix). Yet because it must always be repeated to be recognized as normal/natural, gender is unstable. If gender, then, is itself unstable, so too are other intertwining qualities (like one's status in heteronormativity). Thus what appears as only natural or normal—one's gender, body, sexuality—is not a straightforwardly innate part of one's identity; rather this sense of identity is only an *effect* of the *incessant doing* that must be done in order for one to be readable in the regulatory frame.

Thus this kind of order is revealed as inherently unstable, even panicked, needing constant explanation and reiteration to produce itself as the natural. This order requires copies of copies of copies of what it is producing as the natural. Such an operation leads Butler to observe that "*gender is a kind of imitation for which there is no original*; in fact, it is a kind of imitation that produces the notion of the original as an *effect* and consequence of the imitation itself" (1991, 21, emphasis original). Performativity shows that any gender, any sexuality, any embodied instantiation of an idea or identity is an imitation, an attempt to copy the cultural process by which it is regulated. Their repeatability reveals their instability; the requirement for their continuous repetition to appear natural or stable indicates that they will never be finished.

While Butler thinks that we can never get entirely outside these regulative processes in culture, their necessary repeatability and accompanying instability can make them compelling places to make trouble for norms and their regulatory apparatus. Since one must cite them in or as one's actions, their citationality provides opportunities for subversion. Structured by, but not ultimately determined by, this dynamic, one must cite and repeat the norms of embodiment, but one might find ways to develop subversive repetitions, to "fail to repeat loyally" (Butler 1993, 124). The issue is not *whether* one repeats gendered scripts or cites erotic norms but *how* one does so. Normalization and naturalization are open to rearticulation precisely because they always only work if they are constantly being reinstalled as the normal or the natural, as the practice that must be cited and repeated. Thus Butler (1990, 128–49) proposes that drag highlights the potential for parody and subversion within performativity. One's practice of gender, sexuality, and/or embodiment is not doomed only to be an effect of a heteronormative system, but it can instead be "a practice of improvisation within a scene of constraint" (Butler 2004, 1, see also 15).

Terms such as queer can also function performatively, and not strictly because they connote vexed notions of bodies, sexualities, and genders. They also reflect the possibility to repeat otherwise, even as Butler cautions about the persistent risk or constraint of such an act of subversive affiliation:

> If the term "queer" is to be a site of collective contestation, the point of departure for a set of historical reflections and futural imaginings, it will have to remain that which is, in the present, never fully owned, but always and only redeployed, twisted, queered from a prior usage and in the direction of urgent and expanding political purposes. (1993, 228)

Performativity, then, is not only a concept to be employed in our queer approaches, observing and interrogating their recurrence in materials like Pauline epistles and interpretations; it is also a disposition that defines the tense, slippery, and necessarily reflexive status of queering as a mode of critique and movement toward alliance and resistance.

I summarize some of Butler's key ideas at length because she is referenced in the bulk of the essays in this collection. One recurring technique of these essays is seeking the possibilities for resisting and repeating dynamics in Pauline epistles and interpretations toward other ends. Lindsey Guy imagines the parodic possibilities of the Corinthians' failure to perform expectations around family, children, and economy. Nicolet thinks about the subversive potential of Galatian repetitions, particularly in the ways that monstrous bodies might resist and exceed the disciplinary force of norms. Schwaller opens his essay by considering how histories could be done differently if we noted how dominant discourses around slaves could be performed otherwise: despite constraints, slaveholding power is never as absolute as its holders claimed. Timothy Luckritz Marquis situates his Dionysian disidentification with 2 Corinthians in relation to performativity and the ever-present possibility of interpellation's failure. In my own essay, I seek other possibilities for resistant negotiations within the kyriarchal constraints of the ancient ethos of penetration and domination. As I note above, Dunning situates Butler (particularly Butler 1997) in relation to Derrida, so that the latter may signify otherwise for queer theory and hermeneutics, as we attend to failures of closure and coherence in Paul's anthropological claims. Even in the essay that leaves its theoretical debts most implicit, Jay Twomey describes the willful foreclosures of a fictionalized version of Paul as a space missionary evoking a melancholic heterosexuality (highlighting how normative repetition requires the disavowal of other possibilities).

The citation and use of Butler at so many turns in this collection may not come as a surprise to some readers. After Foucault, she is probably the next most common figure used in queer biblical readings, as evidenced by the bulk of the essays in the landmark collection *Bible Trouble: Queer Readings at the Boundaries of Biblical Scholarship* (Hornsby and Stone 2011). Not only does the title of the collection play upon Butler's *Gender Trouble* (1990), but both of the editors of that collection also contributed the only biblical studies essays in a previous collection on Butler and religion (see Hornsby 2006; Stone 2006). Getting back to the biblical and especially the Pauline trouble in the 2011 collection, Butler's work plays key roles in each of the three essays reflecting on aspects of the Pauline corpus (Townsley 2011; Marchal 2011a; and Twomey 2011). Indeed, as the editor of the present collection, my own persistent engagement with Butler may, if perhaps subconsciously, have primed this particular performative pump (see, for instance, Marchal 2010, 2011b, 2012, 2014b, 2014c, 2014d)!

However, it may be that Butler's value to both feminist and queer approaches (and their overlaps; see Marchal 2014d) has encouraged greater cross-fertilization. To wit: Teresa Hornsby's (2006) aforementioned essay on Butler and the annoying, anointing woman is an analysis specifically of feminist biblical studies as a performative genre. Certainly, works like *Gender Trouble* (1990) are as important for their rethinking of gender normativity toward feminist ends as they are for suggesting (what will be retrospectively described as) queer practices of parody and subversion. This likely accounts for her appearance in Elizabeth A. Castelli's (1994) feminist commentary entry on Romans or Elisabeth Schüssler Fiorenza's (1999) reflections on feminist methodologies. Hornsby's (2005) essay on the gendered sinner in Romans might be the first concerted application of Butler to an aspect of Pauline texts and traditions. Indeed, Hornsby (2005, 157) gestures toward the technique you see repeatedly in many of the present collection's essays though her examination of the gender performance of norms and deviations and her conclusion that the Pauline concept of the sinner has failed to do gender properly.

On the Verge of ... Queering Canons?

From the opening section of this vergical, not terribly surgical introduction, though, stopping at this narration of queer studies, within and beyond biblical studies, I indicate that this introduction would not only be woefully inadequate but would also forcefully whitewash the trajectories and impacts of queer. I have in part repeated the partial and pale centering of one trinity of queer figures—Butler, Sedgwick, Foucault—but two of these scholars resisted this canonization and its various centering and marginalizing effects. Even after venturing some of the definitions I note above, Sedgwick hesitated about keeping queer tethered strictly to same-sex expressions and object choices. Instead she pointed toward a range of work leveraging queer to address dynamics of race, ethnicity, language, nationality, and empire (1993, 8–9). Butler (1993, 227–29) also wondered about the potential exclusions around race, class, age, and gender in the various ways queer has operated. This persistently troubling force of queer could be one of its critical virtues, twisting from previous uses and turning to reflexive critiques and other possible aims and coalitions (228–29).

Even the spectral presence of the already deceased Foucault could be made to trouble this consecrated triad: if so many are willing to enlist him as an icon of queer theory *avant la lettre*, then why not other scholar-advocates from the '70s and '80s? Indeed, the queer of color critique proposed by scholars like Roderick Ferguson (2004) performs other genealogies, particularly with and through women of color feminists. In her hesitation, Sedgwick (only briefly) gestured toward other intellectuals and artists of color, like Gloria Anzaldúa. Yet Anzaldúa coedited the landmark volume *This Bridge Called My Back: Writings by Radical Women of Color* (1981) with Cherríe Moraga more than a decade earlier and published an influential collection of essays and poetry just a few years later (Anzaldúa 1987). In the latter, Anzaldúa complicates notions of clean lineages and clear territories (for queer studies and many other domains)—those that divide and discipline, categorize and target—by introducing the notion of borderlands:

> A borderland is a vague and undetermined place created by the emotional residue of an unnatural boundary. It is in a constant state of transition. The prohibited and forbidden are its inhabitants. *Los atravesados* live here: the squint-eyed, the perverse, the queer, the troublesome, the mongrel, the mulato, the half-breed, the half dead; in short, those who cross over, pass over, or go through the confines of the "normal." (Anzaldúa 1987, 3)

Her evocative description of this zone that is neither territory nor line (it is both border and land) traces how many figures could be assembled together as crossing the domains of the normal—the domains against which queer was defined above. For Anzaldúa, queers are situated and recurrently named as or alongside women, Chicana, dark-skinned, indigenous, marginalized, foreign, or outcast others (1987, 3, 18, 19, 38, 72, 80–81, 82, 84–85, 88). In her best-known essay delineating a new mestiza consciousness (1987, 77–91), the mixtures and crossings of the mestiza and the queer (85) both name and challenge the power of the natural and the normal in their different and ever-shifting forms.

Several scholars have highlighted the formative role that Anzaldúa plays in the development of queer studies (see, e.g., Muñoz 1999; Keating 2009). We might even say that José Esteban Muñoz (1999, 6–7) proposes, if briefly, an alternative trinity of Anzaldúa, Moraga, and Chela Sandoval as he describes and develops reading strategies for queers of color. In the bustling borderlands of biblical interpretation, there has only been occasional interaction with Anzaldúa and Moraga, and mostly from scholars who identify with or as racially minoritized people. Tat-siong Benny Liew (2009) turns to concepts from both Anzaldúa and Butler to reconfigure the Jesus who appears in the Gospel of John as a cross-dressing and border-crossing drag king trickster. Jacqueline Hidalgo (2016, 2018) traces the utopian scripturalizing practices in Moraga's works, particularly in her reuse of the biblical book of Revelation, creation of a queer Chicano codex, and proposal for a queer Aztlán. Manuel Villalobos Mendoza (2011) foregrounds Anzaldúa's notions of borderlands and mestiza consciousness in order to cross interpretive borders around his own body and that of the

Ethiopian eunuch (in Acts 8). As of yet, no biblical interpreter has queerly mixed Anzaldúa or Moraga with the Pauline epistles considered authentic, though Villalobos Mendoza (2014) has followed up his previous work by reading the Pastoral epistles and the others targeted within them *del otro lado* (of the other side).

Anzaldúa's essays and poems repeatedly foreground the mixing, multiplicity, ambivalence, and contradiction of concepts like mestiza and queer: qualities of manifest resonance in queer studies and Pauline studies (and the places where these are increasingly overlapping). Outside of this overlap I am trying to trace, only Efraín Agosto (2018) has begun to grapple with Anzaldúa's work in relation to Paul's letters, in his understanding of the epistles and Puerto Rico as sites of migration and border dwelling in the ongoing contexts of colonialism. The related absence of Anzaldúa in postcolonial approaches to Paul's letters (see e.g., Stanley 2011) is even more striking, given the abundant attention to the mixing and ambivalence within their readings of the apostle or his epistles as examples of hybridity. Still, Anzaldúa's interest in queer figures is unmistakable. She even imagines their exceptional place in culture:

> Being the supreme crossers of cultures, homosexuals have strong bonds with the queer white, Black, Asian, Native American, Latino, and with the queer in Italy, Australia and the rest of the planet. We come from all colors, all classes, all races, all time periods…. Colored homosexuals have more knowledge of other cultures; have always been at the forefront (although sometimes in the closet) of all liberation struggles in this country; have suffered more injustices and have survived them despite all odds. (1987, 84–85)

Though there are manifest reasons to doubt the strong bonds she describes, she highlights how queers of color experience multiple and intersecting dynamics of oppression (and resistances to these) and, further still, how queer identifications should generate broader forms of solidarity and coalition (before Butler or Sedgwick). Obligation causes me to return to various temporal claims about same-sex attraction or orientation later, but at the moment, I focus on how later readers of Anzaldúa have reflected upon the risks and ambivalences around identification.

Muñoz (1999, 138), for instance, explicitly worries that this particular vision of Anzaldúa falsely idealizes such bonding dynamics, particularly given the persistence of racisms within queer culture. Muñoz does stress the potential embedded within the ambivalent, mixed, or mestizo perspectives of minoritized subjects. As a result, he suggests that minorities like queers of color perform disidentification as a distinctive strategy of survival and resistance. Muñoz argues:

> Disidentification is the third mode of dealing with dominant ideology, one that neither opts to assimilate within such a structure nor strictly opposes it; rather, disidentification is a strategy that works on and against dominant ideology. Instead of buckling under the pressures of dominant ideology (identification, assimilation) or attempting to break free of its inescapable sphere (counteridentification, utopianism), this "working on and against" is a strategy that tries to transform a cultural logic from within, always laboring to enact permanent structural change while at the same time valuing the importance of local or everyday struggles of resistance. (1999, 11–12)

Through disidentification, Muñoz highlights the unexpected routes that minoritized viewers, readers, and receivers take in their interaction with dominant culture. To work on, against, and yet also from within these oppressive settings generates other options than those projected through the poles of acceptance or rejection, love it or leave it.[7] Disidentification presents alternative possibilities for the reuse and reconfiguration of prescriptive and pathologizing materials, toward resistance and transformation (see Muñoz 1999, 3, 28, 30, 31, 39, 58, and 71). Thus queers of color do not avoid contact with phobic, stereotyping, or otherwise "bad" objects, since disidentification is "a mode of *recycling* or re-forming an object that has already been invested with powerful energy" (39).

Paul's epistles are certainly those kinds of objects, which is likely why so many of this collection's essays have a marked tendency toward disidentification (for previous queerly biblical uses, see Runions 2011; Stone 2011). Luckritz Marquis most explicitly elaborates upon this practice, citing Muñoz at several turns to discuss this strategy that "tactically and simultaneously works on, with, and against a cultural form" (Muñoz 1999, 12). He carefully traces multiple forms of disidentification, of Paul in relation to Dionysus as a foreign, Eastern preacher; of the Corinthian recipients of this Pauline image in 2 Cor 1–9; and of our reception of this exchange and the composite that scholars call "Pauline studies." But I would venture to

---

7. For a similar refusal to accede to binary options of acceptance or rejection in queer approaches to biblical interpretation, see Stone 2005, 7–22.

say that most of the essays to follow reflect their own ambivalences toward and negotiations of their archives. Each of these are working on and with Pauline images or arguments, typically in order to resist and transform what has been and what can still be done with them.

In conversation with Muñoz, Ferguson (2004, 2–10) has underscored the relevance of disidentification and a different constellation of interlocutors for the development of queer of color critique. As a result, Ferguson explicitly and persistently names "women of color feminism" as the most important component in this development, particularly given how black lesbian feminists were at the vanguard in an analysis of simultaneous and overlapping modes of oppression (throughout but especially 2004, 110–37). Ferguson's work, then, could provide a third trinity of queer theoretical sources, highlighting Audre Lorde, Barbara Smith, and Toni Morrison as black feminists working in the 70s and 80s (see, for instance, Lorde 1984; Smith 1977, 1983; Morrison 1973). Of course, at this point I might be fairly accused of disidentifying with the deifying tendencies of Trinitarian identifications through intentionally multiplying such canonical listings, three by three! Furthermore, Butler and Sedgwick are hardly the only advocacy-oriented scholars to resist such sanctification, particularly as Lorde and Smith (1983) collaborated with other black lesbian feminists to insist upon intersectional politics that interrogated heterosexism alongside and within sexism, racism, and classism in the "Combahee River Collective Statement."

You may not find direct reference to the Combahee River Collective or Smith in what follows, and only the first essay, by Guy, engages Lorde briefly, in order to counter the kind of racist tone policing found in both first- and twenty-first-century contexts. Yet most of the entries in this collection trace and grapple with overlapping and simultaneous vectors of power and privilege, around not only gender and sexuality, but also race and ethnicity. Many of them think through these in light of how Jewish and gentile difference is posed, multiplied, and negotiated. Guy specifically considers the racialized dynamics in the Corinthians' apparent childishness and immaturity. James N. Hoke traces the racialized dimensions of sexual distinctions, demonstrating how ancient Roman and then Paul's Thessalonian arguments relied upon depictions of ethnic others as sexually deviant. Nicolet notes the ethnic resonances of Paul's monstrous arguments about non-Jewish bodies as cast in a racial "no man's land" in Galatians. Midori Hartman specifically foregrounds the role of race alongside animality in introducing her queer approach to those ostensibly former members of the *ethnē* (nations) who pollute Paul's concept of the Corinthian community as particularly prone to a debased and animalistic sexual immorality. Luckritz Marquis also grapples with how Paul might be redirecting the sexually stereotypical association of Eastern others as a celibate Judean wanderer. Twomey puzzles over the ways a science fiction refiguration of Paul problematizes dynamics of race alongside and within gender by setting them in the contact between human and alien. Thus this collection grapples with race and ethnicity in creative and idiosyncratic directions within and beyond the traditionally Pauline focus on Jewish and gentile difference.

While a few of the essays consider enslaved people among the audiences of the letters and subjects of an ancient social system, two of them, Schwaller's and my own, work explicitly in the wake (see Sharpe 2016, 2010) of multiple systems of slavery. Given the ways biblical texts and Paul's letters in particular were employed to justify the Atlantic slave trade and the persistent American slavocracy, these texts carry their own specifically racialized histories and resonances (see especially Johnson, Noel, and Williams 2012). I submit that such vexed heritages indicate the necessity of much greater engagement with black queer studies for queer readers and users of Pauline epistles and interpretations.[8] In turn, I have to admit that my own essay reflects a still partial and inadequate interaction with such work, and thus only partially addresses the haunting heritage of the sexualized dynamics around abjection and receptivity. Much more remains to be done, but gratefully we are already seeing spaces where Lorde, Moraga, Ferguson, and Muñoz are assembled (and in conversation with Hidalgo 2018) among other interlocutors to craft a queer Africana codex for signifying Scriptures otherwise (see, for instance, Thomas 2018).

The appalling aftermaths and haunting heritages suggest not only greater engagement with black queer studies but further conversation and interaction with womanist biblical interpretations. Though I cannot pretend to give an adequate survey of the breadth and depth of womanist work on sexuality, the historical effects of slavery on gendered, sexual, and racial dynamics is a persistent and important topic for womanist scholars in religious and theological studies. Delores Williams's (1993) trailblazing theological work reflected upon the sexual exploitation and coerced surro-

---

8. For black queer studies, see, e.g., Fisher 1996; Cohen 1997; Somerville 2000; Reid-Pharr 2001; Johnson and Henderson 2005; McBride 2005; Stockton 2006; Scott 2010; Holland 2012; Musser 2014; Johnson 2016.

gacy of Hagar as a prototype and a parallel to the situation of more recently enslaved women and their African American descendants. Traci C. West (1999) traces the historical legacy of slavery as a continuing trauma of intimate violence against black women. As with their ancient predecessors, more recently enslaved people were (and are) racially characterized by a presumed promiscuity and availability for sexual uses (see Hartman 1997). Slave systems have generated and deployed a range of figures in order to characterize bodies of color by their especially deviant sexuality, whether they were jezebels, breeders, and bucks (excessive and presumably willing) or mammies and Uncle Toms (asexual yet submissive), and these figurations persist, albeit in altered and even alternating forms into the present (see Collins 2005, 53–85, 119–80). As Kelly Brown Douglas (1999, 31–61) has demonstrated, contemporary forms and norms of black sexuality have been shaped, but not entirely determined, by the legacy of white sexual assault supported and reflected by these racial-sexual types.

In many ways, then, racially minoritized bodies have already been "queered" (so to speak) as departing from what was (or is) considered natural and normal ideals—ideals occupied by only some of the people that one might classify as heterosexual. Outside of religious and theological studies, Cathy Cohen (1997) noted the addition of "Punks, Bulldaggers, and Welfare Queens" to the stigmatizing sexual stereotyping of black people. These racialized figurations have generated reticence, or even silence, for fear of confirming persistent stereotypes that justify racist systems and structures. These ongoing dynamics demonstrate that if queer is meant to chart and counter normalization and naturalization, it must do so in intersectional fashion, grappling with how gender, sexuality, and embodiment overlap and mutually influence race, ethnicity, economy, and empire (among others).

If and when queer approaches to biblical texts and traditions proceed intersectionally, they are drawing upon the labor and theorizations of womanists and women of color feminists. Even the term *intersectionality* was coined by Kimberlé Williams Crenshaw (1989), a black feminist legal scholar and one of the founding figures for critical race theory. As womanist biblical scholars are reaching a critical mass (Smith 2015, 1–13), they are also clarifying the diverse, interdisciplinary approaches they take to such intersectional structures. Gay Byron and Vanessa Lovelace (2016, 9), for instance, emphasize that matters of sexual independence and respectability are key themes for womanist biblical interpretation. The potential for further conversation between womanist and queer can be traced even to the origins of the term womanist, as famously described by Alice Walker. In the first part of her definition, Walker highlighted a popular origin:

> From the black folk expression of mothers to female children, "You acting womanish," i.e., like a woman. Usually referring to outrageous, audacious, courageous or willful behavior. Wanting to know more and in greater depth than is considered "good" for one. (1983, xi)

Byron and Lovelace (2016, 11) suggest that this label was shunned by some black Christian women because of the opening of the second part of Walker's definition: "*Also*: A woman who loves other women, sexually and/or nonsexually" (1983, xi). While the reference to same-sex eroticism between (black) women suggests one clear basis for coalition and solidarity between womanist and queer, I would suggest that the first part of the definition is an even more intriguing basis, as it emphasizes the kinds of disruptive qualities later drafted and resignified for queer. Perhaps it is no surprise, then, that movements such as Black Lives Matter were founded by queer black women and refuse the terms of respectability politics. Queer may be womanist, and womanist may be queer when this work encourages willful and outrageous efforts to counter a politics of respectability and normalcy (for a few intriguing womanist reconsiderations of deviance and respectability, see Clay 2013; Miller 2013; Davis 2016; and Lovelace 2016).

Cathy Cohen (1997) specifically interrogates whether queer activism is prepared to address racisms within and beyond lesbian and gay communities, if other sexually and racially marginalized people—like her essay's titular punks, bulldaggers, and welfare queens—are not (also) the basis for queer coalitional politics. Cohen and others demonstrate the still-contingent relation of queer to radical social and political transformation. If queer is to move with and into its potential, then it would need to remain persistently reflexive, interrogating its strategies and impacts in increasingly intersectional directions. We would need to keep asking, as a special double issue of the journal *Social Text* did, "What's Queer about Queer Studies Now?" (Eng, Halberstam, and Muñoz 2005). The introduction to that collection answers that question by offering an additional and expanding series of questions: "What does queer studies have to say about empire, globalization, neoliberalism, sovereignty, and terrorism? What does queer studies tell us about immigration, citizenship, prisons, welfare, mourning, and human rights?" (2). The sixteen essays that follow these and other questions indicate a different, more capacious terrain for queer studies.

One of the key contributors to that special double issue and the ongoing interrogation of what queer studies is and does is Jasbir Puar. In her essay "Queer Times, Queer Assemblages" (2005) and her pathbreaking book *Terrorist Assemblages: Homonationalism in Queer Times* (2007), Puar traces how liberal nation-states, like the United States, offer a constrained form of inclusion for some lesbian and gay subjects, so long as they attest to the supposed tolerant or progressive status of an imperial center in comparison to regressive or violent others. These others are marked not only by gender and sexual difference, but also and *especially* by their religious, racial, national, and colonial difference. In the context of the (never-ending?) war on terror, these terrorist bodies are religiously racialized Muslims and South Asians, who must be eliminated. A biopolitical inclusion of some figures, like the docile gay patriot, requires the necropolitical exclusion of others, the monster-terrorist-fags (see also Puar and Rai 2002). Queerness can become an alibi for global and imperial violence, for what Puar dubs homonationalism. Sexuality is used to disaggregate subjects who could be in queer solidarity, casting some nation-states and its loyal patriots (straight and gay) as sexually exceptional and casting other populations as inherently perverse and deviant on interlocking racial, religious, and sexual terms and thus deserving of death.

In Puar's work, then, queerness is less an identity than an assemblage of interwoven forces in perpetual motion (see especially 2007, 211–16). The motility and contingency of queer mean that it is capable of both resistance and complicity in the forms and forces of oppression, as the essays by Hoke and Schwaller in this volume indicate.[9] Hoke's chapter specifically redeploys homonationalism to rethink how Paul argues in sexually exceptionalist ways in 1 Thessalonians, potentially offering spaces for the Thessalonian assembly members to be included in Roman imperial concepts of sexual virtue.[10] In such a reading, Hoke refuses to divorce questions of gender and sexuality (often associated with 1 Thess 4:1–12) from those of empire and conquest (in 4:13–5:11). Schwaller foregrounds Puar's conceptualization of queerness as potentially colluding or resistant as a hint for how to approach Paul's slave form in 1 Cor 9 and 2 Cor 11. Queerness cannot be reduced to a celebratory kind of transgression or resistance, as it

---

9. For another, sharp reflection on the roles of both lesbian desire and potential queer complicity for biblical interpretation, without reference to Puar, see Huber 2011.

10. For previous reflections on Puar's relevance for biblical interpretation, see Kotrosits 2014 and Marchal 2014a, 2015a.

can prop up the oppressive material and rhetorical conditions for enslaved people, reflecting their multiple, complicated, yet banal circumstances. In this way Puar's view of queerness mirrors the tension between resistance and complicity intrinsic to slavery discourses in antiquity.

So, perhaps, we should foreground various queer effects and affects as more than occasionally complicit, yet with lingering potentials for disruption and disidentification. This could signal the influence of a different triumvirate, David Eng, Jack/Judith Halberstam, and José Esteban Muñoz, the coeditors of that aforementioned double issue (2005).[11] Halberstam continues to be one of the more creative and prolific writers in queer studies, producing seriously playful and often accessibly queer takes on cultural forms from the art house to the mainstream. Halberstam (1998) famously unmoored masculinity as the exclusive property of males by tracing various practices of female masculinity among lesbians, butches, trans guys, drag kings, and (other) gender queers. Gender variant bodies and transgender narratives are a consistent thread in his later work on temporality (2005) and negativity (2011). Indeed, Halberstam's work remains a sometimes controversial touchstone, or flashpoint, for transgender studies (see, especially Halberstam 2018) and thus ends up reflecting the debts, overlaps, yet clear tensions between queer and transgender studies (see also Stryker 2004).

While Halberstam explicitly appears only a few times in the queer archives of this collection, his work on female masculinity, drag kinging, and the transgender gaze have already influenced a few different attempts at trans biblical readings (Mollenkott 2001; Marchal 2014b; and Hornsby and Guest 2016).[12] However, as Liew highlights in his response, it is possible to read Twomey's analysis of Peter, as the science fiction version of "Paul," apostles to the aliens, *and* a literary embodiment of Halberstam's *In a Queer Time and Place* (2005). In these strange times and bodies, Nicolet's essay is also influenced by trans reclamations of the monstrous, but it goes further back to Halberstam's (1995) first project on Gothic novels to emphasize the disruptive, boundary-troubling potential of the ostensibly inhuman monster. Nicolet draws as much upon Susan Stryker's (1994)

---

11. Halberstam has increasingly, but not consistently, published under the first name of Jack and has admitted to being mostly a free floater when it comes to preferred names and pronouns. See, for instance, Halberstam 2018, 153–54.

12. For other, if still initial, trans approaches to biblical interpretation, see Kolakowski 2000; Tanis 2003, 55–84; Marchal 2011a; Hartke 2018.

daring transgender disidentification with the monster she was called, signifying on, of all things, ancient identifications of monsters and angels as
conduits for extraordinary revelations.

As these interventions indicate, Halberstam's work can also be useful
for thinking queerly in relation to temporality. Thus we have yet another
way of thinking of queerness not as an identity but "as an outcome of
strange temporalities, imaginative life schedules, and eccentric economic
practices" (2005, 1). Queer times and places present "the potentiality of a
life unscripted by the conventions of family, inheritance, and child rear-
ing" (2). Here Halberstam presents generally what Lee Edelman (2004)
poses more specifically, audaciously, even polemically in his critique of
reproductive futurity in *No Future: Queer Theory and the Death Drive*.[13]
Edelman explains that the heart of his argument starts with "a simple
provocation: that *queerness* names the side of those *not* 'fighting for the
children,' the side outside the consensus by which all politics confirms
the absolute value of reproductive futurism" (3). Rather than resisting or
qualifying this structural positioning—and agreeing that the children are
our future—Edelman suggests that the queer should accede to his or her
figural status as resistant to the cult of the Child. Queerness, then, figures the death drive of the social (153) and can reveal the fantasies that
move the social order. In his last major work, Muñoz (2009, 11) aimed to
counter Edelman's antisocial turn by insisting that "queerness is primarily
about futurity and hope.... Queerness is always in the horizon." He adopts
a more utopian approach to the past that just might performatively reveal
an alternative future.

Guy's essay situates us in relation to this larger body of reflections
on queer temporality. Guy even starts with the specifically apocalyptic temporality of Paul's arguments in 1 Corinthians and Halberstam's
(2005, 2) reflections on the HIV crisis.[14] The Corinthian embrace of
childishness and failure reflect a different orientation to time, perhaps
the sort of ecstatic time that Muñoz (2009, 32) presents on the horizon
or that Brandy L. Simula (2013) highlights in BDSM scenes. Edelman's

---

13. For a more thorough contextualization of Edelman, including in relation to
biblical and theological uses of sacred texts and traditions, see Moore, Brintnall, and
Marchal 2018, 8–13; Brintnall 2018.

14. For further reflections on how living and dying with HIV could reflect the
interpretation of Mark, for instance, see Kotrosits 2018. On the multiple Corinthian
apocalypticisms, in relation to multiple queer temporalities, see Marchal 2018.

critique of futurism is made to attend, then, not only to the idealiza-
tion of the future Child, but also to the necessary alienation of labor
in the present. Guy's essay engages these interlocutors more extensively
than any other essay, but issues of time and history haunt nearly every
one of these essays. How could they not as we reach back to discuss
first-century epistles and their interpretations in our queer twenty-first-
century times and places?! Guy and Twomey, then, share an interest in
Halberstam's rethinking of failure. Luckritz Marquis notes the utopian
aims of Muñoz's disidentifications. Schwaller opens his essay by admitting to feeling affective links to enslaved subjects of the past, the sort of
haunting with which my own essay reckons as it puzzles over receiving
different, more porous relations to the past.[15] Huber's response in particular brings out the kinds of melancholic "backwards feeling" (Love
2007) or "bottomy historiography" (Freeman 2010, 109) that queer
approaches take as they negotiate or simply dwell in the tension between
the past and the present.

This melancholia reminds that queer studies has long been formed
and informed by more psychoanalytically inclined thinkers. Understanding Edelman, for instance, requires some working knowledge of Jacques
Lacan, but even some of this collection's favorite queer theorists, such as
Butler and Muñoz, respond to and work with elements from Lacan, Sigmund Freud, or Melanie Klein. These elements of queer studies are less
foregrounded in this collection, outside my all-too-brief reflections on
trauma, melancholia, abjection, and haunting (and conversing with Bersani 1987; Cvetkovich 2003; Cheng 2001; and Freccero 2006). Yet many
queer theorists, such as David Eng (2001, 2010; see also Eng and Kazanjian 2003), have shown how individualized notions of concepts like
trauma or melancholia could be applied to broader sociopolitical—yet
still sexual—conditions of racialization and colonization. Eng persistently
demonstrates the relevance of psychoanalytic theory for engaging racist
social structures and their sexualized fantasies and stereotypes, for Asian
Americans among others.

---

15. Schwaller briefly references Dinshaw (1999) and Freeman (2010), both of
whose works have been considered at greater length for how they could allow interpreters of these epistles to develop a more desirable or pleasurable affective relation
between the past and the present in Marchal 2011b; 2014b; 2018; Menéndez-Antuña
2015; Hoke 2018.

Though this work is not explicitly taken up in the present volume, Liew (2008) has demonstrated the generative potential of mixing psychoanalytic and, or *as*, critical race theory, particularly with and from Asian American studies, with some important insights for queer approaches to Pauline epistles and interpretations. Following Eng's extension of melancholia, for instance, allows Liew to identify Paul's own racialized melancholia as a diasporic member of a denigrated group within the Greco-Roman context (103–5).[16] While his melancholic attachment to another Jewish body of Jesus as a lost object could be deployed in surprisingly depathologizing directions, Paul's own ambivalence about his colonized and thus effeminized position leads to his reinforcement of ancient colonial ideologies of gender and sexuality. As Liew and then the essays by both Hartman and Luckritz Marquis note, Paul's arguments about sexualized offenses and communal belonging in 1 Cor 5–6 could be symptomatic of these dynamics. Liew highlights:

> Paul projects his own abjection and stigmatization as being "feminine" and "morally corrupt" onto women and other sexual dissidents. By duplicating and displacing colonial abjection onto people who are also in different ways already subjected, Paul's resistance against colonization and racialization is greatly compromised.... He is building community on the backs of those whom "everyone" can agree to marginalize and stigmatize. (95)

Here Paul's projection of his own abjection and stigmatization onto others looks like a foretaste of Freud's own ambivalent displacements as a (later) diasporic Jew (see also Gilman 1993; Boyarin 1997).

This work may mostly be in the background of the essays to follow, but Liew's response notes how Freud's notion of the uncanny, or Lacan's *das Ding* as the intrusion of the Real, resonate with this collection's repeated attention to figures of excess or exclusion. Liew stresses that the children, slaves, animals, monsters, and freaks examined in this volume can all fall under the category of the inhuman. Indeed, Dunning's essay revolves precisely around the questions of what counts as the human and its resulting effects on how we could approach texts like Rom 1. Follow-

---

16. Liew is also in conversation with additional, more sociopolitical reuses of melancholia around gender and sexuality (Butler 1990, 57–72) and white supremacy and colonialism (Gilroy 2005).

ing Butler, Derrida, and Étienne Balibar (2017), Dunning reconsiders how the nonperson haunts any articulation of the human. The resulting incoherence reflects the failure of closure in any appeal to system, including when interpreters presume the stability of specific sexual subject positions. While Karen Barad's (2003) conceptualization of the intraactive agency of nonhuman material objects informs Schwaller's essay, and Twomey's essay examines the posthuman potential in the contact between earthlings and aliens, Hartman's essay directly engages the relationship between the queer and the nonhuman (see especially Luciano and Chen 2015). Constructions of human-animal difference trouble the demands to perform a particular norm of humanity, in our times as much as in the first-century context of the Corinthian correspondence. From such an angle, not only are the images in Paul's condemnations and exclusions gendered, sexualized, and racialized, but they are also animalized through his creaturely arguments around the lamb and the yeast. Of course, he is trying to convince the Corinthians to remove one sexually offensive human by transforming him into the yeast polluting their entire rising batch. Yet if they were (re)animated by another creaturely transformation into a lamb, then perhaps the Corinthians would not have minded a little yeast infection!

These interpretive possibilities rise from these essays' persistent attentions to excluded, marginalized, or denigrated elements of Pauline epistles and interpretations, often made possible by their innovative engagement with the dizzying array of directions in which queer studies has developed. Thus far, I have aimed to situate the essays in these directions and signal still further possibilities in increasing interactions between various strands of biblical and queer studies. In doing so, I suggest that we are really on the verge of something here.

Of course, in some ways this collection is just one in a long line of works of biblical scholarship appealing to the possibilities of theory from outside our normal disciplinary confines. Often, this sort of turn to theory evinces the anxiety of the interpreter—that we are somehow way behind other disciplines and domains. Moore's (2001, 7–12) introduction to his often dazzling collection *God's Beauty Parlor* opens with multiple suggestions about how biblical scholars dwell in the outdated assumptions of a far distant galaxy, light years from the mysterious and thrilling nebula of queer theory. Even in its most vanilla forms, biblical scholarship often promises one kind of space-time travel, ostensibly providing access backward to distant times and foreign places. With this collection I suggest that we are in an extraordinary moment of back and forth, reaching back to the first century but no longer in Moore's galaxy behind.[17] Indeed, when I recently went to the web version of *GLQ* (the most prominent queer studies journal) to quickly check a reference, my eyes landed on the site's list of their most-read articles. The first four were Butler's "Critically Queer" (later collected in 1993, 223–42), Stryker's "My Words to Victor Frankenstein..." (1994), Cohen's "Punks, Bulldaggers, and Welfare Queens" (1997), and Luciano and Chen's "Has the Queer Ever Been Human?" (2015). Of course, I have already situated this collection in light of each of these, as many of the essays to follow are influenced by this work (see especially Nicolet and Hartman). This biblical conversation is looking increasingly like a queer convergence, toward a significantly expanding universe of possibilities for our travels on, against, and within Pauline epistles and interpretations.

In introducing a finite collection of essays, I would be colossally foolish to promise a panoramic view of this entire universe or to chart a course for interstellar sexual salvation. To be sure, the various contributors to this volume do not prescribe a new collective course of action, but they do perform an at-times-outrageous range of alternative options for queering our constellations, often through a robust, reflexive, even nimble negotiation of so much (admittedly sometimes dense) theoretical material. For the less initiated, these essays can function as important and illuminating guides into the riotous variety of queer theories circulating outside and, now more than occasionally, within religious or theological studies. Such guides inevitably signal still other possibilities.

Even just returning to the work of Eng indicates other topics relevant for queering Pauline epistles and interpretations. His reflections on *Racial Castration* (2001) suggest alternative analogues or angles on questions about circumcision and the racially gendered bodies that composed and received the epistles and Acts. Critiques from queer diaspora (see Eng 2001, 2010; Manalansan 2003; Gopinath 2005) have some obvious resonances for these movements and stigmatized bodies subsisting in the Jewish diaspora of the Roman Empire, and they could help to trouble normative relationships to kinship and the racialized intimacies of hostlands and homelands. In rethinking the inevitable destinations of these move-

---

17. See Miranda July's (2005) film *Me and You and Everyone We Know*; see also Berlant and Edelman 2014, 20–34.

ments, feminist and queer disability—or crip—approaches (Kafer 2013; McRuer 2006), would significantly reframe how we approach the stigmatized bodies reflected in Paul's correspondence with various communities (though see aspects of Nicolet's essay).[18]

Once we begin considering how social impressions are generated, shared, and maintained, how these often nonconscious sensations resonate within and travel between bodies, we begin to get a feel for the queer territories of affect. Affect theory is only now starting to catch on in biblical studies (see Koosed and Moore 2014; Kotrosits 2015, 2016; Black and Koosed forthcoming), but most of the essays in this collection have been infected with affect, whether they know it or not. Indeed, many of the figures encountered in these ancient epistles and assemblies could be labeled queer or, following Liew, inhuman or, more simply still, just willful subjects (Ahmed 2014). In Guy's hands, the absurd ecstasy of the Corinthians refuses the appeals of both paranoia (see Sedgwick 2003) and cruel optimism (Berlant 2011). Hoke's Thessalonians are untidy vessels in that their affectively mobilized assemblages (Puar 2007) fail to rationally align along simple narratives around complicity and resistance. Nicolet's monsters are scare figures with their potential for wounding or disgust, but in Stryker's intervention, a transgender rage can transform their stigmatizing impacts. Several essays state or simply stage the affective resonances of historical efforts (including especially Hartman, Schwaller, and Marchal). Concerns about contagion (Hartman) and the dynamic relationship between material and discursive practices (Schwaller) transmit affect as well. My own essay is concerned with the trauma and abjection of a past that is not past, one that haunts and drags on in both painful and pleasurable sensations. Twomey, too, wonders about the potential connections of solidarity across bleak conditions. Huber's response underscores (with Love 2007) that many of these desires for the past are both melancholic and nostalgic. Stockton's response demonstrates how the objects that linger in our respective queer archives reflect often-excessive yet necessary affective attachments. Many of us have feelings about these texts and traditions because we have a history with them.

---

18. For some initial uses of crip theory for biblical and rabbinic interpretation, see Solevåg 2016 and Belser 2016. The former discusses castration, the subject of a cutting joke in Gal 5:12 (see the discussion in Marchal 2015b and Nicolet's essay in this volume).

On the Verge of ... Pauline Bodies

And still ... when most of us say the words *queer* and *Paul* in any proximity to one another, our friends and family, lovers and haters, and pastors and other confessional professionals anticipate a conversation about how Paul's letters clearly condemn homosexuality. This typically means an enormous amount of attention devoted to just a few verses in Paul's letters—Rom 1:26–27 and 1 Cor 6:9–10—texts that ostensibly give us not just Paul's but (with Gen 19 and Lev 18 and 20) the *Bible*'s stance on homosexuality. Since Paul's reputation precedes us, the current, most common scholarly response is to situate these brief references and Paul's arguments in general within the historical context of the first century CE. Yet as Heather White's essay and her larger work (2015) demonstrate, this focus is a product of a particular moment, one far more recent than the first century.

From the middle of the twentieth century, interpreters of these texts began insisting upon the historical difference between now and then. Derrick Sherwin Bailey (1955), for instance, maintained that Paul's letters make definite enough references to homosexual practices to discuss them in British ecclesial and political debates. Yet Bailey's emphasis on practice or behavior introduced an important discontinuity, since: "the Bible and Christian tradition know nothing of *homosexuality*; both are concerned solely with the commission of homosexual *acts*" (x). John Boswell (1980) also sought to dissociate homosexuality from Pauline condemnations, but he focused on the language of exchanging or abandoning (in Rom 1:23, 25, 26, 27). Boswell attempted to argue that both homosexual and heterosexual people were known in the Greco-Roman context of the time, but "even more important, the persons Paul condemns are manifestly not homosexual: what he derogates are homosexual acts committed by apparently heterosexual persons" (109). Thus Boswell assumes the source of antigay feelings must be found elsewhere in (later) Christian traditions. Both Boswell and Bailey differentiate acts in ways akin to Foucault's separation of the homosexual from sodomy (discussed above), but toward different ends. Boswell argues for the existence of ancient homosexuals, while Bailey proceeds on the (once-current) modern medical view that homosexuals suffered from an involuntary and interior mental condition. To Bailey, this made the modern homosexual less culpable in his eyes and deserving of a modicum of legal protection afforded by a repeal of sodomy laws.

While not many have been persuaded by Boswell's proposition that we could identify people across the centuries as homosexual, many interpreters preserved the term homosexual in their discussion of Paul's letters, even as they introduce some important historical difference. Robin Scroggs (1983, 122), for instance, insists that Paul "must have had, *could only have had*, pederasty in mind" in texts like Rom 1. For Scroggs, the conceptual and denominational significance of this fact turn in somewhat contradictory fashion. On the one hand, pederasty and homosexuality are different: "The *fact* remains, however, that the basic model in today's Christian homosexual community is so different from the model attacked by the New Testament that the criterion of reasonable similarity of context is not met" (127). This lack of similarity has so great a force that he argues, "The conclusion I have to draw seems inevitable: *Biblical judgments against homosexuality are not relevant to today's debate*" (127). On the other hand, Scroggs persists in identifying homosexuality as the target of biblical judgment, an identification that maintains a (politically and historically fraught) link between pederasty and, or as a kind of, homosexuality. The relatively progressive positions of Scroggs, Boswell, and Bailey often managed to both solidify the notion that the Bible is relevant for present-day debates about (homo)sexuality (even in spite of their claims otherwise) and reflect more recent, modern assumptions of difference.

This difference was highlighted in order to advocate a more compassionate or progressive approach. This might suggest the benefit of a gradual liberalization, even secularization, in our new, different historical era. Yet as White (2015, 1–4, 34–41) highlights, it was sympathetic, liberal, even progressive Protestant ministers and scholars who first inserted the word *homosexuals* into a passage of Pauline condemnation. Using what was thought to be the best and most up-to-date historical and therapeutic knowledge, the scholars on the translation committee of the Revised Standard Version (1946) introduced homosexuals as a translation for two separate (!) words, *malakoi* and *arsenokoitai* (in 1 Cor 6:9), where broader (if differently troubling) terms of effeminacy and abuse once stood (for instance, in the King James Version). A new therapeutic approach initiated a new common sense about the history of Pauline texts and traditions, reflecting an apparent sympathy for homosexuals among some American Protestants, but ironically working contrary to such sentiments. For twentieth-century homosexuals, a shift away from discussions of sodomites was not progress. The new translation narrowed and condensed the meaning of Paul's letter (among other passages) and directed the condemnation in now some of the most explicit terms. If the slightly later, liberal interpreters would insist that history teaches us that this is *not* what these texts meant, then the plain meaning they were contesting was, ironically, the product of only slightly earlier, liberal interpreters!

This attention to a small selection of texts and the certainty that they are relevant for discussions about homosexuality, then, are both products of a particular moment and its still-lingering aftermath. This specific and far more recent origin scrambles the most common coordinates in contemporary discussions of religion and sexuality. These are often posed in oppositional terms: if biblical teachings are religious and ancient (even timeless), then gays and lesbians are modern and secular (see White's essay). Yet this common sense is itself distinctly modern and built upon the incorporation of secular psychological assumptions into a modern biblical translation. Indeed, both conservatives and liberals draw upon the same relatively short tradition of translation. This is the story of how Paul was transformed into a modern authority on sexuality. This more recent history should, in turn, interrogate our (Protestant) desire for the biblical text's original meaning, particularly when we are the ones planting ancient truths in the texts. This history might suggest the strange possibilities of a more proximate—yet still pre-Stonewall—past, the periods often explored by queer scholars such as Muñoz (1999, 2009), Love (2007), and Freeman (2010). These encounters should also trouble any confidence that we can know the effect of our interpretive efforts, whether we are questing for an ancient historical difference or aiming for a contemporary contextualized outcome (or both), without a persistent, even nagging, reflexivity.

Thus Bailey, Boswell, and Scroggs were not the only interpreters operating in the aftermath of this contradictorily ancient innovation. We still pay inordinate attention to the "clobber passages," even if biblical scholars have increased our disciplinary habit of stressing historical difference. I consider this habit at greater length in my essay in this volume (and elsewhere, Marchal 2011b), but it is one I confess I cannot quite shake, a site of unreconciled attachment or continuing disidentification. Even still, I persistently identify with the work of yet another queer threesome—Bernadette J. Brooten (1996), Dale B. Martin (1995, 1996), and Stephen D. Moore (2001, 133–72)—particularly where they address these texts and lingering problems of their historical difference.

Martin, for instance, underscores the specific problems of translation when grappling with the oft-cited "clobber passage," found in 1 Cor 6:9–10. While the RSV renders the Greek pair *arsenokoitai* and *malakoi* with the English "homosexuals," Martin (1996, 118–23) shows that *arsenokoitēs* is extraordinarily rare, poorly attested, and radically uncertain in its meaning, while *malakos* (or "softness") is none of those things—it is easily, yet distressingly familiar in its negative associations with femininity or effeminacy (124–28). Brooten's extensive study of female homoeroticism demonstrates how this same gendered asymmetry is reflected in the broader Greco-Roman context and then in Paul's arguments in Rom 1:18–32. Her convincing commentary on this mightily contested text shows its fit within an ancient context where "'natural' intercourse means penetration of a subordinate person by a dominant one" (1996, 241). The possibility of female-female sexual contact is condemned in this context because females (among or akin to others with lower sociopolitical status, such as slaves, minors, and foreigners) are presumed to be subordinate, passive, and thus receptive. Moore (2001, 146) builds upon Brooten, noting how much Paul's argument in Rom 1:26–27 is "startlingly congruent" with the prevailing emphasis on phallic penetration. Such appalling repetitions lead Brooten (1996, 302) to conclude that churches should not teach Rom 1:26–27 as authoritative, while Moore (2001, 171–72) can only conclude that his work could be a prolegomenon to a radical reformation away from such dynamics.

Not surprisingly, then, many queer readers and users stay away from Paul's letters. It seems easier to imagine, with Robert E. Goss (1993), that *Jesus Acted Up*, more exciting to imagine other biblical figures belonging, with Nancy Wilson (1995), to *Our Tribe*. Both Goss and Wilson refer to the two clobber passages as "texts of terror" (Goss 1993, 90–92; Wilson 1995, 65–66, 94–96), one of several signs of the influence of feminist biblical interpreters, like Phyllis Trible (1984), on queer approaches. Yet liberation oriented interpreters tend to have a greater investment in and identification with biblical texts. This could, in part, account for why Theodore W. Jennings Jr. (2009) devotes an entire study to defending Paul and biblical traditions in general against their common association with the origins of homophobia. Thomas Hanks (2000) develops such liberationist yet apologist tendencies even further, particularly when he casts most of the New Testament authors (including Paul) as sexual minorities. Hanks maintains that the bulk of Paul's letter to the Romans deconstructs the argument he mimes in 1:24–27 (2000, 80–94; 2006), as the entire Pauline corpus reveals a range of liberating messages for oppressed groups like women, slaves, and sexual minorities (2000, 80–199). This identification of Paul as a sexual minority himself, and perhaps even gay, may go as far back as the mid-twentieth-century insertion of "homosexuals" into translations of 1 Cor 6:9. The Italian filmmaker Pier Paolo Pasolini depicts Paul as troubled by same-sex desires in his screenplay for *Saint Paul*, written in the 1960s, long before bishop John Spong (1992) or novelist Gore Vidal (1992), for instance, imagined Paul as a homosexual.[19]

Paul certainly claimed to be unmarried and that this status would be the far better option for anyone who could handle it, particularly given the apocalyptic conditions of his time (1 Cor 7:7–9, 26–40). At times, these letters even seem to be anticipating the queer critiques of reproductive futurity performed by Edelman, Halberstam, and Muñoz (noted above)! This work, then, indicates the importance of both exploring many aspects of the epistles other than the small set of clobber passages and trying out more creative approaches to these texts and traditions. Many queer commentaries, for instance, proceed by way of analogy, if not always exact identification. Several gay-affirmative readings apply Paul's argument against circumcision for (male) gentiles in Galatians to counter claims that homosexuals must change the way they are to count as Christians (see Siker 1994; Bohache 2000; Cheng 2006). Holly Hearon's (2006) entry on the Corinthian correspondence in *The Queer Bible Commentary* multiplies the potential modes of analogy by explicitly attending to multiple voices, reflecting upon the tensions within both the Corinthian and more-recent LGBTIQ communities. It works so well because it, too, learned key lessons from feminist interpretations of these letters and read against the grain of Paul's perspective (especially Wire 1990).

Like Hearon, many of the essays in this collection specifically draw from the insights and techniques first developed in feminist approaches to Pauline epistles and interpretations by Elisabeth Schüssler Fiorenza (1983, 1992, 1999, 2001), Antoinette Clark Wire (1990), and Elizabeth A. Castelli (1991a), and then practiced by a range of scholars (including Kittredge 1998, 2003; Marchal 2006, 2008; and Johnson-DeBaufre and Nasrallah 2011). While only a few imagine the possibilities for a feminist reconstruction or historical reimagination, a majority of the essays here try to decenter Paul's perspective in several different ways, often by reading against the grain of the letters (see, for instance, Guy, Hoke, Hartman, Schwaller, Luckritz Marquis, and Marchal). Many recognize the rhetoricity of our sources for queering Pauline epistles, and several use Schüssler Fiorenza's neologism *kyriarchy* (see 1999, ix; 2001, 1, 118–24, 211) to describe intersecting

---

19. The English translation of this screenplay for *Saint Paul* would unfortunately have to wait until Pasolini 2014.

dynamics of oppression, instead of single-factored terms like patriarchy, slavery, poverty, or empire. Indeed, Schüssler Fiorenza interrogates the politics of othering that accompanies the scholarly politics of identification with Paul (see especially 2000), grappling with a set of dynamics that is strikingly similar to those that have troubled approaches to queer identification. If larger bodies of scholarship would attend to either—or preferably both!—of these discussions, it would signal that biblical studies is really on the verge of some significant and much-needed transformations.

These feminist strategies animate the majority of essays in this collection, but the political and affective pull of identifying (with) what Paul argues still remains rather strong for many readers and users of these texts and traditions. Inevitably, this draws our eyes back to passages like Rom 1:18–32. In a series of important essays (2003, 2004, 2006), Diana Swancutt situates the letter's argument about "unnatural" sexual activity as a stereotypical censure of hypocritical Stoics. Paul repeats ancient gender stereotypes, but his rhetoric of masculinity is "a biting denunciation of *Romanitas*" (Swancutt 2003, 232). Several other interpreters, such as Neil Elliott (2008, 77–85) and Theodore W. Jennings Jr. (2009, 129–55; see also 2013), see allusions to various emperors in the litany of offensive behaviors in the opening chapter of Romans, indicating that the sexual matters are the set-up for a broader anti-imperial critique. In contradistinction to Brooten (1996), Swancutt (especially 2007), and Jennings (2009, 153–54) strongly doubt that the admittedly brief mention of females (in Rom 1:26) refers to female-female sexual contact. It seems clearer that at least some male-male sexual behavior may be alluded to here (Paul is probably punning on receptivity in 1:27), but to anti-imperial interpreters, homoeroticism in general is not the focus; rather, the focus is Paul's critique of specific Roman imperial elites. In the case of Galatians, scholars like Davina Lopez (2008, especially 142) have argued even further that Paul's resistance to Roman imperial ideology is matched by his own transgendered identification as a mother in labor pains in 4:19.

Aspects of these anti-imperial (or postcolonial) approaches to the epistles and interpretations have proven illuminating, but they falter some when they pass over the repeated ways in which the letters deploy gender and sexual stereotypes.[20] Such repetitions complicate our approach to

---

20. For the closely related feminist concerns about mostly single-factored anti-imperial readings of Paul's letters, see Kittredge 2000; Wire 2000; Marchal 2008.

these texts and traditions in several ways. First, the kinds of sexual insult that appear in Paul's letters were rather common in the ancient setting of the Roman Empire (see Knust 2006), making it difficult to insist that their appearance refers to specific historical figures in the letter's arguments or audiences. Second, these stereotyped figures are not just fleeting moments in two isolated—if oft-cited—bashing passages, but they appear in several moments, in most of Paul's letters. This indicates, third, that the letters fit into a broader kyriarchal ambiance, their arguments mark not a difference but a similarity to those Paul is (ostensibly) critiquing. Fourth, this similarity reflects a strikingly colonizing but also racializing perspective shared between the letters and their broader contexts. Thus Swancutt, Jennings, Elliott, and many other interpreters are of course correct in noting that the clobber texts are not strictly about sexuality, let alone our culturally specific perspectives on homosexuality. Yet even as aspects of these letters depart from Roman imperial family values (see D'Angelo 2003), interpreters such as Kwok Pui-lan (2006) and Fredrik Ivarsson (2007) stress the specifically ethnoracial dynamics of texts like Rom 1 and 1 Cor 6, since they operate by targeting people through xenophobic figurations of gentile outsiders or Others who recurrently do the wrong things.[21]

Thus as the histories of both feminist biblical studies and queer studies in general have indicated, queering Pauline epistles and interpretations will need to be dynamic, reflexive, and intersectional. Subjects like gender and sexuality cannot be easily separated from race, ethnicity, religion, or imperialism in these letters and communities, and not only because they often address Jews and gentiles, Romans and their barbarians. A range of scholars have demonstrated how profoundly Paul's letters are shaped not by an alternative view of ethnic or religious difference but precisely through ethnic, racial, and religious rhetorics (C. Martin 1991, 1998; Byron 2002; Kelley 2002; Buell and Johnson Hodge 2004; Buell 2005, 2009; Johnson Hodge 2007). In light of this work, Paul is neither the founder of a universalistic religion nor an advocate for ethnic transcendence. Caroline Johnson Hodge and Denise Kimber Buell (2004, 238), for instance, stress that these letters "define a communal vision in terms of ethnicity—not over against ethnicity." They underscore the ways that ethnoracial dis-

---

21. For some initial indications of the connections and overlaps between postcolonial and queer approaches, see Punt 2010, 2011, as well as Kwok 2006 and Marchal 2015a.

courses are dynamic, simultaneously playing between the poles of fixity and fluidity. The receptions and uses of these epistles, then, are haunted by the not-yet-past pasts of racism in many forms, including those shaped by the historical conditions of slavery, anti-Semitism, and colonialism. Indeed, Buell has persistently reflected on such haunting heritages (2009, 2010, 2014), connecting these pasts and our presents without evading our accountabilities to lingering effects and afterlives. The ambivalences of these heritages reach backward and forward, particularly in the cases of enslaved people in these traditions, highlighting distinctive obstacles and fraught interconnections (see especially Glancy 1998, 2002; and Briggs 2000, 2003).

As I note above, most of the essays in this collection trace and grapple with the overlapping and mutually informing vectors of race, ethnicity, and empire alongside and within gender, sexuality, and embodiment. Jewish-gentile difference is a recurrent and rather expected topic within Pauline studies because so many interpreters esteem Paul as the (Jewish) apostle to the gentiles. Yet the queer approaches taken in this introduction and in the pages to follow present rather unexpected pictures of these dynamics and significantly complicate more common perspectives on the apostle and the epistles we attribute to him. With some of the more recent, creative, and often liberationist-style queer approaches, this collection moves beyond more defensive approaches to the expected prooftexts. Because the approaches developed in this volume are not especially disciplined by this defensive stance, these interpreters tend to push past not only the common texts but even the traditional scholarly focus on the perspective of Paul in favor of more audacious, excessive, twisty, and troubling possibilities. These possibilities bubble up from our encounters and engagements with nearly all of the authentic or undisputed letters. The essays focus on various elements within six of those seven letters, including Romans (Dunning, Marchal), 1 Corinthians (Guy, Hartman, Schwaller), 2 Corinthians (Luck-ritz Marquis, Schwaller), Galatians (Nicolet, Twomey), 1 Thessalonians (Hoke, Marchal), and Philemon (Marchal).[22]

The volume as a whole tends to resist the siren call of the slim but still much-disputed bashing passages, though an attentive reader may notice that they do make their way into three of the last four essays (Marchal,

---

22. For a queer approach to the only "missing" letter in this batch, Philippians, see Marchal 2014c.

Dunning, and White). These are pushed to the back for several reasons (thematically and strategically), but most especially because work on Pauline epistles and interpretations still need a good shove to move into more critical, theoretical, reflexive, and creative directions. If we situate this collection within the odd assemblage called Pauline studies, the approaches taken here especially stand out. Pauline studies is perhaps the least adventurous of the canonically divided subfields within biblical studies, still mostly dominated by traditional or—more candidly—conservative and apologist assumptions and approaches. So while it is certainly important to counter the oppressive, phobic, and stigmatizing uses of Rom 1:26–27 and 1 Cor 6:9–10, it is well past time to take these and many other texts and traditions in other, unanticipated directions.

This volume is one demonstration that this sort of queering of Pauline epistles and interpretations is on the verge of happening. As a collection, it is the most concentrated expression of these bodies on the verge, but it is not the only example. We have only just begun to get into *Bible Trouble* (Hornsby and Stone 2011)! This is why readers should be familiar with a wider range of work. For instance, Swancutt's work is important not only because it marshals a masterful body of evidence about ancient imperial masculinity in order to contextualize texts like Rom 1:26–27.[23] In one of her more creative moments, she addresses contemporary culture wars by turning to recent work on intersex (2006, 70–75) to interrogate assumptions about the "natural" two-sex body.[24] In another, she moves past a discussion of the bashing passages, turning just a few verses after 1 Cor 6:9–10, to highlight the strangely sexualized description of Paul's admonition to unite with the Lord (6:17), with the same verb for uniting, joining, or having sex with a prostitute—*kollōmenos* (repeated in 6:16 and 6:17) (2006, 93–96). Becoming members of Christ's body and receiving his seed (*sperma*) never sounded kinkier! To be sure, this Pauline gender performance still repeats ancient forms of misogyny and hierarchy, but such queer angles on the epistles and interpretations, in light of both ancient

---

23. For further reflections on Paul's letters in terms of masculinity, see also Kahl 2000; Moore 2001, 133–72; Glancy 2003; Larson 2004; Ivarsson 2007; Conway 2008, 67–88.

24. For three other more concentrated reflections on the significance of intersex for biblical interpretation (and perhaps also vice versa), see Gross 1999; DeFranza 2015; Marchal 2015b.

and contemporary settings, suggest far more daring possibilities than enacted in the dry, vanilla versions centered within Pauline studies.

This collection turns the terms of many of the debates deploying parts of Paul's letters, resisting them while twisting them, queering them to show what else can be done with epistles and interpretations. Because queer studies has developed in capacious, even riotous directions, engaging this expanse now helps interpretations of these letters explode along previously unimagined trajectories. The story I am trying to tell in this introduction, and that the contributors collectively demonstrate, is not only about the use of theory but about what we are doing and what we could still do with biblical images, ideas, arguments, and afterlives. These bodies on the verge indicate that we are in an emerging but hopefully extended moment. This collection is one mark of the moment, but another gauge is the 2017 arrival, at different rates, of three dissertations—one last queer trinity!—each using queer theory to grapple with aspects of Pauline epistles and interpretations.[25] Hoke (2017) and Schwaller (2017) are among this volume's fabulous contributors, but Gillian Townsley was unable to participate since she was hard at work adapting her 2011 dissertation into a fabulous book: *"The Straight Mind" in Corinth* (2017). Townsley's project demonstrates the importance of traveling not only with queer partners but beyond canonical versions of queer studies, particularly through her use of Monique Wittig's work. Wittig has provided yet another way to trouble these versions since her influential essay "The Straight Mind" (to which the title of Townsley's dissertation project refers) was first delivered in 1979, but her essays were only collected in 1992 as a result of the critical appreciation and engagement shown in Butler's (1990) *Gender Trouble*. Townsley's work tracing alternative, subdominant views of gender is inspired by Wittig's (2005, 47) call to "lesbianize the heroes of love, lesbianize the symbols, lesbianize the gods and the goddesses, lesbianize Christ, lesbianize the men and the women." Her final chapter graphically displaces the work of an infamously phobic and abusive interpreter (who frankly does not deserve my citation) page by page by progressively adding more and more discussion of Wittig's differently outrageous views of anatomy, degradation, and disgust from the bottom up.

---

25. Another foretaste of this moment could be Dunning's (2014) relatively brief *Christ without Adam*, which deploys some aspects of queer theory in its critique of recent philosophical readings of Paul, mostly along the lines of his previous work (2011) on the Adam-Christ typology among second- and third-century Christian thinkers.

Townsley's monstrous lesbians make furtive appearances in the pages to follow, but so do other bodies on the verge of excess and offense—childish Corinthians, monstrous Galatians, and Thessalonian vessels among them. These bodies reflect the still "open mesh of possibilities, gaps, overlaps, dissonances and resonances, lapses and excesses" (Sedgwick 1993, 8) for our queering encounters with these texts and traditions. These encounters allow us to reassess ancient terms like *porneia*, reveal the cracks where enslaved members negotiated their conditions, disrupt our ideals, challenge the coherence of our systematizing habits, and explode our canons by looking both backward and forward in surprising new directions. This involves an often-decentered and perhaps even wandering Paul, but also more porous interpreters and receivers—embodied animals but not especially exceptional ones—even from within our increasingly approximate attention to such troubling texts and traditions. So many different kinds of bodies, then, are on the verge. There are the bodies of traditions around biblical interpretation, including those that have recently insisted on appeals to only some verses, within certain historically, ethically, and politically constrained frames. The Pauline corpus, too, has been alternately assembled either as a scripturally canonical or a historically authentic body. Each of these bodies contains multitudes: the letters themselves are touchy, even troubling items for queer archives, yet the bodies they address and the many other bodies they construct, like and unlike the one constructed for the author/apostle, suggest still other perilous propositions (for these bodies beside Paul's, see Marchal 2019). Though most scholars like to pose and project otherwise, interpreters and users of these bodies are themselves embodied receivers, engaging in performative recitations and negotiating our academic and affective investments, political and physical desires, and spiritual and sexual sensations.

This is not one body, given for you, but a whole series of *bodies* on the verge—these do not speak with one voice, nor do the essays in this collection. They do not prescribe the one right way to queer Pauline epistles and interpretations. They do significantly expand the repertoire of possibilities for both the texts and the strategies, in attentive but often daring directions. They certainly reflect excessive expertise in the contexts of the first century, but they spill out and stretch beyond these, not only to our current cultural contexts but to more recent history, to contemporary literature that elicits a conflicted futurity, and even to the dissonant comforts and pleasures of our trips to the movies (see Stockton's concluding response). As Stockton's (2017) own work attests, queer approaches to these letters have already begun seeping into other disciplines. We are neither behind nor ahead more cutting edge fields more accustomed to queering interventions; perhaps, on the verge of this moment, our assumed boundaries have never been more porous. Perhaps this is not the case, but the work contained in this volume gives a concerted shove to the silos that separate us by our ostensible specializations, tipping them over and shaking, crossing, even twerking with the bodies tumbling out of them.

Your body, the one that holds these bodies in your own hands, or glances at them flitting before your eyes, should take a tumble with these queer juxtapositions, disidentifications, and reimaginations. We're on the verge of…. These epistles and interpretations prove to be surprisingly prone to both attachments and refusals, frequent decentering and occasional deconstruction. We're on the verge of…. Dwelling with these ambivalences and negotiations, our elaborations and qualifications present disturbing and dazzling possibilities, almost always because they risk verging on queering, approaching so closely to subjects of perverse revulsion and devotion. We're on the verge of…. Leave this last margin or edge of this impossible introduction—it will be worth the trouble.

We're on the verge of…

Works Cited

Agosto, Efraín. 2018. "Islands, Borders, and Migration: Reading Paul in Light of the Crisis in Puerto Rico." Pages 149–70 in *Latinxs, the Bible and Migration*. Edited by Efraín Agosto and Jacqueline Hidalgo. New York: Palgrave.

Ahmed, Sara. 2014. *Willful Subjects*. Durham: Duke University Press.

Anzaldúa, Gloria. 1987. *Borderlands/La Frontera: The New Mestiza*. San Francisco: Aunt Lute.

Bailey, Derrick Sherwin. 1955. *Homosexuality and the Western Christian Tradition*. London: Longmans, Green.

Bailey, Randall C., Tat-siong Benny Liew, and Fernando F. Segovia, eds. 2009. *They Were All Together in One Place? Toward Minority Biblical Criticism*. SemeiaSt 57. Atlanta: Society of Biblical Literature.

Balibar, Étienne. 2017. *Citizen Subject: Foundations for Philosophical Anthropology*. Translated by Steven Miller. New York: Fordham University Press.

Barad, Karen. 2003. "Posthumanist Performativity: Toward an Understanding of How Matter Comes to Matter." *Signs* 28:801–31.

Belser, Julia Watts. 2016. "Brides and Blemishes: Queering Women's Disability in Rabbinic Marriage Law." *JAAR* 84:401–29.

Berlant, Lauren. 2011. *Cruel Optimism*. Durham: Duke University Press.

Berlant, Lauren, and Lee Edelman. 2014. *Sex, or the Unbearable*. ThQ. Durham: Duke University Press.

Berlant, Lauren, and Elizabeth Freeman. 1993. "Queer Nationality." Pages 193–229 in *Fear of a Queer Planet: Queer Politics and Social Theory*. Edited by Michael Warner. Minneapolis: University of Minneapolis Press.

Bersani, Leo. 1987. "Is the Rectum a Grave?" Pages 197–222 in *AIDS: Cultural Analysis/Cultural Activism*. Edited by Douglas Crimp. OB. Cambridge: MIT Press.

Black, Fiona C., and Jennifer L. Koosed, eds. Forthcoming. *Reading with Feeling: Affect Theory and the Bible*. SemeiaSt. Atlanta: SBL Press.

Bohache, Thomas. 2000. " 'To Cut or Not to Cut': Is Compulsory Heterosexuality a Prerequisite for Christianity?" Pages 227–39 in *Take Back the Word: A Queer Reading of the Bible*. Edited by Robert E. Goss and Mona West. Cleveland: Pilgrim.

Boswell, John. 1980. *Christianity, Social Tolerance, and Homosexuality: Gay People in Western Europe from the Beginning of the Christian Era to the Fourteenth Century*. Chicago: University of Chicago Press.

Boyarin, Daniel. 1997. *Unheroic Conduct: The Rise of Heterosexuality and the Invention of the Jewish Man*. Contraversions. Berkeley: University of California Press.

Briggs, Sheila. 2000. "Paul on Bondage and Freedom in Imperial Roman Society." Pages 110–23 in *Paul and Politics: Ekklesia, Israel, Imperium, Interpretation; Essays in Honor of Krister Stendahl*. Edited by Richard A. Horsley. Harrisburg, PA: Trinity.

———. 2003. "Slavery and Gender." Pages 171–92 in *On the Cutting Edge: The Study of Women in Biblical Worlds; Essays in Honor of Elisabeth Schüssler Fiorenza*. Edited by Jane Schaberg, Alice Bach, and Esther Fuchs. New York: Continuum.

Brintnall, Kent L. 2013. "Queer Studies and Religion." *CRR* 1:51–61.

———. 2018. "Who Weeps for the Sodomite?" Pages 145–60 in *Sexual Disorientations: Queer Temporalities, Affects, Theologies*. Edited by Kent L. Brintnall, Joseph A. Marchal, and Stephen D. Moore. TTC. New York: Fordham University Press.

Brooten, Bernadette J. 1996. *Love between Women: Early Christian Responses to Female Homoeroticism.* CSSHS. Chicago: University of Chicago Press.

Buell, Denise Kimber. 2005. *Why This New Race: Ethnic Reasoning in Early Christianity.* New York: Columbia University Press.

———. 2009. "God's Own People: Specters of Race, Ethnicity, and Gender in Early Christian Studies." Pages 159–90 in *Prejudice and Christian Beginnings: Investigating Race, Gender, and Ethnicity in Early Christian Studies.* Edited by Elisabeth Schüssler Fiorenza and Laura Nasrallah. Minneapolis: Fortress.

———. 2010. "Cyborg Memories: An Impure History of Jesus." *BibInt* 18:313–41.

———. 2014. "Hauntology Meets Posthumanism: Some Payoffs for Biblical Studies." Pages 29–56 in *The Bible and Posthumanism.* Edited by Jennifer L. Koosed. SemeiaSt 74. Atlanta: Society of Biblical Literature.

Buell, Denise Kimber, and Caroline Johnson Hodge. 2004. "The Politics of Interpretation: The Rhetoric of Race and Ethnicity in Paul." *JBL* 132:235–51.

Butler, Judith. 1990. *Gender Trouble: Feminism and the Subversion of Identity.* TG. New York: Routledge.

———. 1991. "Imitation and Gender Insubordination." Pages 13–31 in *Inside/Out: Lesbian Theories, Gay Theories.* Edited by Diana Fuss. New York: Routledge.

———. 1993. *Bodies That Matter: On the Discursive Limits of "Sex."* New York: Routledge.

———. 1994. "Against Proper Objects." *dif* 6.2–3:1–26.

———. 1997. *Excitable Speech: A Politics of the Performative.* New York: Routledge.

———. 2004. *Undoing Gender.* New York: Routledge.

Byron, Gay L. 2002. *Symbolic Blackness and Ethnic Difference in Early Christian Literature.* New York: Routledge.

Byron, Gay L., and Vanessa Lovelace, eds. 2016. *Womanist Interpretations of the Bible: Expanding the Discourse.* SemeiaSt 85. Atlanta: SBL Press.

Castelli, Elizabeth A. 1991a. *Imitating Paul: A Discourse of Power.* LCBI. Louisville: Westminster John Knox.

———. 1991b. "Interpretations of Power in 1 Corinthians." *Semeia* 54:199–222.

———. 1994. "Romans." Pages 272–300 in *A Feminist Commentary*. Vol. 2 of *Searching the Scriptures*. Edited by Elisabeth Schüssler Fiorenza, with Ann Brock and Shelly Matthews. New York: Crossroad.

Cheng, Anne Anlin. 2001. *The Melancholy of Race: Psychoanalysis, Assimilation, and Hidden Grief*. RAC. New York: Oxford University Press.

Cheng, Patrick S. 2006. "Galatians." Pages 624–29 in *The Queer Bible Commentary*. Edited by Deryn Guest, Robert E. Goss, Mona West, and Thomas Bohache. London: SCM.

Clay, Elonda. 2013. "Confessions of a Ex-Theological Bitch: The Thickness of Black Women's Exploitation between Jacquelyn Grant's 'Backbone' and Michael Eric Dyson's 'Theological Bitch.'" Pages 93–106 in *Ain't I a Womanist, Too? Third-Wave Womanist Religious Thought*. Edited by Monica A. Coleman. Minneapolis: Fortress.

Cohen, Cathy J. 1997. "Punks, Bulldaggers, and Welfare Queens: The Radical Potential of Queer Politics?" *GLQ* 3:437–65.

Collins, Patricia Hill. 2005. *Black Sexual Politics: African Americans, Gender, and the New Racism*. New York: Routledge.

Combahee River Collective. 1983. "Combahee River Collective Statement." Pages 264–74 in *Home Girls: A Black Feminist Anthology*. Edited by Barbara Smith. New York: Kitchen Table Women of Color.

Conway, Colleen. 2008. *Behold the Man: Jesus and Greco-Roman Masculinity*. New York: Oxford University Press.

Cornwall, Susannah. 2011. *Controversies in Queer Theology*. CCT. London: SCM.

Crenshaw, Kimberlé Williams. 1989. "Demarginalizing the Intersection of Race and Sex: A Black Feminist Critique of Antidiscrimination Doctrine, Feminist Theory and Antiracist Politics." *UCLF* 140:139–67.

Cvetkovich, Ann. 2003. *An Archive of Feelings: Trauma, Sexuality, and Lesbian Public Cultures*. SerQ. Durham: Duke University Press.

D'Angelo, Mary Rose. 2003. "Early Christian Sexual Politics and Roman Imperial Family Values: Rereading Christ and Culture." Pages 23–48 in vol. 6 of *The Papers of the Henry Luce III Fellows in Theology*. Edited by Christopher I. Wilkins. Pittsburgh: Association of Theological Schools.

Darms, Lisa, ed. 2013. *The Riot Grrrl Collection*. New York: Feminist.

Davis, Stacy. 2016. "The Invisible Women: Numbers 30 and the Politics of Singleness in Africana Communities." Pages 21–47 in *Womanist Interpretations of the Bible: Expanding the Discourse*. Edited by Gay L. Byron and Vanessa Lovelace. SemeiaSt 85. Atlanta: SBL Press.

DeFranza, Megan K. 2015. "Virtuous Eunuchs: Troubling Conservative and Queer Readings of Intersex and the Bible." Pages 55–77 in *Intersex, Theology, and the Bible: Troubling Bodies in Church, Text, and Society*. Edited by Susannah Cornwall. New York: Palgrave Macmillan.

Derrida, Jacques. 1988. "Signature, Event, Context." Pages 1–23 in *Limited, Inc.* Edited by Gerald Graff. Translated by Samuel Weber and Jeffrey Mehlman. Evanston, IL: Northwestern University Press.

Dinshaw, Carolyn. 1999. *Getting Medieval: Sexualities and Communities, Pre- and Postmodern*. SerQ. Durham: Duke University Press.

D'Lugo, Marvin, and Kathleen M. Vernon, eds. 2013. *A Companion to Pedro Almodóvar*. West Sussex, UK: Blackwell.

Douglas, Kelly Brown. 1999. *Sexuality and the Black Church: A Womanist Perspective*. Maryknoll, NY: Orbis.

Dunning, Benjamin H. 2011. *Specters of Paul: Sexual Difference in Early Christian Thought*. Div. Philadelphia: University of Pennsylvania Press.

———. 2014. *Christ without Adam: Subjectivity and Sexual Difference in the Philosophers' Paul*. GTR. New York: Columbia University Press.

Edelman, Lee. 2004. *No Future: Queer Theory and the Death Drive*. SerQ. Durham: Duke University Press.

Eisenbaum, Pamela. 2009. *Paul Was Not a Christian: The Original Message of a Misunderstood Apostle*. New York: HarperOne.

Elliott, Neil. 2008. *The Arrogance of Nations: Reading Romans in the Shadow of the Empire*. Minneapolis: Fortress.

Eng, David L. 2001. *Racial Castration: Managing Masculinity in Asian America*. PM. Durham: Duke University Press.

———. 2010. *The Feeling of Kinship: Queer Liberalism and the Racialization of Intimacy*. Durham: Duke University Press.

Eng, David L., Judith Halberstam, and José Esteban Muñoz, eds. 2005. "What's Queer about Queer Studies Now?" *SocT* 23:3–4.

Eng, David L., and David Kazanjian, eds. 2003. *Loss: The Politics of Mourning*. Berkeley: University of California Press.

Ferguson, Roderick. 2004. *Aberrations in Black: Toward a Queer of Color Critique*. CAS. Minneapolis: University of Minnesota Press.

Fisher, Gary. 1996. *Gary in Your Pocket: Stories and Notebooks of Gary Fisher*. Edited by Eve Kosofsky Sedgwick. SerQ. Durham: Duke University Press.

Foucault, Michel. 1988a. *The Use of Pleasure*. Vol. 2 of *The History of Sexuality*. Translated by Robert Hurley. Repr. ed. New York: Vintage.

———. 1988b. *The Care of the Self.* Vol. 3 of *The History of Sexuality.* Translated by Robert Hurley. Repr. ed. New York: Vintage.

———. 1990. *An Introduction.* Vol. 1 of *The History of Sexuality.* Translated by Robert Hurley. Repr. ed. New York: Vintage.

———. 2018. *Histoire de la sexualité IV: Les aveux de la chair.* Edited by Frédéric Gros. CBH. Paris: Gallimard

Freccero, Carla. 2006. *Queer/Early/Modern.* SerQ. Durham: Duke University Press.

Freeman, Elizabeth. 2010. *Time Binds: Queer Temporalities, Queer Histories.* PM. Durham: Duke University Press.

Fuggle, Sophie. 2013. *Foucault/Paul: Subjects of Power.* RT. New York: Palgrave Macmillan.

Gilman, Sander L. 1993. *Freud, Race, and Gender.* Princeton: Princeton University Press.

Gilroy, Paul. 1995. *The Black Atlantic: Modernity and Double Consciousness.* Cambridge: Harvard University Press.

———. 2005. *Postcolonial Melancholia.* WL. New York: Columbia University Press.

Glancy, Jennifer A. 1998. "Obstacles to Slaves' Participation in the Corinthian Church." *JBL* 117:481–501.

———. 2002. *Slavery in Early Christianity.* Oxford: Oxford University Press.

———. 2003. "Protocols of Masculinity in the Pastoral Epistles." Pages 235–64 in *New Testament Masculinities.* Edited by Stephen D. Moore and Janice Capel Anderson. SemeiaSt 45. Atlanta: Society of Biblical Literature.

Gopinath, Gayatri. 2005. *Impossible Desires: Queer Diasporas and South Asian Public Cultures.* PM. Durham: Duke University Press.

Goss, Robert E. 1993. *Jesus ACTED Up: A Gay and Lesbian Manifesto.* San Francisco: HarperSanFrancisco.

Gross, Sally. 1999. "Intersexuality and Scripture." *ThS* 11:65–74.

Guest, Deryn, Robert E. Goss, Mona West, and Thomas Bohache, eds. 2006. *The Queer Bible Commentary.* London: SCM.

Halberstam, Judith. 1995. *Skin Shows: Gothic Horror and the Technology of Monsters.* Durham: Duke University Press.

———. 1998. *Female Masculinity.* Durham: Duke University Press.

———. 2005. *In a Queer Time and Place: Transgender Bodies, Subcultural Lives.* Sexual Cultures. New York: New York University Press.

———. 2011. *The Queer Art of Failure*. JHFCB. Durham: Duke University Press.

Halberstam, Jack. 2018. *Trans*: A Quick and Quirky Account of Gender Variability*. ASN. Oakland: University of California Press.

Halperin, David M. 1995. *Saint Foucault: Toward a Gay Hagiography*. New York: Oxford University Press.

———. 2012. *How to Be Gay*. Cambridge: Belknap.

Hanks, Thomas D. 2000. *The Subversive Gospel: A New Testament Commentary of Liberation*. Translated by John P. Doner. Eugene, OR: Wipf & Stock.

———. 2006. "Romans." Pages 582–605 in *The Queer Bible Commentary*. Edited by Deryn Guest, Robert E. Goss, Mona West, and Thomas Bohache. London: SCM.

Hartke, Austen. 2018. *The Bible and the Lives of Transgender Christians*. Louisville: Westminster John Knox.

Hartman, Saidiya. 1997. *Scenes of Subjection: Terror, Slavery, and Self-Making in Nineteenth-Century America*. RAC. New York: Oxford University Press.

Hearon, Holly E. 2006. "1 and 2 Corinthians." Pages 606–23 in *The Queer Bible Commentary*. Edited by Deryn Guest, Robert E. Goss, Mona West, and Thomas Bohache. London: SCM.

Hidalgo, Jacqueline M. 2016. *Revelation in Aztlán: Scriptures, Utopias, and the Chicano Movement*. BCS. New York: Palgrave Macmillan.

———. 2018. "'Our Book of Revelation … Prescribes Our Fate and Releases Us from It': Scriptural Disorientations in Cherríe Moraga's *The Last Generation*." Pages 113–32 in *Sexual Disorientations: Queer Temporalities, Affects, Theologies*. Edited by Kent L. Brintnall, Joseph A. Marchal, and Stephen D. Moore. TTC. New York: Fordham University Press.

Hoke, James N. 2017. "Under God? A Queer and Feminist Subversion of Submission in Romans." PhD diss., Drew University.

———. 2018. "Unbinding Imperial Time: Chrononormativity and Paul's Letter to the Romans." Pages 68–89 in *Sexual Disorientations: Queer Temporalities, Affects, Theologies*. Edited by Kent L. Brintnall, Joseph A. Marchal, and Stephen D. Moore. TTC. New York: Fordham University Press.

Holland, Sharon Patricia. 2012. *The Erotic Life of Racism*. Durham: Duke University Press.

Hornsby, Teresa J. 2005. "The Gendered Sinner in Romans 1–7." Pages 143–66 in *Gender, Tradition, and Romans: Shared Ground, Uncertain Borders*. Edited by Cristina Grenholm and Daniel Patte. RTHC. New York: T&T Clark.

———. 2006. "The Annoying Woman: Biblical Scholarship after Judith Butler." Pages 71–89 in *Bodily Citations: Religion and Judith Butler*. Edited by Ellen T. Armour and Susan M. St. Ville. GTR. New York: Columbia University Press.

———. 2016. "Introduction: The Body as Decoy." Pages 1–11 in *Transgender, Intersex, and Biblical Interpretation*. Teresa J. Hornsby and Deryn Guest. SemeiaSt 83. Atlanta: SBL Press.

Hornsby, Teresa J., and Deryn Guest. 2016. *Transgender, Intersex, and Biblical Interpretation*. SemeiaSt 83. Atlanta: SBL Press.

Hornsby, Teresa J., and Ken Stone, eds. 2011. *Bible Trouble: Queer Readings at the Boundaries of Biblical Scholarship*. SemeiaSt 67. Atlanta: Society of Biblical Literature.

Huber, Lynn R. 2011. "Gazing at the Whore: Reading Revelation Queerly." Pages 301–20 in *Bible Trouble: Queer Reading at the Boundaries of Biblical Scholarship*. Edited by Teresa J. Hornsby and Ken Stone. SemeiaSt 67. Atlanta: Society of Biblical Literature.

Ivarsson, Fredrik. 2007. "Vice Lists and Deviant Masculinity: The Rhetorical Function of 1 Corinthians 5:10–11 and 6:9–10." Pages 163–84 in *Mapping Gender in Ancient Religious Discourses*. Edited by Todd Penner and Caroline Vander Stichele. BibInt 84. Leiden: Brill.

Jagose, Annamarie. 1996. *Queer Theory: An Introduction*. New York: New York University Press.

Jennings, Theodore W., Jr. 2003. *The Man Jesus Loved: Homoerotic Narratives from the New Testament*. Cleveland: Pilgrim.

———. 2009. *Plato or Paul? The Origins of Western Homophobia*. Cleveland: Pilgrim.

———. 2013. *Outlaw Justice: The Messianic Politics of Paul*. CMP. Stanford: Stanford University Press.

Johnson, E. Patrick, ed. 2016. *No Tea, No Shade: New Writings in Black Queer Studies*. Durham: Duke University Press.

Johnson, E. Patrick, and Mae G. Henderson, eds. 2005. *Black Queer Studies: A Critical Anthology*. Durham: Duke University Press.

Johnson, Matthew V., James A. Noel, and Demetrius K. Williams, eds. 2012. *Onesimus Our Brother: Reading Religion, Race, and Culture in Philemon*. PCC. Minneapolis: Fortress.

Johnson-DeBaufre, Melanie, and Laura S. Nasrallah. 2011. "Beyond the Heroic Paul: Toward a Feminist and Decolonizing Approach to the Letters of Paul." Pages 161–74 in *The Colonized Apostle: Paul through Postcolonial Eyes.* Edited by Christopher D. Stanley. PCC. Minneapolis: Fortress.

Johnson Hodge, Caroline. 2007. *If Sons, then Heirs: A Study of Kinship and Ethnicity in the Letters of Paul.* New York: Oxford University Press.

Kafer, Alison. 2013. *Feminist, Queer, Crip.* Bloomington: Indiana University Press.

Kahl, Brigitte. 2000. "No Longer Male: Masculinity Struggles Behind Galatians 3.28?" *JSNT* 79:37–49.

Keating, AnaLouise, ed. 2009. *The Gloria Anzaldúa Reader.* LAO. Durham: Duke University Press.

Kelley, Shawn. 2002. *Racializing Jesus: Race, Ideology, and the Formation of Modern Biblical Scholarship.* BibLim. New York: Routledge.

Kittredge, Cynthia Briggs. 1998. *Community and Authority: The Rhetoric of Obedience in the Pauline Tradition.* HTS 45. Harrisburg, PA: Trinity.

———. 2000. "Corinthian Women Prophets and Paul's Argumentation in 1 Corinthians." Pages 103–9 in *Paul and Politics: Ekklesia, Israel, Imperium, Interpretation; Essays in Honor of Krister Stendahl.* Edited by Richard A. Horsley. Harrisburg, PA: Trinity.

———. 2003. "Rethinking Authorship in the Letters of Paul: Elisabeth Schüssler Fiorenza's Model of Pauline Theology." Pages 318–33 in *Walk in the Ways of Wisdom: Essays in Honor of Elisabeth Schüssler Fiorenza.* Edited by Shelly Matthews, Cynthia Briggs Kittredge, and Melanie Johnson-DeBaufre. Harrisburg, PA: Trinity.

Knust, Jennifer Wright. 2006. *Abandoned to Lust: Sexual Slander and Ancient Christianity.* GTR. New York: Columbia University Press.

Kolakowski, Victoria. 2000. "Throwing a Party: Patriarchy, Gender, and the Death of Jezebel." Pages 103–14 in *Take Back the Word: A Queer Reading of the Bible.* Edited by Robert E. Goss and Mona West. Cleveland: Pilgrim.

Koosed, Jennifer L., and Stephen D. Moore. 2014. "Introduction: From Affect to Exegesis." *BibInt* 22:381–87.

Kotrosits, Maia. 2014. "The Queer Life of Christian Exceptionalism." *CultRel* 15:158–65

———. 2015. *Rethinking Early Christian Identity: Affect, Violence, and Belonging.* Minneapolis: Fortress.

———. 2016. "How Things Feel: Biblical Studies, Affect, and the (Im)Personal." *BRPBI* 1.1:1–53.

———. 2018. "Queer Persistence: On Death, History, and Longing for Endings." Pages 133–44 in *Sexual Disorientations: Queer Temporalities, Affects, Theologies*. Edited by Kent L. Brintnall, Joseph A. Marchal, and Stephen D. Moore. TTC. New York: Fordham University Press.

Kwok, Pui-lan. 2006. "A Postcolonial Reading: Sexual Morality and National Politics; Reading Biblical 'Loose Women.'" Pages 21–46 in *Engaging the Bible: Critical Readings from Contemporary Women*. Edited by Choi Hee An and Katheryn Pfisterer Darr. Minneapolis: Fortress.

Larson, Jennifer. 2004. "Paul's Masculinity." *JBL* 123:85–97.

Lauretis, Teresa de. 1991. "Queer Theory, Lesbian and Gay Studies: An Introduction." *differences* 3.2:iii–xviii.

Liew, Tat-Siong Benny. 2008. *What Is Asian American Biblical Hermeneutics? Reading the New Testament*. Intersections. Honolulu: University of Hawaii Press.

———. 2009. "Queering Closets and Perverting Desires: Cross-Examining John's Engendering and Transgendering Word across Different Worlds." Pages 251–88 in *They Were All Together in One Place? Toward Minority Biblical Criticism*. Edited by Randall C. Bailey, Tat-siong Benny Liew, and Fernando F. Segovia. SemeiaSt 57. Atlanta: Society of Biblical Literature.

Lopez, Davina C. 2008. *Apostle to the Conquered: Reimagining Paul's Mission*. PCC. Minneapolis: Fortress.

Lorde, Audre. 1984. *Sister Outsider: Essays and Speeches*. Trumansburg, NY: Crossing.

Love, Heather. 2007. *Feeling Backward: Loss and the Politics of Queer History*. Cambridge: Harvard University Press.

Lovelace, Vanessa. 2016. "'We Don't Give Birth to Thugs': Family Values, Respectability Politics, and Jephthah's Mother." Pages 239–61 in *Womanist Interpretations of the Bible: Expanding the Discourse*. Edited by Gay L. Byron and Vanessa Lovelace. SemeiaSt 85. Atlanta: SBL Press.

Luciano, Dana, and Mel Y. Chen. 2015. "Introduction: Has the Queer Ever Been Human?" *GLQ* 21:183–207.

Manalansan, Martin F. 2003. *Global Divas: Filipino Gay Men in the Diaspora*. PM. Durham: Duke University Press.

Marchal, Joseph A. 2006. *Hierarchy, Unity, and Imitation: A Feminist Rhetorical Analysis of Power Dynamics in Paul's Letter to the Philippians.* AcBib 24. Atlanta: Society of Biblical Literature.

———. 2008. *The Politics of Heaven: Women, Gender, and Empire in the Study of Paul.* PCC. Minneapolis: Fortress.

———. 2010. "Giving an Account of a Desirable Subject: Critically Queering Graduate Biblical Education." Pages 199–219 in *Transforming Graduate Biblical Education: Ethos and Discipline.* Edited by Elisabeth Schüssler Fiorenza and Kent Harold Richards. GPBS 10. Atlanta: Society of Biblical Literature.

———. 2011a. "The Corinthian Women Prophets and Trans Activism: Rethinking Canonical Gender Claims." Pages 223–46 in *Bible Trouble: Queer Reading at the Boundaries of Biblical Scholarship.* Edited by Teresa J. Hornsby and Ken Stone. SemeiaSt 67. Atlanta: Society of Biblical Literature.

———. 2011b. "'Making History' Queerly: Touches across Time through a Biblical Behind." *BibInt* 19:373–95.

———. 2012. "Queer Approaches: Improper Relations with Pauline Letters." Pages 209–27 in *Studying Paul's Letters: Contemporary Perspectives and Methods.* Edited by Joseph A. Marchal. Minneapolis: Fortress.

———. 2014a. "Bio-Necro-*Biblio*-Politics? Restaging Feminist Intersections and Queer Exceptions." *CultRel* 15:166–76.

———. 2014b. "Female Masculinity in Corinth? Bodily Citations and the Drag of History." *Neot* 48:93–113.

———. 2014c. *Philippians: Historical Problems, Hierarchical Visions, Hysterical Anxieties.* PGNT 11. Sheffield: Sheffield Phoenix.

———. 2014d. "Queer Studies and Critical Masculinity Studies in Feminist Biblical Studies." Pages 304–27 in *Scholarship and Movement: Feminist Biblical Studies in the Twentieth Century.* Vol. 21 of *The Bible and Women: An Encyclopaedia of Exegesis and Cultural History.* Edited by Elisabeth Schüssler Fiorenza. Atlanta: Society of Biblical Literature.

———. 2015a. "The Exceptional Proves Who Rules: Imperial Sexual Exceptionalism in and around Paul's Letters." *JECH* 5:87–115.

———. 2015b. "Who Are You Calling a Eunuch?! Staging Conversations between Feminist and Queer Biblical Studies and Intersex Advocacy." Pages 29–54 in *Intersex, Theology, and the Bible: Troubling Bodies in Church, Text, and Society.* Edited by Susannah Cornwall. New York: Palgrave Macmillan.

———. 2018. "How Soon Is (This Apocalypse) Now? Queer Velocities after a Corinthian Already and a Pauline Not Yet." Pages 45–67 in *Sexual Disorientations: Queer Temporalities, Affects, Theologies*. Edited by Kent L. Brintnall, Joseph A. Marchal, and Stephen D. Moore. TTC. New York: Fordham University Press.

———. 2019. *Appalling Bodies: Queer Figures before and after Paul's Letters*. New York: Oxford University Press.

Martin, Clarice J. 1991. "The *Haustafeln* (Household Codes) in African American Biblical Interpretation." Pages 206–31 in *Stony the Road We Trod: African American Biblical Interpretation*. Edited by Cain Hope Felder. Minneapolis: Fortress.

———. 1998. "'Somebody Done Hoodoo'd the Hoodoo Man': Language, Power, Resistance, and the Effective History of Pauline Texts in American Slavery." *Semeia* 83–84:203–33.

Martin, Dale B. 1995. "Heterosexism and the Interpretation of Romans 1:18–32." *BibInt* 3:332–55.

———. 1996. "*Arsenokoitēs* and *Malakos*: Meanings and Consequences." Pages 117–36 in *Biblical Ethics and Homosexuality: Listening to Scriptures*. Edited by Robert L. Brawley. Louisville: Westminster John Knox.

Matthews, Shelly. 2017. "'To Be One and the Same with the Woman Whose Head Is Shaven' (1 Cor 11:5b): Resisting the Violence of 1 Corinthians 11:2–16 from the Bottom of the Kyriarchal Pyramid." Pages 31–51 in *Sexual Violence and Sacred Texts*. Edited by Amy Kalmanofsky. Cambridge, MA: Feminist Studies in Religion Books.

McBride, Dwight A. 2005. *Why I Hate Abercrombie and Fitch: Essays on Race and Sexuality*. Sexual Cultures. New York: New York University Press.

McRuer, Robert. 2006. *Crip Theory: Cultural Signs of Queerness and Disability*. CF. New York: New York University Press.

Menéndez-Antuña, Luis. 2015. "Is There a Room for Queer Desires in the House of Biblical Scholarship? A Methodological Reflection on Queer Desires in the Context of Contemporary New Testament Studies." *BibInt* 23:399–427.

Miller, Monica R. 2013. "'I Am a Nappy-Headed Ho': (Re)Signifying 'Deviance' in the Haraam of Religious Respectability." Pages 123–37 in *Ain't I a Womanist, Too? Third-Wave Womanist Religious Thought*. Edited by Monica A. Coleman. Minneapolis: Fortress.

Mollenkott, Virginia R. 2001. *Omnigender: A Trans-religious Approach*. Cleveland: Pilgrim.

Moore, Stephen D. 1994. *Poststructuralism and the Bible: Derrida and Foucault at the Foot of the Cross*. Minneapolis: Fortress.

———. 2001. *God's Beauty Parlor: And Other Queer Spaces in and around the Bible*. Contraversions. Stanford: Stanford University Press.

Moore, Stephen D., Kent L. Brintnall, and Joseph A. Marchal, 2018. "Introduction: Queer Disorientations; Four Turns and a Twist." Pages 1–44 in *Sexual Disorientations: Queer Temporalities, Affects, Theologies*. Edited by Kent L. Brintnall, Joseph A. Marchal, and Stephen D. Moore. TTC. New York: Fordham University Press.

Moraga, Cherríe, and Gloria Anzaldúa, eds. 1981. *This Bridge Called My Back: Writings by Radical Women of Color*. Watertown, MA: Persephone Press.

Morrison, Toni. 1973. *Sula*. London: Allen Lane.

Moxnes, Halvor. 2003. "Asceticism and Christian Identity in Antiquity: A Dialogue with Foucault and Paul." *JSNT* 26:3–29.

Muñoz, José Esteban. 1999. *Disidentifications: Queers of Color and the Performance of Politics*. CSA. Minneapolis: University of Minnesota Press.

———. 2009. *Cruising Utopia: The Then and There of Queer Futurity*. Sexual Cultures. New York: New York University Press.

Musser, Amber Jamilla. 2014. *Sensational Flesh: Race, Power, and Masochism*. Sexual Cultures. New York: New York University Press.

Nicolet-Anderson, Valérie. 2012. *Constructing the Self: Thinking with Paul and Michel Foucault*. WUNT 2/324. Tübingen: Mohr Siebeck.

Pasolini, Pier Paolo. 2014. *Saint Paul: A Screenplay*. Translated by Elizabeth A. Castelli. London: Verso.

Puar, Jasbir K. 2005. "Queer Times, Queer Assemblages." *SocT* 23:121–39.

———. 2007. *Terrorist Assemblages: Homonationalism in Queer Times*. NW. Durham: Duke University Press.

Puar, Jasbir K., and Amit S. Rai. 2002. "Monster, Terrorist, Fag: The War on Terrorism and the Production of Docile Patriots." *SocT* 20:117–48.

Punt, Jeremy. 2010. "Power and Liminality, Sex and Gender, and Gal 3:28: A Postcolonial, Queer Reading of an Influential Text." *Neot* 44:140–66.

———. 2011. "Queer Theory, Postcolonial Theory, and Biblical Interpretation: A Preliminary Exploration of Some Intersections." Pages 321–41 in *Bible Trouble: Queer Readings at the Boundaries of Biblical Scholarship*. Edited by Teresa J. Hornsby and Ken Stone. SemeiaSt 67. Atlanta: Society of Biblical Literature.

Reid-Pharr, Robert F. 2001. *Black Gay Man: Essays*. With a foreword by Samuel R. Delaney. Sexual Cultures. New York: New York University Press.

Rubin, Gayle. 1984. "Thinking Sex: Toward a Radical Theory of the Politics of Sexuality." Pages 267–319 in *Pleasure and Danger: Exploring Female Sexuality*. Edited by Carole S. Vance. London: Pandora.

Runions, Erin. 2011. "From Disgust to Humor: Rahab's Queer Affect." Pages 321–41 in *Bible Trouble: Queer Readings at the Boundaries of Biblical Scholarship*. Edited by Teresa J. Hornsby and Ken Stone. SemeiaSt 67. Atlanta: Society of Biblical Literature.

Schippert, Claudia. 1999. "Too Much Trouble? Negotiating Feminist and Queer Approaches in Religion." *ThS* 11:44–63.

———. 2011. "Implications of Queer Theory for the Study of Religion and Gender: Entering the Third Decade." *RelGen* 1.1:66–84.

Schüssler Fiorenza, Elisabeth. 1983. *In Memory of Her: A Feminist Theological Reconstruction of Christian Origins*. New York: Crossroad.

———. 1992. *But She Said: Feminist Practices of Biblical Interpretation*. Boston: Beacon.

———. 1999. *Rhetoric and Ethic: The Politics of Biblical Studies*. Minneapolis: Fortress.

———. 2000. "Paul and the Politics of Interpretation." Pages 40–57 in *Paul and Politics: Ekklesia, Israel, Imperium, Interpretation; Essays in Honor of Krister Stendahl*. Edited by Richard A. Horsley. Harrisburg, PA: Trinity.

———. 2001. *Wisdom Ways: Introducing Feminist Biblical Interpretation*. Maryknoll, NY: Orbis.

Schwaller, Tyler, 2017. "The Use of Slaves in Early Christianity: Slaves as Subjects of Life and Thought." PhD diss., Harvard University.

Scott, Darieck. 2010. *Extravagant Abjection: Blackness, Power, and Sexuality in the African American Literary Imagination*. Sexual Cultures. New York: New York University Press.

Scroggs, Robin. 1983. *The New Testament and Homosexuality: Contextual Background for Contemporary Debate*. Philadelphia: Fortress.

Sedgwick, Eve Kosofsky. 1990. *Epistemology of the Closet*. Berkeley: University of California Press.

———. 1993. *Tendencies*. SerQ. Durham: Duke University Press.

Segovia, Fernando F., and Mary Ann Tolbert, eds. 1995. *Reading from This Place*. 2 vols. Minneapolis: Fortress.

Shaner, Katherine A. 2017. "Seeing Rape and Robbery: *Harpagmos* and the Philippians Christ Hymn (Phil. 2:5–11)." *BibInt* 25:342–63.

Sharpe, Christina. 2010. *Monstrous Intimacies: Making Post-slavery Subjects*. PM. Durham: Duke University Press.

———. 2016. *In the Wake: On Blackness and Being*. Durham: Duke University Press.

Siker, Jeffrey S. 1994. "Homosexual Christians, the Bible, and Gentile Inclusion: Confessions of a Repenting Heterosexist." Pages 179–94 in *Homosexuality in the Church: Both Sides of the Debate*. Edited by Jeffrey S. Siker. Louisville: Westminster John Knox.

Simula, Brandy L. 2013. "Queer Utopias in Painful Spaces: BDSM Participants' Interrelational Resistance to Heteronormativity and Gender Regulation." Pages 71–100 in *A Critical Inquiry into Queer Utopias*. Edited by Angela Jones. New York: Palgrave Macmillan.

Smith, Barbara. 1977. *Toward a Black Feminist Criticism*. Trumansburg, NY: Crossing.

———, ed. 1983. *Home Girls: A Black Feminist Anthology*. New York: Kitchen Table Women of Color.

Smith, Mitzi J. 2015. "Introduction." Pages 1–14 in *I Found God in Me: A Womanist Biblical Hermeneutics Reader*. Edited by Mitzi J. Smith. Eugene, OR: Cascade.

Solevåg, Anna Rebecca. 2016. "No Nuts? No Problem! Disability, Stigma, and the Baptized Eunuch in Acts 8:26–40." *BibInt* 24:81–91.

Somerville, Siobhan B. 2000. *Queering the Color Line: Race and the Invention of Homosexuality in American Culture*. SerQ. Durham: Duke University Press.

Spong, John Shelby. 1992. *Rescuing the Bible from Fundamentalism: A Bishop Rethinks the Meaning of Scripture*. New York: HarperOne.

Stanley, Christopher D., ed. 2011. *The Colonized Apostle: Paul through Postcolonial Eyes*. PCC. Minneapolis: Fortress.

Stockton, Kathryn Bond. 2006. *Beautiful Bottom, Beautiful Shame: Where "Black" Meets "Queer."* SerQ. Durham: Duke University Press.

Stockton, Will. 2017. *Members of His Body: Shakespeare, Paul, and a Theology of Nonmonogamy*. New York: Fordham University Press.

Stone, Ken. 2001. "Queer Theory and Biblical Interpretation: An Introduction." Pages 11–34 in *Queer Commentary and the Hebrew Bible*. Edited by Ken Stone. Cleveland: Pilgrim.

———. 2005. *Practicing Safer Texts: Food, Sex, and Bible in Queer Perspective*. Queering Theology. London: T&T Clark International.

———. 2006. "The Garden of Eden and the Heterosexual Contract." Pages 48–70 in *Bodily Citations: Religion and Judith Butler*. Edited by Ellen T. Armour and Susan M. St. Ville. GTR. New York: Columbia University Press.

———. 2011. "Queer Reading between Bible and Film: Paris Is Burning and the 'Legendary Houses' of David and Saul." Pages 75–98 in *Bible Trouble: Queer Reading at the Boundaries of Biblical Scholarship*. Edited by Teresa J. Hornsby and Ken Stone. SemeiaSt 67. Atlanta: Society of Biblical Literature.

Stryker, Susan. 1994. "My Words to Victor Frankenstein above the Village of Chamounix: Performing Transgender Rage." *GLQ* 1:237–54.

———. 2004. "Transgender Studies: Queer Theory's Evil Twin." *GLQ* 10:212–15.

Sugirtharajah, R. S., ed. 1991. *Voices from the Margin: Interpreting the Bible in the Third World*. Maryknoll, NY: Orbis.

Swancutt, Diana M. 2003. "'The Disease of Effemination': The Charge of Effeminacy and the Verdict of God (Romans 1:18–2:16)." Pages 193–233 in *New Testament Masculinities*. Edited by Stephen D. Moore and Janice Capel Anderson. SemeiaSt 45. Atlanta: Society of Biblical Literature.

———. 2004. "Sexy Stoics and the Rereading of Romans 1.18–2.16." Pages 42–73 in *A Feminist Companion to Paul*. Edited by Amy-Jill Levine with Marianne Blinckenstaff. London: T&T Clark.

———. 2006. "Sexing the Pauline Body of Christ: Scriptural Sex in the Context of the American Christian Culture War." Pages 65–98 in *Toward a Theology of Eros: Transfiguring Passion at the Limits of Discipline*. Edited by Virginia Burrus and Catherine Keller. TTC. New York: Fordham University Press.

———. 2007. "*Still* Before Sexuality: 'Greek' Androgyny, the Roman Imperial Politics of Masculinity and the Roman Invention of the *Tribas*." Pages 11–61 in *Mapping Gender in Ancient Religious Discourses*. Edited by Todd Penner and Caroline Vander Stichele. BibInt 84. Leiden: Brill.

Tanis, Justin. 2003. *Trans-gendered: Theology, Ministry, and Communities of Faith*. Cleveland: Pilgrim.

Thomas, Eric A. 2018. "The Futures Outside: Apocalyptic Epilogue Unveiled as Africana Queer Prologue." Pages 90–112 in *Sexual Disorientations: Queer Temporalities, Affects, Theologies*. Edited by Kent L.

Brintnall, Joseph A. Marchal, and Stephen D. Moore. TTC. New York: Fordham University Press.

Townsley, Gillian. 2011. "*The Straight Mind* in Corinth: Problematizing Categories and Ideologies of Gender in 1 Corinthians 11:2–16." Pages 247–81 in *Bible Trouble: Queer Reading at the Boundaries of Biblical Scholarship*. Edited by Teresa J. Hornsby and Ken Stone. SemeiaSt 67. Atlanta: Society of Biblical Literature.

———. 2017. *"The Straight Mind" in Corinth: Queer Readings across 1 Corinthians 11:2–16*. SemeiaSt 88. Atlanta: SBL Press.

Trible, Phyllis. 1984. *Texts of Terror: Literary-Feminist Readings of Biblical Narratives*. OBT 13. Philadelphia: Fortress.

Turner, William B. 2000. *A Genealogy of Queer Theory*. American Subjects. Philadelphia: Temple University Press.

Twomey, Jay. 2011. "The Pastor and His Fops: Gender Indeterminacy in the Pastor and His Readers." Pages 283–300 in *Bible Trouble: Queer Reading at the Boundaries of Biblical Scholarship*. Edited by Teresa J. Hornsby and Ken Stone. SemeiaSt 67. Atlanta: Society of Biblical Literature.

Vidal, Gore. 1992. *Live from Golgotha*. New York: Random House.

Villalobos Mendoza, Manuel. 2011. "Bodies *Del Otro Lado* Finding Life and Hope in the Borderland: Gloria Anzaldúa, the Ethiopian Eunuch of Acts 8:26–40, *y Yo*." Pages 191–221 in *Bible Trouble: Queer Reading at the Boundaries of Biblical Scholarship*. Edited by Teresa J. Hornsby and Ken Stone. SemeiaSt 67. Atlanta: Society of Biblical Literature.

———. 2014. *When Men Were Not Men: Masculinity and Otherness in the Pastoral Epistles*. BMW 62. Sheffield: Sheffield Phoenix.

Walker, Alice. 1983. *In Search of Our Mothers' Gardens*. San Diego: Harcourt Brace Jovanovich.

West, Traci C. 1999. *Wounds of the Spirit: Black Women, Violence, and Resistance Ethics*. New York: New York University Press.

White, Heather R. 2015. *Reforming Sodom: Protestants and the Rise of Gay Rights*. Chapel Hill: University of North Carolina Press.

Williams, Delores S. 1993. *Sisters in the Wilderness. The Challenge of Womanist God-Talk*. Maryknoll, NY: Orbis.

Wilson, Nancy. 1995. *Our Tribe: Queer Folks, God, Jesus, and the Bible*. San Francisco: HarperSanFrancisco.

Wire, Antoinette Clark. 1990. *The Corinthian Women Prophets: A Reconstruction through Paul's Rhetoric*. Minneapolis: Fortress.

———. 2000. "Response: The Politics of the Assembly in Corinth." Pages 124–29 in *Paul and Politics: Ekklesia, Israel, Imperium, Interpretation: Essays in Honor of Krister Stendahl*. Edited by Richard A. Horsley. Harrisburg, PA: Trinity.

Wittig, Monique. 1992. *The Straight Mind and Other Essays*. Boston: Beacon.

———. 2005. "Some Remarks on *The Lesbian Body*." Pages 44–48 in *On Monique Wittig: Theoretical, Political, and Literary Essays*. Edited by Namascar Shaktini. Urbana: University of Illinois Press.

Wasting Time at the End of the World: Queer Failure, Unproductivity, and Unintelligibility in 1 Corinthians

Lindsey Guy

Time is of the essence in 1 Corinthians. Paul underscores his ethical injunctions with language of the "present crisis" (7:26), warning that "the form of this world is passing away" (7:31) and that the community should "prepare [it]self for battle" (14:8).[1] There is a suggestion of temporal collapse in these warnings, compatible with what Jack Halberstam (2005, 2) writes of as *queer temporality*: the sense of impending crisis creates heightened awareness of "the constantly diminishing future [that] creates a new emphasis on the here, the present, the now." On the brink of the apocalyptic horizon, the Corinthian community is negotiating contextual ethics exactly predicated on this crisis.

While Elizabeth Freeman (2007, 160) writes that through Bourdieu's *habitus* "we can see most clearly how time makes bodies and subjects," we may also find the reverse: in studying bodies and subjects, we may learn what sort of time or times they inhabit. Queer temporality is valuable for denaturalizing time, as it interrogates the seemingly compulsory relations of past to present and present to future, "once one leaves the temporal frames of bourgeois reproduction and family, longevity, risk/safety, and inheritance" (Halberstam 2005, 6). Normative understandings of progress and progression demarcate social identity, with queer time in particular critiquing the dominant re/productive paradigm.[2]

---

1. Unless otherwise indicated, all biblical translations are mine.

2. I use the term *re/productive* here to gesture to the close ties between construction of the family and capitalist production.

Paul and the Corinthian community apparently agree that normative constructions of time and sexuality should be disrupted, though
they disagree as to how this should be accomplished. In reconstructing
1 Corinthians's discourse on sex as intraqueer discussion, we may find
the apocalyptic to be a tool for social disruption, lending credibility to
nonnormative or antisocial identities. Particularly drawing upon the construction of the Corinthian women prophets as sketched by Antoinette
Clark Wire (1990), and tracing the motifs of childishness, unprofitability,
and unintelligibility, this essay explores how an apocalyptic ethos height-
ens queer un/belonging.

My methodology draws on feminist reconstruction and reimagination
of the recipient community but moves away from any countervalorization
and toward queer antagonism, characterized by a skepticism toward the
desirability of authority, leadership, or intelligibility altogether.[3] The Corinthians' ethical reorientation imagined in this essay disputes authority
and social status *through* the queer and irreverent time of the apocalypse;
that everyone is mutually lowered to irrelevance after the apocalyptic crisis
has revealed that we are all wasting our time.

Queer Childhood and Childishness

The letter's ethics are persistently predicated upon themes of adulthood,
growth, and maturity. Paul implores the Corinthians to grow into adults
in Christ, to "put away childish things" and join him as adults in the
apocalyptic crisis. But in a childish sort of way, my hermeneutic embraces
childishness as a deliberate retention of all that is disruptive, mischievous, antisocial, and queer. As I rehabilitate the motif of childishness in
1 Corinthians, I argue alongside Kathryn Bond Stockton (2009) and Jack
Halberstam (2005) that such childishness deliberately performs a queer
critique of re/productive time and expectations. I position the Corinthian
community, particularly the constructed Corinthian women prophets, as
performing flagrant, resistant, joyful childishness. This argument leans
into Paul's rhetoric of his own maturity and his paternal(istic) relationship
to the Corinthians in order to interrogate the assumed value of leadership,
authority, or credibility. In constructing the ways in which the Corinthians

---

3. Wire is the primary feminist scholar with whom this essay thinks, but similar work has been done by Elisabeth Schüssler Fiorenza (1987), Elizabeth A. Castelli
(1991a, 1991b), and Melanie Johnson-DeBaufre and Laura Nasrallah (2011).

"talk back" to Paul (itself an accusation of childishness), we may find a counternarrative of apocalyptic resistance to heteronormative structures of power, performed with ecstatic irreverence.

Perhaps the Corinthians accused by Paul of childishness may not have intended to be contrary or irrational; perhaps they considered their own actions to be perfectly reasonable and mature. I claim them, however, as de/constructed subjects of childhood, whose presence questions the sociorhetorical value of childhood and childishness when they are divorced from the trajectory of proto-adulthood. This resistant reading suggests a counternarrative of the prophets' *willful* unbelonging, of ecstasy and unintelligible bodily expression as deconstruction of the demands of being civilized, responsible, or mature.

Stockton's 2009 monograph *The Queer Child* explores the queer excesses of childhood, beyond the narratives of maturation that privilege re/productive adulthood. The instability and indefinability of childhood— particularly of gay childhood, of children who do not progress toward heteronormativity—creates "a frightening, heightened sense of growing toward a question mark. Or growing up in haze. Or hanging in suspense— even wishing time would stop, or just twist sideways, so that one wouldn't have to advance to new or further scenes of trouble" (3). The queerness of childhood is an indictment of the rhetoric of reproductive futurity—such as the "think of the children" sloganeering critiqued by Lee Edelman in his 2004 monograph *No Future*—and particularly underscores how the rhetorical use of childhood normatively works in service of defining adulthood, maturity, or productivity.

As Stockton writes, childhood innocence is a paradox:

> From the standpoint of adults, innocence is alien, since it is "lost" to the very adults who assign it to children. Adults retrospect it through the gauzy lens of what they attribute to the child. And adults walk the line— the impossible line—of keeping the child at once what it is (what adults are not) and leading it toward what it cannot (at least, as itself) ever be (what adults are). (2009, 30–31)

Childishness is the bits of time that heteronormativity left behind, that cling to queerness; queerness is the childhood that one fails to jettison appropriately.

Halberstam, working with Stockton's model of a non-re/productive "growing sideways," proposes childhood and childishness as queer failure.

The 2011 monograph *The Queer Art of Failure* denaturalizes the construction of childhood as anticipatory "pre-adulthood," suggesting that childhood is instead best characterized and defined by its excesses and nonmaturational growth. Queer "antidevelopment" is a failure of the heteronormative trajectory, one that may be recognized "as a way of refusing to acquiesce to dominant logics of power and discipline and as a form of critique" (73, 88). On the queer time of childhood, Halberstam explains:

> the child is always already queer and must therefore quickly be converted to a proto-heterosexual by being pushed through a series of maturational models of growth that project the child as the future and the future as heterosexual. Queer culture, with its emphasis on repetition, horizontality, immaturity and a refusal of adulthood, where adulthood rhymes with heterosexual parenting, resists a developmental model of substitution and instead invests in what Stockton calls "sideways" relations, relations that grow along parallel lines rather than upward and onward. This queer form of *antidevelopment* requires healthy doses of forgetting and disavowal. (73)

As Joseph Marchal (2018, 52) has recently demonstrated, the temporality of 1 Corinthians may be better characterized as multiple and fragmented; Elizabeth Freeman's concept of temporal drag "helps one register the simultaneous copresence of different timelines here … reflecting two different practices of the Corinthians." Though Paul's rhetoric primarily relies on normative household power structure, the occasional slippage of time or power deconstructs his claims to authority. Marchal demonstrates that since time is not compulsory, neither are its velocity nor its trajectory, as Paul and the Corinthians negotiate their communal ethos "with what rate one aims to change conditions, positioned in particular directions, aiming for different points, over time—what velocity—we assemble, disrupt, and alter" (58). The Corinthian embrace of childishness realizes the power of multiple temporalities simultaneously, finding their identity in the past and future, or the past *as* future. The deconstructed, parodic household emerging from these unstable trajectories undoes itself, demonstrating the precarity of its own authority.

The rhetoric of Corinthian children and familial authority comes, of course, from Paul himself. He asserts his authority over them as an intimate, household matter. The Corinthian church members are "infants in Christ" (3:1) and "my dear children" (4:14), while Paul variously puts himself in the role of mother or wet nurse (3:2), "your father through the gospel" (4:15), tutor or disciplinarian (4:21), or shepherd (9:7). Paul's role as paterfamilias has been frequently noted by scholars; for example, Todd Penner and Caroline Vander Stichele (2004, 12) note the political investment of "*why* the 'household' is so important to Paul: it is his 'public stage' in Corinth and beyond; the projection of his ability to control, order, and dominate." The prevalence of Paul's rhetoric of parenting and his insistence that their conflicts should remain "family affairs" (as he does with regard to lawsuits in 1 Cor 6 and prophesying before outsiders in 1 Cor 14) stand as moments of anxiety within the text. They imply that this is ongoing rhetoric within their community or relationship—to a greater or lesser degree of acceptability for the Corinthians. But apocalyptic urgency (does the *ekklēsia* have *time* to grow up?) reveals how normative time compels even metaphorical families. Conversely, we may understand the Corinthian church to be "growing sideways" under apocalyptic pressure.

Paul himself draws upon inverted structures of power from the outset of the letter, asking, "Has God not made foolish the wisdom of the world?" (1:20). While he does not often identify himself as a child, he does identify with other disposable and dishonored demographics.[4] (As he writes variously: "I came to you in weakness, with great fear and trembling" [2:3]; the apostles are "the garbage of this world" [4:13]; "though I am free I have made myself a slave" [9:19].) The simultaneous claims of maturity and abjection destabilize the metaphor that Paul is constructing. His self-lowering undercuts his own claim to be the paterfamilias—if, as per Penner and Vander Stichele, he controls, orders, and dominates in the view of the larger world, then in the household of the Corinthian church, he himself fails at the socially prescribed role of fatherhood. To what end is the *ekklēsia* a household, or their relations familial, in light of this breakdown of authority?

Certainly Paul is not conceding his authority over them—a "father" who is "least of all" still, to him, bears Christ's wisdom and authority. Elizabeth A. Castelli (1991a, 111) suggests that these familial metaphors create a double bind of obligation: Paul is at once authority over and distinct from the Corinthians, but he is also familiar to and unified with them. And Reider Aasgaard (2007, 144), citing Castelli but focusing on the

---

4. While he speaks of his own childhood in 13:11 and identifies himself as a fetus in 15:18, he inverts the imagery of being given milk in 9:7 as evidence of his authority, not childhood. Elsewhere in his letters, he infrequently identifies as a child (a fetus in Gal 1:15, a nursing child in 1 Thess 2:7, and an orphan in 1 Thess 2:17). See Aasgard 2007.

child rather than the parent, notes that Paul reflects the standard values of antiquity, which "perceived [children] to be unfinished: they were humans-to-be." If Paul inverts family dynamics as he inverts wisdom and power, then he does not do it completely. Nor, I would argue, are the Corinthians performing perfected, virtuous childhood (the sort of kid you can take out in public)—rather, the mischievous, chaotic sort. This imperfect, incomplete performance of heteronormativity might be better read as a failure of household, of chrononormativity, and of maturity.

Gillian Townsley reads 1 Cor 11 with Judith Butler, and I follow her work in considering the weight of performativity within the letter. Townsley writes that Paul, while at points expressing support of "gender equality and mutuality," still thinks with a binary, naturalized conception of gender: "He invokes 'nature' as a way of setting the necessary limits of gendered life, including the threat of shame and dishonor for those who transgress such boundaries" (2006, 17.8). Conversely, if the Corinthians are taking part in "a repeated recitation of their gender-blurring performances," then they destabilize the categories that Paul has attempted to stabilize (17.9).

In the same vein, I suggest that we might read the prescribed categories of parent and child as both performative and parodic. In parody, Butler (1990, 146) sought "the possibility for a repetition that is not fully constrained to reconsolidate naturalized identities." In reading the narrative of Paul's relationship to the Corinthians as a denaturalized, failed/failing family that grows sideways together, we find space for them to talk back, as some children so often do.

Paul associates maturity with spiritual wisdom early in the letter, in order to establish his argument of virtuous societal inversion and place the Christ community over against Greek paganism or philosophy. Despite ostensibly celebrating foolishness (1:20), he does not vindicate it at any length, instead relapsing into the language of wisdom again quickly: "Among the mature [*teleiois*] we do speak wisdom, though it is not a wisdom of this age or of the rulers of this age.... But we speak God's wisdom, secret and hidden" (2:6–7). *Mature* may also be rendered as *perfected*—and while the former translation carries physical connotations (i.e., a fully grown human or animal), the latter carries metaphysical connotations. This ambiguity conforms to what we have already seen in Paul's meta/physical slipperiness, of the spiritual economy and productivity he champions.

Paul positions himself as an exceptional bearer of God's wisdom, not only superior to the Greek wisdom teachers but also to the Corinthian community, which has fallen short of its potential and is therefore *imma-*

ture. "I could not speak to you as spiritual people, but rather as people of the flesh, as infants [*nēpiois*] in Christ," he belittles them. "I fed you with milk, not solid food. Even now you are still not ready, for you are still of the flesh. For as long as there is jealousy and quarreling among you, are you not of the flesh?" (3:1–3). While this passage evokes a maternal image, the parallel paternal relationality occurs shortly thereafter: "I am not writing this to make you ashamed, but to admonish you as my beloved children [*tekna*].... Indeed, in Christ Jesus I became your father through the gospel" (4:14–15).

The rhetoric *is* obviously meant to evoke shame, though. To refuse the Corinthians an equal place within adulthood is infantilizing at best and gaslighting at worst, and even if they (or I) ultimately reclaim childishness, Paul obviously does not intend it to liberate them or even take them seriously. Children are lesser; children are neither fully social participants nor knowledgeable enough to be; children are inexperienced and of little utility. He implies that a mismatch of physical and emotional age is unnatural, writing of how he progressed appropriately: "When I was a child, I ... reasoned like a child; but when I became an adult, I put an end to childish things" (13:11). The "childish things" that he specifically identifies are quarreling (3:3) and prophesying (13:8–12)—and regarding the latter, the image of barbarian *or infantile* babbling is appropriate. The communal ethics evoked by these passages also shame the Corinthians through an association of children with selfishness. Adulthood and maturity are marked by sacrifice on behalf of those weaker (and perhaps more childlike?) than oneself. Again, the rhetoric of moralized asceticism and delayed gratification indicates the force of futurity upon present day politics.

The extent of his rebuke is "You're being childish!"—an accusation that cannot be properly denied without exactly affirming it ("*Nuh-uh!*"). But proper adulthood, to Paul, is marked by asceticism and paranoia. One should always already expect the worst future—the most precarious future, that they may not survive—as the most mature orientation. Eve Kosofsky Sedgwick writes about the pressures of paranoia, anticipation, and fear upon the constructed future. Paranoia is a paradox:

> The unidirectionally future-oriented vigilance of paranoia generates, paradoxically, a complex relation to temporality that burrows both backward and forward: because there must be no bad surprises, and because learning of the possibility of a bad surprise would itself constitute a bad surprise, paranoia requires that bad news be always already known. (2003, 130)

Sedgwick's paranoia does not itself account for childhood: the paranoid temporality only "burrows backward" as far as rational adulthood, at which point adults seem to have agency to affect the future. But Paul's rhetoric often aligns itself with Sedgwick's paranoia: it is the mature way to be in the world, anticipating the worst because anticipation is mature and profligacy is immature. For example, concerning prophesying and spiritual gifts, Paul writes, "Let all things be done for building up" (14:26). Even in the scene of the imminent apocalypse, even when the world's "present form is passing away" (7:29), this logic is aligned with cautious asceticism. The anticipation of linear and unbroken progress is the generational logic that Halberstam critiques. But as Halberstam and Stockton have both noted, the sideways relationality of childhood disrupts linear re/productive futurity—and, I argue, it also disrupts the paranoia that drives anticipatory asceticism. Halberstam (2011, 3) writes that "failure preserves some of the wondrous anarchy of childhood," and a juxtaposition with Sedgwick suggests that an embrace of failure *of anticipation* would create an atemporal, recursive future childhood.

With childish anarchy and carelessness, the Corinthian church has not "put away the childish things" of unproductivity and unintelligibility. Looking to Halberstam's critique of the compulsory "maturational models of growth" to which children are subjected, we find Paul anxiously herding the immature Corinthians toward the imminent re/productive future that approaches, and he herds himself toward the same, since he seems at least as invested in his own maturity as anyone else's. Indeed, the *ekklēsia* might find an unusual ally in C. S. Lewis when he writes that it is in fact anxious adherence to adulthood that signals true immaturity:

> Critics who treat "adult" as a term of approval, instead of as a merely descriptive term, cannot be adult themselves. To be concerned about being grown up, to admire the grown up because it is grown up, to blush at the suspicion of being childish; these things are the marks of childhood and adolescence.... When I was ten, I read fairy tales in secret and would have been ashamed if I had been found doing so. Now that I am fifty I read them openly. When I became a man I put away childish things, including the fear of childishness and the desire to be very grown up. (1966, 25)

The construct of mature adulthood, particularly as *inevitable* except in embarrassing cases of arrested development, is predicated upon economic interests. Adults are responsible re/productive citizens, while children are an investment at best and a waste at worst. An embrace of childishness undermines the dominating pressure to "grow up already," interrogating the vested interests inherent in such pressures. The millennial-coined term *adulting* has recently marked this same break-down: a generation-wide impostor's syndrome that implies adulthood is somewhere between unpleasant and impossible to maintain.[5] Adult-hood is not compulsory, but it does serve as the foundation for many conservative, hegemonic, re/productive ideals.If we instead construct a denaturalized or parodic family out of Paul's relation to the Corinthians, we may find Paul and the church performing "queer lives [that] seek to uncouple change from the supposedly organic and immutable forms of family and inheritance" (Halberstam 2011, 70). Paul himself seems con-flicted about the generational logic he puts forward; even as he ushers the church toward maturity as their self-appointed father, he also denies the normative logic of family in favor of asceticism and chastity. I note that his deconstruction of the family is incomplete: "Those who have wives should live as though they did not" (7:29), but he does not add, "Those who have children (or parents!) should live as though they did not." And perhaps he should.

Butler writes, "The injunction to *be* a given gender produces necessary failures, a variety of incoherent configurations that in their multiplicity exceed and defy the injunction by which they are generated" (1990, 145). I suggest that the incoherence of family, fatherhood, and chrononormativity throughout Corinthians produces a family done in drag, with relation-ships that mimic and also conspicuously fail normative expectations in order to discursively de/construct their familial relationships. In other words, perhaps the Corinthians should call Paul not Father but *Daddy*. Like drag, ageplay creates an erotic, self-aware, performative relationship that is at least as interested in its own deviation and failure as in its success. It provides a self-aware space to negotiate, interrogate, and defy house-hold power dynamics, but there is always a safeword and respite from the imposed hierarchy. And Corinthian childishness, as I show in the next section, is predicated upon deconstructions of chrononormative success and progress, including economic failure.

---

5. First used in Kelly Williams Brown's "adultingblog" in 2011, the word *adulting* is now prominent across the internet, typically in sentiments such as "adulting is hard" or "I can't adult today."

Queer Economics and Unproductivity

Having considered childishness as a queer virtue, I explore further the failed economy as a failure to *just grow up already*. The epistle consistently draws upon language of investment and profit in order to justify current austerity: Paul invokes profiting (*symphero*) in conjunction with the Corinthians's moral "investments" in their future: " 'All things are lawful for me,' but not all things are profitable," he quotes twice (6:12, 10:23).[6] Conversely, he positions economic profligacy as childishness: the *ekklēsia* members who do not anxiously hoard resources (if only righteousness, in this instance) and anticipate the future will be ruined. But in reading the Corinthian stance of unproductivity as a deliberate critique of Paul's re/ productivity, we might discover a queer economy among them, one that supports profligacy as an act of reckless faith.

Queer time is frequently noted as anticapitalist in its interests: Halberstam's queer failure is also economic failure; Stockton's queer childhood is precarious in part because children are not yet appropriately economized citizens; Edelman's repro-futurity is predicated upon the Protestant work ethic and moralization of self-denial; Sedgwick's paranoia fears the capitalist society that will let its residents die for not being appropriately anticipatory or successful. The economic conflict of 1 Corinthians, between the community's childish profligacy and Paul's pragmatism, underscores how straight time and profitability are predicated upon one another and how queer resistance may mutually destabilize their relationship.

In Edelman's (2004, 21) formulation of reproductive futurity, heteroadulthood is marked by paranoid asceticism; the only responsible way to live is to withhold present pleasures for future ones, particularly for "the future envisioned for a Child who must never grow up." Genealogical logic and chrono-heteronormativity anticipate the endless idea of the Child, of reproducing in an obvious and linear fashion. Edelman writes that this

---

6. The NRSV chooses to translate the stem *symphero* with variations on *benefit* or *advantage*. Material wealth, however, would seem to be a contentious and resonant point for the circumstances: from Dale B. Martin's (1995) argument that the Corinthian community was socioeconomically divided, to the disagreement about provisions made for Paul (9:3–18), to "the collection for the saints" (16:1–5). I therefore translate *symphero* with explicitly economic connotations to highlight the stresses suggested by the rhetoric.

perpetuates a "coercive universalization" in which "the image of the Child ... serves to regulate political discourse—to prescribe what will *count* as political discourse—by compelling such discourse to accede in advance to the reality of a collective future whose figurative status we are never permitted to acknowledge or address" (11).

José Esteban Muñoz (2009, 22) writes that *straight time* is an "autonaturalizing temporality" that obscures its own particular contours and implications. I suggest that the re/productive script of time is especially so, naturalizing its own investments of body, time, and labor within a self-contained narrative of *productivity as good citizenship*. This is what Edelman has shown above: the narrative of the biological imperative of the Child asserts not only the need for normative family structure but also the need for self-alienating labor to support said family. Thus if straight time is autonaturalizing, per Muñoz's critique, it is because the overarching system of capitalism compels it to be. Queer time, conversely, refuses the logic of progress and productivity, embracing pleasure and, per Halberstam (in the 2007 *GLQ* roundtable on queer temporalities), "engag[ing] in activities that probably seem pointless to people stranded in hetero temporalities" (Dinshaw et al. 2007, 181–82).

Halberstam argues in *The Queer Art of Failure* that queerness, as a rejection or resistance to normative social values, should embrace failure as a virtue. To achieve within a normative system is to adhere to—and excel at—following its rules; thus if queerness has any aspirations of being disruptive, it must "fail spectacularly" (2011, 5). Halberstam deconstructs the paradox of capitalism in relation to this failure: it is "a system that equates success with profit and links failure to the inability to accumulate wealth even as profit for some means certain losses for others" (88). This shadow narrative of loss and failure represents a queer economics, marked by "the association of failure with nonconformity, anticapitalist practices, nonreproductive life styles, negativity, and critique"; it runs counter to "heteronormative common sense [that] leads to the equation of success with advancement, capital accumulation, family, ethical conduct, and hope" (89).

Halberstam terms the economics of this ideology a "rejection of pragmatism" (89); I expand further in the same direction and identify queer, non-re/productive utilization of time as *profligacy*. If straight time is moralized according to capitalist ideals, then queer time must dissociate time from morality and from economy, and this term profligacy carries such (in)appropriate connotations of amorality and scandal. If neither productivity nor the future itself is compulsory any longer, then *action* is no longer obligated to *purpose*. In the shadow of the apocalypse, this is particularly interesting: its temporal collapse would seem to undermine cautionary asceticism, since there's little future left for which to plan.[7] Yet the apparent disagreement or discussion at stake between Paul and the Corinthians is as much about the economy of the apocalypse as anything, that he still urges asceticism and investment in a future that is rapidly closing. In Paul's theology, present austerity promises forthcoming reward, suggesting an economic pragmatism that has placed its faith in the cautious logic of straight time.

Throughout the letter, while Paul is utterly uninterested in normative family life, his call to asceticism still follows the logic of re/productive paranoia.[8] "'All things are lawful,'" he quotes the profligate Corinthian slogan, "but not all things are profitable"—that is, current actions are an investment in the future (6:12). Or in another iteration: "All things are lawful, but not all things are profitable.... Do not seek your own advantage, but the advantage of the other" (10:23–24). "The other" (presumably the weaker members of the community) serve the same purpose as Edelman's future Child: the future and thus the entire ethos of the community should be oriented toward their (future, hypothetical) well-

---

7. This motif—that the imminent apocalypse is reasonable cause for hedonism, recklessness, and chaos—is found persistently in postapocalyptic pop culture. The 2012 film *Seeking a Friend for the End of the World* most cheerily exemplifies this trope, as people hold "end of the world parties" with every manner of vice. While the 1993 film *Groundhog Day* is not a proper apocalypse, one character muses that if there were no tomorrow, "that would mean there would be no consequences, there would be no hangovers. We could do whatever we wanted!" A historical example may be found in Thucydides's *History of the Peloponnesian War*, in describing the plague of 430 BCE: "Nor was this the only form of lawless extravagance which owed its origin to the plague. Men now coolly ventured on what they had formerly done in a corner, and not just as they pleased, seeing the rapid transitions produced by persons in prosperity suddenly dying and those who before had nothing succeeding to their property. So they resolved to spend quickly and enjoy themselves, regarding their lives and riches as alike things of a day.... No one expected to live to be brought to trial for his offenses, but each felt that a far severer sentence had been already passed upon them all and hung ever over their heads, and before this fell it was only reasonable to enjoy life a little. Such was the nature of the calamity, and heavily did it weigh on the Athenians; death raging within the city and devastation without." (2.53.1–54.1 [Crawley])

8. The only times he addresses *actual* childhood is his own childhood in 1 Cor 13 and the question of children from mixed marriages in 1 Cor 7.

being. Edelman (2004, 148) writes that the entire structure of capitalist repro-futurity is predicated upon the threat of the dead Child: "Tiny Tim survives at our expense in a culture that always sustains itself on the threat that he might die." The entire economy is organized around this imaginary future citizen, at the expense of real, present residents; as Edelman writes, "That figural Child alone embodies the citizen as an ideal, entitled to claim full rights to its future share in the nation's good, though always at the cost of limiting the rights 'real' citizens are allowed" (11). And Paul *is* imagining citizenship, for he writes that if one prophesies without interpretation as the women prophets do, then one is a *barbaros* (14:11), a senseless babbler and racialized outsider. For Paul, good citizenship is productive citizenship.

His rhetoric consistently thinks of time in terms of productivity and wealth accumulation. "Already you have become rich!" he admonishes the Corinthians. "Quite apart from us, you have become kings!" (4:8). The wealth in question is the high status they have metaphysically gained in becoming "wise in Christ" (4:10), and as Dale Martin has noted in his 1995 book *The Corinthian Body*, Paul's economics rely more on maintaining a united, unpolluted body rather than a hierarchically organized one. Martin speculates that ultimately Paul is aiming to mend a socioeconomic rift in the Corinthian community by "convinc[ing] those of high status in the Corinthian church to imitate him in accepting a position of low status" (67). While offering metaphorical wealth and status to all members of a socioeconomically diverse community does disrupt normative class structure, especially with the motif of inverted hierarchy (wise/foolish in 1 Cor 1, greater/lesser honor in 1 Cor 12), Paul's repeated appeals to *profit* continue to valorize productivity and elite belonging within a slippery rhetoric of elite spiritual economy.

As Halberstam (2011, 89) writes, every story of success implies a shadow narrative of failure, one that is often more interesting than the predetermined narrative of what success looks like. And the situation of the prophets provides a pointed contrast to Paul's straight time ethos. The unproductive performance of prophesying disrupts the logic of straight time, gesturing to the futility of it all. The prophets will *lose* at the *apocalypse*. The queer economics of profligacy construct an ethos of apocalyptic failure, which privileges the present over the future and obscurity over status. Instead, the Corinthian gospel of failure declares, "Already you have been made poor! Quite apart from us you have been made losers."

The Queerness of Unintelligibility

The feminist scholarship regarding the Corinthian women prophets has demonstrated the ways in which they disrupt majoritarian space and time. Their alternative belonging is defined by a shared sense of purpose, with performance of metaphysical compression of space and time, in prophesying. Contrary to the feminist interpretations that have embraced the legitimacy of prophesying as a demonstration of alternative authority, I suggest that a hermeneutic of queer time deconstructs *purpose* and *productivity* as the foundations of authority, thereby dismantling the social hierarchies constructed on political and spiritual economies.[9] Queer unintelligibility—a performance that *means* nothing, especially not anything intelligible or useful to dominant discourses—is helpful for dismantling oppressive epistemologies and compulsory belonging. The queer ecstatic time of José Esteban Muñoz and Brandy L. Simula demonstrate how ecstatic performance expresses unbelonging to the present order and a longing for something different.

Muñoz proposes queer time as both a palliative and a strategy of resistance to the hegemonic present. For Muñoz (2009, 1), queerness is marked by its potentiality and its horizonality—it is not yet here and perhaps never can be, but it is the mechanism by which oppressed peoples can remove themselves briefly from "the here and now [that] is a prison house." Specifically, in resisting compulsory straight time, queer horizonality is

> a modality of ecstatic time in which the temporal stranglehold that I describe as straight time is interrupted or stepped out of. Ecstatic time is signaled at the moment one feels ecstasy, announced perhaps in a scream or grunt of pleasure, and more importantly during moments of contemplation when one looks back at a scene from one's past, present, or future. (32)

Simula, using Muñoz as the methodology of a sociological study, theorizes ecstatic time in relation to queer subcultures, particularly BDSM[10]

---

9. On prophesying as a demonstration of alternative authority, see, for example, Wire (1990, 112): "Rather than putting the women in a new subordination by withholding certain knowledge and demanding instead their love and dependence, the one God has given them all things. Their one obligation to God, if it can be called that, is to exercise this authority fully and not abdicate it in fear of offending others."

10. Bondage and discipline, dominance and submission, sadism, and masochism.

practitioners and scenes. For her subjects, queer time enables resistance to heteronormativity and regulated performance of gender. She examines BDSM encounters that "occur in settings that are spatially and temporally demarcated from everyday experiences or what participants refer to as 'vanilla life'" (2013, 79). Ecstatic time and space create exceptional opportunities for nonnormative performativity. As one of Simula's interview subjects describes how the BDSM scene allows them to both explore and transgress gender performance, the ecstatic experience opens space to "express other aspects of my gender identity maybe that I don't get to express ordinarily. So it's about relaxing in a lot of ways. It's about transgressing. Transcending" (80). Connecting this scene of erotic taboo to Muñoz's ecstatic "scream or grunt of pleasure," I offer that such extraordinary bodily performances signal expression that is unintelligible to the dominant culture. This unintelligibility, whether vocal or corporeal, indicates uncivilized irrationality and may be read as a rebuke of the extent to which bodily control itself is a mark of civilization.

In 1 Corinthians, prophesying without interpretation is the most significant threat to the unity of the body politic; thus it is also a conflict of economy. Unintelligible prophesying is both socially and spiritually useless, Paul writes, because "if I pray in a tongue, my spirit prays but my mind is unproductive (*akarpos*)" (14:14). The minds of the prophets are literally *fruitless*.[11] The associations of time, efficiency, and profit are strengthened by the apocalyptic imagery to which Paul appeals when he demands intelligibility of prophecy: "If the trumpet gives an unintelligible (*adēlos*) sound, who will prepare themselves for battle?" (14:8). To Paul, the rapid approach of the future necessitates a single, dominant discourse, particularly in conformity to "fruitful" ethics.

The strategy by which Paul uses this logic for social control is apparent in his injunctions against prophesying. Feminist scholars have demonstrated through rhetorical criticism of 1 Corinthians that the Corinthian women prophets were an alternative source of divine authority, disrupting and challenging the practical, masculinist theology asserted by Paul. As Castelli (1991b, 215) writes, the nature of prophecy as "self-authorizing, mobile, and unaccountable to other forms of authority" defies control and has "caused Paul's own claims to authority to pale significantly."

---

11. While Paul chooses the vocabulary of *sympherō* over *karpos* in 1 Corinthians, *karpos* elsewhere in the epistles denotes the same conceptual matrix of benefit/advantage/profit (e.g., Rom 6:21–22).

Uncontrolled power cannot be put efficiently to purpose, and perceived purposelessness seems central to Paul's irritation with the prophets—he accuses them of *wasting everyone's time*. He poses the rhetorical question, "If I come to you speaking in tongues, how will I benefit [*ōphelēsō*] you unless I speak to you in some revelation or knowledge?" (14:6). Paul's (comm)unity-driven ethos insists upon a singular construction of time, such that he can only understand the unintelligible (to him) and unproductive prophesying as *obstruction* of that purposeful time.

But we might read resistance, such as that offered in the ecstatic experiences of Simula's queer BDSM practitioners, into the act of untranslated prophesying instead. Ecstasy and unintelligibility perform deconstruction of the requirement of civility and majoritarian respectability. The multivocality of the prophets presents alternatives to Paul's pragmatic, re/productive future. We might imagine their ecstatic performance alongside BDSM. As one of Simula's (2013, 80) subjects says, the experience of a scene "allows one's conscious[ness] to go somewhere else. You hit this meditational phase where everything disappears around you, you do not feel bound to the moment. Time does not matter. Where you are doesn't matter, how you are doesn't matter. Free, that's the real key. You feel free." Feeling timeless, feeling unbound, marks this performance as standing outside of normative (or, if you would prefer, vanilla) life and normative society.

Conversely, homogeneity and erasure run throughout Paul's ethic and may be similarly resisted with coded, minority-intelligible, or unintelligible expression. Wire (1990, 143–44) describes the circumstances of Paul's privileging of the majority as contextual rather than ideological, but it nevertheless limits his ethics. "It is not accurate to say that Paul reduces the constructive social value of the spoken word to its rational context. He keeps his focus on communication.... But Paul takes the hearer rather than the speaker as his touchstone, rejecting tongues because the hearers do not understand them." So Paul chides the prophets, "So it is with you: if in a tongue you utter speech that is not intelligible, how will anyone know what is being said? You might as well be speaking into the air" (14:9). We might see his rebuke as analogous to what Muñoz (2009, 30) terms *gay pragmatism*—a counterculture's move toward majority accommodation and assimilation, with "gay pragmatic political strategies that tell us not to dream of other spatial/temporal coordinates but instead to dwell in a broken-down present." Paul is fundamentally pragmatic, and the dangers of such are self-evident when he tells slaves to "remain as you are," for example, in a "broken-down present" that does not fit them (7:21). Paul works within the confines of an abusive structure; we can easily imagine that opposition to him comprises the queer dreamers who reject this, people who are not so comfortable or content as he is.

Comprehensibility by the majority is antithetical to the construction of subculture. Incomprehensibility may reverse the binaries of insider/outsider and privileged/disadvantaged, but it simultaneously deconstructs these designations. Muñoz (2009, 60–62) uses stickering and wheatpasting as an example of the coding of queer expression—the existence of queer resistance stickers at a site conveys as much as the actual messages written on them. We may read the prophets in the same manner: *that* they express may be more significant than *what* they express.

The rhetoric of civility and civilization in his rebuttal of the prophets is racialized: "For if I do not know the meaning/power [*dynamin*] of a sound, I will be a barbarian to the one speaking, and the one speaking will be a barbarian to me" (1 Cor 14:11). This evokes inflammatory connotations of racial and cultural unbelonging. Performing unintelligibly to the hegemonic culture, within Paul's logic, justifies marginalization, if not exile. Demands of minority accommodation for majority *hearing* are a frequent but subtle aggression, often found in the racist tone argument that delegitimizes voices raised by people of color. When Paul writes to the community, "If in a tongue you utter speech that is not intelligible, how will anyone know what is being said," Audre Lorde (1984, 125) answers him, "I speak out of direct and particular anger at an academic conference, and a white woman says, 'Tell me how you feel but don't say it too harshly or I cannot hear you.' But is it my manner that keeps her from hearing, or the threat of a message that her life may change?"

It is this threat that the Corinthian community poses to Paul and to readers. The performative childishness, unproductivity, and unintelligibility found in rereading Corinthians do not have to be reprimanded or denounced. But rather than positioning the prophets as alternative authority figures, I find that reading them as *unauthoritative* reveals pointed countercultural ethics within the Corinthian circumstances. To find (or construct) a demographic that does not want power, does not want success, does not want majoritarian understanding—or perhaps understanding at all—reorients the letter. Rather than framing the conflict between or among competing authorities in Corinth, the conflict becomes one of authorities versus *anti*-authority. And while Paul disrupts hierarchy in his own way with his ethos of *homonoia* and unity, the prophets' imagined resistance represents challenges to the value of either unity or order altogether.

Halberstam writes that "the bleak and angry territories of the antisocial turn" provide

> the jagged zones within which not only self-shattering but other-shattering occurs. If we want to make the antisocial turn in queer theory we must be willing to turn away from the comfort zone of polite exchange in order to embrace a truly political negativity, one that promises, this time, to fail, to make a mess, to fuck shit up, to be loud, unruly, impolite, to breed resentment, to bash back, to speak up and out, to disrupt, assassinate, shock, and annihilate. (2011, 110)

None of these desires is incompatible with queer ecstasy, but they are incompatible with respectability politics, gay pragmatism, capitalism, and vanilla sex. The antiglamour of voluntarily losing in a competitive system reveals the unsustainable manipulation of cultural narrative—to tell everyone they can be winners in a world that needs losers is, in Lauren Berlant's (2011) term, cruel optimism. I read the prophets as resistant not because they perform Paul's mode of authority just as well as he does (or better!) but because their absurd, ecstatic performance might reveal just how fragile authority—his specifically but also generally—really is. We might imagine the Corinthians talking back, in expression that may or may not be in words: "You're being childish!" A shrug, "Yeah, so?"

Works Cited

Aasgaard, Reidar. 2007. "Paul as a Child: Children and Childhood in the Letters of the Apostle." *JBL* 126:129–59.

Berlant, Lauren. 2011. *Cruel Optimism*. Durham: Duke University Press.

Butler, Judith. 1990. *Gender Trouble: Feminism and the Subversion of Identity*. TG. New York: Routledge.

Castelli, Elizabeth A. 1991a. *Imitating Paul: A Discourse of Power*. LCBI. Louisville: Westminster John Knox.

———. 1991b. "Interpretations of Power in 1 Corinthians." *Semeia* 54:199–222.

Crawley, Richard, trans. 1903. *Thucydides' Peloponnesian War*. London: J. M. Dent.

Dinshaw, Carolyn, Lee Edelman, Roderick A. Ferguson, Carla Freccero, Elizabeth Freeman, Judith Halberstam, Annamarie Jagose, Christopher Nealon, and Tan Hoang Nguyen. 2007. "Theorizing Queer Temporalities: A Roundtable Discussion." *GLQ* 13:177–95.

Edelman, Lee. 2004. *No Future: Queer Theory and the Death Drive*. SerQ. Durham: Duke University Press.

Freeman, Elizabeth. 2007. "Introduction." *GLQ* 13:159–76.

Halberstam, Judith. 2005. *In a Queer Time and Place: Transgender Bodies, Subcultural Lives*. Sexual Cultures. New York: New York University Press.

———. 2011. *The Queer Art of Failure*. JHFCB. Durham: Duke University Press.

Johnson-DeBaufre, Melanie, and Laura S. Nasrallah. 2011. "Beyond the Heroic Paul: Toward a Feminist and Decolonizing Approach to the Letters of Paul." Pages 161–74 in *The Colonized Apostle: Paul through Postcolonial Eyes*. Edited by Christopher D. Stanley. PCC. Minneapolis: Fortress.

Lewis, C. S. 1966. "On Three Ways of Writing for Children." Pages 22–34 in *Of Other Worlds: Essays and Stories*. San Diego: Harvest.

Lorde, Audre. 1984. *Sister Outsider: Essays and Speeches*. Trumansburg, NY: Crossing.

Marchal, Joseph A. 2018. "How Soon Is (This Apocalypse) Now? Queer Velocities after a Corinthian Already and a Pauline Not Yet." Pages 45–67 in *Sexual Disorientations: Queer Temporalities, Affects, Theologies*. Edited by Kent L. Brintnall, Joseph A. Marchal, and Stephen D. Moore. TTC. New York: Fordham University Press.

Martin, Dale B. 1995. *The Corinthian Body*. New Haven: Yale University Press.

Muñoz, José Esteban. 2009. *Cruising Utopia: The Then and There of Queer Futurity*. Sexual Cultures. New York: New York University Press.

Penner, Todd, and Caroline Vander Stichele. 2004. "Unveiling Paul: Gendering Ethos in 1 Corinthians 11:2–16." *LD* 2:1–21.

Schüssler Fiorenza, Elisabeth. 1987. "Rhetorical Situation and Historical Reconstruction in 1 Corinthians." *NTS* 33:386–403.

Sedgwick, Eve Kosofsky, with Adam Frank. 2003. *Touching Feeling: Affect, Pedagogy, Performativity*. SerQ. Durham: Duke University Press.

Simula, Brandy L. 2013. "Queer Utopias in Painful Spaces: BDSM Participants' Interrelational Resistance to Heteronormativity and Gender

Regulation." Pages 71–100 in *A Critical Inquiry into Queer Utopias.* Edited by Angela Jones. New York: Palgrave Macmillan.

Stockton, Kathryn Bond. 2009. *The Queer Child: or, Growing Sideways in the Twentieth Century.* SerQ. Durham: Duke University Press.

Townsley, Gillian. 2006. "*Gender Trouble* in Corinth: Que(e)rying Constructs of Gender in 1 Corinthians 11:2–16." *BCT* 2:1–14.

Wire, Antoinette Clark. 1990. *The Corinthian Women Prophets: A Reconstruction through Paul's Rhetoric.* Minneapolis: Fortress.

Be Even Better Subjects, Worthy of Rehabilitation: Homonationalism and 1 Thessalonians 4–5

James N. Hoke

The end of 1 Thessalonians betrays a Pauline form of homonationalism. This is the crux of this essay's exegetical argument. I support this claim by showing how the normative alignments analyzed in contemporary politics by queer theorists can help us discover queerness (and attempts to restrict and exclude it) in its first-century manifestations. Doing so, I argue, requires placing Paul's letters within the context of Roman imperialism, which opens space to find other queer wo/men around Paul's letters and enhances our understanding of queer theory in the present.[1]

Homonationalism emerges, intentionally and unintentionally, out of tactics that bring together sexual exceptionalism, homonormativity, and the political—often imperial-like—goals of the United States as a nation. This brief definition, which overviews Jasbir K. Puar's original theorization, may be less clear than the term itself; it offers a road map, however, for the concepts that must be presented to understand homonationalism in its original—and then its first-century—context. In addition, the development of this definition helps us understand queerness in regard to the first-century Roman world of Paul's letters.

"Exceptionalism," writes Puar, "paradoxically signals *distinction from* (to be unlike, dissimilar) as well as *excellence* (imminence, superiority)" (2007, 3, emphasis added). Linking exceptionalism to discourses surrounding sexuality, Puar shows how language of sexual morality is often used by persons or groups to signal their exceptional—that is, superior— sexual behavior. Their status as exceptional, however, does not just make

---

1. I use *wo/men* following Elisabeth Schüssler Fiorenza's theorization (see 2001, 57–59, 108–9).

them distinguished: their similar language simultaneously distinguishes them *from* an exceptional—that is, dissimilar and thus deviant—Other. The dissimilarity of the latter, framed in terms of sexual immorality, confirms the superiority of the former (36). Puar terms this linked process "sexual exceptionalism"—being exceptionally sexually moral produces bodies that are sexually immoral exceptions (3–11).[2]

Queer theorists often identify and critique manifestations of heteronormativity—the ways in which society assumes straightness to be normal for all persons, an assumption that is built into social structures, regulations, and institutions (Warner 1993). Considering sociopolitical victories for LGBTIAQ+ rights, from the overturning of antisodomy laws (2003) to the repeal of "Don't Ask, Don't Tell" (2010) and the nationwide legalization of same-sex marriage (2015), alongside the increasing visibility and influence of wealthy gay persons (mostly cis men), norms have slightly shifted so that certain nonstraight persons are included. Such inclusion, however, presumes that one's only deviance from heteronormativity is not being heterosexual. Otherwise, these persons live according to the same norms and regulations of straightness: in a stable, monogamous relationship (ideally marriage), having a good job, raising children, staying fit, and generally looking like gay replicas of the "traditional family," typically imagined as white.[3] Lisa Duggan (2000, 50; see also Puar 2007, 38–39) names this inclusion—and the ways it has come to structure and regulate gay lives—homonormativity.

In homonationalism, Puar (2007, 1; see also Kaplan 2004, 1–18) denotes how the conforming inclusion fostered by homonormativity weds with strategies of sexual exceptionalism, a wedding fostered by the national politics of the United States, a nation that is more and more "coming out of the closet" as a contemporary manifestation of empire. Looking at discourses of sexuality within the "war on terror," Puar (2007, 37–78) argues that the United States establishes, via sexual exceptionalism, its dominion by virtue of its superior sexuality and its valuation of inclusion vis-à-vis the deviant-yet-homophobic sexualities of terrorists. In so doing, the United States makes space for new tactics wherein homonormative gay subjects can perform their patriotism and align themselves

---

2. These sexualized distinctions are also racialized, working in tandem with politics of whiteness as ascendant in the US context (Puar 2007, 24–32).

3. Puar emphasizes connections between homonormativity and the policing, regulation, and repression of sexuality (2007, 9–10).

with national interests.[4] Although the nation still privileges and bases its values on traditional heterosexuality, homonationalism permits certain LGBT persons (almost exclusively white, affluent, monogamous, cis gay men) to present themselves as "subjects worthy of rehabilitation" (38). Thus exceptional gays align with national sexual values (monogamy and the acceptance of homosexuality as patriotic) by excepting other bodies as deviant and perverse (e.g., nonmonogamous sexual practices, the presumed rejection of homosexuality based on perceptions of race/religion) (37–51, see also 3–11). Homonormative lives become political via sexual exceptionalism: they conform to and justify the control of and war against sexual deviance, particularly that of the terrorist, which threatens both national virtue and security.

Obviously, Puar combines the terms *homo* and *nationalism*—whose origins and theorizations lie in modernity and postmodernity—to coin a neologism that theorizes tactics that arise in a particularly twenty-first-century, post-9/11 Age of Terror. One may understandably find the use of such terms troubling or anachronistic when applied to first-century texts and contexts that were penned prior to the invention of nations and homosexuality.[5] As this essay's use of Puar shows, however, homonationalism holds

---

4. Notable gay/queer participation in these discourses of patriotic inclusion consists of the uplifting of "gay heroes" on 9/11 (e.g., Mark Bingham and Father Mychal Judge, both white men), the rise in the appearance of the US flag in publicly gay spaces (including an image of two young, fit, shirtless [or naked], white men closely wrapped in the flag, with the caption "Come Together"), and the encouragement of "gender patriotism"—conforming to stereotypical social gender roles as a performance of national solidarity (Puar 2007, 41–43).

5. On the invention of homosexuality in the nineteenth century, some classicists/theorists, following Foucault, have insisted that the term—and contemporary sexual expressions it conveys—cannot be accurately applied to first-century persons, since the dominant view of sexuality constructed it quite differently from the modern view (Foucault 1988b, 187). Halperin (1990, 15–18) is perhaps most exemplary and insistent on this point. Other classicists, however, most notably Brooten (1996) and Richlin (1993), who also acknowledge and analyze the dominant constructions of first-century sexuality, have shown how the dominant construction of sexuality does not capture the experience of all ancient wo/men, some of whom loved or experienced attraction in ways similar to modern ideas of homosexuality, even if they did not have the terms to theorize their attraction. Though there are certainly differences between first-century and contemporary wo/men, lesbians, and gays, there are important and undeniable continuities that are effaced by temporal restrictions enforced on certain contemporary terms.

far too much theoretical potential to be restricted to settings where homos and/or nationalism literally apply. Homonationalism theorizes strategies for rehabilitating certain broadly queer bodies that prove exceptional in the eyes of dominant powers. These alignments have occurred and will occur far beyond the temporal limitations of the term's composite parts. Like queerness and the assemblages that motivate Puar's (2007, 204–22) work, homonationalism exceeds its origins. Ultimately, Puar's theorization is affective, meaning that forces like homonationalism can shift, morph, and adapt to different settings—spatial and, as this essay shows, temporal.[6] Indeed, homonationalism's malleable quality makes it useful for theorizing Paul's letters as participants in discourses surrounding first-century sexuality and Roman imperialism.[7]

Similar to modern constructions of sexuality (though differing on specific terms), *Romosexuality* was governed by norms: certain sexual acts and desires were natural while others were unnatural (Foucault 1986a, 17–25; Winkler 1990, 17–23; Brooten 1996, 249–58, 175–86; Moore 2001, 140–43).[8] What was considered natural, however, were sexual practices that mirrored the social structure of Roman kyriarchy: men over women, free over slave, citizen over foreigner.[9] Those at the top of Roman society

---

There is considerably less discussion about the continuities between modern and postmodern understandings of nationalism and the imperialism of first-century Rome, but the similarities and usefulness for theorizing these continuities is emphasized and established by Shumate (2006).

6. This understanding comes from the crossings between queer theory and affect theory. Puar draws especially from Massumi 2002 and Ahmed 2004. For a good introductory overview of affect theory and its trends, its background, and different vectors within it, see Seigworth and Gregg 2010. On affect theory and its relation to biblical studies, see Koosed and Moore 2014.

7. Puar's work since 2007 supports the temporal flexibility of homonationalism. Puar clarifies that homonationalism is neither an "identity positioning" nor "an adjective" but is instead an *analytic of apprehension* (2017, 123). In other words, homonationalism moves, shifts, and adapts to new conditions in order to maintain efficacy even as structures of power change—or it operates as an assemblage (117–25; see the final section of this essay).

8. The term *Romosexuality*, which riffs on homosexuality by combining *Rome* with (*homo*)*sexuality*, comes from the conference theme upon which Ingleheart 2015 is based. See esp. pp. 1–25.

9. *Kyriarchy* is a neologism coined by Elisabeth Schüssler Fiorenza (see 1999, 5–6; 2001, 118–24; 2011, 8–11) to capture these intersecting hierarchies by which power is constructed to permit the rule (*archē*) of the lord/master (*kyrios*).

(i.e., freeborn male citizens) were naturally "impenetrable penetrators," able to penetrate those socially beneath them (Walters 1997, 30; Parker 1997, 48–49; Williams 2010, 178–97). What Romans deemed natural, therefore, is synonymous with what queer theory labels normative. Naturalness, like normalness, was defined and regulated according to prevailing sociosexual-political considerations.

Deviating from the norms of this sociosexual-political nature, unnatural sexuality, queer from Rome's perspective, was any sexual act that did not replicate the kyriarchal norms. Romosexuality engendered a first-century form of sexual exceptionalism: those exceptionally able to ascribe to these norms ruled society while excepting from its ranks the majority of others unable to do so and, therefore, deemed immoral (Marchal 2015, 95–99; Hoke 2017, 243–50, 269–75). "The exceptional proves who rules," as Joseph A. Marchal (2015) observes.

The existence of first-century Roman sexual exceptionalism would permit first-century tactics of homonationalism. Rome's conquered subjects could attempt to align their sexual values and practices to the elite ideals in order to see themselves—and potentially be seen by the Roman state as—worthy of rehabilitation. Roman imperialism, therefore, crafts the rules and framework to a game that (purportedly) anyone can win and creates competition amongst its subjects. Some conquered subjects develop homonationalistic tactics for playing a game that most/all were destined to lose. Versions of these tactics can be seen in Paul's letters, including 1 Thessalonians. To uncover how homonationalism operates in the earliest extant Pauline epistle, I show how sexuality and politics are inseparable in 1 Thessalonians by placing together two passages typically read as separate units: 4:1–12, which contains ethical instructions typically discussed in conversations about gender and sexuality, and 4:13–5:11, which contains an eschatological vision of the *parousia kyriou* (the lord's coming) often discussed with regard to Paul's politics.[10] By analyzing the wedding of politics and sexuality in both passages, I show how Paul's replication of Rome's sexually exceptional morality continues beyond its overt appearance in 4:3–5, encouraging Thessalonian Christ followers to be better Romans and therefore subjects worthy of rehabilitation in Roman

---

10. Pointing out this trend, Johnson-DeBaufre (2010, 90–91) draws attention to the fact that questions of gender and women's visibility in the Thessalonian community disappear into an assumed "generic congregation" when imperial ideology is discussed with respect to Paul's eschatological discourse.

imperial culture. Ultimately, Paul's ethical eschatology imagines a future that remains Roman, even when ruled by Christ. The essay ends by considering how these homonational ideas could participate in a conversation with the wo/men in Thessalonikē's *ekklēsia*, who perhaps still propagated some queerness.

Imperial Ideologies in Paul's (Sexual) Ethics: 1 Thessalonians 4:1–12

Homonationalism appears in 1 Thessalonians when its alignments with Roman politics and Romosexuality become more visible. It is crucial to observe that when Puar (2007, 10) theorizes homonationalism, she insists that "there is no organic unity or cohesion among homonationalisms; these are partial, fragmentary, uneven formations, implicated in the pendular momentum of inclusion and exclusion, so dissipating as quickly as they appear." Homonationalism and its tactics are not rigid; indeed, it is its fragmentary nature that permits different homonationalisms across the United States and the world today and that makes it possible to find its fragmentary resonances in ancient Rome. Uncovering some of these resonances, the first subsection focuses on 1 Thess 4:3–5 to show how its instructions on sexual ethics repeat the ideal and ethnic stereotypes of Romosexuality, making this an example of sexual ethics that reproduce Roman ideals of sexual exceptionalism. The second subsection turns to the broader framework of 1 Thess 4:1–12 to show how Paul frames his sexually exceptional ethics within the projects and goals of Roman imperialism and social mobility. This subsection situates Paul's aligning tactics with those of other, roughly contemporaneous writers, Philo of Alexandria and Dionysius of Halicarnassus. Both authors came from communities of conquered Roman subjects, and both attempted to align their respective Jewish and Greek values with Roman virtue. By showing how Paul's ethics in 4:1–12 align with imperial ideologies through normative sexual exceptionalism, homonationalism emerges as an apt description for Paul's ethical tactics.

Romanormativity and Sexual Exceptionalism in 1 Thessalonians 4:3–5

In 1 Thessalonians, sexuality appears most overtly in 4:1–12, where Paul relates ethical instructions regarding, among other issues, sexual morality. In 4:3–5, Paul exhorts, "For this is God's will, your holiness: that you refrain from *porneia*, that each of you knows to obtain your own vessel in holiness and honor—not in desire's passion, just as, indeed, the *ethnē* who do not know God."[11] Much ink has been spilled trying to determine exactly what Paul's instructions mean. They clearly involve sex and sexuality, given the references to *porneia* in 4:3 and *epithumia* ("desire") in 4:5. The meaning of *porneia*, however, is broad and contested, well beyond the bounds of Paul's letters, though coming from a root that specifies it as prostitution. By the first century, the term *porneia* often refers more broadly to unspecified acts and behaviors considered to be "sexual immorality" (LSJ, s.v. "πορνεία").[12] Likewise, while *mē en pathei epithumias* ("not in desire's passion") conveys the desires and passion that motivate and lead to uncontrolled and immoral sexuality, the directive the phrase modifies— *to heautou skeuos ktasthai* ("to acquire one's own vessel")—is especially vexing. The specific direction is completely unclear. In particular, to what does *skeuos* refer: a literal clay vessel ("or implement of any kind"; LSJ, s.v. "σκεῦος")? a woman? a penis? a slave? And, after that, what does *ktasthai* ("procure for oneself," "acquire," "obtain," potentially "control"; LSJ, s.v. "κτάομαι") mean in relation to this ambiguous vessel (Yarbrough 1985, 68–73; Elgvin 1997; Malherbe 2000, 226–29; Bruce 1982; 83–84; Gaventa 1998, 51–56; Konradt 2001; Bassler 1995; Glancy 2002, 59–63)?

Instead of asking or determining the specifics of *what* Paul's sexual morality was in 4:3–5, here I consider *how* and *why* Paul frames such directives, especially as they relate to and replicate Romosexuality.[13] As in Paul's writings, Roman morality usually restricted and condemned acts classified as *porneia*, and, even more emphatically, Roman men were to control their

---

11. Unless otherwise noted, all translations from ancient texts are my own.

12. Especially since prostitutes were typically enslaved women, it is not surprising that prostitution becomes a metonymy for all sexual immorality. On the complexity of the term's meaning, see Rousselle 1988; Gaca 2004; Harper 2011; Glancy and Moore 2011.

13. In other words, I assume that 1 Thess 4:1–8 contains instructions that referred to specific sexual practices (of which his audience seem to have been aware), but I do not think we can ever fully reconstruct what Paul prohibits and permits in using these terms. Furthermore, I do not see much value in knowing the answer to such questions, as they have little relevance to modern debates on sex and sexuality. Finally, in focusing on these questions of *why* and *how*, I hope to decenter Pauline authority from the interpretation of this passage. A similar distinction can be found in Yarbrough 1985, 3. His monograph, however, and its analysis of 1 Thess 4:3–8 focus on sexual morality specifically through the lens of marriage. He concludes that Paul's idea of marriage and morality is not distinct from that of Greco-Roman moral philosophy (77, 31–63).

desires (*epithumia*) and passions (*pathos*) (Martin 2006, 65–76; Edwards 1993, 57; Malherbe 2000, 229–30; Bruce 1982, 84). Having too much sex, having sex with the wrong sorts of people, and having sex in the wrong position were evidence of uncontrolled and excessive desire (Foucault 1988b, 63–77). All of these desires and behaviors were deemed unnatural for the true Roman *vir*; they deviated from the norms of Romosexuality (Walters 1997, 32; Gleason 1995, 159; Conway 2008, 15–34; Knust 2006, 28; Edwards 1993, 34–62). Because desire was associated with lack of self-control, it is rare to find references to a person having a single immoral desire—where there is one, there are many. In other words, immoral passions and desires compounded and accompanied one another, in addition to excessive desire for food, drink, and luxury (Foucault 1988b, 85–184). Connected with desire and self-control, regulating sexual morality among citizens was considered crucial for maintaining imperial rule. If a Roman could not control his own desire, as defined by imperial sexual mores, then how could he be fit to control and rule over others (Edwards 1993, 57; Richlin 1993, 553; Williams 2010, 137–76; Marchal 2015, 95–96; Martin 2006, 65–76; Knust 2006, 32–47; Conway 2008, 21–29; McDonnell 2006, 3; Smith 2007, 315–16)?

Although Rome's regulations regarding sexual mores were largely concerned with its citizens, Roman ideals and concerns surrounding natural sexual praxis were known by subjects throughout the empire's conquered and incorporated territories. For example, we see the ideals being disseminated through Augustan marriage and adultery laws, continued by his successors (Treggiari 1991, 37–80, 262–319; D'Angelo 2007, especially 70). These conquered and incorporated territories—that is, *ethnē* ("nations")— formed the empire, but their inhabitants were distinguished from Romans of Rome as both conquered *ethnē* (as seen in their depictions in Roman conquest imagery) and as *peregrini* ("foreigners"/"strangers") (Lopez 2008; Noy 2000).[14] Even though Romans thought most sexual practices among its *ethnē* to be queer vis-à-vis these elite norms, Romosexuality offered a model to which conquered *ethnē*, perhaps especially those with upwardly mobile aspirations, might attempt to conform—in essence, *Romanormativity* (Hoke 2017, 93–94, 340–42).

The hopes of inclusion or upward mobility that foster these normative alignments are rarely made explicit by the dominant regime. Puar (2007,

---

14. I follow Davina Lopez (2008, esp. 119–63) here and read Paul's use of *ethnē* through the lens of representing nations conquered by Rome.

40–51, 61–67) observes how homonormative and homonational tactics presume a new normal in twenty-first-century US culture that openly includes certain gays who raise children in stable marriages; their alignment with traditional national values permits the United States to proclaim its value of inclusion. Puar notes, however, that from the vantage point of the state, the promised inclusion is largely illusory—homonational gays tout national inclusivity even as the nation does not fully include them (currently seen, e.g., in so-called religious freedom laws) (10, 78).[15] Thus homonationalism is "a facile construction that is easily revoked, dooming the exceptional queers to insistent replays and restagings of their exceptionalisms" (78). In similar ways, via the virtues of Romosexuality, Romanormativity offers opportunities for nonelite Roman subjects to align their sexual virtue with that of Rome's elite as a means of an upward mobility that was illusory.[16] Paul can be seen as drawn into such normativity via his repetitions of Romosexual virtues (controlling desire and passions) and condemnations of immorality (*porneia*) in 1 Thess 4:3–5.

Rome's imperial sexual exceptionalism, therefore, presented Romans as uniquely able to adhere to its sexual mores. Roman sexual slander, which presumed predilections toward unnatural sexuality, was frequently associated with and applied to non-Romans (Gleason 1995, 3–54; Knust 2006, 28–35; Shumate 2006, 19–32). Such slander, Knust observes, reinforced Rome's rigid sociosexual-political hierarchies: "In this way, invective cat-

---

15. At the time of writing *Terrorist Assemblages* in 2007, Puar observes how the illusion of inclusion is shattered by the realities of then-president Bush's rigid defense of marriage as a heterosexual institution as well as the then-active "Don't Ask, Don't Tell" policy that governed the US military.

16. Certainly, Rome granted citizenship—one signal of upward mobility—to some of its conquered/incorporated inhabitants; those granted citizenship, however, were often the exceptions rather than the rules; often, they were already elite. Most foreigners were not citizens in the first century; see Noy 2000, as well as Lavan 2013, 32–37. We find that the granting of citizenship was frequently accompanied by a public display, a boon for Rome as much as for its new citizen (who likely financed it). These displays would proclaim the subject's extreme loyalty to Rome, as seen in the second-century example of *Iulianus Zegrensis* (Julian the Zegrensian); see Oliver 1972, 336, 339. Such bestowals and their public proclamation sustained the promise of citizenship and upward mobility precisely by encouraging the proper imperial-patriotic mores exemplified by (usually) already-elite *ethnē*. A similar situation can be seen in the freedom and upward mobility of slaves and freedpersons; see Knust 2006, 27–28; Weaver 1967.

egories were extended to indict entire nations and peoples. At the same time, these categories reinforced a definition of gender and status that favored freeborn citizen men by associating women, slaves, foreigners, and barbarians with weakness in the face of desire" (Knust 2004, 167; see also Smith 2007, 315–16; Marchal 2015, 97). Who else but a Roman could be Romosexual?

A similar sexual exceptionalism appears in 1 Thess 4:5: "not in lust's passion, as is in the case of the *ethnē* who do not know God" (*mē en pathei epithumias kathaper kai ta ethnē ta mē eidota ton theon*). Contrasted with the believers' "holiness and honor" in the ambiguous act of acquiring a vessel, this lustful sexual excess is placed upon the *ethnē*, from whom the Christ followers of Thessalonikē are being distinguished. Like Rome's slanderous associations between unnatural sexuality and foreigners, 4:5 associates sexual deviance—that is, passions that involve uncontrolled desire—with the unnatural and ungodly behaviors practiced among the *ethnē* around Thessalonica.[17] Paul employs the language of sexual morality in order to firmly secure a boundary between Christ followers and these supposedly deviant *ethnē*.[18] Thus the Romanormative alignments in 4:3–5 also employ sexual exceptionalism: they rely on an ethnic other, cast as sexually deviant, from whom those aspiring to appear normal can distinguish themselves.

This boundary marker is necessary because the Thessalonian Christ followers live among and, indeed, are from these *ethnē*. In 1 Thess 1:9, Paul already distinguishes the Thessalonian Christ followers from the religious practices of those around them. Paul praises this assembly because it is well known and reported "how you turned to God from idols in order to be enslaved to a living and true god." Because the Thessalonian Christ followers were among these *ethnē*, they had adhered to their practices in terms of religious ritual and worship of deities. Paul distinguishes his audience of *ethnē* from these former practices and, presumably, the

---

17. Yarbrough (1985, 84–86) notes that Paul's language is similar to what Romans used against barbarians, but he denies this as the source of Paul's language because Paul uses the language of Jewish marital morality. See also Smith 2007, 315–16. These Jewish influences on Paul cannot be discounted, but it should be noted that Jewish moralists, rabbis, and philosophers (notably Philo, discussed later) are also influenced by Greco-Roman morality and can even display instances of Romonormativity.

18. For another elaboration of these sexually exceptional tactics in 1 Thess 4:5, see Marchal 2015, 107–9.

people and groups who practice them. Bringing in 4:5, these *ethnē* who do not know God are presumably worshipping idols as the Thessalonian Christ followers once did. Quite probably, Paul and his audience would have these most proximate idol-worshipping *ethnē* in mind. If the Thessalonian Christ followers have already distanced themselves from the idol worship that surrounds them, now they are reminded that they must also distance themselves from the sexual practices associated with these *ethnē*. Thus Paul's language of sexual morality further distinguishes Thessalonian Christ followers from the *ethnē* around them.

By contrasting their slanderous "desire's passion" with the Christ followers' purer sexuality, Paul "somatizes" ritual purity, as Thomas (2010, 122–24; see also Yarbrough 1985, 79) argues, by making sexual behaviors central to "holiness and honor."[19] As she compares Paul's ethics with those of neighboring cultures (based upon literary and epigraphic evidence), Thomas concludes, "Thus ironically, the ideals of sexual morality so critical to Paul as a boundary marker for his community did not differ between Jews and Gentiles. Both groups negatively sanctioned the same sexual practices" (120). Read with this background, Paul's instructions about sex in 1 Thessalonians were clearly not unique; they conformed to the standard mores of many communities—whether Roman, Jewish, or another *ethnē*—who used sexual purity to draw boundaries between themselves and others, where the others are almost always simultaneously sexually deviant and ethnically different.

In 1 Thess 4:3–5, Paul primarily parrots Roman sexual morality, including the fact that barbaric *ethnē* were sexually immoral: they cannot control their lustful passions for one another. The Thessalonian Christ followers have already turned away from their worship of the idols, and Paul now reminds these followers to distinguish themselves, via their sexual praxis, from those practiced among the non-Roman *ethnē* around them. Just as good Romans controlled their vessels (whatever they may be) and avoided unnatural liaisons, the *ekklēsia* should also remain pure and therefore honorable in the eyes of their superiors. Via Romanormative sexual morality, these verses draw clear boundaries between them and other *ethnē* and remove any (former) connections with them. Through such

---

19. She further observes how purity language—which Paul uses most frequently when discussing sexual morality—is crucial for drawing group boundaries because it cements communal identity and creates parameters for policing members; see Thomas 2010, 114–15, 117.

sexual exceptionalism, Paul associates Christ followers as most proximate to elite Romans in terms of their sexual virtues and practices (see Smith 2007, 315–16).

In somewhat similar terms, Marchal (2015, 107–9) spelled out how Roman sexual exceptionalism is apparent in 1 Thess 4:3–8 in ways that disrupt any easy identification of Paul standing against Rome and its empire. But could this sexual exceptionalism be further specified as homonationalism—that is, a tactic by which Thessalonian Christ followers attempt to present themselves not only as virtuous but also, therefore, as worthy of inclusion *by Rome and its ruling elite* into the upper tiers of its society? Indeed, I am arguing that Paul's sexual exceptionalism in 4:3–5 is a tactic that folds into a larger homonational impulse that Paul has woven into 1 Thessalonians. Sexuality is not isolated into this single passage. It affects and is affected by—and is woven into—Paul's ethics, theology, and politics.[20] By turning to spaces where sexuality is less obvious, I show how 1 Thess 4:3–5 participates in Pauline homonationalism.

"Being Even Better" among Rome's Subjects: Framing 4:3–5 in Homonationalism

To see how homonationalism might occur in 1 Thessalonians, the sexual exceptionalism of 4:3–5 should be situated within its wider framing in 4:1–12, which should furthermore be placed in the context of the writings of some of Rome's other conquered subjects.[21] In 4:1, Paul transitions to these ethical instructions and introduces them as a reminder of "how you must live and please God." He ends this first sentence with the explanation that these living standards are necessary *hina perisseuēte mallon* ("so that you may be even better"), a phrase that recurs in the unit's final sentence: *parakaloumen de hymas, adelphoi, perisseuein mallon* ("we encourage you, siblings, to be even better"; 4:10b). Thus Paul emphasizes that *perisseuein mallon*—being even better—is an ultimate goal of following these instructions, including the sexually exceptional ethics of 4:3–5. Such abundance (indeed, *perisseuō* is often translated as "to abound" here) among the

---

20. A point Moore (2001, 169–72) makes about Rom 1:18–32 in relation to the remainder of this epistle.

21. Yarbrough (1985, 67–68) makes this point as well. His framework of 1 Thess 4:1–12 focuses on Paul's use of *peripateō* ("to live") and how Paul focuses generally on the moral lifestyle of Christ assemblies.

Thessalonians suggests several interesting implications. What sorts of abundance or great increase might Paul have in mind?

In general terms, *perisseuō* denotes abundance in the sense of being more than enough or going beyond what is sufficient, expected, or required (LSJ, s.v. "περισσάκις"). As such, in addition to meaning "to abound," it can be used to connote overflow and superfluity, and, with respect to persons, it can connote superiority, advantage, or betterness. While translating *perisseuō* as "to abound" in 1 Thessalonians conveys many of these senses, the warmly positive sense of abundance misses some of the negative and neutral meanings of this term, as well as its meaning vis-à-vis the context of Roman conquest and morality. In a more neutral sense, the term refers to one amount exceeding another in a comparison of quantities. For example, when Philo of Alexandria observes that it is impossible for humans to divide quantities equally, he states that one segment inevitably falls short and is lacking (*endeō*) and the other is more abundant in quantity (*perisseuō*; *Her.* 142).[22]

Appropriately, Philo's usage of *peritteuō* (i.e., the Attic form of *perisseuō*) divides unevenly, and its negative implications abound in greater frequency. In *De Iosepho*, Philo writes:

> The means of sustenance are managed by only myself, who can distribute and apportion them, with respect to necessary need, to each of those who lacks them so that it neither produces excess among those using it for luxury nor falls short among those using it for completing their lack. (243)

In this instance, nourishment is allowed to exceed in this way by those prone to *tryphē*, "luxury"—in the sense of delicacy, softness, or daintiness (LSJ, s.v. "τρῦφή"). Because of this association with softness—and implicitly effeminacy—*tryphē* and its accompanying excesses were viewed negatively in Roman thought (Knust 2006, 32–35). If elite Roman virtue prioritized moderation and self-control, then luxury was a sign

---

22. In *Her.* 192, Philo observes how the Israelites were able to evenly distribute manna so that no one went hungry and no one took it in excess (*perisseuō*) of their need. Philo also occasionally uses the term positively when God is the subject or, when discussing the combined experiences on earth of joy and grief (both coming from God), the "better" experience (i.e., joy) exceeds the amount of the other (grief); see, respectively, *Conf.* 137; *Abr.* 205.

of inherent immoderation, even as all elite Romans lived in comparative luxury. Similar to sexual mores, the exceptional ones set the rules that established the boundary between necessary nourishment and luxurious excess. In *De Iosepho*, Philo's use of *perisseuō* signals negative superfluity: it means crossing this boundary by those who go beyond basic nourishment (*trophē*). This superfluous abundance should be avoided by a good manager or ruler (such as Joseph), whose ruled subjects can be presumed less able to control their superfluous desires.

A similar connection between abundance and vice can be found in book three of *Legum Allegoriae*. Philo writes: "Passion [*to pathos*] abounds [*peritteuei*] in the foolish [mind], which does not have a remedy in the soul, with which it repels the doom that comes from the senses and their sensations" (3.200).[23] In this instance, the excess that *perisseuō* produces is not wealth, recognition, or joy but *to pathos*, passion—the same passion exhibited by *ethnē* in 1 Thess 4:5. It is clear that this is uncontrolled passion—associated with folly (and feminine expressions of pain and grief)—the precise excess that Roman virtue dictated should be self-controlled in the minds and bodies of men, particularly those fit to rule. What we see in these examples is that, though excess or abundance can be good when it applies to good qualities/virtues (and God), it is often dangerously superfluous and signals a lack of self-control with respect to diet and passion. The verb *perisseuō* emphasizes the exceptionalism of Roman virtue, where rule is justified by excessive wealth and power while preventing unwanted and dangerous excess (usually with respect to desire and the body).

Philo is not alone in this application of Roman values to *perisseuō*. In his *Antiquitates Romanae*, Dionysius of Halicarnassus relates negotiations for a peace between the Romans and the Albans (circa 670 BCE), which resulted in the uniting of Rome and Alba Longa (as a vassal state until its eventual conquest/full incorporation into Rome) (3.1–21). In the midst of these negotiations, the king of the Romans describes how the Albans were once stronger and more prominent than Rome and the Romans, but

---

23. In the Loeb translation, Colson and Whitaker translate *to pathos* more specifically as "grief," which is certainly the specific passion being discussed allegorically with respect to the woman's punishment in Gen 3:16; Philo and the LXX from which he quotes, however, employ more specific terms for grief in this discussion, and while Philo still has grief in mind here, it seems he connects it to the more general passions that abound in less controlled minds and souls (which, of course, also include lust and overindulgence).

this is no longer the case. Thus he proclaims of Rome: "It would therefore have been impossible, three generations after its construction, for there to be such a city with regard to its greatness and power—unless there was more than enough manliness and sensibility in it" (*Ant. rom.* 3.11.9). What appears to abound among Rome's founders and early rulers are the good qualities and virtue that lead to self-control and moderation. Dionysius presents Rome, from its foundation, as exceptional: its prominence and dominance stem from its abundant virtue—that is, its excessive (manly) ability to control excess.

Philo's and Dionysius's uses of *perisseuō* are especially relevant because, although both authors were comparatively wealthier and of higher standing, neither was Roman. Philo was an Egyptian Jew; Dionysius was Greek. Philo's writings frequently present Jewish history, figures, traditions, and ethics in an alliance with Roman values and politics (often in distinction to the values and traditions of Greeks and, especially, Egyptians) (Niehoff 2001). Similarly, in his history of Rome, Dionysius "hopes to reconcile his Greek readers to their subjection to Rome" (Cary 1937, xiii). By presenting a full history of Rome, Dionysius emphasizes how Rome's current dominion is due not only to their present virtue (alongside their conquest via military might) but also to the presence of this virtue from Rome's founding and throughout most of its history (i.e., the *mores maiorum*; see Res. gest. divi Aug. 8.13–15; Horace, *Carm.* 3.16–20, *Saec.* 56–60; Zanker 1988, 156–62; Edwards 1993, 34–62). By emphasizing the abundance of Roman virtue, Dionysius continues the alignment of Greek and Roman values and implicitly encourages virtuous subjection from his audience, furthering or continuing their successful incorporation into Roman rule. Among other tactics, their use of *perisseuō* demonstrates how both Dionysius and Philo present Roman values and traditions to their Greek and Jewish audiences by adapting them to their own histories and traditions and, ultimately, encouraging model subjection.

Paul's use of *perisseuō* to frame 1 Thess 4:1–12 carries similar implications: *be even better.* Paul urges them to abound in their adherence to Roman virtue, most notably in sexual terms that distinguish them from the other *ethnē* around them. By becoming abundantly Roman, Paul and the Thessalonians presumably hope to gain a share in Roman abundance. They are loyal Roman subjects whose virtues both sustain Rome's rule and make them subjects worthy of abundant rehabilitation. Paul's use of *perisseuein mallon* as a framework for his ethical instruction, which includes the sexually exceptional ethics of 4:3–5, begins to encourage a homonational presentation of the Thessalonian Christ followers as being abundantly Roman with respect to their virtue.

This homonational framework becomes more emphatic in the final exhortation in 4:10b–12: "We encourage you, brothers and sisters, to be even better [*perisseuein mallon*] and aspire to keep quiet, mind your own business, and work with your hands, just as we instructed you, so that you can live respectably toward those outside and not need anyone else." Paul's first exhortation to be even better (4:1) is specified by the instructions that follow, including those on sexual morality in 4:3–5. In 4:10b–12, being even better is also qualified—in this case, with encouragements to keep a low profile and to look respectable to outsiders.

In particular, 4:11 includes an aspiration to keep quiet, *philotimeisthai hēsuchazein*. The verb *philotimeomai* combines *phileō* ("love," "affection") with *timē* ("honor"), the Roman virtue that already defined Christ followers' sexual morality in 4:4. The verb's typical meaning is to love or seek after honor, and it was often used to mean "to be ambitious" or "to compete or vie for honor" (LSJ, s.v. "φιλοτιμέομαι"). Thus in the same section of his *Antiquitates*, Dionysius describes the Roman general Tullus responding to Fufetius's (the ruler of the Alba Longa) objections about Roman infighting. Tullus asserts that the competition between societal factions in Rome increases its inhabitants' contributions to the common good. He says, "For we compete for the honor—the youth with the elders, and the settlers with those who beckoned them in—of who among us does more for the common good" (*Ant. rom.* 3.11.8). Honor (and therefore greater status), then, belongs to those who contribute most to the common good, and in Dionyius's portrayal of an idealized (ancient) Roman society, this meant that everyone (e.g., young/old, newcomer/inhabitant) could compete for it on equal grounding.

When, as in 1 Thess 4:11, *philotimeomai* is used with a subordinate infinitive, it can mean to strive or aspire to do something, but given its more general meaning and use, the verb retains implications of competition and ambition for honor and honorable status when it is used with an infinitive. When Paul uses the verb in 2 Cor 5:9, he speaks of a competitive ambition to please God: "We are therefore ambitious [*philotimoumetha*], whether we are at home or abroad, to be pleasing to him [Christ, *ton kyrion*]."[24] Alternatively, the main clause could be rendered

---

24. Apart from its usage here and in 1 Thessalonians, Paul uses *philotimeomai* on one other occasion—in Rom 15:20.

as "We compete for the honor ... to be pleasing to him." While Paul focuses on the exhortation to please Christ, the ambition to do so implicitly introduces a sense of competition. Even if everyone wins, some will be better than others in their striving—that is, some will please Christ more honorably. Similarly, when Paul uses *philotimeomai* in 1 Thess 4:11, it implies that some can be more honorable than others.

But in 1 Thessalonians, Paul's encouragement to *philotimeisthai hēsychazein* is different: competing for honor by keeping quiet, maintaining the peace, and, then, "minding your own business" (*prassein ta idia*) gives more explicit direction than the general encouragement to compete to be pleasing to Christ in 2 Corinthians. If, by using *philotimeomai* in general, Paul adopts and adapts the Roman value *timē* into his ideas for following Christ, in 1 Thess 4:11 he parrots Roman expectations for honorable behavior from the *ethnē* it ruled: do not cause disruption. If most *ethnē* drew imperial attention when they were rebellious or otherwise causing disturbances, the path to Roman honor required *ethnē* to avoid notice from imperial authorities—*philotimeisthai hēsychazein*, vie for honor by keeping quiet. Ironically, avoiding imperial notice really meant that those who remained quiet could be ignored and passed over in terms of gaining honor.[25] Though citizenship was granted to a small number of already elite subjects among Rome's *ethnē*, the *pax Romana* could be maintained with few of the empire's conquered subjects really rising in status.[26]

---

25. Translating as "be ambitious to be quiet," Bruce (1982, 90–91) calls the language oxymoronic in his discussion. Malherbe (2000, 246–50) discusses the term alongside the ideas among contemporary Greco-Roman philosophers (e.g., Plutarch, Dio Chrysostom, Seneca) about desiring to withdraw from public politics to quietly wax eloquent.

26. Except for a small, praiseworthy elite among various *ethnē* who were able to rise, to a degree, in status and attain Roman honor (such as Julian the Zegrensian of n. 16). Even if they were praised for their fidelity to Rome and their role in not disturbing the peace, however, their rise in status was related to both their wealth and their political prowess. One might reasonably inquire about Paul's status as a Roman citizen, as he is presented in Acts (though it is decidedly unclear as to his citizenship status in the authentic epistles). While my essay may be making the implicit presumption that Paul is not a Roman citizen, it should be noted that if he did have citizenship status, it does not affect the hopes and visions he conveys to *ethnē* who likely did not. Indeed, if Paul stands with these *ethnē* as a citizen, his status models the exceptional promises of Rome and reinforces the benefits of modeling their *mores* (potentially also reifying Paul's authority as a model to imitate).

Of course, Paul imagines an empire ruled by God and Christ, not Caesar, so it could be said that even if his ethics largely replicate honorable behavior in Roman terms, God's reign will eventually reward anyone and everyone who can adhere to these standards. It is equally plausible, however, that when Paul exhorts the Thessalonians to proper (Roman) behavior in the present, Paul also has present imperial honors and recognition in mind. Indeed, Paul's direction is reminiscent of Rom 13:1–7, where he infamously implores Rome's Christ followers to submit to "prevailing authorities," not rebel, and to pay their taxes.[27] Paul essentially exhorts a similar sort of submission—aligning one's sexual behavior with imperial mores and therefore not behaving "like the *ethnē*" (4:3–5) and behaving exceedingly better, keeping quiet, and minding one's own affairs (4:10b–12 and 4:1–2)—evincing, at least, a desire to not attract attention by disturbing the peace.

Indeed, Paul specifies that these silent alignments *are* meant to curry favor or good judgment from human observers in the present. In 4:12, he states that the reason for behaving in the ways described in 4:10b–11 is so that the Thessalonians can live "respectably (*euschēmonōs*) towards those outside." The adverb *euschēmonōs* literally means "good appearance" and it was often used to describe respectability and decency, especially, by the first century CE, in terms of honor and nobility (LSJ, s.v. "εὔσχημος"). Respectable living was primarily associated with those who held honorable status. For the Thessalonian Christ followers, gaining such respectability requires, in part, living according to the directions in 4:1–12: adhere to Rome's sexual virtues, vie for honor, and be as good as possible (see also Hoke 2017, 300).[28]

Furthermore, this respectability comes *from the eyes of outsiders.* Their respectable lives are specifically intended toward those outside. They hope that these outsiders will notice their good appearance, their confor-

---

27. Note, furthermore, the resonances between 1 Thess 4:12 (above) and Rom 13:8: "Owe nothing to no one except for loving reciprocally. For whoever loves completes a different law." While they differ in content, the parallels between these passages point to potential connections in Paul's development of ideas of submission to Rome and performance of its *mores* and, indeed, his homonationalism. I uncover Pauline homonationalism in Rom 13:1–14 in Hoke 2017, 239–306.

28. Johnson-DeBaufre and Nasrallah (2011, 169) briefly call attention to this verse and how, in heroic Pauline interpretation, it places the community into a stance of accommodation while Paul emerges as the "counter-cultural persecuted hero."

mity to Roman morality, their quiet, nonsubversive tending to their own affairs and judge them as respectable subjects—even *honorable* Romans. These ethical alignments do more than prepare the Thessalonian Christ followers to excel in an empire ruled by God and Christ. By being even better than their competition for honor, they demonstrate how and why Paul's ethical instructions align with first-century Roman virtues: by living according to these standards, they are presenting themselves respectably toward those outside.

Ultimately, then, these exhortations and instructions to be even better in 1 Thess 4:1–12 align and present Christ followers as respectable—as subjects worthy of rehabilitation and admittance into the upper tiers of Roman honor *in the present*. Respectable, silent living requires adhering to Romosexuality and, in particular, not behaving like other rebellious, indulgent, sexually deviant *ethnē* who evoke the ire found in Roman slander. These behavioral alignments present Christ followers as better, respectable Romans. They win the competition for honor by wedding strategies of Romanormativity (aligning their mores to those of Rome) and sexual exceptionalism (they are better Romans *because* they are unlike sexually deviant ethnic others)—ultimately supporting the imperial *pax Romana*. These ethical directions are ultimately strategies of Pauline homonationalism.

Though manifested in certain tactics and strategies, as a complex assemblage, homonationalism—especially in the case of Paul—is not a fully conscious decision. In both the US and Roman contexts, those in power (in whose images norms are shaped) create the conditions whereby those subject to and oppressed by their power can seek competitive avenues that might permit some to appear respectable, gain recognition, and gain more (but ultimately limited) inclusion among the upper sociopolitical echelons. Paul's strategies attempt to take advantage of these conditions, and as they seek this avenue, they develop, both unwittingly and intentionally, their own version of homonationalism.

Sexuality in Paul's Political Eschatology: 1 Thessalonians 4:13–5:11

Given the not fully realized and fragmentary nature of Paul's homonationalism, it is possible that these tactics can even be embedded within a sociosexual-political ethics that simultaneously resists and seeks to overturn Rome's power. The eschatological explanations and exhortations in 4:13–5:11, which immediately follow Paul's politically sexual ethics, are more often seen as representative of a politically resistant Paul. If this section of the epistle offers a political vision that imagines Rome's overthrow in a triumphal procession led by Jesus and directed by God (see Koester 1997, Míguez 2012), then such politically resistant rhetoric could seemingly contradict the possibility of Pauline homonationalism. Though these verses may imagine a world over which God and Jesus (and therefore not Caesar) will rule, Paul continues to employ Romanormative and sexually exceptional ideas and tactics. His political vision ultimately replicates an ideology of an empire that is decidedly Roman—just without Rome. Given the continuation of these tactics, this vision is not incompatible with the homonationalism found in 4:1–12.

Unfortunately, readings of 4:13–5:11 usually ignore questions of gender and sexuality, segmenting 4:13–5:11 as the political and/or eschatological section of the letter in distinction to 4:1–12, which deals with gender, sexuality, and ethics (Johnson-DeBaufre 2010, 90–92). Just as the sexual ethics in 4:1–12, however, are also embedded in first-century Roman politics (as seen in the previous section), 4:13–5:11 also stresses sexual ethics that align with Romosexuality. For example, the language of Romosexuality is especially apparent in 5:4–8:

> You, siblings, are not in darkness, so that the day will not catch you as a thief. For you are all sons of light and sons of day. We do not belong to night or darkness. Therefore, let us not sleep away like the rest but let us stay awake and be sober. For those who sleep sleep at night, and those who get drunk get drunk at night. However, we, because we belong to the day, should be sober, wearing a cuirass of trust and love and a helmet, salvation's hope.

Paul emphasizes the contrast between day and night and declares that his audience (as well as himself) belong to the day, the time of sobriety. Night, as Paul notes explicitly, is the time when people get drunk, a vice, like that of sexual excess, that was indicative of a lack of self-control and discouraged in elite Roman morality. "Moderation, or self-mastery, was frequently discussed in terms of mastery of the passions, especially lust and anger, but also self-restraint in eating, drinking, and luxury in general," writes Conway (2008, 24). Furthermore, lack of moderation—notably including drunkenness—was considered to be non-Roman, the province of Greeks and other conquered *ethnē*. Knust (2006, 33) observes, "Some Roman authors claimed that wasting money on prostitutes and wild drinking parties was a Greek trait, a characteristic of 'Greek leisure' (*otium*), something that had unfortunately infected Rome." In remaining awake and sober, those of the day demonstrate their *virtuous* mastery over bodily needs.

This mastery does not merely qualify them to be rewarded or saved on the lord's day; it proves that they have achieved Romanormativity and are therefore most fit to rule over and dominate others, in particular those less sober and alert. Meanwhile, those who get drunk and sleep prove to be unfit to rule: their destruction is justified by their behavior, which befits those of subordinate status. Alongside their superior sexual mores, as Roman men touted their superior and virtuous self-control, they castigated the dangers and lack signaled by drunkenness and, more broadly, nighttime. Roman authors, most notably Tacitus, describe Rome's military prowess as being due to this self-control: because they remained properly sober, Romans remain prepared and vigilant at night, while their barbarian enemies (notably the Germans) lack preparation due to their nighttime revelries (*Ann.* 1.50; see Shumate 2006, 96–97; Hoke 2017, 292–305; Smith 2007, 315). This lack of self-control and vigilance proclaims the inevitableness of Roman victory alongside its right to rule.

Paul's night and day binary with respect to the behavior of Christ followers aligns with this Roman ideology of self-control as the purview of the day. The echoes of Roman sexual morality in these binaries connect Paul's sexual ethics to the project of empire and conquest. Additionally, the militaristic imagery of 5:8—the cuirass and the helmet—makes connections between self-control, preparation for battle/conquest, and rights to rule that are similar to those of Rome.[29] Not only does the armor convey military might, but the values this armor demonstrates—especially *pistis* ("trust," traditionally translated "faith") and *sōtēria* ("salvation")—were also Roman virtues that the emperor purported to bestow upon conquered *ethnē* incorporated into the empire (Koester 1997; Georgi 1997). This linking of imperialism and the right to rule with sexual control and morality draws the homonationalism of 4:1–12 into a Romanormative eschatology.

Throughout 1 Thess 4:13–5:11, Paul describes an eschatological vision of the *parousia* and *hēmera kyriou* ("the lord's/master's coming and day"). His description continues to employ the political, militaristic, and

---

29. The cuirass was an important part of Rome's visual propaganda that displayed its military dominance; statues, including that of Augustus, depicted Roman men donning a cuirass, which was in turn decorated to depict his and Rome's victories over various *ethnē*; see Lopez 2008, 38–42; Janssen 2014; Smith 2007, 316.

Romosexual rhetoric of the Roman Empire (Koester 1997; Smith 2007, 308).[30] In Paul's letters, *kyrios* is consistently applied to Jesus as an honorific title that conveys his sociopolitical power: Rome's elite rulers were its *kyrioi*, the lords and masters of their households and, by extension, society. As such a lord, Jesus, in 4:15–17, arrives triumphantly in what Paul proclaims will be a *parousia* announced with trumpets accompanying a battle cry. Such an arrival marks Jesus, who follows the familiar footsteps of Roman imperial conquerors and takes the form of a new divinely appointed ruler, who presumably will replace the human emperor and his regime.

Paul defines Jesus's return as *tēn parousian tou kyriou* (4:16). Continuing the language of Rome's *imperium* and its conquest of foreign nations, this recalls the arrivals of Roman imperial officials who visited Roman territories, which had been incorporated into the empire through conquest and/or the threat of military might (Harrison 2011, 56–59). For example, the term announced, with indications of their divine status, Germanicus's acclaimed arrival in Egypt (18–19 CE) and Hadrian's arrival in Greece, and its Latin equivalent appears on coins minted for Nero's visits to Corinth and Patras (Harrison 2011, 56–57). Since these visits were celebrated and commemorated publicly, they simultaneously reminded inhabitants of Rome's rule through its military prowess and victories. These arrivals celebrate the stability and peace brought (or imposed) upon these territories by Roman rule while emphasizing the original militaristic arrival of Rome's empire through its expansive conquest. Often, as Lopez (2008, 113–17) shows, these triumphal processions included the bodies of captive *ethnē*, dressed and portrayed according to Roman stereotypes, in ways that emphasized the empire's defeat and mastery over these ethnic others, now incorporated as Roman subjects. These triumphal imperial visits participated in the broader project of Roman propaganda that reinforced its ideologies and secure Rome's rule, ensuring that all subjects knew and performed their place vis-à-vis Rome.[31]

---

30. This does not mean that it does not also draw from ideas found in the Hebrew Bible and other Jewish texts (which were also written in imperial contexts), as emphasized in Malherbe 2000, 290–91; Bruce 1982, 109–11.

31. These embodied processions complement the message conveyed in visual and written media from the first century. In these depictions, Roman rule is further conveyed through a gendered hierarchy in which men—in reality, only *Roman* men— were on top. Lopez (2008, 49–50) notes that most frequently the victorious Roman

Jesus's *parousia* in 1 Thess 4:15–17 conveys a similar ideology of conquest. The language of battle cries and trumpets in 4:16 emphasizes these aspects and implies that Jesus's arrival signals a military victory that was the imperial norm. The most frequent usages of both battle cry (*keleusma*) and trumpet (*salpinx*) can be found in descriptions of battles and territorial conquest—that is, the language of Roman expansion (LSJ, s.vv. "κέλευμα," "σαλπιγγωτός"). In these terms, Jesus's return replaces the emperor and his elite advisors with a new *kyrios*, one who is presumably loyal to a different divine power—namely, God. Such a replacement can be read to have anti-Roman implications, as it hopes to establish true peace and justice, most notably for loyal devotees of God and followers of Christ (Koester 1997; Míguez 2012, 133–55; Oakes 2005, 315–18). By replicating the language of imperial conquest, however, Paul retains Rome's imperial ideology, especially in terms of its establishment of peace through conquest and its gendered ideals of domination and control.[32]

Paul's use of imperial imagery continues in chapter 5: "Whenever they say, 'Peace and security,' then sudden destruction is set upon them, like labor pains upon a pregnant woman, and they certainly will not escape" (5:3). Following Helmut Koester's (1997, 162; see also Weima 2012) suggestion, many scholars acknowledge that this "peace and security" was likely a political slogan, equivalent to the Latin *pax et securitas*, that is "best ascribed to the realm of Roman political propaganda."[33] Thus the "they" who speak in 5:3 (and upon whom sudden destruction will later fall) refers to Rome's rulers, especially the elite *kyrioi* ("masters" or "lords") at the apex of imperial society. According to Paul's eschatology, this empire that proclaims peace and security is unaware of just how insecure its borders are; imperial conquest merely established a fragile peace through military

---

emperors and armies, always male, lord over the defeated nations, usually imagined as female. For an especially poignant visual example, see her discussion of Emperor Claudius subduing the nation of Britannia in a relief from the Sebasteion at Aphrodisias in Lopez 2008, 1–3.

32. Though Moss and Baden (2012) do not fully dispel these Roman connections, they emphasize the similarities of these verses to the rabbinic tradition and Jewish apocalypticism in the first centuries CE. Of course, these concepts were also grounded in experiences of empire for rabbis, Paul, *and* Thessalonian wo/men.

33. White (2013, 2014) is skeptical that "peace and security" was an actual Roman slogan, but he does admit that both terms have roots in Greco-Roman political traditions (however he attributes *eirēnē/pax* to Rome and *asphaleia* to the Hellenistic tradition).

might that placed many nations and peoples under its control. When read as foretelling the destruction of the *pax Romana* and the downfall of its rulers and their sociopolitical security, Paul's politicized eschatology in 1 Thess 4:13–5:11 is typically seen as containing a message of liberation that resists Rome and its imperial domination (Míguez 2012, 133–55; Smith 2007, 310–11; Koester 1997, 166).

In 5:3, Paul depicts as vulnerable the Roman peace and security that was portrayed and typically seen as inevitable and impenetrable. Paul's language of imperial conquest, however, replicates Rome's kyriarchal structure, just as his ethics, which do not stop at 4:12, repeat Romosexuality. Casting this fragile peace and security in feminized terms, Paul retains the hierarchal gendered ideology of Roman rule: to be feminine is to be more vulnerable and less powerful than the masculine ideal. The male *kyrioi* rule the household and the empire, and it is masculine virtue that permits a peaceful, secure, and invulnerable rule. In 5:3, however, when the peaceful and secure rulers are defeated, they are depicted as women, echoing Roman representations of male emperors standing over defeated women who represented the *ethnē* they conquered (see Lopez 2008, 42–45). According to Paul, Rome is about to become the conquered female, under the more masculine and self-controlled authority of God and Jesus, the true *kyrios*.

Still, the *parousia* of 1 Thess 4:13–5:11 is effectively and entirely Roman—just without Rome. In Paul's imagination, Jesus's coming may change who rules, but, since he replicates the moral language of Roman conquest, his vision does not shift the sexually exceptional status of those in power who rule over deviant others. Reading 4:13–5:11 in isolation, Paul's ideas can appear resistant—at least, discontent enough to hope for a power shift. When it is set alongside 4:1–12, more complex negotiations and alignments with Rome and its rule emerge. Politics and sexuality inseparably influence both of these passages, not to mention the entire epistle and beyond. Homonationalism, furthermore, develops and manifests in diverse, fragmentary, and sometimes contradictory ways. Its tactics can be sensed in isolated passages, but its complex assemblage of meanings, affects, and effects are best sensed when traditionally separate units are considered together. Indeed, while this essay limits itself to the span of 4:1–5:11, it is highly probable that even more complex dimensions of homonationalism could be developed with a reading of 1 Thessalonians from "Paul" (*Paulos*), at the start of 1:1, to "with y'all" (*meth' humōn*), the final words of 5:28.

Ultimately, the fact that 1 Thess 4:1–5:11 can simultaneously rehabilitate Christ followers as moral Roman subjects and imagine Rome's demise reveals more ways that homonationalism operates, in the first century as well as today. Some first-century Christ followers and some twenty-first-century gays may imagine themselves taking over and running the world, but, in their present, they employ tactics that align their sexual mores as participants in the political project of the prevailing nation/empire so as to become rehabilitatable subjects: homonationalism. These homonational strategies rehabilitate the systems they hope to replace, allowing kyriarchal power to perpetuate practices at the expense of persons whom these tactics exceptionalize and exclude.

Pauline Homonationalism and Queer Vessels in Thessalonica

We can never assume that any text or author plays easily into any binary of domination or resistance (sexual, imperial, social, etc.). As biblical scholars working with theories of intersectionality have already begun to point out, questions of sexuality, gender, race, class, and empire are always connected, and one must be especially aware and cautious when any one factor is either privileged or ignored (e.g., Johnson-DeBaufre 2010; Johnson-DeBaufre and Nasrallah 2011; Marchal 2008; Lopez 2008). Puar's work with the concept of assemblages conceives of identities in fluid terms and considers the ways different aspects of identity are shifting, moving, and melding as diverse bodies (human and nonhuman) interact (Puar 2007, 211).[34] These porous conglomerations—a term that could also describe first-century *ekklēsiai*—can impel those who engage biblical texts and contexts to consider how empire, ethnicity, gender, and sexuality interact together in spaces where some of these issues bubble up to the surface while others are less apparent (Hoke 2017; see also Marchal 2011, 393–94; 2014, 171–74).

Traditionally, the segmentation of 1 Thess 4:1–12 and 4:13–5:11 has allowed for the isolation of questions of empire and conquest from those of gender and sexuality. Such treatment prevents a more assemblaged, queer reading that can reveal how both sets of questions can and should be considered throughout 1 Thess 4–5 and, by extension, throughout the

---

34. Puar 2012 clarifies this distinction and elaborates on the relations between intersectionality and assemblage.

epistle. By treating these two passages together, my analysis demonstrates how considering the relationships between empire, ethnicity, gender, and sexuality reveals ways in which Paul's tactics aligned with and reinforced ideologies of the imperial elite, especially the ethnic and sexual hierarchies that perpetuated its kyriarchy. Similarly, Puar aptly demonstrates that, through homonationalism, certain brands of modern queer rhetoric, though attempting to resist certain norms, participates in an overarching nationalistic/imperial project that accepts certain persons within its group boundaries while violently dispelling others. Likewise, Paul's sexual morality and eschatology participate in their own homonationalism that weds most closely the values of the believing communities with those of the Roman imperial elite.

Ultimately, Puar's identification of homonationalism and her conceptualization of identity as assemblage is framed as a project within *queer* theory: her purpose is to think alongside other queer bodies struggling to unravel kyriarchy.[35] Though Christ followers who participated in Thessalonikē's *ekklēsia* (and Paul alongside) can be called nonnormative (as having come from the *ethnē*), does this necessarily make them into queer subjects susceptible to the allures of homonationalistic stratagems yet open to the possibility of shattering gendered/sexual/ethnic binaries? "Queerness," as Puar (2007, xv) asserts, "irreverently challenges a linear mode of conduction and transmission: there is no exact recipe for a queer endeavor, no a priori system that taxonomizes the linkages, disruptions, and contradictions into a tidy vessel." Perhaps just as the ambiguous *skeuos* ("vessel") of 1 Thess 4:4 is difficult to control, so also participants gathered in the Thessalonian *ekklēsia* cannot be contained within a tidy vessel of queer/nonqueer, *ethnē*/elite, or pro/anti-empire. Although Paul's ethical and eschatological ideas attempt, through an ancient form of homonationalism, to make Christ followers less queer vis-à-vis Romanormativity and sexual exceptionalism, these ideas were not the only ways that Christ followers thought, moved, acted, and reacted in their gatherings. Paul's letters, particularly those written to Corinth and Galatia, bear witness to the fact that some wo/men expressed other opinions, embodied diverse expressions of sexuality, claimed authority and leadership, and acted in ways that

---

35. Likewise, the Christ followers in Thessalonikē are clearly *struggling* against some form of oppression, i.e., *thlipsis* (1 Thess 1:6; 3:3, 7); see Johnson-DeBaufre 2011, 95–98.

deviated from Paul's ideals. Paul is just one voice and body among many in Thessalonikē's *ekklēsia* (Johnson-DeBaufre and Nasrallah 2011).

Although there is less direct evidence of the debates and contestations that moved through the *ekklēsia* in Thessalonikē, we know that these Christ followers gathered together and raised questions (such as the question of what will happen to those who have died prior to Jesus's *parousia*, which seems to have compelled Paul to write). Furthermore, based on material evidence, we know that wo/men were there, and we can assume that this *ekklēsia* held together a gathering of diverse bodies with different ideas and experiences that affected how and why they followed Christ (Johnson-DeBaufre 2010, 91–103). While these wo/men's reactions to Paul's words (whether voiced or gestured) have been lost to history, the fact of their presence serves as a reminder that, if *ekklēsia*-l bodies were queer vis-à-vis Rome, then this queerness could have allowed some Thessalonians to dissent and move away from Paul's homonationalism. It is possible, to differing and even miniscule degrees, that some experienced following Christ as a means of exceeding, breaking free of, or relinquishing control over the tiny, tidy vessels imposed by Rome and its sociosexual-political dominance.

Reading 1 Thess 4:1–5:11 through the lens of queerness opens space for understanding this community as one with layers of multiple identities that affect their (and our) experiences of the gendered, sexual, and imperial language of Paul's letter. This lens continues to emphasize the overlaps between biblical interpretation and queer theory in ways that spill issues of empire, ethnicity, race, gender, sexuality, ancient history, and the modern world out of their separate vessels. In so doing, this spilling and mixing has revealed strategies of homonationalism in Paul's letter to Thessalonikē in order to warn of the ways that even countercultural spaces and uncontainable identities can still (sometimes) easily become a space for empire.

Works Cited

Ahmed, Sara. 2004. *The Cultural Politics of Emotion*. New York: Routledge.

Bassler, Jouette M. 1995. "σκεῦος: A Modest Proposal for Illuminating Paul's Use of Metaphor in 1 Thessalonians 4:4." Pages 53–66 in *The Social World of the First Christians*. Edited by Wayne A. Meeks. Minneapolis: Fortress.

Brooten, Bernadette J. 1996. *Love between Women: Early Christian Responses to Female Homoeroticism.* CSSHS. Chicago: University of Chicago Press.

Bruce, F. F. 1982. *1 and 2 Thessalonians.* WBC 45. Waco, TX: Word.

Cary, Ernest. 1937. Introduction to Dionysius of Halicarnassus, *Roman Antiquities: Books 1–2.* Translated by Ernest Cary. LCL 319. Cambridge: Harvard University Press.

Conway, Colleen M. 2008. *Behold the Man: Jesus and Greco-Roman Masculinity.* Oxford: Oxford University Press.

D'Angelo, Mary Rose. 2007. "Gender and Geopolitics in the Work of Philo of Alexandria: Jewish Piety and Imperial Family Values." Pages 63–88 in *Mapping Gender in Ancient Religious Discourses.* Edited by Todd C. Penner and Caroline Vander Stichele. BibInt 84. Leiden: Brill.

Duggan, Lisa. 2000. *The Twilight of Equality: Neo-Liberalism, Cultural Politics and the Attack on Democracy.* Boston: Beacon.

Edwards, Catharine. 1993. *The Politics of Immorality in Ancient Rome.* Cambridge: Cambridge University Press.

Elgvin, Torleif. 1997. " 'To Master His Own Vessel': 1 Thess 4.4 in Light of New Qumran Evidence." *NTS* 43:604–19.

Foucault, Michel. 1988a. *The Care of the Self.* Vol. 3 of *The History of Sexuality.* Translated by Robert Hurley. Repr. ed. New York: Vintage.

———. 1988b. *The Use of Pleasure.* Vol. 2 of *The History of Sexuality.* Translated by Robert Hurley. Repr. ed. New York: Vintage.

Gaca, Kathy. 2004. *The Making of Fornication: Eros, Ethics, and Political Reform in Greek Philosophy and Early Christianity.* HCS. Berkeley: University of California Press.

Gaventa, Beverly Roberts. 1998. *First and Second Thessalonians.* IBC. Louisville: Westminster John Knox.

Georgi, Dieter. 1997. "God Turned Upside Down." Pages 148–57 in *Paul and Empire: Religion and Power in Roman Imperial Society.* Edited by Richard A. Horsley. Harrisburg, PA: Trinity.

Glancy, Jennifer A. 2002. *Slavery in Early Christianity.* Oxford: Oxford University Press.

Glancy, Jennifer A., and Stephen D. Moore. 2011. "How Typical a Roman Prostitute Is Revelation's 'Great Whore'?" *JBL* 130:551–69.

Gleason, Maud. 1995. *Making Men: Sophists and Self-Presentation in Ancient Rome.* Princeton: Princeton University Press.

Halperin, David M. 1990. *One Hundred Years of Homosexuality: And Other Essays on Greek Love.* NAW. New York: Routledge.

Harper, Kyle. 2011. "*Porneia*: The Making of a Christian Sexual Norm." *JBL* 131:363–83.

Harrison, James R. 2011. *Paul and the Imperial Authorities at Thessalonica and Rome.* WUNT 273. Tübingen: Mohr Siebeck.

Hoke, James N. 2017. "Under God? A Queer and Feminist Subversion of Submission in Romans." PhD diss., Drew University.

Ingleheart, Jennifer, ed. 2015. *Ancient Rome and the Construction of Modern Homosexual Identities.* Oxford: Oxford University Press.

Janssen, David. 2014. "The Roman Cuirass Breastplate Statue and Paul's Use of Armour Language in Romans 13:12 and 1 Thessalonians 5:8." *Colloq* 46:55–85.

Johnson-DeBaufre, Melanie. 2010. "Gazing upon the Invisible: Archaeology, Historiography, and the Elusive Women of 1 Thessalonians." Pages 73–108 in *From Roman to Early Christian Thessalonikē: Studies in Religion and Archaeology.* Edited by Laura Nasrallah, Charalambos Bakirtzis, and Steven J. Friesen. HTS 64. Cambridge: Harvard University Press.

———. 2011. "A Monument to Suffering: 1 Thessalonians 2:14–16, Dangerous Memory, and Christian Identity." *JECH* 1:91–118.

Johnson-DeBaufre, Melanie, and Laura S. Nasrallah. 2011. "Beyond the Heroic Paul: Toward a Feminist and Decolonizing Approach to the Letters of Paul." Pages 161–74 in *The Colonized Apostle: Paul through Postcolonial Eyes.* Edited by Christopher D. Stanley. PCC. Minneapolis: Fortress.

Kaplan, Amy. 2004. "Violent Belongings and the Question of Empire Today: Presidential Address to the American Studies Association, October 17, 2003." *American Quarterly* 56:1–18.

Knust, Jennifer Wright. 2004. "Paul and the Politics of Virtue and Vice." Pages 155–74 in *Paul and the Roman Imperial Order.* Edited by Richard A. Horsley. Harrisburg, PA: Trinity.

———. 2006. *Abandoned to Lust: Sexual Slander and Ancient Christianity.* GTR. New York: Columbia University Press.

Koester, Helmut. 1997. "Imperial Ideology and Paul's Eschatology in 1 Thessalonians." Pages 158–66 in *Paul and Empire: Religion and Power in Roman Imperial Society.* Edited by Richard A. Horsley. Harrisburg, PA: Trinity.

Konradt, Matthias. 2001. "Εἰδέναι ἕκαστοω ὑμῶν τὸ ἑαυτοῦ σκεῦος κτᾶσθαι…: Zu Paulus' sexualethischer Weisung in 1 Thess 4,4f." *ZNW* 92:128–35.

Koosed, Jennifer L., and Stephen D. Moore. 2014. "Introduction: From Affect to Exegesis." *BibInt* 22:381–87.

Lavan, Myles. 2013. *Slaves to Rome: Paradigms of Empire in Roman Culture*. Cambridge: Cambridge University Press.

Lopez, Davina C. 2008. *Apostle to the Conquered: Reimagining Paul's Mission*. PCC. Minneapolis: Fortress.

Malherbe, Abraham J. 2000. *The Letters to the Thessalonians*. AB 32B. New York: Doubleday.

Marchal, Joseph A. 2011. " 'Making History' Queerly: Touches across Time through a Biblical Behind." *BibInt* 19:373–95.

———. 2014. "Bio-Necro-*Biblio*-Politics? Restaging Feminist Intersections and Queer Exceptions." *CultRel* 15:166–76.

———. 2015. "The Exceptional Proves Who Rules: Imperial Sexual Exceptionalism in and around Paul's Letters." *JECH* 5:87–115.

Martin, Dale B. 2006. *Sex and the Single Savior: Gender and Sexuality in Biblical Interpretation*. Louisville: Westminster John Knox.

Massumi, Brian. 2002. *Parables for the Virtual: Movement, Affect, Sensation*. PCI. Durham: Duke University Press.

McDonnell, Myles. 2006. *Roman Manliness: Virtus and the Roman Republic*. Cambridge: Cambridge University Press.

Míguez, Nestor O. 2012. *The Practice of Hope: Ideology and Intention in 1 Thessalonians*. Translated by Aquíles Martínez. PCC. Minneapolis: Fortress.

Moore, Stephen D. 2001. *God's Beauty Parlor: And Other Queer Spaces in and around the Bible*. Contraversions. Stanford: Stanford University Press.

Moss, Candida, and Joel S. Baden. 2012. "1 Thessalonians 4.13–18 in Rabbinic Perspective." *NTS* 58:199–212.

Niehoff, Maren. 2001. *Philo on Jewish Identity and Culture*. TSAJ 86. Tübingen: Mohr Siebeck.

Noy, David. 2000. *Foreigners at Rome: Citizens and Strangers*. London: Duckworth.

Oakes, Peter. 2005. "Remapping the Universe: Paul and the Emperor in 1 Thessalonians and Philippians." *JSNT* 27:301–22.

Oliver, James H. 1972. "Text of the Tabula Banasitana, A.D. 177." *AJP* 93:336–40.

Parker, Holt N. 1997. "The Teratogenic Grid." Pages 47–65 in *Roman Sexualities*. Edited by Judith P. Hallett and Marilyn B. Skinner. Princeton: Princeton University Press.

Puar, Jasbir K. 2007. *Terrorist Assemblages: Homonationalism in Queer Times*. NW. Durham: Duke University Press.

———. 2012. "'I Would Rather Be a Cyborg than a Goddess': Becoming-Intersectional in Assemblage Theory." *philoSOPHIA* 2:49–66.

———. 2017. *The Right to Maim: Debility, Capacity, Disability*. ANIMA. Durham: Duke University Press.

Richlin, Amy. 1993. "Not before Homosexuality: The Materiality of the Cinaedus and the Roman Law against Love between Men." *Journal of the History of Sexuality* 3:523–73.

Rousselle, Aline. 1988. *Porneia: On Desire and the Body in Antiquity*. Translated by Felicia Pheasant. Oxford: Blackwell.

Schüssler Fiorenza, Elisabeth. 1999. *Rhetoric and Ethic: The Politics of Biblical Studies*. Minneapolis: Fortress.

———. 2001. *Wisdom Ways: Introducing Feminist Biblical Interpretation*. Maryknoll, NY: Orbis.

———. 2011. *Transforming Vision: Explorations in Feminist The*logy*. Minneapolis: Fortress.

Seigworth, Gregory J., and Melissa Gregg. 2010. "An Inventory of Shimmers." Pages 1–25 in *The Affect Theory Reader*. Edited by Melissa Gregg and Gregory J. Seigworth. Durham: Duke University Press.

Shumate, Nancy. 2006. *Nation, Empire, Decline: Studies in Rhetorical Continuity from the Romans to the Modern Era*. London: Duckworth.

Smith, Abraham. 2007. "The First and Second Letters to the Thessalonians." Pages 304–22 in *A Postcolonial Commentary on the New Testament Writings*. Edited by Fernando F. Segovia and R. S. Sugirtharajah. BP 13. London: T&T Clark.

Thomas, Christine M. 2010. "Locating Purity: Temples, Sexual Prohibitions, and 'Making a Difference' in Thessalonikē." Pages 109–32 in *From Roman to Early Christian Thessalonikē: Studies in Religion and Archaeology*. Edited by Laura Nasrallah, Charalambos Bakirtzis, and Steven J. Friesen. HTS 64. Cambridge: Harvard University Press.

Treggiari, Susan. 1991. *Roman Marriage: Iusti Coniuges from the Time of Cicero to the Time of Ulpian*. Oxford: Clarendon.

Walters, Jonathan. 1997. "Invading the Roman Body: Manliness and Impenetrability in Roman Thought." Pages 29–43 in *Roman Sexualities*. Edited by Judith P. Hallett and Marilyn B. Skinner. Princeton: Princeton University Press.

Warner, Michael, ed. 1993. *Fear of a Queer Planet: Queer Politics and Social Theory*. Minneapolis: University of Minnesota Press.

Weaver, P. R. C. 1967. "Social Mobility in the Early Roman Empire: The Evidence of Imperial Freedmen and Slaves." *PP* 37:3–20.

Weima, Jeffrey A. D. 2012. "'Peace and Security' (1 Thess 5.3): Prophetic Warning or Political Propaganda?" *NTS* 58:331–59.

White, Joel R. 2013. "'Peace and Security' (1 Thessalonians 5.3): Is It Really a Roman Slogan?" *NTS* 59:382–95.

———. 2014. "'Peace' and 'Security' (1 Thess 5.3): Roman Ideology and Greek Aspiration." *NTS* 60:499–510.

Williams, Craig A. 2010. *Roman Homosexuality*. 2nd ed. Oxford: Oxford University Press.

Winkler, John J. 1990. *The Constraints of Desire: The Anthropology of Sex and Gender in Ancient Greece*. New York: Routledge.

Yarbrough, O. Larry. 1985. *Not Like the Gentiles: Marriage Rules in the Letters of Paul*. SBLDS 80. Atlanta: Scholars Press.

Zanker, Paul. 1990. *The Power of Images in the Age of Augustus*. Translated by Alan Shapiro. Detroit: University of Michigan Press.

Monstrous Bodies in Paul's Letter to the Galatians

Valérie Nicolet

Monsters in Our Closets

Various monsters populate the closets of our imagination. There are the monsters of literature and cinema, various vampires, freaks, and creatures that scare and scar us. These all reveal something about popular conceptions of monstrosity and beg the question: what is a monster? Various authors help delineate features and characteristics of the monstrous.

Often, monsters display some physical deformity. The classic example here might be Frankenstein's monster. In Mary Shelley's novel (*Frankenstein or the Modern Prometheus*, 1818), it is the monster's body that functions as the "locus of fear" (Halberstam 1995, 28). For Frankenstein's monster, life among human beings is rendered impossible because of his external aspect. The most powerful dimension of physical deformity lies in the presupposition that it reflects some inner flaw.[1] The monster's expres-

A heartfelt word of thanks is due especially to the editor of the volume, Joseph Marchal, as well as to the reviewers of Semeia Studies for their thorough comments on earlier versions of this article. They have helped me develop this into a much better piece. All shortcomings are due to my own limited means. I also gratefully recognize the key insights of Mikael Larsson at the University of Uppsala in discussing monsters and their potential. I dedicate this article to the queer students at my teaching institution. Their courage humbles and inspires me, and I am grateful for the community they embody.

1. This aspect is present in New Testament texts, where deformities and handicaps are often associated with sin. See, for example, how John 9:2 has Jesus's disciples ask after the origin of a man's blindness: "His disciples asked him, 'Rabbi, who sinned, this man or his parents, that he was born blind?'" This perspective is also reflected in miracle stories where Jesus's healing is presented as bringing salvation. See, for example, the dialogue between Jesus and the woman with a flow of blood as narrated

sion of its self-identity has no value, cannot be trusted, does not correctly reflect the interiority of the individual, because its outside appearance contradicts the monster's self-analysis. As Judith Halberstam highlights, even language that typically conveys humanity is rendered distrustful by the physical aspect of the monstrous creature (44; see also Sullivan 2006). The monster cannot be trusted, not even about what it might say about itself. Thus no matter what the monster might express or declare, the legitimacy of its discourse is discounted. Susan Stryker notes that, "through the filter of this official pathologization, the sounds that come out of my mouth can be summarily dismissed as the confused ranting of a diseased mind" (2006, 249). Yet it can also be reclaimed. Stryker, for instance, reacts to the ways she and other trans people have been cast as monstrous by taking up the term to perform a critique and an ambivalent identification, even reclamation, of the term and of trans identity.

In this essay I proceed in three steps to show how reflections on monsters can dialogue with a reading of Galatians. First, I develop elements that define monsters, their functions, and their queering potential. Second, I identify the traces of monstrous bodies in Galatians, focusing on four types: uncircumcised bodies, female and maternal bodies, Paul's stigmatized and pregnant body, and finally the new body of the Christ believers. The essay concludes with a reflection on the queer possibilities of critique and reclamation of monsters. Through my analysis of Galatians, I show not only how monsters highlight the fragility of constructions of normalcy but also how they make us think about the possibilities of communities made up of different types of bodies stitched together, challenging the notion of ideal bodies and perfect communities.

Halberstam shows that physical deformity alone does not a monster make. Her analysis of Shelley's *Frankenstein*, which inaugurates her history of the Gothic, identifies several features of monstrosity, which I briefly present here. Halberstam (1995, 36) insists that the monster "can never be one thing, never represent only a singular anxiety." On the contrary, the monster is formed out of a great many things, "bits and pieces of life and death, of criminals and animals, animate and inanimate objects," and the danger is for it to break down "into his constitutive parts" (36–37). In this potential for breaking down, for decomposition,

---

in Matt 9:21–22: "Indeed she said to herself: 'If I only touch his cloak, I will be saved.' And Jesus turned around and seeing her he said: 'take heart, daughter! Your faith has saved you. And from that hour, the woman was saved.'"

Halberstam sees the monster as escaping identity and as the motor that makes modern readers want to fix the monstrosity down to one dimension. When readers can pinpoint the monstrosity to some features, or even to a single aspect, of the monster, they are also in the position to construct what is truly human in contrast. But, as Halberstam says, in its refusal to be pinned down to one dimension only, "the monster, in fact, is where we come to know ourselves as never-human, as always between humanness and monstrosity" (37). The monster exemplifies how all identities are constructed (38).

This constructed aspect of both monsters and humans highlights another dimension of how monsters function (as in Gothic novels such as *Frankenstein*). The monster in *Frankenstein* lives on the margins and breaks boundaries. His dwellings stress how he can only survive on the edge of humanity. When the monster and his creator encounter one another for the first time again after the creation of the monster, it is in the Alps, a wilderness that seems outside of time and space. Similarly, when the creator pursues his creature to the bitter end, he finally glimpses the monster at what seems like the end of the world, the southern pole. Yet monsters not only roam at the boundaries, in the wilderness; they also challenge the limits drawn by human beings. Halberstam (1995, 44) writes: "In *Frankenstein* the complexity of the monster—it walks, it talks, it demands, it pursues, it rationalizes and shows emotions—confuses the politics of purity in which every dirty thing is marked and will pollute if not eliminated." Boundaries concerned with what it means to be physically human, to live with others, to show appropriate emotions for each gender collapse in Frankenstein's creation (44).

This crossing of boundaries is perhaps made even clearer in another Gothic novel, Robert Louis Stevenson's *Strange Case of Dr. Jekyll and Mr. Hyde* (1886). Here identity is double and unstable: "Each one depends upon the hidden presence of the other and each must perform and inscribe the doubleness and instability of the identity they share" (Halberstam 1995, 60). Monster and human are no longer separated; they belong to the same person. Thus Halberstam indicates how these works are "narratives that produce ideological and interpretive strategies for readers to recognize the human and distinguish between human and monster" (56). Monsters, by breaking boundaries, highlight the same boundaries and discipline readers in seeing what are the appropriate racial, social, familial, sexual and gender norms. Beyond the differences between various incarnations of the monstrous, "the monster, therefore, by embodying what is not human, produces the human as a discursive effect" (45). The monstrous contributes to normalization.

With the notions of normalization and disciplining, classic concepts and targets for queer critique, we have already moved from the features of monsters toward their functions. What do monsters do? Of course, each monster works differently depending on its story and its setting. When Stryker (2006, 247) writes her own letter to Frankenstein, reflecting on her transsexuality and the response in gay and lesbian communities, she presents herself as a monster and insists that "monster" came "to refer to living things of anomalous shape or structure, or to fabulous creatures like the sphinx who were composed of strikingly incongruous parts, because the ancients considered the appearance of such beings to be a sign of some impending supernatural events."[2] Monsters, then, could, serve a warning function. They alert "fellow creatures" that the "seams and sutures" found in Frankenstein's monster and in the transsexual body might well be discovered in every creature (247). In this way, they warn and scare, but they do much more. Indeed, Stryker here connects monsters to creatures more familiar to readers of Paul's letters: "Monsters, like angels, functioned as messengers and heralds of the extraordinary. They served to announce impending revelation, saying, in effect, 'Pay attention; something of profound importance is happening'" (247). Monsters are angelic—perhaps prophetic—figures requiring, even demanding, greater attention.

In Shelley's *Frankenstein*, these functions are intensified because the monster escapes the control of his master. Independently of his master, he constructs an identity and a purpose for himself, which "exceeds and refutes the purpose of the master" (Stryker 2006, 248). As Stryker notes, Frankenstein's success in creating a live creature also precisely marks his failure; he is unable to control it. Halberstam insists that monsters contribute to normalization, yet, as she also suggests, this process of normalization and disciplining can never be total. This approach resonates with Judith

---

2. Her article appeared first in 1994, in *GLQ*. She documents the violence experienced by transsexuals in the gay community at the time. See, for example, Stryker 2006, 245 and 246. One would hope that in twenty or so years, the situation for transgender and transsexual people inside the gay community has improved (the inclusion of the T, in the LGBTQ acronym might be a small indication of this evolution). In the 2016 "marche des fiertés" in Paris, the rights of trans people were the main theme. See the poster for the 2016 pride at https://tinyurl.com/SBL0699j. In any case, Stryker's point about the function of monsters remains valid.

Butler's analysis of the creative and subversive potential of abjection and particularly repetition. If the repetition of norms creates spaces where subjects are formed, where we find "bodies that matter," the repetitions "are never simply replicas of the same" (1993, 172). Rather, they create spaces where other bodies, abject beings, can be produced, "those who are not yet 'subjects,' but who form the constitutive outside to the domain of the subject" (xiii). Monsters have the capacity to escape and break the limits created by their own masters.[3] Frankenstein experiences it painfully.

Butler insists that this process of reiteration and repetition calls into question the existence of norms, of the law itself. Law does not exist outside or before its repetition. Law is only the reiteration of principles of laws, of norms of conduct, that then creates the law and gives it its authority (Butler 1993, xxii–xxiii; see also Marchal 2012, 209–27). Butler, of course, is building upon Michel Foucault's (1980, 1982, 1990, 1995) conceptualization of power, through his analysis of discourse in particular. Discourse can have a repressive dimension; it limits what can be said and who can speak, and yet it also produces spaces where one can resist. As "a multiplicity of force relations" (1990, 93), power is dynamic, circulates between people, and can be used to resist power itself.

Queerness exposes this disciplinary process of repetition, the artificiality of the law, and creates spaces to repeat the norms differently. As Joseph Marchal (2012, 210) notes, queer is not only an identity (and perhaps it should never be an identity [see for a discussion Brintnall 2013]), but it can be "more of a disposition, a mode of examining the processes that cast certain people and practices into categories of normal and abnormal and then of interrogating the various effects of such processes." In their ability to exceed and refute the purpose of the master, monsters provide a critique of normalization and create spaces of resistance and improvised repetition. As Halberstam (1995, 27) argues, "the monster always represents the disruption of categories, the destruction of boundaries, and the presence of impurities and so we need monsters." This need for monsters also questions the way we relate to our embodied being. Critique or disgust toward the monstrous implies that we construct a proper way to relate to our body, our embodied self. There is an ideal form to which we aspire

---

3. For Butler (1993, 169–85), this is what takes place with the term *queer*, which has been reclaimed with a positive signification. This also comes close to Homi Bhabha's (1994) understanding of mimicry.

that the monster challenges. Monsters have the potential to question the desire for an ideal body.

Tracing Monstrous Bodies in Galatians

While I am not saying that Paul employs characters as obviously and immediately monstrous as Frankenstein's creature or Mr. Hyde, I am reading Galatians with an attention to finding who the monsters are, as Halberstam, Stryker, and Butler help us to think about them. I also want to see how these identified monsters in Galatians function and for whom they are monsters. I suggest one can identify (at least) four types of monstrous bodies in Galatians, deployed differently according to Paul's rhetorical purpose. Indeed, as monsters do, these types burst out of neat category boundaries, since circumcised bodies are often imagined as or alongside female bodies, Paul's body is described like a feminized body (though he was among the male circumcised), and each of these kinds of bodies were among the baptized bodies in Christ.

First, we encounter, throughout the letter, the bodies of those circumcised and those who are uncircumcised. Toward the end of the letter, Paul even alludes to the castrated body (Gal 5:12). In his discussion of circumcision and foreskin, Paul eventually reverses the traditional Jewish distinction, which he seems to uphold at the beginning of the letter (2:15) and which sees the nations, those with a foreskin, as outside the bounds of the covenant. At the end of Gal 4, those who make it inside the covenant are the Christ believers with a foreskin; those who are perceived as monstrous and need to be thrown out in the wilderness are the non-Jewish Christ believers who are thinking about circumcision. Here those traditionally outside of the normative boundaries of God's people (uncircumcised polytheists) gain access to the God of Israel. Those uncircumcised bodies who are now part of the people of God threaten the boundaries of Israel, its purity. Traditionally perceived as occupying the peripheries of the people of God, roaming with the monsters that are kept there, they now move to the center of the people of God.[4] Paul, and those with whom he is in conflict in Galatians, must negotiate this move from periphery to center. Paul, in insisting that the non-Jews remain uncircumcised, emphasizes the

---

4. For an analysis of monsters as threatening God and the order that God establishes at creation, see Angelini 2013.

non-Jews' abnormality, their deviance from the norms. Thus he has some work to do in the letter in order to make this monstrous insertion of uncircumcised non-Jews into the people of God acceptable and even desirable. One of the ways in which he attempts to normalize the monstrous characteristic of his uncircumcised polytheists is through his use of the female enslaved body, our second type of monstrous body.

Second, inside this broader frame of subject and abject, female, and specifically maternal, bodies function in a powerful way to define monstrosity. In Gal 4:22–31, Paul constructs the body of the slave woman as a repellent for those of the nations who would consider becoming circumcised. Here Paul finds support in the traditional hierarchical organization of the Roman Empire, which would have placed the body of a slave woman and her illegitimate offspring on the lowest rung of the social structure. Yet in two other places, Paul seems instead to upset this traditional hierarchy: when he presents the barren woman as invited to rejoice (4:27) and when he refers to himself as a birthing mother (4:19). Who is the monster now?

Third, in an apparent destabilization of patriarchal structures, Paul presents himself as both a maternal and an otherwise stigmatized body. Two chapters after depicting himself as a mother in labor, he points to his own branded, stigmatized body (6:17). This can be further associated with Paul's reference to his weakness in Gal 4:13, which had the potential to elicit disgust in those who saw him (4:14). Here we come closest to an explicit description of Paul's physical aspect as monstrous: his outside appearance has the potential to provoke scorn and contempt, and it puts the Galatians to the test. I reflect on the way these apparently belittling self-references might function for our understanding of Paul in this epistle, especially when these self-references are put in dialogue with passages that violently attack those who are perceived by Paul as opposing his gospel (1:7–10; 2:4, 11–13; 5:12; 6:12–13).

Fourth, and finally, in Gal 3:27 Paul talks of those who have been baptized as having clothed themselves in Christ. They are one in Christ (3:28). This language is developed more explicitly around the notion of the body in 1 Cor 12:12–13: "For just as the body is one and has many members, and all the members of the body, though many, are one body, so it is with Christ. For in the one spirit, we were all baptized into one body—Jews or Greeks, slaves or free—and we were all made to drink of one spirit."[5]

---

5. I use the NRSV for biblical quotations, sometimes with my own modifications.

One can wonder what this new hybrid and recreated body is and how this body would have functioned for those usually experiencing exclusion from a society privileging free, adult males. In terms of the monstrous, when unprivileged members of the ancient Mediterranean world (slaves, females, but also—for Jews—Greeks, if one listens to Gal 3:28) don Christ, they acquire characteristics normally reserved for a specific elite, like freedom and masculinity. In this crossdressing, those usually constrained to the abject cross the line and enter subject space, where their bodies matter. Their integration has the potential of queering the composition of the community itself, bringing in "bits and pieces of life and death" (Halberstam 1995, 36) and challenging the normativity of the group.

Reading for monsters in Galatians challenges traditional understandings of Paul as the champion of universalism and identifies this universalism as geared first and foremost toward free adult males in the ancient world. Tracing monsters exposes this apparent universalism and uses queer interpretations to challenge the normalizing effect of presenting some people as monstrous and to reflect on what it would be like to occupy the place of the monster in Paul's letter.

Circumcising Bodies

As Paul reflects in Gal 2:15 ("we are Jews by nature, and not sinners from among the nations"), Jews often cast the nations as unclean and impure because of their moral status (see Fredriksen 2002, 237). Their position outside the people of God highlights more clearly the privileges of those within the boundaries of the people: the adoption, the glory, the covenants, the giving of the law, the worship, the promises, the patriarchs, and the Messiah (see Rom 9:4–5). Nations remain "inherently profane" (Klawans 1995, 292) because they worship idols (Fredriksen 2002, 237). In terms of boundaries, their race keeps nations outside of the people of God and makes them at best guests in the temple.[6]

Part of what is at stake with the non-Jews, to whom Paul specifically addresses himself (he presents his mission as "bringing the good news of the son to the nations"; 1:16), is thus a redrawing of the boundaries of the people of God to include the nations. This inclusion signifies a change of

---

6. For a discussion of Jewish-polytheist relationships, see Fredriksen 2002; Cohen 1989; Rajak 1992.

identity for the nations, which means they will no longer so clearly violate the limits of the people of God. Before the advent of Christ, the nations were perceived as marginal entities outside the boundaries of the people of God, abject entities from which Jews had to be separated in order to preserve their status as God's chosen people. Through Christ's faith and obedience, the nations are rendered holy and separate and identified as God's elect. Their previous monstrous essence, which kept them outside of the people of God, is erased because Christ shows perfect obedience to God on the cross and inaugurates the eschatological age by reconciling polytheists to God (Gal 2:16). All that is asked of them is that they put their trust in the figure of Christ (Gal 2:16), as they know that for them the path to the God of Israel is through the eschatological impact of the faith of Christ.

Still, the nations are not freed from their ethnic belonging and thus are not freed from their ethnic monstrosity. On the contrary, it might be reinforced by what Paul demands. Paul asks that they turn away from polytheistic worship but not abandon their ethnic identity: they remain nations, now associated with the promises made to Israel, but as nations. As Paula Fredriksen (2010, 244) puts it, they are indeed part of the people of God, but not of the people of Israel. In his inclusion of the non-Jews, Paul remains particularistic and maintains ethnic differences within the people of God (Johnson Hodge 2005, 2007; Fredriksen 2002, 2010). In terms of race, the non-Jewish Christ believers in Galatia are abnormal. They bring something of their previous monstrosity, lived on the periphery of the people of God, directly within the chosen people, thus threatening the purity of the people. At the same time, they could potentially also appear monstrous to Roman authorities in the province. Indeed, if the Jews had their own way of participating in the emperor cult (Rajak 1984), those uncircumcised polytheists who abandoned their ethnic gods would also cross religious and cultural boundaries for the Romans. If they underwent circumcision, they would join a recognizable, and recognized, group "that participated (via the Jewish community) in the public veneration of the emperor" (Hardin 2008, 112) and would thus abate the threat of persecution from Roman authorities, normalizing their status and identity. In addition, they would no longer bring their abject nature into the midst of the people of God. Through circumcision and thus through ethnic assimilation within the people of God, their status would be normalized. It would no longer be a case of monstrous periphery suddenly invading the center, but it would simply be marginal individuals being assimilated, ritually enculturated, within God's people, occupying a normal place inside the divine economy. This is precisely what Paul rejects (Kahl 2010; Hardin 2008), to the point that in Gal 2:7, Paul even presents himself as entrusted with the gospel of the foreskin.[7] In terms of the categories of monstrosity we have evoked before, Paul's eschatological polytheists do not fit the traditional ethnic demands of the people of God. Their ethnicity should keep them on the margins of the people of God, but they have now penetrated the boundary and are fitted within the people of God without being assimilated to the Jews. What lay outside the boundaries, the abject, is now part of the subject space and has access to its privileges. Inside the subject space, the polytheists can embody the new identity given to them, can repeat the norms of being in Christ, but in their repetition, if we follow Butler and Halberstam, they will modify and change the subject space; they might exceed the master's purpose.[8] When the peripheral monsters move into the center, they might have the potential to queer the space traditionally defined as God's people. In antiquity—and we see examples of this being discussed in other letters in the Pauline corpus—they might modify not only the group's eating habits (1 Cor 8), but perhaps also the shape of marriage in the community (1 Cor 7), the right to speak and prophesy (1 Cor 11:2–16), and even the relationship between slaves and master (Philemon).

The presence of these marginalized expolytheists has an impact on the circumcised; in addition, or to be more precise, it has an impact on those who would advocate circumcision for the polytheists. The distinction is important for Pauline scholarship: Galatians does not have much to say about the role and destiny of Israel (the word *Israel* is used once in 6:16) or of the Jews as a community (in contrast to Rom 9–11).[9] The letter

---

7. The NRSV translates "gospel for the uncircumcised"; *akrobustia* literally designates the foreskin, the prepuce. By extension, those who have a foreskin are the uncircumcised. In this expression, though, it seems that Paul plays with the bodily dimension associated with circumcision and uncircumcision.

8. One can see that concern in the way in which Paul attends to the sexual immorality he attributes to the polytheists. For Paul, polytheist sexuality, which he constructs (accurately or not) in terms of immorality, impurity, prostitution, homosexuality, needs to be erased and replaced with virtues previously inaccessible to polytheists (Rom 13:12–13; 2 Cor 6:6–7; Gal 5:22–23; Phil 4:8–9).

9. *Ioudaios* is used only four times in Galatians, in the context of the discussion with Cephas (Gal 2:13, 14, 15) and in 3:28 to affirm the uselessness of the distinction Jew-Greek to enter in the people of God.

is concerned primarily with those who propose that polytheists should be circumcised in order to belong to the people of God, thus eliminating (or at least removing) the physical mark of the non-Jews's monstrosity, making them more normal. This group, which is not easily identifiable, is strongly criticized by Paul, but it is not Israel or the Jews.[10] If they are first introduced, it seems, as pseudobrothers in Gal 2:4 (where they are distinguished from the leaders of the community in Jerusalem), they are further discussed and criticized in the allegory presented in Gal 4:21–31 and at the end of the letter, in chapters 5 and 6. The bodies seeking to circumcise (themselves or others) are imagined as a specific kind of monstrous female body, one that Paul will use to make the monstrosity of the uncircumcised Christ believers less repelling. Interestingly, Paul can thus embrace a certain kind of marginality—symbolized by the uncircumcised, formerly polytheist Christ believers—while also constructing his own monsters in order to convince his audience of his own position.

Maternal Bodies

In the allegory found in Gal 4:21–31, one woman is portrayed as frightening by Paul. This woman is Hagar (4:24). She is introduced as the *paidiskē* (4:22), the young female slave with whom Abraham had a child according to the flesh (4:23). Both indications, slavery and flesh, associate this mother of one of Abraham's sons with realities that Paul criticizes in Galatians and place Hagar firmly on the margins of what is deemed acceptable and desirable by Paul. In the previous section (4:1–7), Paul emphasizes the contrast between being a slave and being a son (4:7) and affirms the identity of free sons of God for his addressees. Flesh is also often criticized by Paul. For example, at the beginning of the section where Paul directly turns to the Galatians (3:1), he reminds them that ending with the flesh now would be denying the work of the spirit (3:3). Later, in Gal 5 and 6, he associates flesh with negative desires and behaviors, paralleling what one also finds in Rom 8. Thus there would be no positive association with the first two attributes—slavery and flesh—describing Hagar in Gal 4.

The slave girl is then presented as one of the two covenants, the one bearing children for slavery (Gal 4:24). She is named for the first time. She

---

10. J. Louis Martyn (1997, 118–20), for instance, calls this group "Teachers." Fredriksen (2002, 256–57) reconstructs their position as "a Jewish *mission* to the Gentiles."

is Hagar, the present Jerusalem, in slavery with her children (4:25). At the
end of the allegory she is presented as the one thrown out, with her son,
the one whose son will not inherit with the son of the free woman (4:30).
This expulsion of Hagar is enacted through a quote of Gen 21:10 (LXX),
which gives it added significance and impact. The destiny of Hagar, as the
slave mother, excluded from the covenant with her slave children, makes
it clear that those who feel a solidarity with her will not participate in the
inheritance promised to the sons of God (Gal 4:7). In addition, they will
be returned to the wilderness, the space where monsters are kept, and to
the margins from where they have just escaped. Here too, categories of
center and periphery play an important role in defining what should be
considered acceptable or not by Paul's addressees. One can read the alternative created by Paul in the following manner: the non-Jews can remain
uncircumcised and be nontraditional participants in the people of God,
potentially perceived as profane by circumcised Jews, or circumcise and
join the marginal Hagar in the wilderness. I imagine that Paul hoped that
the monstrous aspects of Hagar would be sufficient to discourage those
who might think of getting circumcised. Who are those whom Paul associates with Hagar? They are those, as Paul indicates at the beginning of the
analogy (4:21), who want to be under the law, those who want to pursue
circumcision as a way of being further integrated into the people of God.
They are, then, those who would compromise their non-Jewish ethnicity
by becoming Jews. These, Paul insists, far from taking part in the promises
reserved for the son of the free woman, will share in the destiny of the
slave girl, Hagar, thrown into the desert and excluded from participating
in the inheritance.

Set up by Paul as the monster, Hagar is supposed to discourage those
who might be tempted to regularize their abnormal ethnic status through
circumcision. As Stryker indicates, as a monster, one of her functions is
to warn and discourage the would-be circumcised. She is the scare figure
that should dampen the resolution of those who want to avoid persecution by becoming Jewish. Ironically, she is now associated with Jewishness,
symbolized in the ritual of circumcision, even though she is precisely
understood as representing the alien, the non-Jew. In Paul's allegory, it is
the free woman, the one whose son is born according to the promise, that
is associated with those who will inherit. This categorization is in keeping with biblical tradition. Sarah is the mother of Isaac, through whom
the people of Israel will be formed. But she is now also the ancestor of the
non-Jews, who are taking part in the promises reserved for Israel. Faced

with this allegory, the Galatians can either associate—in a counterintuitive move—with Sarah and Isaac but without practicing circumcision, or they can be thrown in the desert with Hagar and miss the promises and the inheritance. In the allegory set up by Paul, circumcision has the reverse effect that it should normally have. Far from associating the circumcised with Sarah, it connects them with Hagar, the alien slave woman thrown in the wilderness.

For the Galatians, it is better to remain uncircumcised within the people of God than follow the monster Hagar into the wilderness! Those who advocate circumcision are presented as inviting the Galatians down the path of Hagar. Hagar—and the path of circumcision—is presented as a monster created to discourage non-Jewish Christ believers to circumcise. This monster is intended to make the abnormal case of the uncircumcised male participant in the people of God more acceptable by associating him with the traditional path to membership in the people of God—namely, inheritance and genetics. We do not know if this strategy of the scare figure was successful for Paul. But we do know that the monster expelled in the wilderness by Paul has unleashed a terrible history of reception, detrimental to the relationships both between Judaism and Christianity and between Christianity and Islam (Trible and Russell 2006).

In addition to being associated with Hagar and her descendants, those advocating circumcision and those considering circumcision are further criticized. Immediately following the allegory (and thus confirming the identification of Hagar with those advocating circumcision [and not with Israel]), Paul warns those who would let themselves be circumcised that they render Christ useless (Gal 5:2). In exasperation and, it seems, out of reasonably argued explanations, Paul exclaims ten verses later: "I wish those who unsettle you would castrate themselves!" (5:12). Having connected those advocating circumcision with slavery and flesh, he further challenges the masculinity of the pseudobrothers by voicing his desire for their castration. The status of those advocating circumcision is moved even further from the pole of maleness and thus rendered even less desirable for Paul's male audience.[11] This association with lesser males contributes to marginalizing the advocates of circumcision, pushing them toward periphery and abjection. Finally, in 6:12 and 6:13, Paul accuses those who try to compel circumcision of hypocrisy and boasting. They do not

---

11. For gender construction in antiquity, see Burrus 2007.

advocate circumcision out of respect for the law but because they fear persecution.[12] Furthermore, they themselves do not obey the law (suggesting in fact that these pseudobrothers might not even be Jewish); they merely want to boast in the flesh of those who would have let themselves be circumcised. Paul's construction of his opponents has succeeded in making them hypocritical, boastful, and effeminate, and thus less desirable. In this construction, the female body, particularly the penetrated slave body of Hagar, is used to insure the success of Paul's argumentation.

Hagar proves useful in constructing the advocates of circumcision in Galatians as undesirable, effeminate bodies, rendering them in fact monstrous for antiquity. Hagar's body, in antiquity, as the body of a slave, subjected to rape by her masters, is characterized by a lack of control and passivity. There would be no benefit in associating oneself with this body.[13] In his use, Paul agrees with the ideology surrounding the body of slave women in antiquity (see Marchal 2012, 221). If one identifies Hagar as a monster, then one of the effects of Paul's use of her body is to delineate what kind of body is acceptable and recognized in the community: the free, male, unpenetrated, and uncircumcised body of those in Christ. Bodies that do not correspond to these characteristics are relegated to the margins of the community, or even to the wilderness. As Marchal writes, any other way of thinking about the bodies of those in Christ is "akin to slavery" (222). These bodies, however, particularly the female and enslaved bodies, as we will see below, might have a way of coming back into the community when they are offered a new identity in putting on Christ (Gal 3:27).

Paul also presents two other mothers, seemingly in a more positive manner. In Gal 4:27, through a quote from Isa 54:1 (LXX), Paul introduces the figure of the childless woman, the desolate woman, who will rejoice because her children will be numerous.[14] As is already clear from the story of Sarah and Abraham, the Hebrew Bible evaluates sterility negatively, a

---

12. This fear of persecution accords well with Hardin's 2008 and Kahl's 2001 hypothesis that a fear of Roman reprisals lies behind the will to circumcise in Galatians.

13. Elizabeth Castelli (1991, 32) quotes Philo, QE 1.8 as an example of the female gender's undesirability: "For progress is indeed nothing else than the giving up of the female gender by changing into the male, since the female gender is material, passive, corporeal, and sense-perceptible, while the male is active, rational incorporeal, and more akin to mind and thought."

14. Gal 4:27 reads: "For it is written: 'Rejoice, you childless one, you who bear no children, burst into song and shout, you who endure no birth pangs; for the children of the

view one also finds in later Second Temple Jewish literature.[15] Here Paul, following Isaiah, reverses the curse experienced by the barren woman, and he makes her the better of the two women. Marchal (2012, 221) rightly notes that this use of the two women reduces them to the maternal and to their function as "receptacles for male seed." In addition, as it opposes two paths of access to the God of Israel (a covenant marked by the flesh and a covenant characterized by the promise), Paul's allegory also opposes the two women and renders any solidarity between them impossible. In theory, Hagar and Sarah have more in common with one another than with Abraham, and yet the story in both Genesis and Paul's retelling of it pits them against one another, to the advantage of the male figure (Reinhartz and Walfish 2006, 117–20). The retrieval of the desolate body of the barren woman is not sufficient to bring the female body back from the margins. Hagar, as the enslaved, alien woman, is rejected in the wilderness, a wilderness she can escape only (and at this only partially) in the history of reception.[16] In Gal 4, the treatment of Hagar reinforces the normativity of the free male as the correct embodiment of being in Christ, thus problematizing Paul's universalism often deduced from Gal 3:28.

Paul's Maternal and Stigmatized Body

Even Paul's application of maternal imagery to himself does not quite do the trick of making the female body acceptable. The third mother in Galatians is thus Paul himself: "My little children, whom I am birthing again until Christ is formed in you" (4:19). The image of Paul as a birthing mother is startling, at least for readers of the twenty-first century informed by gender-critical analyses of the ancient world, where a male

---

desolate woman are more numerous than the children of the one who is married." The quotation of Isa 54:1 (in italics) corresponds to the LXX text (at least to Rahlfs's edition).

15. For example, Protevangelium of James records Anna and Joachim's despair upon not having children (ch. 1 for Joachim's distress, and chs. 2 and 3 for Anna).

16. The history of reception of Hagar is a good example of how monstrous bodies can signify. She has been represented negatively in Christian usage, as well as by rabbis (where she is associated with the dangers of sex with a foreigner) but she has received a positive story in Muslim reception, and has been used powerfully in womanist interpretations as an ally for the cause of African-American women, showing how the monster in this case escapes its master (be it Paul or Sarah and Abraham). For more details, see Trible and Russell 2006 and, more recently, Kartzow 2013, Sherwood 2014, and England 2018.

embodying female characteristics would move down in the patriarchal hierarchy (see McNeel 2014, 169). Interpreters argue about whether it was indeed so. Margaret Aymer (2009, 187) sees Paul as embodying the Roman matron who "cries out against the impiety of her children—who owe her their very lives—because they are 'putting her through childbirth' all over again." As Jennifer Houston McNeel (2014, 166) summarizes, for Aymer and others (like McKinnish Bridges 2008) "Paul's maternal meta-phors" in the end serve to "reinforce the androcentrism of the letters and Paul's domination of his churches." McNeel also remarks, however, that when one views Paul instead as collaborative, "his maternal metaphors can be understood as highly relational, affectionate illustrations of Paul's countercultural views" (169).[17] McNeel highlights that this interpretive dilemma cannot be solved precisely because images of maternity in Paul occupy a middle ground between egalitarian and authoritarian (171). For her, they reflect the ambiguous power contained in the cross (171). From a perspective informed by Foucault's understanding of power, Paul's dis-course has a repressive dimension; it limits what can be said and what can be done, and yet it also produces spaces where one can resist pre-cisely some of the patriarchal implications of Paul's disciplining. Maternal metaphors and the power they carry reflect this understanding of power as dynamic, both disciplining and empowering. In this ambiguity, Paul's self-presentation as a pregnant mother, and thus as a transgendered body, holds monstrous potential.

For the first century, the maternal body of Paul may or may not have been perceived as countercultural. In the male maternal body, transgres-sion occurs because the male is associated with femininity, and yet the maternal body, especially in Roman imperial culture, marked the femi-nine power of upper-class Roman women who "became *matronae* and expressed their civil obedience through the act of childbirth" (Nelson 2016, 20). Today, as in antiquity, the monstrous maternal body of Paul might function in ways that go beyond its disciplining effect, beyond the warning it sends to the community whom Paul is controlling. The mater-nal body creates a potential space of identification for those who do not correspond to the normalized male body of antiquity and of the contem-porary world. One might desire to step into the feminized, pregnant body

---

17. She mentions as representatives of the collaborative interpretation of Paul: Schüz 2007; Hooker 1996; Ehrensperger 2007. Marchal (2012) notes a similar ambigu-ity in the way the maternal image is interpreted (and in the image itself).

of Paul and occupy the place of the monster. Its use will then go beyond Paul's rhetorical move in embodying motherhood. If one becomes the monster that Paul is for but a few moments in the letter, one must think of the power and influence afforded to bodies that mainstream occidental culture often finds difficult to classify and accept, including trans, drag, and intersex people. Marchal indicates that occupying the space of the monster might give an opportunity to create a new kind of community, precisely because of the solidarity experienced in sharing traumatic experiences. He even sees this community of solidarity embodied in the way the Galatians received Paul's stigmatized body when he first visited them (Gal 4:13–14) (Marchal 2010, 176). Embracing weakness and physical difference from the norms might be one of the powers afforded to those who occupy the space of the monstrous.

Paul indicates that he visited the Galatians because of a weakness in the flesh (Gal 4:13) and that this weakness represented a trial for those who welcomed him (4:14). In alluding, even fleetingly, to his own monstrosity in his self-presentation, Paul can positively remark on the welcome of the community. The members of the community could have despised him and even spit him out in disgust (*ekptuō*), but that is not what they did. In addition, Paul's flirting with monstrosity, when he uses terms that evoke physical deformity, allows Paul to reflect on his own self-worth, which might explain why the Galatians did not reject him. In 6:17, he notes that he himself carries the stigmata of Jesus in his body. Paul seems to be playing with practices that transform the body, whether it be religious tattoos that would identify him as belonging to Jesus, reference to the troubles caused by his missions, or slavery marks (Betz 1979, 323, 324). This marking of the body could call into question Paul's own explanation of it, making it a mere attempt to rationalize something that scripts him as vulnerable and irrational. Many insist that the monster cannot make sense of its own deformity. The ancient context might go against this explanation: stigmata here identify Paul as the one who physically embodies Christ and who can represent him in a Christophany, wherein weakness reveals the true nature of the person (Gal 4:13–14). In his "self-description as a representative of the crucified Christ," Paul is able to show his "worth, his manly pursuits, the scars from wounds received in battle" (Betz 1979, 323–24).[18] This is not so

---

18. Quoting Quintilian, *Inst.* 6.1.21.

much humiliation as it is showing off, and his addressees would have perceived it as such (323). In contrast to those he opposes, who are presented as pseudobrothers (Gal 2:4), hypocrites (2:11–13), potentially castrated (5:12), and ashamed of the cross (6:12), Paul is not afraid of wearing Christ on his own skin, thus demonstrating his valor and manhood. As a result, Paul reinforces the fact that his own way of embodying the gospel is the only one acceptable. He represents masculinity, while his adversaries are feminized.

As Marchal (2010, 177) points out, the Galatians might have "negotiat[ed] their communal embodiment differently (as likely indicated by their nonaggressive treatment of the strange visitor [Gal 4:13–14])." They welcomed Paul as a "messenger of God, like Christ Jesus" (Gal 4:14), despite his monstrous appearance. Thus they recognized in the deformed figure of Paul precisely what Paul says he represents: an incarnation of Christ Jesus. One might ask whether this was due, as Paul seems to suggest, to his own exceptional value as "apostle not by humans or through a human, but through Jesus Christ" (1:1) or due to the Galatians' own interpretation of the message that Paul presented to them—in particular, the baptismal formula found in 3:28 and the conviction that they are now clothed in Christ (3:27). I suggest that the polyvalence of monstrosity makes both explanations possible. The queer body of the person wearing Christ now allows for the welcoming of the monster. Yet a reflection in terms of monstrosity also opens up another interpretation: when Paul presents himself as the ideal messenger, the one who represents Christ, he can also attribute to himself the angelic qualities of some monsters, as Stryker has identified them. In that case, Paul would appear as a "herald of the extraordinary" (Stryker 2006, 247) and alert the Galatians to the potency of his message and his person. There was but one wise choice for this community when confronted with this powerful angelic being: to welcome him, despite his unorthodox, monstrous, appearance.

Bodies Clothed in Christ

Paul describes the newly baptized Christ believers as having put on Christ in Gal 3:27. A similar image is found in 4:19, a verse I already discussed in relation to birthing imagery. I highlight the purpose of Paul's birth pangs: to have Christ be morphed in the Galatians. Here it is as if the body of the Galatians is transformed in a new form, corresponding to the Christ ideal. In connection with Butler's reflection on repetitions and norms, one touches here on the creative potential of the monstrous body to resist norms and use the interstice of repetition to create ways of embodying Christ that diverge from the norm established by Paul. Indeed, for Paul, to get out of childhood (4:1), one must become a male heir (4:6–7). For Paul, the normative Christ believer is the free, adult male, described in 4:28–5:1 (see Punt 2012, 2013, 2014).

Yet putting on Christ opens the possibility to repeat queerly. In light of the clothing imagery and the categories in the baptismal formula quoted in 3:28, it is hard to resist thinking of the Christ believers as somehow embodying Christ in drag, sublimating their identity through the vestments of Christ, and thus revealing their true essence and identity as sons of God, an identity that might not have corresponded to what Paul wanted. Jeremy Punt warns against seeing too much space for resistance in this alternative embodiment of Christ. Because Paul's use of family language "[replicates] the reigning sociocultural values…, opportunities for serious counter-cultural and other deviations from socially acceptable practice were limited" (Punt 2013, 165). Nevertheless, even if the actualization of these deviations is historically unlikely, their possibility remains. The disciplining and reiteration of the norms with which Paul engages indicate that the materialization of the proper Christ body (to use Butler's [1993, xii] language) is never a given: "bodies never quite comply with the norms by which their materialization is impelled." Thus there is potential instability, which might turn the norms against themselves and produce "rearticulations that call into question the hegemonic forces of that very regulatory law" (xii). Even the community of baptized bodies might function as this new hybrid and recreated body, since it mattered to Paul to have a community composed of both Jews and non-Jews, slaves and free, males and females. Baptism produces a community of composite people stitched together. When females, slaves, and children put on Christ, the results might have looked different from what Paul expected. This cross-dressing of baptized bodies opens up the possibility—a possibility that Paul (and tradition after him) will want to shut down in privileging more traditional-looking communities—of a body of Christ in transition, with feminized bodies potentially accessing privileges usually reserved for males. There are traces of these transgender bodies, for example, in the story of Thecla, who dresses as a male to start her own mission, or in the passion of Perpetua, who becomes male when she has a vision of her combat in the arena on the eve of her martyrdom.[19] Such nonconforming bodies and "moments of slippage" (Castelli 1991, 49) recall that monsters might arise and question Paul's disciplining power. They warn us not to imagine that we know what Christ-like communities should look like.

To briefly go back to the monstrous categories identified previously, cross-dressing and cross-dressed Christ believers now have bodies made of different parts, parts that do not necessarily belong together. In terms of the ancient world, we find females dressed as male figures, slaves embodying free persons, and polytheists belonging to the people of the God of Israel. Halberstam noted that monsters threaten to decompose into their various parts (think of Frankenstein's monster in particular) and use the different components of their identities in ways that can challenge the norms. The cross-dressed Christ believers own that same possibility in their new identities, and, in embodying Christ in their own way, they destabilize the norms upheld by ancient societies. Paul's efforts in disciplining their embodiment of Christ aim at stabilizing the boundaries that the Galatian Christ believers question.

Queering Monsters: Possibilities for Critique and Reclamation?

Given the potential for a queer embodiment of Christ, this last section offers some reflections on what it would mean to occupy the place of the monster in Paul's letter, taking to heart Halberstam's (1995, 27) exhortation: "We need to recognize and celebrate our own monstrosities." Yet it also proceeds more ambivalently around the monster as a figure of reclaimed perversity, as Stryker (2006, 246) did when she explored "the dark power of [her] monstrous identity without using it as a weapon against others or being wounded by it [herself]." The four overlapping types of monsters I trace in Galatians could function in a variety of ways: they could celebrate, wound, resist, or reveal like other monsters do, like angelic "messengers and heralds of the extraordinary" (247).

In their warning function, they might be repulsive precisely because they indicate the fragility of constructions of normalcy. If not careful, any

---

19. In Acts Paul 4.15, Thecla arranges her tunic like a man's mantle to go find Paul. In Pass. Perp. 10.7, Perpetua sees herself becoming a man to fight an Egyptian. One could also mention the end of Gospel of Thomas (logion 114), where Jesus indicates that he will make Mary male, making her like male spirits. For Gos. Thom. 114, making women male guarantees access to the kingdom of heaven.

human body might well step over the line and find itself on the side of the monstrous. To make sure that this does not happen, Paul sets up a high price to pay: he threatens the ones who proclaim another good news with anathema (Gal 1:8–9) and separation from Christ (Gal 5:4), and he underlines their hypocrisy (Gal 6:13). Precisely this discourse designed to warn and scare might be used to underscore the porosity of the boundaries that Paul is trying to preserve. The letter to the Galatians reflects Paul's own anxieties about nature and flesh, as indicated by the monstrous figures he deploys but cannot quite shake. He tries to use monsters to create or maintain boundaries, but monsters can subsist on the margins, frequently threatening to cross or decompose these boundaries, particularly those around identity.

We do not have the evidence necessary to determine whether the Galatians might have recognized the artificiality of Paul's rhetoric to circumscribe monsters and humans. Today, though, a queered reading engaging Stryker's self-identification with the monstrous suggests a few possibilities. Where Paul tried to normalize and discipline his audience by using Hagar as a monstrous symbol for the circumcisers, one can recognize that these and other monstrous bodies in Galatians (including other maternal bodies, Paul's own stigmatized body, and the baptized body of the community) escape the control of their masters and refuse to be pinned down to any one dimension of these claims to a separate and pure identity. Indeed, when all of these bodies are stitched together in the letter, especially where they already overlap and assemble with each other, the community itself, baptized as different bodies into one collective body, begins to look monstrous, formed out of a great many things. These monsters could just reveal how constructed Pauline and other ancient arguments about bodies and communities were.

Critical readings of Paul's language of grace are thus necessary to avoid reproducing a language that ends up excluding Hagar, the enslaved, alien woman (and others monstrously aligned with her). The presence of monsters at the outskirts of biblical texts highlights the need for a critique of the Bible's participation in the creation of a patriarchal society and culture. Standing next to Hagar allows the interpreter to produce a story of God standing with the monsters against the dominant readings of the white middle and upper class.[20] Standing in the place of the monsters

---

20. See, for example, the use of Hagar in womanist readings, Williams 1993. For a critical reading of Williams, see Harrison 2004.

shows that the strict boundaries that Paul aims to produce are intended to protect the new communities from the monsters. Ironically, these strict boundaries are needed precisely because society, by trying to defend its values, produces the monsters against which one needs to defend oneself, thus upholding the boundaries that produced the monster in the first place.

The monster's potential lies in the fact that it can make disciplining strategies explode and threaten boundaries. As Stryker (2006, 253) indicates, "transgender rage furnishes a means for disidentification with compulsorily assigned subject positions.... Through the operation of rage, the stigma itself becomes the source of transformative power." Once the monster has done the hard work "of constituting [itself] on [its] own terms, against the natural order," the monster is no longer indebted to its master and is free to transform the world (254). Halberstam (1998, 59), however, underscores that occupying the space of the monster can be a dangerous and hurtful strategy, especially outside of theoretical and academic approaches. There is a risk—especially for white, heterosexual, cisgender, able persons—of idealizing and romanticizing the position of the monster and continuing to function with the assumption that monsters are the Other, that they can in some ways be fixed or saved through faith. Miracle stories in the New Testament exemplify this position. They present Jesus as fixing and healing sick and disabled bodies, setting up a strong preference for able and healthy bodies (for example, Mark 5:25–34 and 10:46–52, where faith leads to salvation after Jesus's healing act; Mark 2:17 // Matt 9:12 // Luke 5:31, the logion about Jesus as physician coming to call the sinners; and Mark 2:1–12 // Matt 9:1–8 // Luke 5:17–26, where healing and pardon of sins are closely connected). This preference is also found in the Levitical instructions preventing anyone with a defect from serving as a priest (Lev 21:17–23; see Solevåg 2016, 92). Perhaps one can question this desire for health and ideal forms of embodiment and use Paul's disabled and stigmatized body as an entry way to problematize our relationship to an ideal body.

To idealize the theological potential of monsters is treacherous. One cannot claim to speak for those experiencing otherness or marginalization. Perhaps all I can do is problematize the notion of the ideal body and reflect upon ways that allow me to see all forms of embodiment as "transmogrifications," within a "process of (un)becoming strange and/or grotesque, of (un)becoming other" (Sullivan 2006, 561). I can become the Other as well. The stigmatized body of Paul, as well as the body of the

Christ believer in drag, might invite us to step out of the binary process that associates the making of humans with the making of monsters. These bodies, as well as the broken body of Christ on the cross, question the notion of the ideal, able body. Who can tell what the body of the Christ believer clothed in Christ should look like? The body could be an androgynous, transgender, cross-dressed body, with practices that "cross over, cut across, move between, or otherwise queer socially constructed sex/gender boundaries" (Stryker 2006, 254, n. 2). Monsters question the belief in the possibility of inhabiting one's body without tensions and difficulties. Monsters underline the distance and foreignness one might experience toward one's body and render one particularly attentive to the "(im)possibility of such an ideal form of embodied being" (Sullivan 2006, 555). Monsters expose this desire for the utopian body, and they thus might reduce the distance between what is qualified as valid or invalid bodies, normal or abnormal bodies.

With Stryker and Halberstam, through the approaches of Butler and Foucault, we could come to see monsters not only as figures of reclaimed perversity but also as figures that critique normalizing arguments about nature and flesh, identity and community. Monsters remind us of the dangers associated with the creation of norms and of the need to acknowledge and critique the frailty of the boundaries that we keep building and erasing. In Galatians, the community accepted the deformed, maternal, and stigmatized body of Paul "like an angel" (4:14). Monsters, these "heralds of the extraordinary" (Stryker 2006, 247), encourage us to work toward stitched-up communities that skillfully disassemble and reassemble various bits of the identities that Paul desperately seeks to bound together. As "patron saints of our blissful imperfection," monsters have the potential to liberate us from knowing what perfect communities should look like and how they should function.[21] They revel in the decomposition of identity and stand as ambiguous and even queer figures of reclamation and critique, to which we should attend in our community building and in our reading of biblical texts.

---

21. Quote from Guillermo del Toro's acceptance speech for Best Director at the 2018 Golden Globes (https://www.youtube.com/watch?v=ykv23HpruCo).

Works Cited

Angelini, Anna. 2013. "Méthodes taxinomiques comparées: Dan Sperber et Mary Douglas à propos des animaux hors catégorie." *Yod* 18:http://yod.revues.org/1834.

Aymer, Margaret. 2009. "'Mother Knows Best': The Story of Paul Revisited." Pages 187–98 in *Mother Goose, Mother Jones, Mommie Dearest: Biblical Mothers and Their Children.* Edited by Cheryl A. Kirk-Duggan and Tina Pippin. SemeiaSt 61. Atlanta: Society of Biblical Literature.

Betz, Hans Dieter. 1979. *Galatians: A Commentary on Paul's Letter to the Churches in Galatia.* Hermeneia. Philadelphia: Fortress.

Bhabha, Homi. 1994. *The Location of Culture.* London: Routledge.

Brintnall, Kent L. 2013. "Queer Studies and Religion." *CRR* 1:51–61.

Burrus, Virginia. 2007. "Mapping as Metamorphosis: Initial Reflections on Gender and Ancient Religious Discourses." Pages 1–10 in *Mapping Gender in Ancient Religious Discourse.* Edited by Todd Penner and Caroline Vander Stichele. Leiden: Brill.

Butler, Judith. 1993. *Bodies That Matter: On the Discursive Limits of "Sex."* London: Routledge.

Castelli, Elizabeth. 1991. "'I Will Make Mary Male': Pieties of the Body and Gender Transformation of Christian Women in Late Antiquity." Pages 29–49 in *Bodyguards: The Cultural Politics of Gender Ambiguity.* Edited by Julia Epstein and Kristina Straub. London: Routledge.

Cohen, Shaye J. D. 1989. "Crossing the Boundary and Becoming a Jew." *HTR* 82:13–33.

Ehrensperger, Kathy. 2007. *Paul and the Dynamics of Power: Communication and Interaction in the Early Christ-Movement.* LNTS 325. London: T&T Clark.

Englard, Yaffa. 2018. "The Expulsion of Hagar." *RelArts* 22:261–93.

Foucault, Michel. 1980. "Two Lectures." Pages 78–108 in *Power/Knowledge: Selected Interviews and Other Writings, 1972–1977.* Edited by Colin Gordon. New York: Pantheon.

———. 1982. "The Discourse on Language." Pages 215–37 in *The Archeology of Knowledge.* Translated by Alan Sheridan Smith. New York: Pantheon.

———. 1990. *An Introduction.* Vol. 1 of *History of Sexuality.* Translated by Robert Hurley. Repr. ed. New York: Vintage.

———. 1995. *Discipline and Punish: The Birth of the Prison.* Translated by Alan Sheridan Smith. Repr. ed. 1995. New York: Vintage.

Fredriksen, Paula. 2002. "Judaism, Circumcision, and Apocalyptic Hope: Another Look at Galatians 1 and 2." Pages 235–60 in *The Galatians Debate: Contemporary Issues in Rhetorical and Historical Interpretation*. Edited by Mark D. Nanos. Peabody, MA: Hendrickson.

———. 2010. "Judaizing the Nations: The Ritual Demands of Paul's Gospel." *NTS* 56:232–52.

Halberstam, Judith. 1995. *Skin Shows: Gothic Horror and the Technology of Monsters*. Durham: Duke University Press.

———. 1998. "Between Butches." Pages 57–66 in *Butch/Femme: Inside Lesbian Gender*. Edited by Sally Munt. London: Cassel.

Hardin, Justin K. 2008. *Galatians and the Imperial Cult: A Critical Analysis of the First-Century Social Context of Paul's Letter*. WUNT 2.237. Tübingen: Mohr Siebeck.

Harrison, Renee K. 2004. " 'Hagar Ain't Workin,' Gimme Me Celie': A Hermeneutic of Rejection and a Risk of Re-appropriation." *USQR* 58.3–4:38–55.

Hooker, Morna D. 1996. "A Partner in the Gospel: Paul's Understanding of His Ministry." Pages 83–100 in *Theology and Ethics in Paul and His Interpreters: Essays in Honor of Victor Furnish*. Edited by Eugene H. Lovering Jr. and Jerry Sumney. Nashville: Abingdon.

Johnson Hodge, Caroline. 2005. "Apostle to the Gentiles: Constructions of Paul's Identity." *BibInt* 13:270–88.

———. 2007. *If Sons, Then Heirs: A Study of Kinship and Ethnicity in the Letters of Paul*. New York: Oxford University Press.

Kahl, Brigitte. 2010. *Galatians Re-imagined: Reading with the Eyes of the Vanquished*. PCC. Minneapolis: Fortress.

Kartzow, Marianne Bjelland. 2013. "On Naming and Blaming: Hagar's God-Talk in Jewish and Early Christian Sources." Pages 97–119 in *In the Arms of Biblical Women*. Edited by Mishael M. Caspi and John T. Greene. Piscataway: Gorgias.

Klawans, Jonathan. 1995. "Notions of Gentile Impurity in Ancient Judaism." *AJSR* 20:285–312.

Marchal, Joseph A. 2010. "Bodies Bound for Circumcision and Baptism: An Intersex Critique and the Interpretation of Galatians." *ThS* 16:163–82.

———. 2012. "Queer Approaches: Improper Relations with Pauline Letters." Pages 209–27 in *Studying Paul's Letters: Contemporary Perspectives and Methods*. Edited by Joseph A. Marchal. Minneapolis: Fortress.

Martyn, J. Louis. 1997. *Galatians. A New Translation with Introduction and Commentary.* AB 33A. New York: Doubleday.

McKinnish Bridges, Linda. 2008. *1 and 2 Thessalonians.* Macon: Smyth & Helwys.

McNeel, Jennifer Houston. 2014. *Paul as Infant and Nursing Mother: Metaphor, Rhetoric, and Identity in 1 Thessalonians 2:5–8.* ECL 12. Atlanta: SBL Press.

Nelson, Brooke. 2016. "A Mother's Martyrdom: Elite Christian Motherhood and the *Martyrdom of Domnina*." *JFSR* 32:11–26.

Punt, Jeremy. 2012. "*He Is Heavy … He's My Brother*: Unravelling Fraternity in Paul (Galatians)." *Neot* 46:153–71.

———. 2013. "Pauline Brotherhood, Gender and Slavery." *Neot* 47:149–69.

———. 2014. "Masculinity and Lineage in the New Testament in Roman Times." *Neot* 48:303–23.

Quintilian. *Quintilian II: Books IV–VI.* Translated by H. E. Butler. LCL. Cambridge: Harvard University Press, 1966.

Rajak, Tessa. 1984. "Was There a Roman Charter for the Jews?" *JRS* 74:107–23.

———. 1992. "The Jewish Community and its Boundaries." Pages 9–28 in *The Jews among Pagans and Christians in the Roman Empire.* Edited by Judith Lieu, John North, and Tessa Rajak. London: Routledge.

Reinhartz, Adele, and Miriam-Simma Walfish. 2006. "Conflict and Coexistence in Jewish Interpretation." Pages 101–25 in *Hagar, Sarah, and Their Children: Jewish, Christian, and Muslim Perspectives.* Edited by Phyllis Trible and Letty M. Russell. Louisville: Westminster John Knox.

Schüz, John Howard. 2007. *Paul and the Anatomy of Apostolic Authority.* SNTSMS 26. Louisville: Westminster John Knox.

Sherwood, Yvonne. 2014. "Hagar and Ishmael. The Reception of Expulsion." *Int* 68:286–304.

Solevåg, Anna Rebecca. 2016. "No Nuts? No Problem! Disability, Stigma, and the Baptized Eunuch in Acts 8:26–40." *BibInt* 24:81–99.

Stryker, Susan. 2006. "My Words to Victor Frankenstein above the Village of Chamounix [sic]: Performing Transgender Rage." Pages 244–56 in *The Transgender Studies Reader.* Edited by Susan Stryker and Stephen Whittle. New York: Routledge.

Sullivan, Nikki. 2006. "Transmogrification: (Un)becoming Other(s)." Pages 552–64 in *The Transgender Studies Reader.* Edited by Susan Stryker and Stephen Whittle. New York: Routledge.

Trible, Phyllis, and Letty M. Russell eds. 2006. *Hagar, Sarah, and Their Children: Jewish, Christian, and Muslim Perspectives.* Louisville: Westminster John Knox.

Williams, Delores S. 1993. *Sisters in the Wilderness: The Challenge of Womanist God-Talk.* Maryknoll, NY: Orbis.

A Little *Porneia* Leavens the Whole:
Queer(ing) Limits of Community in 1 Corinthians 5

Midori E. Hartman

This is one side of the story: the *ekklēsia* (Christ community) at Corinth has a recurring habit of courting *porneia* (sexual immorality).[1] The community's members were once *ta ethnē* (the nations) of a cosmopolitan city famed for its embrace of the cult of Aphrodite and its associated sexual practices.[2] In following Christ, they supposedly gave up the primacy of

I extend my gratitude to the following people, without whom this essay could not have been realized in its present state: Melanie Johnson-DeBaufre for her pedagogy and support in the course from which the first version of this essay originated; Stephen D. Moore for his help with further developing the material several years later; Tat-siong Benny Liew for his response paper feedback on an earlier version of this essay presented at the 2016 Annual Meeting of the Society of Biblical Literature, especially for his push for more attention to race and ethnicity; Steed V. Davidson for his editorial insights and changes; and, finally, Joseph A. Marchal for his invitation to the "Queering Pauline Epistles and Interpretations" panel at the 2016 Annual Meeting of the Society of Biblical Literature and this volume, as well as for his help with the revision process. Any infelicities are mine and mine alone. All translations come from the NRSV and the JSB unless otherwise noted.

1. The NRSV translates *ekklēsia* as "the church," which has distinctly established Christian connotations for a community that is still undergoing processes of self-definition and does not call to mind the term's root notions of public "assembly" or "congregation." I offer "Christ community" above as a means of both attending to the root of the term and acknowledging their focus on Christ. There are, however, more radically inclusive translations that highlight the democratic potential behind *ekklēsia*, for example Elisabeth Schüssler Fiorenza's (2016) "congress of wo/men."

2. I translate *ta ethnē* as "the nations" instead of the NRSV's "pagans" for two reasons: it subverts the connotations of the latter translation, and "the nations" better aligns the conversation with the topic of ethnicity. Here I acknowledge that modern associations of the nation-state may affect how the translation "the nations" for *ta*

that cosmopolitan identity and its standards in exchange for becoming members of the corporate body of Christ. This transfer was made possible only at a great price—Christ's own crucifixion—which requires a present obligation to intracommunal policing in order to keep the *ekklēsia* pure by keeping *porneia* out. First Corinthians 5 reveals the failure of this communal obligation in allowing an unorthodox relationship of a son taking up with his father's *gynē* ("woman"), which makes him and the relationship *ponēros* ("wicked"). Chastisement and correction toward a purified unity are the necessary cure to prevent divine wrath; the history of Israel speaks to the imminence of this truth.

This could be the other side of that story: the *ekklēsia* at Corinth is not unified over what it means to live their new lives in Christ, especially when it comes to membership limits and behavior. The issue stems from the fact that one of their guides is an absent-yet-present figure, one who has a particular preoccupation with what he says is *porneia*, but he is not so forthcoming with the details about what that exactly means (Gaca 2003, 120). First Corinthians 5 reveals a conflict of interpretation over what liberation from one's past can mean when it comes to sexual expression. If the community has been invited to imagine themselves as no longer *ta ethnē*, could that also mean that they are no longer beholden to that old identity's morality? Perhaps some envision true liberation from the world as a queer embrace of the opposite of the status quo, as seen in the reported relationship between the son and the woman. What could a rejection of normative paradigms of propriety mean for a people who are invited to reject the world that taught them such paradigms? What are the limits of community here?

A queer reading of Paul's rhetoric of intracommunal policing in 1 Cor 5 provides the chance to explore the radical possibility of the *ekklēsia*'s interpretation of the Christ message. While Paul's interests and anxieties drive the first perspective above, this essay embraces the second perspective, which considers queer possibilities for imagining what a new life in

---

ethne is received and that these associations do not correspond to the first-century CE conceptualization of *ta ethnē*. I understand *ta ethnē* as functioning in exclusionary terms within the New Testament context, namely, as a collective noun for those who are not Jewish or part of the Christ community, i.e., gentiles (LSJ, s.v. "ἔθνος," 2b). I also use "Greco-Roman society/context" as an approximate synonym within this essay, which is a sign of the extremely broad function that it serves for Paul in his naming of the specific nature and obligations of the Christ community.

Christ means, even willfully against Paul. As I suggest that we read it, the racial-ethnic reasoning of being ex-*ethnē* opens up the interpretive space to embrace new ways of being and relating to others that could involve what wider society considered *porneia*, as witnessed in the tolerance of the *ponēros* relationship. This is contrary to Paul's imperative that the community should consider its gift of a new identity as making them accountable to an ethic of purification out of obligation to Christ's crucifixion. In 1 Cor 5, Paul justifies his ethic of purification by inviting the community to imagine its present role in history as mirroring the history of Israel that has been ritualized in the language of festivals marking liberation (the Feast of Unleavened Bread and Passover).

This essay, then, is a queer reading of the intersection(s) of animality, sexuality, and racial-ethnic logic that Paul introduces in his exhortation to communal self-policing against *porneia* in 1 Cor 5. I argue that the community's division over the *ponēros* relationship and Paul's command to excise the man like yeast (*zumē*) reveals rather than suppresses the embedded potentiality of *porneia* within the multiplicity that is the body of Christ. Although Paul justifies communal self-policing by connecting it to the Christ event in the language of paschal sacrifice (5:7b), his invocation to imagine *porneia* elimination in the terms of ritual purification language also introduces its inability to be (completely) erased. *Porneia*, in its sense as an ambiguous and anti–status quo possibility, animates the community's imagination of what being ex-*ethnē* can mean, including a potential embrace of what the *ethnē* would reject.

Queer Theory at the Intersection(s) of
Animality, Sexuality, and Racial-Ethnic Logic

To queer is to "disrupt heteronormative knowledges and institutions, and the subjectivities and socialities that are (in)formed by them and that (in) form them" (Sullivan 2003, v). Important in this definition is the emphasis on the critique of normative knowledges *and* institutions. When we consider what this means for the study of Paul as a figure entangled in empire, Marchal (2012, 210) reminds us to lean into *queer* as a verb, in which we can challenge "an arrangement of power and privilege, or … interpret queerly by attending to certain dynamics." In the case of 1 Corinthians, Paul's exhortation of the *ekklēsia* to keep the communal body of Christ pure appears to strive for a queer resistance to the status quo of imperial life by challenging dominant systems of relationships and values. Consider, for example, Paul's support of nonnormative behavior such as celibacy (1 Cor 7:1, 7–8, 25–26, 29) or his subversion of social mores in favor of addressing the needs of the "weak" versus the desires of the "strong" (1 Cor 8).

If, however, queering invites the (self-)questioning of the deep and unspoken presuppositions about what is normal, then Paul's rhetoric misses much of the mark when it comes to addressing sexuality and gender performance.[3] This is because his perspective on sexual relationships reinscribes the power and privilege of normative marriage as established by Roman standards, if the requirements of chastity cannot be met (see 1 Cor 7:2–5, 9–16, 36–40). This invites the question of who is left out of such paradigms and who stands the most to benefit from their exclusion.

Race and animality can help us address the exclusions of the queer. As a range of queer of color scholarship has highlighted (Ferguson 2004; Somerville 2000; Muñoz 1999), claims of sexual and gender difference have long been deployed to pathologize and police racially minoritized groups. As Cathy J. Cohen's (1997) critique of the frameworks used for queer theory has stressed, the radical potential of queer's interrogation of normativity can be met when it grapples with the ways that marginalized people, including African Americans, have been cast as pathologically estranged from proper kinship and marriage practices. One clear lesson from these exclusions and omissions is that for queer approaches to be queer, they must be intersectional.

Animality studies resonates with and elaborates on these intersectional aims. As Matthew Calarco frames it:

> Much like the critique of essentialism in feminism, queer theory, and race studies, theorists in animal studies seek to track the ways in which the concept of "animality" [i.e., the being of animals] functions to demarcate humans clearly from animals and establish homogeneities among what appear to be radically different forms of animal life. (2008, 2–3)

As a theoretical lens, animality forces us to confront the nonhuman other that troubles our normative anthropocentric perspectives and presumptions of rationality-based subjecthood in the world.[4] In bringing together the queer and the nonhuman, we can ask, with Dana Luciano and Mel Chen

---

3. For critique of Paul's rhetoric concerning gender performance in 1 Corinthians, see Wire 1990 and Townsley 2017.

4. Influential works include Derrida 2002 and Haraway 2008. For examples of

(2015, 186), "Has the queer ever been human?" In other words, how does the queer problematize normative demands to perform a certain kind of humanity? As a result, Chen (2012, 11) stresses that "'queer' refers, as might be expected, to exceptions to the conventional ordering of sex, reproduction, and intimacy, though it at times also refers to animacy's veering-away from dominant ontologies and the normativities they promulgate."

In considering this, we ought to remember that there are subtle ways that animality can be used to assert both the human and the normative. Take, for example, the fact that animalized language is used to dehumanize minorities out of their humanity, or that we uncritically accept and apply heteronormative gender and reproductive narratives of humans to animals.[5] Animality becomes referential to the human, either as a lack of humanity or mimicry of its normative standards. This is seen most strongly in how dehumanization and minoritization become one and the same through an ethos of speciesism, which reinscribes the system of exclusion and oppression by forcing people to argue for their humanity (see Peterson 2013). There remains a hierarchy to who/what can claim to be the most normative, thus most human. As seen in Paul's use of the nonhuman in 1 Cor 5, animality is used to demarcate certain people from the community within an ethnoracial logic of boundary making and maintenance.

Animality and racism intersect at the point at which the dehumanization of people is justified through a logic of speciesism—namely, our treatment of animals as wholly other to us. In treating certain people—for example, slaves—as unequal in their humanity to others, this abuse creates a resonance with our treatment of animals, a point that Marjorie Spiegel (1983) calls "the dreaded comparison." We avoid confronting the similarities between the abuse of animals and the abuse of certain people because of the intense dissonance it causes within us; to acknowledge it would demand that we confront our justification of systematic abuse of other beings, both in the past and in the present.[6] Attempts to resist such dehumanization

---

the intersection between animality and biblical studies, see Moore and Kearns 2014; Koosed 2014; Stone 2016a, 2016b; Moore 2017.

5. On such interconnection(s) between animality, race, and/or gender, see Haraway 1990; Birke 1995; Elder, Wolch, and Emel 1998; Peterson 2013; and Kim 2015.

6. Alexander G. Weheliye (2014, 10–11) raises an excellent critique to this point in showing how scholars replicate a particular pattern: often, they do not explain how it comes to be that blackness and chattel slavery have become connected, why the desire to claim human freedom necessarily leads to the dehumanization of nonhuman

through an insistence on humanity "can only reinscribe the speciesist logic that initiates their exclusion" in the first place (Peterson 2013, 2).

Demanding one's humanity does not change a social system that prioritizes certain human groups and attributes over others. The demand of the individual on behalf of (a) community must become a critique of the larger system's categories that uphold its biopolitics. This includes paying attention to how value-imbued notions of ethnicity and race are wielded to categorize beings as "full humans, not-quite-humans, and nonhumans," as seen in Alexander G. Weheliye's (2014, 3) theory of categorization via "racializing assemblages" and Achille Mbembe's (2017) theory of how the creation of blackness as a racial category equates with the nonhuman in the logistics of exclusion. These insights help us to consider the ways in which certain people can be made nonhuman through communal rejection of their subjectivity and how using fear about being drawn into the web of exclusion concretizes communal boundaries.[7]

This relationship between racial-ethnic exclusion, sexual immorality, and the creaturely is present in 1 Cor 5, especially in how Paul invites the Corinthians to imagine themselves as inhabiting a new corporate identity. His choice to use the *ethnē* to shame the *ekklēsia* is a form of self-definition that Denise Kimber Buell (2005, ix) calls "ethnic reasoning," in which a group may conceptualize their identity through comparison and contrast with large corporate collectives. The Corinthian *ekklēsia* is populated by members who were once *ta ethnē*; they were supposed to renounce their

---

others, or why black subjects "must bear the burden of representing the final frontier of speciesism."

7. As illustrations of the stakes of this threat, recent films such as *Get Out* (2017), *Advantageous* (2015), and *Transfer* (2010) invite us to think about the commodification of black and other minoritized bodies as upgrades for dying or old bodies of the elite, which signifies the decimation of nonwhite personhood within a system that already marginalizes postslavery blackness, refugees, and other minorities. While these films are pointing to the racist and capitalist system that commodifies the same bodies it rejects from equality, they also invite us to consider how certain people can be made nonhuman through a communal rejection of their subjectivity. In 1 Cor 5, Paul demands that the son (the *ponēros*) be sent to his own "sunken place" (cf. the void where the conscious souls of black people are put when their bodies are taken in *Get Out*) outside of the *ekklēsia*, as he is no longer truly part of *ta ethnē*; nevertheless, if the community follows Paul's command, he has served as an embodiment of the kind of *porneia* that can no longer be tolerated, a kind of teachable moment for the community.

cosmopolitan identity in exchange for the benefits of being in the *ekklēsia*. Paul reminds them of this fact in 1 Cor 12:2: "You know that when you were *ethnē*, you were enticed and led astray to idols that could not speak." As Cavan W. Concannon (2014, xi) puts it:

> The *ethnē*, constructed in Paul's rhetoric as people characterized by idolatry, have become not-*ethnē* by changing their cultic practice. Paul's reasoning assumes a connection between cultic practice and ethnic identity: to change one's cultic practices and allegiances is also a means of changing one's ethnicity, becoming no longer *ethnē* but now something else.

In terms of Paul's ethnic reasoning, the *ekklēsia* is different from the *ethnē*, but the community has somehow become "worse" than before they received this new identity because they allowed a relationship that is beyond the pale for Roman social and legal norms (1 Cor 5). We can see the rhetorical extension of this logic with Tat-siong Benny Liew (2008, 93), who observes that "Paul's 'reversed condemnation' of the Corinthians makes him, though a diasporic and colonized Jew, come across as more Greco-Roman than the Greco-Romans when it comes to matters of sexual 'purity.' "

This present reading of Paul's call to sexual purity against *porneia* suggests that the Corinthian embrace of the ex-*ethnē* identity became a queer interpretation beyond Paul's imagination of what "new lives in Christ" could be. Paul's use of biblical precedent and rituals of Jewish history to justify his exclusion of the man uses animality in such a way that it reveals the inability to completely erase the potentiality of *porneia*.

Porneia: New Lives in Christ

> It is actually reported that there is sexual immorality among you, and of a kind that is not found even among the nations; for a man is living with his father's woman. And you are arrogant! Should you not rather have mourned, so that he who has done this would have been removed from among you?
>
> —1 Cor 5:1–2 (NRSV, modified)

According to Paul, those within the *ekklēsia* who support the son who takes up relations with his father's "woman" introduce a problem of discord in the community by allowing *porneia*. The man is a *ponēros*, one of the *pornoi* (the sexually immoral) that Paul has warned them not to allow within their own community (5:9–11). Paul frames the community's allowance of the man as an act of arrogance and pride, since it defies biblical and legal prohibitions against adultery and incest.[8] The unnamed woman is not the son's biological mother and we have no account of the father's position on the relationship, although by Roman legal standards, his property rights were being infringed.[9] If the family was elite, perhaps this relationship reflects Pauline concerns over the strong being stumbling blocks for the weak in the community, similar to the letter's concerns about the pride of eating habits (see 1 Cor 8).[10]

---

8. See Deut 22:22, "If a man is found lying with another man's wife, both of them—the man and the woman with whom he lay—shall die. Thus you will sweep away the evil from Israel," and 23:1, "No man shall marry his father's former wife, so as to remove his father's garment." According to Roman law, this relationship was prosecutable because it constituted adultery and incest, the seriousness depending upon whether the father was alive or not. Richard A. Horsley (1998, 78) presumes that the father is dead. Given, however, that the relationship would have been legally permissible if the father had been dead, Paul's point that this relationship was extreme even for the *ethnē* implies that the father is most likely alive (Winter 2001, 46–49). We can presume Paul's use of *gynaika* (*gynē*) and not *mētēr* means that she was not the man's biological mother, yet this still would have been considered incest by Roman legal standards (Winter 2001, 49). C. H. Talbert (1987, 19) attributes Paul's problem with the relationship to the fact that allowing incest would offend the wider world to the point of preventing their possible salvation.

9. Note that while Paul is invested in promoting the settling of intracommunal problems within the community itself (see 1 Cor 5:9–13; 6:1–8), from a legal standpoint, involved parties were still held accountable to Roman law. Take, for example, the father, who could be charged with pimping if he chose not to divorce his wife and prosecute her, as adultery became a public offense with the *Lex Iulia* of Augustus (Edwards 1993, 39).

10. Given the number of high-status individuals that Paul could convert in Corinth—which was a problem, as seen through the examples of unequal eating practices in the community (1 Cor 8)—there is a chance that the status of the men of 1 Cor 5 contributes to this issue of power and the privileges of high versus low status, as Paul consistently emphasized that the strong had to model good behavior for the weak (see 1 Cor 8, 10). More informative for this issue of intracommunal conflict may be the woman's status, as she appears to be the object of contest between the rights of the father versus the rights of the son in the community's eyes. Scholars presume that she is an outsider to the community because there is no command to exile her, as exists for the son, which would be the Roman punishment for adultery in this period, along with loss of citizenship and property. See Horsley 1998, 79; Winter 2001, 46, 52; Rosner 1994, 61 n. 4.

While we cannot know the details, one thing is clear: *some* in the community felt that this relationship was not the appropriate way to live their new lives in Christ as a community, and Paul agrees by stating that it is an act of *porneia* beyond the pale, even for Greco-Roman society itself (the *ethnē*). This marks the community as less than that which they were supposed to be transcending: their past as the *ethnē*. Thus, to Paul, it is an affront to the divine gift to include them within God's people, as suggested by the language of a unified and hierarchal body of Christ (see 1 Cor 12).

We can unpack why Paul chose to frame the *ponēros* relationship as a communal threat. Kathy L. Gaca (2003, 119–20) has shown that the attention that the Pentateuch and Paul give to forbidden sexual activity is marked by how it directs God's people away from full devotion to God, in comparison with "permissible sexual conduct [that] shows strict devotion." Moreover, the threat is more than the individual's act of misconduct: allowing individuals who engage in actions that amount to rebellion against God's will bring about divine abandonment or destruction of the community (127). Here we may read Paul's quotation of an injunction to expel the *ponēros*—"Drive out the *ponēros* from among you" (1 Cor 5:13b; see also Deut 13:5; 17:7)—as such a warning. But because this is not the first time that Paul has had to warn the *ekklēsia* about *porneia* (1 Cor 5:9), it seems that the community does not have the same sense of apocalyptically driven moral threat that compels Paul, which causes him to bring his argument back to biblical language and imagery (albeit perfunctorily brief in nature).

Against Paul, we may ask how his language presumes malignant intent in the community's behavior because it challenges his own interpretation of how to live new lives in Christ. His reading of the reported situation: the couple's relationship signals a sexual immorality that is not even approved by Paul's foil for the *ekklēsia*, the *ethnē*, about which some in the community seem to be overly boastful (5:1–2). As a setup to an ethnoracial argument of exclusion, we can see that the *ponēros* in this reading represents "the constitution of the Other not as similar to oneself but as a menacing object from which one must be protected or escape, or which must simply be destroyed if it cannot be subdued" (Mbembe 2017, 10).[11] Liew (2008, 79)

---

11. Paul's focus on the deviance and threat of the *ponēros* son fits with other Roman discourses on sex, which Skinner (1997, 5) notes are "engrossed with departures from established norms, chiefly because they employ putative anomalies in gender role and

offers that the gentile Corinthian community's anxiety over their conversion and new status in the world would have given them incentive to "try to separate religious affiliation from racial/ethnic filiation," as embodied in Paul's own "stigmatized racial/ethnic body as colonized Jew." The *ponēros* therefore marks an event of the colonized—Paul and the Corinthian *ekklēsia*—trying to navigate the "absent presence of the Roman colonization and racialization" over inclusion that, when taken with subsequent cases of *porneia* in the letter, "ends up duplicating and reinforcing a larger ideological imperative to establish and eschew abject bodies" (97, 96).

Yet there is another reading, on the other side of the coin from the one Paul offers: one person's idea of pride might in fact be excitement, joy, and liberation. What if the *ponēros* relationship is one interpretation of the new freedom to live outside societal constructions determined by a world that already minoritizes and excludes them on the basis of their affiliations to the Christ movement? Such an approach is a community-focused extension of Richard A. Horsley's (1998, 79) suggestion that "perhaps ... the enlightened fellow had achieved a freedom from restrictive traditional patriarchal norms such that an alliance of love was now possible." To read for aspects of communal acceptance is a challenge to Bruce W. Winter's (2001, 53) point that "given the criminal nature of the act, it seems unlikely that church members flaunted or glorified in the son's activity as some misplaced example of Christian freedom that allowed even incest." While we ought to be skeptical of Paul's interpretation of boasting, why not consider the existence and tolerance of the *ponēros* as a positive rejection of the legal standards and procedures of their social milieu?[12] To read the case of 1 Cor 5 this way is to suggest that while Paul's rhetoric is an attempt to close the window on sexual expression and relations within the community, it is not a given that all would see or agree with his version of sexuality, nor that they would see that as the most pressing matter in living their new lives as ex-*ethnē*.[13]

---

moral irregularities as symbolic frameworks for identifying and denigrating alterity in class, ethnicity, lifestyle, and political agenda."

12. Skepticism is especially warranted considering that Paul delegitimizes the power of lawsuits and the courts in 1 Cor 6 as the means and place to solve their problems.

13. Take, for example, the sexual ethics of 1 Cor 7, which posits marital sexuality as a concession to prevent worse forms of *porneia* outside the normative and legally bonded pair—like the son and his father's woman in 1 Cor 5.

Furthermore, the relationship signals disunity in the communal body of Christ in that there are factions, but factionalism seems to be a major factor in the *ekklēsia's* interbody politic (see 1 Cor 1:10–17). Casting out the *ponēros*, the willful subject and avatar of the community's tendency toward *porneia*, is not the panacea Paul hopes it will be (or at least is suggesting to his audience). It certainly could help with inter- and intracommunal optics of what the *ekklēsia* represents in Corinth, as they are still working out how to be mixed up with the world (*kosmos*) from which they so long to leave. Paul's drive to make sure the community limits itself as a means of protection against divine wrath by using terror quotations from Hebrew Scripture can be read as a sign of a man who is no longer in control of his message as it is being interpreted by the community. This one example of living new lives in Christ queers what the wider Greco-Roman society deems to be appropriate social relations by embracing behavior that is typically understood as its opposite—namely, the presence and allowance of what the social milieu would deem *porneia*.

In what follows, I examine how Paul frames and justifies his ethic of communal policing with biblical festival metaphors, especially how he uses the creaturely aspects of yeast as contagion and Christ the paschal lamb as gift and obligation to do so. He seeks to help the community see that the history and ritual of Israel's liberation matches their present project of making history: honoring Christ's gift of liberation (crucifixion as *pascha*) by communal policing of the purity of the *ekklēsia*. The efficacy, however, of marrying the two histories to signal the limits of the communal body of Christ is questionable, as Paul feels he has to keep reminding them of the danger of *porneia*, tied to God's wrath. *Porneia* can and will persist. What if we are to read the *ponēros* relationship as an example of communal exploration against Paul's anxiety over divine retribution and his own attempts to assert authority over the contentious and multiplicitous *ekklēsia* in Corinth?

Yeast: Contagion or Constitutive Impurity?

Your boasting is not a good thing. Do you not know that a little yeast leavens the whole batch of dough? Clean out the old yeast so that you may be a new batch, as you really are unleavened.... Therefore, let us celebrate the festival, not with the old yeast, the yeast of malice and evil, but with the unleavened bread of sincerity and truth.

—1 Cor 5:6–7a, 8

The members of the *ekklēsia* of Corinth are invited to imagine themselves as active participants in an ongoing, history-making process of purifying a corporate body that exceeds them and their own motivations as individuals. In 1 Cor 5, Paul uses Exod 12:17's divine command to excise yeast (*zumē*) from one's house for the Feast of Unleavened Bread as a guide for the *ekklēsia*'s own project of purifying the community of *porneia*.[14] Since the former is a ritual act of honoring God's liberation of Israel, Paul wants his audience to see that the rejection of the *ponēros* would be a similar act of honoring the divine liberation of the ex-*ethnē* via Christ's crucifixion. The moral imperative moving forward is framed as intracommunal policing to prevent other individual motivations from threatening the entire project of keeping the community pure enough so that it is not judged by God and found wanting in the end (see 1 Cor 5:12–13a).

A queer reading of Paul's invitation here involves a rejection of the idea of purity itself. As a modern theory against purity offers, "purism is a de-collectivizing, de-mobilizing, paradoxical politics of despair" (Shotwell 2016, 9). Purity is presented as a single-trajectory, teleologically driven project, one without compromise because it is strengthened by an ethos of repetitive rejection of whatever is considered an impurity at the moment. Indeed, in more recent settings, claims about pollution and toxicity operate in raced, classed, and queered ways (Chen 2012, 159–221). Purification can be made to imply finitude and homogeneity, even as it can only deliver repetition and heterogeneity within collective multiplicity.

Although Paul sees the *ponēros* as a sign that the community must continue to self-police against *porneia*, implying that he is aware that this is not a one-time deal, he still imagines a stable trajectory toward becoming a community that God will not forsake if they follow his direction only. The language of ritual introduced by the feast implies repetition that is also an acknowledgment of the inchoate potential of *porneia* that can never be completely excised, periodically bubbling up

---

14. Exod 12:17–20: "You shall observe the [Feast of] Unleavened Bread, for on this very day I brought your ranks out of the land of Egypt; you shall observe this day throughout the ages as an institution for all time. In the first month, from the fourteenth day of the month at evening, you shall eat unleavened bread until the twenty-first day of the month at evening. No leaven shall be found in your houses for seven days. For whoever eats what is leavened, that person shall be cut off from the community of Israel, whether he is a stranger or a citizen of the country. You shall eat nothing leavened; in all your settlements you shall eat unleavened bread."

to feast like the yeast that makes its home in aging batches of dough. Paul connects nonnormative relationships and prideful creaturely idolatry, using them to define humanity's history elsewhere.[15] Thus it follows that Paul would interpret this *ponēros* relationship through the lens of pride. He calls the community "puffed up" (*pephysiōmenoi*), echoing the observation of the rising process of bread as yeast feeding off sugar and expelling carbon dioxide in the baking process. Whether or not the community was boasting in their allowance of this case of *porneia*, the issue remains for Paul that action must be taken to remove this polluting factor from the lump of dough (*phyrama*), lest it ruin the corporate body and inspire similar acts that are beyond the pale of both Pauline and Greco-Roman propriety.

Given that this is not the first time Paul has had to teach them about the problem of *porneia* (see 1 Cor 5:9), it seems that the *ponēros* is not a bug but a feature of the community's imaginative potential of what it means to live as ex-*ethnē* in Christ. What would it mean to read the ever-present *porneia*-yeast connection as an invitation to deconstruct the limitations of defining communal ethics according to societal norms of behavior that reify the status quo? What if the *ekklēsia* is not wrong for its pride but is rather engaging in a responsive ethic of inclusion of the heterogeneity of queerness—an ethnic that did not need to be considered a stumbling block, but a liberative reading of new life and possibility?

Julian Yates (2017) would direct us to think about how yeast is one of many nonhuman figures that have helped us in co-making our reality as we have known it. Yeast is copartner in the basic processes of bread making by humans, such that its excision became part of a core Hebrew tradition that marks a people as set apart by God, honored in ritual repetition of their history, able to be used as a metaphor of communal policing. That Paul can use yeast in such a way reveals its lasting impression—perhaps even its inevitability to be a constant figure in the dough. In this way, we can think about how Paul's call to excise the human equivalent of yeast in the *ekklēsia*, the *ponēros*, cannot represent the once-and-for-all end to the problem of *porneia* in the community. Regardless, Paul would have the community imagine this to be their ethical responsibility to the Christ event by framing it as *pascha*.

---

15. See Rom 1:18–32. For more, see Moore 2000 and Brooten 1996.

Paschal Lamb: Ethical Obligations of the Ex-*ethnē*

For our paschal lamb, Christ, has been sacrificed.

—1 Cor 5:7b

As scholars have noted, this sacrificial metaphor is not a reference to atonement theology (Stowers 1994, 211), but it does follow common convention by describing sacrifice as "gift or service or thank-offering" (Ullucci 2011, 76). Yet it is not a simple metaphor or a throwaway line; Christ the *pascha hēmōn* exceeds normal expectations of sacrifice as gift giving because Christ becomes both the one who sacrifices (himself) and the one who is sacrificed.[16] This is no ordinary gift; there can therefore be no ordinary response by the *ekklēsia*, according to Paul. His purpose in emphasizing this sacrifice par excellence is to hold the community accountable to his version of communal ethic as a form of reciprocal gratitude. Jane Lancaster Patterson (2015, 123) offers that the "metaphors of the Passover unite this gentile community to the historical people of God.... This identification is important not only for defining the community in relation to outsiders ... but for establishing defining principles within the community."[17] Even if Christ the Passover lamb is not the *ekklēsia*'s "moral model" (123), he is the focal point of obligation in the Pauline framework of ethical behavior, one that favors Paul's version of living one's life in Christ.

Note that Paul presents this reference to Christ the sacrificed (*etuthē*) paschal lamb in the middle of a larger conversation inviting the community to imagine his call to self-police as mapping onto the ritual of Feast of Unleavened Bread. First Corinthians 5:7b equates Christ's crucifixion with a key ritual of Passover sacrifice as it is described in Exodus, yet its lack of detail produces more questions than answers here and elsewhere in the letter.[18] Even if the metaphor merely reflects the "knowledge that

---

16. While it may be argued that Christ's agency in this line is too ambiguous to make the above claim, it can be further supported by the resonances between this passage and the language of Phil 2, in which Paul exhorts that Christ's self-lowering to the form of a slave and subsequent crucifixion as an act of humility is a mindset that the community should imitate.

17. For an extensive review of scholarship on Passover references and for explication of Paul's layering of metaphors throughout 1 Corinthians, see Patterson 2015, 117–57.

18. If the sacrificial meat of the *pascha hēmōn* is eaten, then who "ate" Christ? The limitations of this essay mean that more work can and should be done concerning the

Christ's death occurred during Passover" (Keck 1988, 39), the purpose of the sacrifice for Paul's rhetoric ascribes more weight to it than a throw-away metaphor or reference. This is because the *ekklēsia*'s new identity is dependent upon the community understanding that it must animalize that which they are not or that which they are no longer part of (the *ethnē*, the *kosmos*), as defined by who can and cannot be in the community (e.g., the *ponēros*). This logic echoes Paul's overt rhetoric of negatively animalizing his opposition elsewhere.[19] The potency behind this rhetoric follows Paul's point that animals are not considered to be within the community—that is, the body of Christ.[20]

Paul justifies his exhortation to clean out members that make the *ekklēsia* disordered, in this case "unleavened" (*azumos*). The Christ event is reintroduced as a means of excluding those within the *ekklēsia* who would pollute it. After all, Paul says "I wrote to you in my letter not to associate with sexually immoral persons (*pornoi*)—not at all meaning the immoral of this world" (5:9–10), but the ones that come from within the community itself (5:11). They must self-regulate, for God will take care of the *kosmos* (5:12–13). This essay asks: aside from the relationship between the *ponēros* and "his father's woman" who else falls into this category of sexually immoral persons who must be excised? Or, perhaps more worry-ingly, who might find themselves slotted into this category at some later date, given Paul's reticence to define *porneia*?

In this way, anyone who is identified as *pornos* within the community functions as the nonhuman—they cannot be part of the *ekklēsia*, especially if they will be unaccepted by the larger Greco-Roman world. By locating the *ponēros* relationship outside the limits of society broadly and of the *ekklēsia* in particular, Paul seeks to dehumanize the man out of his ability to claim multiple communities, or even personhood within a biopolitical framework. Within the framework of ethnoracial reasoning, Paul would

---

implications of this in other portions of 1 Cor, especially when it concerns eating meat sacrificed to idols (1 Cor 8 and 10), as well as portions that concern the Lord's Supper (1 Cor 11).

19. For example, "beware of the dogs" (Phil 3:2). Consider also, perhaps, "If with merely human hopes I fought with wild animals at Ephesus, what would I have gained by it?" (1 Cor 15:32) as a metaphor for his opposition at Ephesus, when brought together with the reference in 1 Cor 16:8 to Paul's "many adversaries" in Ephesus.

20. See in 1 Cor 15:39 the Genesis-driven point that the differences between the flesh of humans and the flesh of other creatures explicate the importance of the embodiedness of the resurrection (Ketchum 2013).

say that the *pornoi* are like the *ethnē* (again): peopleless, defined by their aberrance and not kinship. The community's only path forward is to kick such deviants out in order to preserve the community's claims to their identity as humans and as followers of Christ, which he can justify through the animalizing metaphor of Christ the paschal lamb.

Conclusions

If 1 Corinthians as a whole is an attempt to transform factionalism into unity, then it is Paul's attempt to tamp down diversity in favor of a limited range of approved and status quo–informed ways of being in and in relation to the body of Christ. Interpreters who see themselves aligned with the latter ethic of communal policing on behalf of a (homogenized) unity most likely interpret the diversity and queer potentialities of *porneia* that 1 Cor 5 introduces as threatening. To read with Paul is to control the options and possibilities of others that threaten his understanding of proper behavior, which is predetermined by his own acceptance of the morality of those whom he is resisting: the *ethnē*.

Yet Paul's first letter to the Corinthians reveals that the limits of the corporate body of Christ are in constant negotiation and that what constituted *porneia* was one marker for exclusion. As Liew (2008, 95) notes, Paul "is building community on the backs of those whom 'everyone' can agree to marginalize and stigmatize." The unanswerable question that remains is whether or not everyone agreed. A more answerable question—and a more relevant approach—is to ask how we might use this text today in a way that acknowledges the queer possibility within the *ekklēsia* when reading against Paul's prescriptive rhetoric in his attempts to center himself as an authority figure, positioned between yeast and the lamb.

This essay explores how Paul sought to connect Christ's crucifixion with an obligation to perform a limited and normative set of behaviors concerning sexuality in the *ekklēsia*. In highlighting the connection between the Christ event and being not-*ethnē*, Paul's rhetoric leans into an idea that this one act of sacrifice defines their communal identity, for which the Corinthian *ekklēsia* must give thanksgiving in the form of policing its boundaries against *porneia*. When criticizing the people and behaviors that he ascribes to *porneia* in 1 Cor 5, Paul's vision of the communal body of Christ purposefully reflects the same valuation of the imperial system that it is rejecting. Queer possibilities are closed and disavowed, rejected from the body of Christ as less human than even their wider Greco-Roman context would afford them.

This essay, however, offers that Paul's choice to frame his exhortation to self-police in terms of ritual cleansing (Feast of Unleavened Bread) and obligatory thanksgiving (Passover) reveals a queer potentiality of *porneia* in spite of Paul's teleological goal of creating a clean communal body of Christ. Rather than reading the *ponēros* relationship as destructive, this essay imagines its acceptance—whether a partial tolerance or an embrace—in an already factionalized community to be a queer interpretation of imagining what being ex-*ethnē* could mean.

The rhetoric of Paul's letter pits different nonhuman creatures against each other in order to pit different members of the Corinthian *ekklēsia* against each other. The yeast and lamb, then, are juxtaposed, urging the audience to sacrifice and expel one because the other was already sacrificed. These differences are not only animalized, for the yeast carries a racialized association of people who are too much like the *ethnē*. What would it mean to try to reanimate an *ekklēsia* of both yeast and the lamb? What if they or what if just *we* refuse the terms of how Paul builds community through stigmatization and marginalization, racialization and animalization? This could mean tracing the alternative rising from within the batch of arguments he has mixed.

This reading does not insist upon the respectability of these *ekklēsia* members, or ourselves, but it does recognize that claims of sexual immorality and impropriety have often, even persistently, been racialized and animalized. Indeed, even Chen (2012, 14, 89–126) describes how notions of "wrong marriage" and "improper intimacy" characterize queer animality, terms that well describe Paul's arguments about the man tainted by a contaminating *porneia*. For Paul, the *ponēros* relationship signals such an improper intimacy: between the dehumanized son and a(n all but erased) female human, and between this yeast and the *ekklēsia*. In resisting these rhetorics, we can imagine not only the inclusion of the previously dehumanized but also a larger reconsideration of the communal systems that Paul's letters and so many of their interpreters try to enforce.

The task of queer interpretation, then, is to think in creative creaturely ways about the racializing and animalizing elements of sexuality and embodiment. Indeed, these arguments already queer the human-animal difference by imagining the redemptive function of a human transformed into a creature (see also Moore 2017). The sacrificed lamb rises; it survives and persists and then some. But here another human has been transformed into yeast, a creature that doubles as a rising agent too. If one follows Paul's arguments, one might be inclined to imagine a roasted fate for this yeasty man (in the company of Satan, 1 Cor 5:5). But it appears that Paul must convince at least some members of the *ekklēsia* to make this association. Could they—can we—imagine the yeast that also nourishes as also rising, as a lamb once roasted rose? Some saw the presence of this yeast in their community differently, or perhaps just more lightly, or leavenly. But rethinking a community of both the yeast and the lamb reflects just some of the potential of *porneia*, beyond contamination and impurity.

Works Cited

Birke, Lynda. 1995. "Exploring the Boundaries: Feminism, Animals, and Science." Pages 32–54 in *Animals and Women: Feminist Theoretical Explorations*. Edited by Carol J. Adams and Josephine Donovan. Durham: Duke University Press.

Brooten, Bernadette J. 1996. *Love between Women: Early Christian Responses to Female Homoeroticism*. CSSHS. Chicago: University of Chicago Press.

Buell, Denise Kimber. 2005. *Why This New Race: Ethnic Reasoning in Early Christianity*. New York: Columbia University Press.

Calarco, Matthew. 2008. *Zoographies: The Question of the Animal from Heidegger to Derrida*. New York: Columbia University Press.

Chen, Mel Y. 2012. *Animacies: Biopolitics, Racial Mattering, and Queer Affect*. PM. Durham: Duke University Press.

Cohen, Cathy J. 1997. "Punks, Bulldaggers, and Welfare Queens: The Radical Potential of Queer Politics?" *GLQ* 3:437–65.

Concannon, Cavan W. 2014. *"When You Were Gentiles": Specters of Ethnicity in Roman Corinth and Paul's Corinthian Correspondence*. Syn. New Haven: Yale University Press.

Derrida, Jacques. 2002. "The Animal That Therefore I Am (More to Follow)." Translated by David Wills. *CI* 28:369–418.

Edwards, Catharine. 1993. *The Politics of Immorality in Ancient Rome*. Cambridge: Cambridge University Press.

Elder, Glen, Jennifer Wolch, and Jody Emel. 1998. "Race, Place, and the Bounds of Humanity." *SocAn* 6.2:183–202.

Ferguson, Roderick. 2004. *Aberrations in Black: Toward a Queer of Color Critique*. CAS. Minneapolis: University of Minnesota Press.

Gaca, Kathy L. 2003. *The Making of Fornication: Eros, Ethics, and Political Reform in Greek Philosophy and Early Christianity*. HCS. Berkeley: University of California Press.

Haraway, Donna J. 1990. *Primate Visions: Gender, Race, and Nature in the World of Modern Science*. New York: Routledge.

———. 2008. *When Species Meet*. Posthumanities 3. Minneapolis: University of Minnesota Press.

Horsley, Richard A. 1998. *1 Corinthians*. ANTC. Nashville: Abingdon.

Keck, Leander E. 1988. *Proclamation Commentaries: Paul and His Letters*. 2nd ed. Philadelphia: Fortress.

Ketchum, Matthew. 2013. "The Metaphysical Menagerie of 1 Corinthians 15: Resurrection, Humans, and Animals." Paper presented at the Mid-Atlantic Regional Meeting of the Society of Biblical Literature, Baltimore, March 14.

Kim, Claire Jean. 2015. *Dangerous Crossings: Race, Species, and Nature in a Multicultural Age*. Cambridge: Cambridge University Press.

Koosed, Jennifer L., ed. 2014. *The Bible and Posthumanism*. SemeiaSt 74. Atlanta: Society of Biblical Literature.

Liew, Tat-siong Benny. 2008. "Redressing Bodies in Corinth: Racial/Ethnic Politics and Religious Difference in the Context of Empire." Pages 75–97 in *What Is Asian American Biblical Hermeneutics? Reading the New Testament*. Honolulu: University of Hawai'i Press.

Luciano, Dana, and Mel Y. Chen. 2015. "Introduction: Has the Queer Ever Been Human?" *GLQ* 21:183–207.

Marchal, Joseph A. 2012. "Queer Approaches: Improper Relations with Pauline Letters." Pages 209–27 in *Studying Paul's Letters: Contemporary Perspectives and Methods*. Edited by Joseph A. Marchal. Minneapolis: Fortress.

Mbembe, Achille. 2017. *Critique of Black Reason*. Translated and introduced by Laurent Dubois. JHFCB. Durham: Duke University Press.

Moore, Stephen D. 2000. "Sex and the Single Apostle." Pages 133–72 in *God's Beauty Parlor: And Other Queer Spaces in and around the Bible*. Contraversions. Stanford: Stanford University Press.

———. 2017. *Gospel Jesuses and Other Nonhumans: Biblical Criticism Post-poststructuralism*. SemeiaSt 89. Atlanta: SBL Press.

Moore, Stephen D., and Laurel Kearns, eds. 2014. *Divinanimality: Animal Theory, Creaturely Theology*. TTC. New York: Fordham University Press.

Muñoz, José Esteban. 1999. *Disidentifications: Queers of Color and the Performance of Politics.* CSA. Minneapolis: University of Minnesota Press.

Patterson, Jane Lancaster. 2015. *Keeping the Feast: Metaphors of Sacrifice in 1 Corinthians and Philippians.* ECL 16. Atlanta: SBL Press.

Peterson, Christopher. 2013. *Bestial Traces: Race, Sexuality, Animality.* New York: Fordham University Press.

Rosner, Brian S. 1994. *Paul's Scripture and Ethics: A Study of 1 Corinthians 5–7.* AGSU 22. Leiden: Brill.

Schüssler Fiorenza, Elisabeth. 2016. *Congress of Wo/men: Religion, Gender, and Kyriarchal Power.* Cambridge: Feminist Studies in Religion Books.

Shotwell, Alexis. 2016. *Against Purity: Living Ethically in Compromised Times.* Minneapolis: University of Minnesota Press.

Skinner, Marilyn B. 1997. "Introduction: *Quod multo fit aliter in Graecia* …" Pages 3–25 in *Roman Sexualities.* Edited by Judith P. Hallett and Marilyn B. Skinner. Princeton: Princeton University Press.

Somerville, Siobhan B. 2000. *Queering the Color Line: Race and the Invention of Homosexuality in American Culture.* SerQ. Durham: Duke University Press.

Spiegel, Marjorie. 1983. *The Dreaded Comparison: Human and Animal Slavery.* New York: Mirror Books.

Stone, Ken. 2016a. "Animal Difference, Sexual Difference, and the Daughter of Jephthah." *BibInt* 24:1–16.

———. 2016b. "Animating the Bible's Animals." Pages 444–55 in *The Oxford Handbook of Biblical Narrative.* Edited by Danna Nolan Fewell. Oxford: Oxford University Press.

Stowers, Stanley K. 1994. *A Rereading of Romans: Justice, Jews, and Gentiles.* New Haven: Yale University Press.

Sullivan, Nikki. 2003. *A Critical Introduction to Queer Theory.* New York: New York University Press.

Talbert, C. H. 1987. *Reading Corinthians.* New York: Crossroad.

Townsley, Gillian. 2017. *"The Straight Mind" in Corinth: Queer Readings across 1 Corinthians 11:2–16.* SemeiaSt 88. Atlanta: SBL Press.

Ullucci, Daniel C. 2011. *The Christian Rejection of Animal Sacrifice.* Oxford: Oxford University Press.

Weheliye, Alexander G. 2014. *Habeas Viscus: Racializing Assemblages, Biopolitics, and Black Feminist Theories of the Human.* Durham: Duke University Press.

Winter, Bruce W. 2001. *After Paul Left Corinth: The Influence of Secular Ethics and Social Change.* Grand Rapids: Eerdmans.

Wire, Antoinette Clark. 1990. *The Corinthian Women Prophets: A Reconstruction through Paul's Rhetoric.* Minneapolis: Fortress.

Yates, Julian. 2017. *Of Sheep, Oranges, and Yeast: A Multispecies Impression.* Posthumanities 40. Minneapolis: University of Minnesota Press.

"A Slave to All": The Queerness of Paul's Slave Form

Tyler M. Schwaller

There is pleasure in reading history for its slippages, for the cracks through which dominant discourses might have been resisted and performed otherwise. Imagining the possibilities for oppressed subjects of the past to act creatively over and against the forces of marginalization and subjugation can likewise inspire and empower individuals and communities in the present. I was unfamiliar with queer historiographical work underscoring these sorts of affective links across time when I began my study of slavery and early Christianity, but I felt it.[1] I felt it as I wondered, following the lead of Jennifer A. Glancy (1998), whether enslaved persons would have been counted as full members of the *ekklēsiai* in Christ when they had no control over the sexual uses of their bodies, being denied the sort of self-control with which Paul was so deeply concerned. I felt the urgency of such critical analysis being animated, in no small part, by debates raging within contemporary Christian churches over the inclusion, or not, of LGBTQ+ Christians. The question of who can count authentically as Christian, then or now, is not merely an academic or historical exercise.

In turn, for Paul to call himself a "slave of Christ" (Gal 1:10; Rom 1:1; Phil 1:1) and "slave to all" (1 Cor 9:19), and especially for Christ to be figured as a slave (Phil 2:7), suddenly felt ripe with radical potentials. Whatever Paul meant, might those who were enslaved have been able to understand and recognize themselves as exemplary, as uniquely identified with and representative of Christ? We do not have firsthand accounts from enslaved persons themselves, but asking the question poses possibilities, for instance, of exposing the inadequacy of Paul's injunction to shun *porneia* and excise its perpetrators from the body of Christ (1 Cor

---

1. Now, of course, I am informed by the influential work of Dinshaw 1999, among others, especially Freeman 2010.

6:12–20).[2] If the enslaved, who could be and frequently were prostituted, could be a model for Paul—"slave of Christ" and "slave to all"—as well as for the form of Christ, then enslaved persons could stand ever ready to queer Pauline teaching on sex, to slip beyond and even to critique its repressive, myopic strictures.[3] And if paying attention to the enslaved of antiquity can show us how Paul's writing on sex two millennia ago was problematically exclusive, perhaps contemporary queers can teach something similar today. There is pleasure and power in queer historiography, in alliances forged across time with those who resist and exist beyond dominant ideals.

In this essay, I read this Pauline discourse of slavery—in particular, Paul's self-identification as a slave to all in 1 Cor 9:19—for its queerness.[4] But rather than celebrating queerness in terms of resistance, as readers might expect from my introductory paragraphs and as much queer scholarship and political organizing importantly do, here I follow Jasbir Puar (2005, 2007) in elaborating also the complicity of queerness in propping up dominant material and discursive practices. My reasons are twofold.

First, it is too easy to dismiss Paul's self-representations as a slave as merely metaphorical or rhetorical.[5] Slavery was a thoroughgoing element of Roman society, essential to social, political, and economic life. The banality of slavery in turn can make the enslaved appear mundane, their use both for physical labor and philosophical thought a rather obvious,

---

2. On the meaning of *porneia* and the shift from the morally neutral classical Greek sense of sex that does not violate a free woman's honor, generally with a prostitute or enslaved person, to a catch-all for condemned sexual behavior in Paul's writing and Second Temple Jewish texts, see Harper 2012, 2013, 86–93. On the problem of *porneia* for the enslaved, see Glancy 1998. See also Hartman's essay in this collection.

3. For a thorough treatment of the sexual use of the enslaved and its implications for understanding early Christian writings, see Glancy 2002. See also Marchal 2011; Briggs 2000.

4. I am deploying the term *queer* to function not as a descriptive category of identity but as an analytical tool aimed at investigating the terms by which any person or group is marked as standing outside prevailing ideals and values, as shamefully other. As Stephen D. Moore explains, "'queer' is a supple cipher both for what *stands over against* the normal and the natural to oppose, and thereby define, them, and what *inheres within* the normal and the natural to subvert, and indeed pervert, them—this opposition and subversion privileging, but by no means being confined to, the mercurial sphere of the sexual" (2001, 18).

5. For a survey of slavery metaphors, see Byron 2003b.

uncritical extension of elite prerogative.[6] Yet while slavery was persistent and pervasive, the rendering of certain bodies as existing so far outside elite, free ideals as to be regarded as entirely unfree is not unremarkable. Reading the material-discursive production of slavery as a form of queering can foreground how ostensibly banal discursive uses of slaves participate in the production of enslaved bodies. That is, the attention that queerness as an analytic draws to fleshly bodies reminds us that discourses of slavery are not merely metaphorical, abstracted from the materiality of enslavement, but they shape and are shaped by the bodies and lives of the enslaved. This, in turn, can be generative for reimagining how enslaved persons may have navigated the constrictive but ever-constructed (hence prone to being reworked) constraints of enslavement.[7]

Second, I propose a method of interpreting queerly that expands the scope of when and how we can read for the enslaved in, or behind, extant early Christian literature, with a particular focus here on the Pauline tradition. It is not, I argue, that we only see "real" enslaved persons when the enslaved are directly addressed, as in 1 Cor 7:21–22. Nor is it that the ability to see the enslaved as actors depends upon reading against the grain of injunctions toward obedience, implying actual enslaved resistance, as in 1 Tim 6:1–2. It is certainly important to highlight evidence of enslaved persons' capacities to resist their master's authority, and such interpretive strategies have been indispensable for undermining rhetorics of domination (e.g., Schüssler Fiorenza 2009). At the same time, there is the danger that agency and subjectivity may be reduced to one's ability or desire to resist, valuing certain modes of action and being over others.[8] By analyzing the queerness of slavery underlying Roman discourses of enslavement, and their particular reiterations within early Christian texts, in terms not only of resistance but also of complicity, I leave open the possibility for recognizing enslaved persons' roles and responses to their circumstances as multiple, multivalent, and not always directed toward freedom, which is not to discount strategies aimed toward one's

---

6. See the critique of Callahan, Horsley, and Smith 1998.

7. On the idea that, short of inflicting death—a power that must certainly be taken seriously—domination is never quite absolute, see Butler 1993.

8. See Saba Mahmood 2001 on the privileging of Western secular-liberal articulations of freedom, especially within feminist discourses. Mahmood argues for recognizing forms of agency that are not necessarily synonymous with resistance to relations of domination.

own advantage or basic survival.[9] Moreover, I work to make sense of how it is that Paul's self-identification as a slave does not eschew queerness (as if it were only imaginable that Paul would call himself a slave if doing so were indeed banal) but rather deploys the queerness of slavery toward ends that demonstrate Paul's freedom as exceptional. By reading queerly, it is possible to bring the influence of enslaved people's lives and activities on Pauline slavery discourses, and vice versa, more clearly into view.

The Queerness of Roman Slavery

I follow Puar's elaboration of a critical queer framework that "resists queerness-as-sexual-identity (or anti-identity) ... in favor of spatial, temporal, and corporeal convergences, implosions, and rearrangements" (2005, 121). Puar explains that "there is no entity, no identity to queer, rather queerness coming forth at us from all directions, screaming its defiance" (127). In this way, queerness is not a thing but a doing. It is not that the enslaved are inherently queer, as if inhabiting a fixed identity to be recognized and named as such. Instead, to echo Puar's language for the ways certain subjects are prefigured as queer, "queerness is always already installed in the project of naming" the slave, insofar as the enslaved are construed as ever potentially disruptive to the social-material reification of elite ideals (127). Enslaved persons do not simply occupy a status opposite that of free persons but are characterized fundamentally as bearing capacities to undermine the interests of free elites, socially, materially, and philosophically (Joshel and Petersen 2014, 13–17).

Aristotle named the slave in terms of lack. Slaves are "naturally" ruled over (*Pol.* 1254b21–24), since they have just enough virtue, in inverse proportion to the virtue of the master, to be obedient and diligent in their tasks (*Pol.* 1260a33–b5). For many Romans, though, slavery was not natural but a consequence of fate, of the ability for some to conquer and rule over others (Dig. 1.5.4.1; Gaius, *Inst.* 1.3.2). Enslaved persons are made, not only through physical constraints but through their discursive construction and legal categorization as akin to animals, rightfully owned and necessarily brought under control (Bradley 2000; Harrill 2013; Gardner 2011, 415–19, 423). Even upon manumission, freedpersons carried

---

9. On reading archaeological remains for the multiple roles and tactics of resistance and survival among the enslaved, see Joshel and Petersen 2014.

the *macula servitutis*, or "stain of slavery," suggesting that an element of queerness—that conspicuous otherness and lack—remained, making freedpersons always somewhat morally suspect (Mouritsen 2011, 10–35). A recurrent discursive strand from Aristotle to predominant Roman thought, then, is the idea that the enslaved are queerly human, marked as outside the bounds of ideal humanity—things, instruments, and animals. The enslaved person is not only one who is subject to the control of a master but one whose supposed natural lack of control is a threat to the ideals of the free and of kyriarchal rule.[10] There is an apparent need for vigilant surveillance and the ability to delineate status, lest the uncontrolled enslaved body become capable of infecting the communal body.[11] This is demonstrated by debates in the Roman Senate over whether enslaved persons should be marked with clearly identifiable clothing (Seneca, *Clem.* 1.24.1; see Bradley 1994, 87–89, 95–99). The idea was ultimately rejected, since it would be too great a threat if the enslaved could readily identify one another and so act together to resist and potentially overthrow the ideals of freedom constructed by elites.[12]

But this does not tell the whole story of the queerness installed in the project of naming the slave. Here again I take cues from Puar, who expounds queerness in a way that moves away from "queerness exclusively as dissenting, resistant, and alternative (all of which queerness importantly is and does) [and] underscores contingency and complicity with dominant formations" (2005, 122). We ought not to look for queerness in slavery only where the enslaved are shown especially as shameful or as resisting. In fact, we should be attentive both to social-material practices aimed at constraining the always potentially disruptive bodies of the enslaved, as well as to the ways enslaved persons themselves could negotiate the coercive terms of enslavement.[13] The Roman practice of manumission held out the promise of freedom, so there were incentives for the enslaved to do enslavement well (Hopkins 1978, 99–132). By this, I do not suggest

---

10. Conversely, effective mastery over the enslaved exemplifies the ideals of free elites. See Harrill 2006, 22–25.

11. We find a clear example in 1 Cor 6:14–20, with its particular implications for the enslaved in light of the lack of enslaved persons' control over their own bodies.

12. On resistance to slavery in the Roman world and yet the general stability of the slave system, see Bradley 1989, esp. 18–45.

13. For the idea that resistance can be measured by the constraints placed upon the enslaved, see Shaw 1998, 49.

primarily absolute obedience but also savvy maneuverings that may not have radically undermined institutional slavery but could work toward an enslaved person's own advantages or at least survival. As such, the queerness of slavery inheres in the dynamic between how enslaved bodies are prefigured as potentially disruptive and yet also as capable of being masterfully controlled, or at least appearing to be.

Under this logic, then, there is an ideal slave: one whose queerness is kept in check and whose obedience proves quite useful. By understanding queerness as not only resistant but also complicit in reiterating elite ideologies, it is possible to understand Paul's representations of his enslaved form as simultaneously productive for his argumentation and potentially disruptive to it. Such contingency highlights the text's openness to a variety of responses.

"A Slave to All"

Writing to the Corinthians, Paul declares dramatically, "I made myself a slave to all so that I might gain the greater number" (1 Cor 9:19).[14] The enslaved, ideal and otherwise, would have been well known at Corinth. After the city was razed by the Romans in 146 BCE, Julius Caesar refounded Corinth in 44 BCE, and the colony came to be populated by a significant number of freedpersons and traders (Spawforth 1996). As an important port between east and west, Corinth was a key site for trade (Millis 2010; Slane 2000; Concannon 2014, 47–74). Benjamin W. Millis (2010, 33) has argued that the city "was made attractive to a group of colonists who could make it a viable and successful commercial enterprise." Alongside a relatively elite stratum of freedpersons who were likely quite adept at negotiating economic exchanges, we should assume also that enslaved persons' integral role in trade was commonplace in Corinth (Nasrallah 2014b; Horsley 1998, 103).[15] The Corinthians would have been intimately familiar with the roles of the enslaved, especially in commerce.

This socioeconomic background is generally not taken into account when reading Paul's language of self-enslavement, with attention given

---

14. Translations are my own unless otherwise noted.

15. Paul's letter itself gives indications of the usefulness of enslaved persons for undertaking tasks on behalf of free persons, including communicating across long distances, mentioning the coming of Fortunatus and Achaius (possible slave names) to refresh Paul's spirit (1 Cor 16:17–18).

instead to philosophical tropes.[16] Discussion of 1 Cor 9 has centered largely around Paul's rhetoric and how the chapter functions in the broader outline of Paul's argumentation.[17] His assertion of freedom and apostleship, with particular concern for the rights of an apostle, comes between treatments of food sacrificed to idols (1 Cor 8) and idolatry (1 Cor 10). Some scholars have considered chapter 9 to represent a disjuncture (Weiss 1910, xxxix–xliii, 211–13; Schmithals 1973), but it is possible to view continuity in terms of rights that might be claimed, such as eating food offered to idols (ch. 8), paying for apostolic efforts (ch. 9), or the lawfulness of all things (10:23), but which should nonetheless be avoided lest weaker persons be led astray (Chow 1992, 107–12, 130–41; Marshall 1987; Mitchell 1991, 130–38; Theissen 1982, 121–43). Under this scheme, Paul is paradigmatic of restraint that serves the interests of the whole community. Paul's concern in ch. 8 that certain practices might prove an obstacle to the weak, such as eating food offered to idols, finds resolution in the way Paul sets himself up as an example of what is required to gain the weak (Martin 1990, 77–80; Mitchell 1991, 246–48).[18]

Against the backdrop of asserting his free status in the first half of 1 Cor 9 ("Am I not free? Am I not an apostle?" [9:1]), in 9:19 Paul makes the claim that he has made himself a slave to all ("For being free from all, I made myself a slave to all so that I might gain [*kerdēsō*] the greater number"). Earlier in the letter, Paul had already identified himself generally with manual (i.e., slavish) labor (e.g., 1 Cor 4:12) and here goes further by declaring his slave status.[19] Many scholars read this passage without giving particular attention to Paul's slave form, suggesting that his enslavement primarily stands as evidence of humility and love for others in service of the gospel (e.g., Thiselton 2000, 701; see also Nasrallah 2014a, 566). In contrast, Dale

---

16. Laura S. Nasrallah (2014a) foregrounds the material context of the letter and reads 1 Cor 9 in light of temple practices, including issues of pay and the use of the enslaved as ritual experts (on enslaved people as ritual experts, see Shaner 2018). See also Cavan W. Concannon's discussion of Paul's malleable self-representation, not only in terms of rhetoric and philosophy but as embedded in the social-material setting of Roman Corinth (2014, 27–46).

17. For the basic contours of scholarly debate, see Thiselton 2000, 661–63.

18. Scholars debate the structural integrity of 1 Cor 9, but Mitchell (1991, 249–50) asserts that it sensibly follows upon 1 Cor 8 as a "digress" or, in Mitchell's terms, an "exemplary argument."

19. On Paul's discussion of "strong" and "weak" as operating primarily in terms of status, see Theissen 1982, 121–43; Martin 1990, 119.

B. Martin (1990, 87–108, 127–28) foregrounds Paul's slavery language in order to argue that Paul's rhetoric, particularly his self-representation as a slave, sets forth a model of leadership opposed to the apparent "benevolent patriarchalism" of at least some Corinthian leaders—that is, their assertion of social hierarchy as essential, elites being morally superior.[20] Paul instead identifies his authority as coming from his master, Christ, and finds power from below by gaining popularity with the masses, following the Greek demagogic model of the leader as a kind of slave to all.[21]

Martin (1990, 92) identifies the model of the enslaved leader as recurring frequently enough in Greco-Roman political rhetoric to be termed a topos. The general concept holds that an effective leader assumes a servile position so as to accommodate the needs of the people (91–100). Invective against leaders who would call themselves slaves to the many often included charges that the true motives were selfish gain, but "someone could defend any populist by asserting that he acted purely in the interests of the public" (99; see also Finley 1962). Martin reads Paul as developing this concern for the common good, culminating in Paul's assertion that he makes himself a slave to all. While Paul makes this claim of self-lowering explicitly, he sets it up in the first part of 1 Cor 9 by saying that he proclaims the gospel out of necessity (*anagkē*; 9:16), not of his own will (*hekōn*) but out of constraint (*akōn*; 9:17). Martin (1990, 71–77) identifies these terms as markers of slave status: "It is clear … that in both popular understandings and moral philosophy, slavery was linked with compulsion and involuntary behavior. Words appearing in such contexts include ones used by Paul: *anagkē, akōn, hekōn*" (74). In these ways, Paul constructs himself as quintessentially enslaved and as a leader.

Martin importantly highlights the vocabulary of manual labor, especially under compulsion, in order to demonstrate the image of Paul's enslavement as central to Paul's argument. Verse 17 is key: "For if I do this [proclaim the gospel] of my own free will [*hekōn*], I have a wage (from hire) [*misthon*], but if unwillingly [*akōn*], I am entrusted with management [*oikonomian*]."[22] The force is twofold. Within elite discourses, working

---

20. See also Glad 1995 on the tradition of educators exhibiting flexibility to adapt themselves to the weak.

21. Against the idea that Paul is Christ's slave in 1 Corinthians, but instead that he positions himself as a "freewill servant of Christ," see Byron 2003a.

22. On the comparison between working for a *misthos* and being entrusted with an *oikonomia*, see Martin 1990, 80–85; see also Malherbe 1994; Byron 2003b, 245–53.

for a wage, a *misthos*, often carried unfavorable connotations; though a *misthos* would not always be compensation specifically for manual labor, working out of need to receive pay similarly signaled inferiority (George 2011, 403). Paul's claim to work under compulsion, and more precisely as a slave, hardly seems any more admirable, but the crucial distinction is that Paul says he receives not standard wages but an *oikonomia*. Effectively, Paul is set up as Christ's *oikonomos*, or household manager. Though working under the legal and social constraints of slavery, a slave-manager could command a great deal of respect, in proportion with the prestige of the slave's master.[23] Hence, as Martin argues, Paul's entrustment with an *oikonomia*, presumably that of Christ, is superior to the compensation of a wage laborer, if not monetarily then almost certainly in terms of philosophical cachet.[24] The logic goes that Paul appeals to the lower class by becoming a manual laborer. At the same time, he invites those who find manual labor distasteful, yet who may also know the topos of the enslaved leader, to follow his example of self-lowering.

Using the Enslaved to Gain the Greater Number

Martin's argument is compelling for expounding some of the text's possible resonances, but there is an even more proximate context for Paul's argumentation than philosophical rhetoric. I expand the scope to consider also the real economic advantages of using the enslaved to make gains in the Roman world. Notice Paul's repeated use of the verb *kerdainō*, which means literally "to gain or derive a profit or advantage":

> For being free from all, I made myself a slave to all so that I might gain [*kerdēsō*] the greater number. To the Jews I became as a Jew so that I might gain [*kerdēsō*] the Jews. To those under the law I became as one under the law—not being under the law myself—so that I might gain

---

23. An *oikonomos* was often but not always an enslaved person, as Martin (1990, 16–14, 74–75) acknowledges. See also Byron 2003b, 243–44.

24. Arzt-Grabner et al. (2006, 353–57) read *oikonomia* in light of *anagkē*, which finds widespread use in documentary papyri for a variety of actions that people are compelled to perform. In the papyrological record, *oikonomia* appears often as a public office for which one might be expected, or compelled, to carry out services without a wage. It may be that Paul refers to a common social practice whereby he pursues unpaid labor as a matter of fulfilling the duties of an office with which he has been entrusted, in this case by God.

[*kerdēsō*] those under the law. To those without the law I became as one without the law—not being without God's law but keeping within the law of Christ—so that I might gain [*kerdēsō*] those without the law. I became weak to the weak so that I might gain [*kerdēsō*] the weak. To all people I have become all things so that I might in all ways save some. (1 Cor 9:19–22)

Commentators have tended to generalize the sense of *kerdēsō* to mean something like "to win over" (Thiselton 2000, 701–3; Fitzmeyer 2008, 368–69; Daube 1947; see also Mitchell 1991, 243–49). But taking into account both the context of the letter and Roman practices of using enslaved persons to make gains, we ought to give a more literal reading.[25]

Considering the context of Corinth as a freedperson's colony and its significance as a site for trade, it is important to note that commercial enterprises in the Roman world relied heavily on the enslaved. Enslaved persons were valued primarily for their production, for the profits that could literally be gained through their use. In urban centers, enslaved and freedpersons often carried out business transactions on behalf of their masters, acting not as independent agents but as extensions of the master (Bodel 2011, 316; Gardner 2011, 415–16; Nasrallah 2014b, 60–61). Enslaved persons also performed skilled labor in workshops to produce a variety of wares (Kehoe 2007, 563; Bradley 1994, 58–64; Joshel 1992). The economics of slavery centered largely on the profits of slave labors with gains going primarily to slaves' owners (Jongman 2007, 595). Alan Watson (1987, 107) explains the particular efficacy of enslaved labor in trade: "What is immediately striking [about Roman regulations for economic exchanges] is that the configuration of the rules means that in commerce a slave can do much more for his master than an extraneous free person could." The reason, quite simply, is that anything that came into an enslaved person's possession, with few exceptions, would be possessed by that slave's owner, since the enslaved themselves could not

---

25. To be sure, LSJ, s.v. "κερδαίνω," includes "win" within the primary sense of gaining or deriving a profit. Still, I contend that the argument of Paul's apologia in 1 Cor 9 is chiefly articulated in terms of economic exchange, with Paul's enslavement as the central image. That Paul concludes by making clear his motivation to save or keep (*sōsō*) what is gained further underscores the materiality of the discourse. I am grateful to Quigley (2018), whose dissertation examines the pervasiveness of theoeconomic rhetoric in the letters of Paul, for calling my attention to the primary economic use of *kerdainō*.

legally hold property of any kind.[26] This is spelled out in Gaius's *Institutes*, compiled in the late second century CE and an important source for earlier Roman laws:

> Whatever children in our power and slaves in our ownership receive by *mancipatio* [formal process for transferring certain types of property, including slaves] or obtain by delivery, and whatever rights they stipulate for or acquire by any other title, they acquire for us. For a person who is in our power can have nothing of his own. (*Inst.* 2.87 [Watson])

The gain of the slave is ultimately the gain of the master.

This begs the question: Who is the master of the slave Paul? To whom would all this gain accrue? Elsewhere in his letters, Paul introduces himself a slave of Christ (Phil 1:1; Gal 1:10; Rom 1:1), but in 1 Cor 9:19, he is more broadly a slave to all. If we consider Paul as a slave of Christ on loan to the Corinthians, the concerns and argument of chapter 9 are legible within the parameters of Roman rules for making acquisitions through enslaved persons. Roman law allowed the right of a usufruct (Gaius, *Inst.* 2.91–92). A usufruct was a kind of temporary borrowing; one (in this case "all") would be granted the right both to use and to enjoy the fruits of another person's property, including the products or effects of the labor of that person's slave. During the period of usufruct, any gains made in connection with the enslaved person's own work or the affairs of the borrower would accrue to and be enjoyed by the borrower (Watson 1987, 103–8). Paul is the property of Christ, loaned to the Corinthians, and the Corinthians enjoy the fruits of Paul's slave labor. He provides an inventory of his own gains: Jews, those under the law, those outside the law, and the weak. These so-called gains are the product of a man who is "slave to all," and thus, according to the logic of Roman law regarding usufruct, they presumably accrue to the community of Christ followers at Corinth.

---

26. Enslaved persons could, however, maintain a *peculium*, or assets available for them to manage, though the *peculium* was technically still under the power of the slaveholder. This may have proved especially useful for commerce, since the master's liability could be limited only to *peculium* funds whenever it was made clear that transactions were based on the *peculium*. On the benefits of using the *peculium* in commerce, and so also the usefulness of employing the enslaved to carry out economic transactions, see Kirschenbaum 1987, 31–88; de Ligt 2007. Evidence for this practice, however, is scant and debated; see esp. Andreau 2004.

A free person, contrary to a slave, could claim the gains for himself. Paul is emphatic that he *could* claim the privileges of freedom, but he does not do so in order to "gain the greater number." He becomes a slave to fulfill the logic that his labor profits not only Christ but the Corinthians. Paul is on the defensive in 1 Cor 9, offering an apologia for his freedom and apostleship. He does so by defending his value to the Corinthians on the basis of his self-enslavement. Against apparent contestation over his authority, Paul uses the efficacious role of the enslaved person in trade— something quite familiar to the Corinthians—to claim that, of all who might call themselves apostles, he is most advantageous to the Corinthians because he is slave to all.

Paul's slave form here is one that seems to eschew queerness, not exemplify it. This slave Paul does not seem concerned that he might be confused with someone lacking self-control. He is the idealized slave. Such a representation, though, is not novel. Literary depictions of the enslaved sometimes functioned to demonstrate elements of self-mastery. In the *Life of Aesop*, whose fables go back as far as the fifth century BCE, with extant versions dated to around the turn of the common era, the enslaved Aesop is shown to be extraordinarily wise.[27] Aesop typifies a literary pairing of enslaved person and philosopher (Fitzgerald 2000, 26–27). He frustrates his owner, Xanthos, with cunning misunderstandings of instructions. When Xanthos finally commands Aesop to do nothing more or less than precisely what he is told, Aesop responds in the most literal ways possible, to comic, and pointed, effect. Asked to "cook lentil" for a dinner party, Aesop prepares just a single lentil. His cleverness demonstrates not only that the enslaved are not automatons, but a slaveholder should not even desire such, since the enslaved person's initiative is necessary for order to be maintained (27).

Aesop's ingenuity serves to teach about proper mastery (Hopkins 1993; Daly 1961, 53–54; Harrill 2006, 22). In an ironic twist, the one figured as requiring control shows how a master must manage potential chaos through proper understanding of human relationships, something the enslaved person is equipped to do well. The wise master responds deftly to dynamic circumstances, recognizing that short of guaranteeing absolute obedience, mastery over others begins with self-mastery.

---

27. On the multiple versions of fables about Aesop, dating, and comparison with the gospels, see Wills 1997, 23–50.

The second-century physician Galen likewise makes this case, also in relationship to the enslaved but from the reverse perspective. In his treatise *The Diagnosis and Cure of the Soul's Passions*, Galen cautions against responding to an enslaved person's perturbing actions, or inaction, with fits of rage, urging that sufficient time be taken to hold the passions in check (Galen, *Aff. dig.* 4 [Harkins 1963, 37–41]). A master's response should be well reasoned rather than impulsive. While such discourses have as their primary concern the ways free men are philosophically self-controlled, they depend upon what the enslaved do or do not do. The discursively inscribed slave body is not wholly descriptive of the enslaved in the social-material world, but it is also not abstracted from real anxieties over the dynamic, contingent relations between enslaved and free(d)persons.

To emphasize the queerness of slavery is to keep in mind the ever-present potential for disruptions to the ideal. Queerness threatens to spill past the edges of Paul's carefully circumscribed rhetoric. Paul, like Aesop, is a resourceful slave who knows how to navigate his circumstances to his gain, and both Paul and Aesop reflect something of the responsibilities entrusted to the enslaved in the world.[28] At the same time, there is danger that their activities as enslaved persons will provoke disorderly, undesirable responses. What if those Corinthians who receive Paul's letter, or who know Paul, do not understand Paul's slave form to perform the relatively respectable duties of the managerial slave he projects himself to be? After all, slave-managers would not have been the only enslaved persons traversing the streets of Corinth. Prostitutes were often enslaved persons pimped out by their owners, and we know from 1 Cor 6 that Paul is concerned over prostitution at Corinth (Glancy 1998). Paul's rhetoric in 1 Cor 9 puts on display a desirable, even exceptional slave body. But an enslaved person could not choose her or his own work (Joshel 1992). What if Paul's enslaved body were put to different kinds of uses? What effect might it have had to receive these words among myriad forms of enslaved bodies, both living bodies and those represented in art and literature?[29]

---

28. Paul is like Aesop in another respect: Aesop is described as having a hideous physical form, something against which Paul also contends and that he works to his best advantage in 2 Corinthians, as discussed below.

29. Here I follow the example of David L. Balch (2003). Balch reads Paul's discussions of suffering—Christ's and his own—alongside artistic depictions of scenes of suf-

The Queerness of Paul's Slave Form

Paul might have been careful to control his rhetoric, but he could not constrain the responses to it. He puts himself forward as an ideal slave, one capable of accruing great gains to the benefit of all, over and against those who would work for a wage. In this way, Paul shows forth an exceptional queerness.[30] Though he labors, the perfect obedience exhibited in his well-trained, malleable body brings successes untainted by the perversion of freedom associated with the need to be paid. And yet Paul's performance as a slave to all is convincing to the extent that he cannot control how his enslaved form is both perceived and put to use.[31] The queerness of slavery cannot be perfectly contained, and keeping in mind its disruptive potential helps to make sense of the way Paul re-presents his body in 2 Corinthians.

From 2 Corinthians, it seems, that at least some in Corinth mocked Paul for slavishness signaled by his corporeal vulnerabilities. Paul moves from defending his apostleship on the basis of his value as a slave to all (1 Cor 9) to defending himself against the invective of opponents by boasting, ironically, of his apparently slavish weakness (2 Cor 10–13). In a long list of the hardships he has endured (2 Cor 11:23–28), it is particularly striking that Paul begins by recounting his toil and suffering, including countless blows, lashings, and beatings by rod (11:23–25). The remainder of Paul's catalogue of adversity—highlighting danger in travel, hunger, and immense daily pressures (11:25–28)—might well have been read as showcasing heroic endurance (Harvey 1996, 99). Yet as Glancy (2004) argues, Paul's whipped body would likely have been read as servile. In the context of the first-century CE Roman world, battle wounds signified manly persistence and achievement (Leigh 1995), but scars on one's back from repeated lashings heralded a whippable body, which was a dishonorable body (Glancy 2004, 107–13). While enslaved persons were

---

fering in Greek and Roman myth, asking what might have been the effects of reading Paul's words in spaces that may have been decorated with such images.

30. Puar (2007, esp. 2–11, 48–49) underscores the complicity of queerness with dominant ideologies by arguing that queer narratives in the United States have functioned at times in the service of nationalism, what she terms homonationalism: "That is, queerness is proffered as a sexually exceptional form of American national sexuality through a rhetoric of sexual modernization that is simultaneously able to castigate the other as homophobic *and* perverse, and construct the imperialist center as 'tolerant' but sexually, racially, and gendered normal" (2005, 122).

31. On the dynamics of controlling enslaved bodies, see Bradley 1984.

not the only ones to experience corporal punishment, the violability of one's body was a distinctly slavish quality, certainly unbefitting a free man (Bauman 1996).

As Albert J. Harrill (2006, 37–44) has shown, making physiognomic distinctions between enslaved and free bodies was common in writings from Aristotle through the Roman imperial period. Associating moral characteristics with the form and appearance of particular bodies served to reinforce social hierarchies, especially the difference between slave and free (Mouritsen 2011, 10–35). As such, invective against opponents frequently included charges of failing to live up to the standards of idealized masculinity (i.e., free, self-controlled, inviolable, and authoritative; see Gleason 1995). Harrill argues that this sort of invective is deployed against Paul by competing teachers, facetiously dubbed "superapostles" by Paul, who mock his dishonorable body in order to undermine his standing among the Corinthians. Paul's weaknesses signal his lack of capacity to exercise authority over others (*auctoritas*). Instead of working to overturn this representation outright, Paul follows a Cynic-Socratic tradition of rejecting such physiognomic logic by underscoring the value of humility (Harrill 2006, 53–54). In addition, Harrill follows Abraham Malherbe (1983) in reading Paul's valorization of his beaten body as akin to Homer's Odysseus flagellating himself and appearing like a slave to gain entry into Troy (*Od.* 4.240–250). In this way, "Paul defends himself by taking the tag of the slave *schēma* that connects his struggle to that of Odysseus, a famous counterexample of the danger that confidence in outward appearance brings to strongholds under siege" (Harrill 2006, 56).

Harrill makes a compelling case for reading Paul's self-representation in 2 Cor 10–13 as drawing upon and participating in competing philosophical discourses over the significations of (enslaved and free male) bodies. In terms of his beaten body, it is plausible that Paul had Odysseus in mind as a model for undermining the reliability of physiognomic assumptions.[32] Even so, it not entirely necessary to turn to philosophical and literary works to consider the force of Paul's argumentation in its social-material context. Whatever rhetorical tactics Paul had in mind, the Corinthians would not have needed to be familiar with physiognomic handbooks or the tale of Odysseus's self-flagellation to read the scars on

---

32. Yet Glancy (2004, 129, n. 113) makes the key point that Paul does not flagellate himself as Odysseus does. Still, Harrill (2006, 55–56) contends that this is in line with the ways Paul regularly overlooks and changes details of source material.

a person's back. Within an *ekklēsia* that included both enslaved persons and masters and a city accustomed to the buying and selling of humans as chattel, dishonorable associations with the marks of whips and rods would have been poignant (Glancy 2004, 134).

For Paul to boast of his beatings, as Glancy argues, is not to assert valor but to identify with Christ. Paul owns up to the beatings his body has taken and imbues them with deeper meaning. As he has said to the Corinthians, he is "always carrying in the body the mortification/death (*nekrōsis*) of Jesus" (2 Cor 4:10).[33] Paul's response to the criticisms of the superapostles is thus both strategic and theological (Glancy 2004, 135). Whether or not Paul has Odysseus in mind when working to undercut the physiognomic invective of the superapostles, there is a more obvious and relevant connection to make. The scars on Paul's body re-present a narrative presumably held in common by the whole *ekklēsia*, namely, the passion of Christ, which itself has slavish associations (Phil 2:6–7).

In the comparison between Paul's self-representation as slave to all in 1 Cor 9 and his beaten body in 2 Cor 11, we can see something of the queerness inscribed in slavery—both its potentially disruptive effects as well as its repetition of slaveholding ideologies. As a slave to all, Paul shows himself to be the most respectable sort of slave, one who performs significant functions on behalf of a prominent patron, or patrons, and does so thoughtfully and effectively.[34] He is even exemplary, modeling service that is to the advantage of all. The queerness of slavery—that is, that which is conceptualized as outside the prevailing ideals of the free elite—is managed in such a way as to "gain the greater number," which works to shore up Paul's own social standing. As Puar observes, complicity with dominant material-discursive arrangements can be constitutive of queerness, not just resistance.

At the same time, to insist upon queerness as constitutive of slavery, even where it seems most contained or even effaced, is to insist upon the potential for queer disruptions, for the perversion of the ideal. This has historiographical implications, particularly toward recognizing that discourses of slavery, inasmuch as they perpetuate the queerness of slavery, are never quite stable. That is, what Paul intends by invoking slavery

---

33. Bearing marks (*stigmata*) of Christ is a recurring theme for Paul (Glancy 2004, 131–34).

34. On the link between the power of the enslaved and that of the owner, see Martin 1990, 56–57.

discourses is too narrow a scope to account for the meaning, implications, and provocations of his writing. We must also consider how such discourses interface with the social-material circumstances of enslavement, since Paul both draws upon and engages a world in which there are enslaved persons and masters.

No matter how carefully circumscribed the conception of slavery and the enslaved body, as with Paul's self-representation as a dutiful slave to all, the slave form carries with it the queerness installed in the naming and constraining of the enslaved. This is evident in the dramatic shift from Paul's self-representation as a slave in 1 Cor 9 to the superapostles' mocking of his weak, slavish body in 2 Cor 10–12. Not only is Paul unable to control the response to his claims to apostleship, as if any author could ever guarantee singular interpretation, but the queerness of his slave form has spilled into the open, its monstrous marks of violability on full display. Granted, to deride Paul's whipped and beaten body would not necessarily have depended upon him first calling himself a slave, only then opening himself up to this sort of invective. But the uneven deliberation over the value, or not, of Paul's body and work as related to his apostleship and authority is tied up with the discursivity and materiality of enslavement.[35] What is said about slaves and how slaves' bodies are (re)presented, regulated, and active in the world come to bear on Paul—slave of Christ, slave to all, and beaten apostle.

Even so, some might be inclined to say that Paul empties slavery of any queerness by deploying slavery rhetorically and philosophically, abstracted from the lives of those who are enslaved in the world, from those who are marked as queer. Indeed, Harrill (2006, 37; see also Gleason 1995, xxviii) makes such a claim regarding "the Roman physiognomic polarity of free and slave," proposing that it "has little to do with actual slaves, but only between free men and slavish free men.... In other words, the reference is *literary*, not social, description." While this is an important caveat insofar as Paul's perspective should not stand as sufficiently describing the lives of the enslaved, it is also insufficient insofar as it dislodges discourses of slavery from the social-material realities of enslavement. The machinations of enslavement are simultaneously discursive and material.[36] The

---

35. This is intrinsically connected with the ways that discourses of power in 1 Corinthians more broadly are played out on and through bodies (Castelli 1991).

36. My understanding of the mutual constitution of discourse and materiality is significantly informed by Barad 2003.

bodies and lives of the enslaved are regulated in accord with slaveholding ideologies made manifest through particular material arrangements
and practices (Joshel and Petersen 2014).[37] In turn, enslaved persons act,
often in dynamic relation to free(d)persons, in ways that may provoke a
response, such that the social-material enactments of the enslaved inform
and shape discourses of slavery.[38]

Said more simply, without enslaved persons in the world, whose bodies
are acted upon but who also act, there can be no legible discourses of slavery.[39] For Paul to call himself a slave of all does not make sense, especially
in a way modeled on the role of the enslaved in accruing gains for their
masters, if there are no enslaved persons who do this work. Philosophical
debates over physiognomy, as well as rhetorical invective in physiognomic
terms, may take distinctions between free men as their primary aim, but
they are meaningful insofar as discursive delineations between slave and
free have real effects in the world. When the superapostles impugn Paul's
slavish body, this is not abstracted from the repetitive lashings that regularly mark certain bodies as ever suspect and dishonorable.

Reading Paul Queerly

To underscore the queerness of enslavement when reading ancient slavery discourses is to insist that representations of the enslaved and slavery
should not be disentangled from the bodies and lives discursively and
materially figured as queer, as nonideal. Paul might not literally have
been enslaved nor interested in describing the lives of the enslaved. Yet
in identifying as a slave and defending his slavish body, he re-presented

---

37. More generally, on the ways discourses shape social-material practice, which
in turn constrains people's lives to varying degrees, see Rivera 2014.

38. On the potentials for interpellations to be resisted, see Butler 1997, esp. 10–16.
The responses provoked belie elite fantasies of absolute control, evincing the contin-
gencies inhering in dynamic human relations.

39. One might argue that language of slavery can still be meaningful today even
where there is no chattel slavery (though we ought to interrogate the tactics of making
such language "relevant," such as by substituting "servant" for "slave," as often happens
in English translations of the Bible). Yet especially in the United States, with its own
history of enslavement, we see how ideologies of slavery are not relegated to the past
but persist in new forms, continuing to circumscribe and mark certain bodies as ever
vulnerable to constraint, abuse, and exploitation, as poignantly underscored by Kimberly Juanita Brown (2015).

material-discursive practices that shaped and were shaped by dynamic, contingent relations between enslaved and free(d)persons in the social-material world. Likewise, these discourses were informed by the presence and activities of the enslaved, whose so-conceived potential to undermine elite ideals could never be wholly restrained, always leaving open possibilities for the disruption of slaveholding logics.

Paul may have set himself up as an exemplar, but he did so by imitating enslaved and freedpersons. Even as his rhetoric evinces a level of unease over the perception of his labors, neither Paul's hedging nor the elite discourses that degrade manual work stand as fully representative. Enslaved and freedpersons themselves regularly took a different view of their labors (Martin 1990, 124). This is best evidenced by monuments and inscriptions of freedpersons. While distinct from the enslaved in terms of status, freedpersons, as formerly enslaved, demonstrated that the skills cultivated and put to use in both slavery and freedom could be a source of pride (Petersen 2006, 114–17; George 2011). In some places, the disproportionately high representation of freedpersons in epigraphic and visual evidence might be attributed to the desire to avow status, and it is not insignificant that this was often done by identifying with work, not concealing it (Mouritsen 2011, 127–28; Petersen 2006, 114). Thus even though "Paul uses his manual labor as an example in chapter 9 of his social self-lowering," recognizing this as fundamentally degrading is not the only interpretive option (Martin 1990, 123). Paul may have perpetuated discourses that functioned to shore up the mastery of free persons, but his exploitation of the slave form can also be read differently through a framework rooted in the value, and perhaps values, of the enslaved and freed.

Paul's writing and logic is embedded in a particular slavish corporal idiom bound up with material-discursive practices of enslavement.[40] Emphasizing also the queerness of slavery opens up consideration of how Paul's complicity with the dominant ideology of slaveholding simultaneously poses potential for disruptions as his words reverberate through the social-material world. Just as the discursive construction of slaves as "rightly" brought under control could not ensure the absolute control of the enslaved in the social-material world (see, e.g., Joshel and Petersen 2014, 140–42), so, too, the rhetorical invocation of the slave form would

---

40. On this point, I take inspiration from Glancy's (1998, 2002, 2004) insistence on the corporeality of slavery discourse.

be subject to contingency and unpredictability in its reception and treatment. Take, for instance, the problem raised in the introduction to this essay, which follows Glancy's incisive analysis. Paul's instruction in 1 Cor 6:18 to shun or, more literally from the Greek (*pheugete*), to flee *porneia* would not have been an option for the enslaved, who could be compelled into sexual service for their owners or through prostitution (Glancy 1998). Paul appears to have been perfectly content exploiting the queerness of the slave form when it worked to demonstrate his exceptional apostleship, but he was not concerned about the sexual exploitation of the enslaved, at least not in his extant writing. Yet by shining the spotlight on the slave form, its "queerness coming forth at us from all directions" (Puar 2005, 127), it is possible that we begin to imagine enslaved persons as queering Paul's injunctions against *porneia*. The enslaved may well have filled the gap of Paul's apparent disregard with embodied responses that took his words otherwise, confronting more directly the exploitative social-sexual arrangements forced upon the enslaved. We can imagine enslaved persons literally fleeing *porneia*.

The discourses of Roman jurists do present as legitimate the option for enslaved persons to flee (*fugio* in Latin) from their owners in cases of extreme abuse, at least for a time, including to seek out another free(d) person to intercede on her or his behalf (e.g., Dig. 21.1.17). Did enslaved persons, and even free(d)persons who owned or interacted with the enslaved, hear Paul's injunction to flee *porneia* as highlighting the sexual use of the enslaved as a form of egregious cruelty from which an enslaved person could rightly flee? We do not have sufficient evidence to answer affirmatively.[41] But we can imagine how Paul's words rubbed up against the social-material realities of slavery in ways that might not just have confirmed their controlling practices but could also have generated responses that disrupted and reshaped enslavement, even subtly so.[42]

---

41. There are some later negative examples, like the use of an enslaved woman as a sexual stand-in for her newly abstinent mistress in the Acts of Andrew, but evidence from early Christian sources for the everyday lives of the enslaved in general is too scant to make broad claims.

42. For example, enslaved persons did, in fact, run away from their masters for any number of reasons. To do so successfully would have required concealing the scars on the body, since such physical marks were often used as the basis for identification in public notices about runaway slaves (Fuhrmann 2012, 21–43). To conceal and re-present the body to the advantage of an escaped slave would certainly have been precarious, subject to capture and punishment in a way not represented by Paul. Still,

I am not arguing that the queerness of slavery means disruptions and alternative responses were infinitely possible. Instead, I insist upon viewing the tension between resistance and complicity as intrinsic to slavery discourses. Paul's slave form is legible because of the work enslaved persons do, materially and discursively, to make gains, fulfill obligations, and reflect something of mastery. Insofar as the proper performance of slavery conforms to and confirms slaveholding ideology, it is not such a surprise for Paul to embrace the role of the slave as particularly useful. At the same time, the queerness of the enslaved, imputed to justify control and constraint, threatens always to undermine that control. Just as masters could not guarantee that enslaved persons would act according to the masters' desires, we should not assume that Paul's deployment of the figure of the enslaved always accomplished his intentions. To read Paul's language and rhetoric as embedded in and not abstracted from the social-material world of Roman slavery shifts attention beyond Paul's aims toward the presence and influence of the enslaved.

Works Cited

Andreau, Jean. 2004. "Les esclaves 'hommes d'affaires' et la gestion des ateliers et commerces." Pages 111–26 in *Mentalités et choix économique des Romains*. Edited by J. Andreau, J. France, and S. Pittia. Pessac: Ausonius.

Arzt-Grabner, Peter, Ruth Elisabeth Kritzer, Amfilochios Papathomas, and Franz Winter. 2006. *1. Korinther*. PKNT 2. Göttingen: Vandenhoeck & Ruprecht.

Balch, David L. 2003. "Paul's Portrait of Christ Crucified (Gal. 3:1) in Light of Paintings and Sculptures of Suffering and Death in Pompeiian and Roman Houses." Pages 84–108 in *Early Christian Families in Context: An Interdisciplinary Dialogue*. Edited by David L. Balch and Carolyn Osiek. Grand Rapids: Eerdmans.

Barad, Karen. 2003. "Posthumanist Performativity: Toward an Understanding of How Matter Comes to Matter." *Signs* 28:801–31.

Paul's anxieties over the presentation of his body might remind us of the slippages inherent in the performativity of status. There are different stakes and limitations for the enslaved in comparison with Paul, but Paul's rhetoric, just as much as the actions of enslaved persons, operates within the material-discursive practices of enslavement and status-making, which are dynamic and contingent.

Bauman, Richard A. 1996. *Crime and Punishment in Ancient Rome*. London: Routledge.

Bodel, John. 2011. "Slave Labour and Roman Society." Pages 311–36 in *The Ancient Mediterranean World*. Vol. 1 of *The Cambridge World History of Slavery*. Edited by Keith Bradley, Paul Cartledge, David Eltis, and Stanley L. Engerman. Cambridge: Cambridge University Press.

Bradley, Keith. 1984. *Slaves and Masters in the Roman Empire: A Study in Social Control*. Bruxelles: Latomus.

———. 1989. *Slavery and Rebellion in the Roman World, 140 B.C.–70 B.C.* Bloomington: Indiana University Press.

———. 1994. *Slavery and Society at Rome*. Cambridge: Cambridge University Press.

———. 2000. "Animalizing the Slave: The Truth of Fiction." *JRS* 90:110–25.

Briggs, Sheila. 2000. "Paul on Bondage and Freedom in Imperial Roman Society." Pages 110–23 in *Paul and Politics: Ekklesia, Israel, Imperium, Interpretation: Essays in Honor of Krister Stendahl*. Edited by Richard A. Horsley. Harrisburg, PA: Trinity.

Brown, Kimberly Juanita. 2015. *The Repeating Body: Slavery's Visual Resonance in the Contemporary*. Durham: Duke University Press.

Butler, Judith. 1993. *Bodies That Matter: On the Discursive Limits of "Sex."* New York: Routledge.

———. 1997. *Excitable Speech: A Politics of the Performative*. New York: Routledge.

Byron, John. 2003a. "Slave of Christ or Willing Servant? Paul's Self-Description in 1 Corinthians 4:1–2 and 9:16–18." *Neot* 37:179–98.

———. 2003b. *Slavery Metaphors in Early Judaism and Pauline Christianity: A Traditio-Historical and Exegetical Examination*. WUNT 2/262. Tübingen: Mohr Siebeck.

Callahan, Allen Dwight, Richard A. Horsley, and Abraham Smith. 1998. "Introduction: The Slavery of New Testament Studies." *Semeia* 83–84:1–15.

Castelli, Elizabeth A. 1991. "Interpretations of Power in 1 Corinthians." *Semeia* 54:197–222.

Chow, John K. 1992. *Patronage and Power: A Study of Social Networks in Corinth*. JSNTSup 75. Sheffield: JSOT Press.

Concannon, Cavan W. 2014. *"When You Were Gentiles": Specters of Ethnicity in Roman Corinth and Paul's Corinthian Correspondence*. Syn. New Haven: Yale University Press.

Daly, Lloyd W. 1961. *Aesop without Morals: The Famous Fables, and a Life of Aesop*. New York: Thomas Yoseloff.

Daube, David. 1947. "χερδαίνω as a Missionary Term." *HTR* 40:109–20.

Dinshaw, Carolyn. 1999. *Getting Medieval: Sexualities and Communities, Pre- and Postmodern*. SerQ. Durham: Duke University Press.

Finley, Moses I. 1962. "Athenian Demagogues." *PP* 21:3–24.

Fitzgerald, William. 2000. *Slavery and the Roman Literary Imagination*. Cambridge: Cambridge University Press.

Fitzmeyer, Joseph A. 2008. *First Corinthians*. AB 32. New Haven: Yale University Press.

Freeman, Elizabeth. 2010. *Time Binds: Queer Temporalities, Queer Histories*. PM. Durham: Duke University Press.

Fuhrmann, Christopher J. 2012. *Policing the Roman Empire: Soldiers, Administrations, and Public Order*. Oxford: Oxford University Press.

Gardner, Jane F. 2011. "Slavery and Roman Law." Pages 414–37 in *The Ancient Mediterranean World*. Vol. 1 of *The Cambridge World History of Slavery*. Edited by Keith Bradley, Paul Cartledge, David Eltis, and Stanley L. Engerman. Cambridge: Cambridge University Press.

George, Michele. 2011. "Slavery and Roman Material Culture." Pages 385–413 in *The Ancient Mediterranean World*. Vol. 1 of *The Cambridge World History of Slavery*. Edited by Keith Bradley, Paul Cartledge, David Eltis, and Stanley L. Engerman. Cambridge: Cambridge University Press.

Glad, Clarence E. 1995. *Paul and Philodemus: Adaptability in Epicurean and Early Christian Psychagogy*. NovTSup 81. Leiden: Brill.

Glancy, Jennifer A. 1998. "Obstacles to Slaves' Participation in the Corinthian Church." *JBL* 117:481–501.

———. 2002. *Slavery in Early Christianity*. Oxford: Oxford University Press.

———. 2004. "Boasting of Beatings (2 Corinthians 11:23–25)." *JBL* 123:99–135.

Gleason, Maud W. 1995. *Making Men: Sophists and Self-Representation in Ancient Rome*. Princeton: Princeton University Press.

Harkins, Paul W., trans. 1963. *Galen: On the Passions and Errors of the Soul*. Columbus: Ohio State University Press.

Harper, Kyle. 2012. "*Porneia:* The Making of a Christian Sexual Norm." *JBL* 131:363–83.

———. 2013. *From Shame to Sin: The Christian Transformation of Sexual Morality in Late Antiquity*. Cambridge: Harvard University Press.

Harrill, J. Albert. 2006. *Slaves in the New Testament: Literary, Social, and Moral Dimensions.* Minneapolis: Fortress.

———. 2013. "Slavery and Inhumanity: Keith Bradley's Legacy on Slavery in New Testament Studies." *BibInt* 21:506–14.

Harvey, Anthony E. 1996. *Renewal through Suffering: A Study of 2 Corinthians.* SNTW. Edinburgh: T&T Clark.

Hopkins, Keith. 1978. *Conquerors and Slaves.* New York: Cambridge University Press.

———. 1993. "Novel Evidence for Roman Slavery." *PP* 138:3–27.

Horsley, Richard A. 1998. *1 Corinthians.* ANTC. Nashville: Abingdon.

Jongman, Willem M. 2007. "The Early Roman Empire: Consumption." Pages 592–618 in *The Cambridge Economic History of the Greco-Roman World.* Edited by Walter Scheidel, Ian Morris, and Richard P. Saller. Cambridge: Cambridge University Press.

Joshel, Sandra R. 1992. *Work, Identity, and Legal Status at Rome: A Study of the Occupational Inscriptions.* Norman: University of Oklahoma Press.

Joshel, Sandra R., and Lauren Hackworth Petersen. 2014. *The Material Life of Roman Slaves.* Cambridge: Cambridge University Press.

Kehoe, Dennis P. 2007. "The Early Roman Empire: Production." Pages 541–69 in *The Cambridge Economic History of the Greco-Roman World.* Edited by Walter Scheidel, Ian Morris, and Richard P. Saller. Cambridge: Cambridge University Press.

Kirschenbaum, Aaron. 1987. *Sons, Slaves, and Freedmen in Roman Commerce.* Washington, DC: Catholic University of America Press.

Leigh, Matthew. 1995. "Wounding and Popular Rhetoric at Rome." *BICS* 40:195–215.

Ligt, Luuk de. 2007. "Roman Law and the Roman Economy: Three Case Studies." *Lat* 66:10–25.

Mahmood, Saba. 2001. "Feminist Theory, Embodiment, and the Docile Agent: Some Reflections on the Egyptian Islamic Revival." *CultAnth* 16:202–36.

Malherbe, Abraham J. 1983. "Antisthenes and Odysseus, and Paul at War." *HTR* 76:143–73.

———. 1994. "Determinism and Free Will: The Argument of 1 Corinthians 8 and 9." Pages 231–55 in *Paul in His Hellenistic Context.* Edited by Troels Enberg-Pedersen. London: T&T Clark.

Marchal, Joseph A. 2011. "The Usefulness of an Onesimus: The Sexual Use of Slaves and Paul's Letter to Philemon." *JBL* 130:749–70.

Marshall, Peter. 1987. *Enmity in Corinth: Social Conventions in Paul's Relation with the Corinthians.* WUNT 2/23. Tübingen: Mohr.

Martin, Dale B. 1990. *Slavery as Salvation: The Metaphor of Slavery in Pauline Christianity.* New Haven: Yale University Press.

Millis, Benjamin W. 2010. "The Social and Ethnic Origins of the Colonists in Early Roman Corinth." Pages 13–35 in *Corinth in Context: Comparative Studies on Religion and Society.* Edited by Steven J. Friesen, Daniel N. Schowalter, and James C. Walters. Leiden: Brill.

Mitchell, Margaret M. 1991. *Paul and the Rhetoric of Reconciliation: An Exegetical Investigation of the Language and Composition of 1 Corinthians.* HUT 28. Louisville: Westminster John Knox.

Moore, Stephen D. 2001. *God's Beauty Parlor: And Other Queer Spaces in and around the Bible.* Contraversions. Stanford: Stanford University Press.

Mouritsen, Henrik. 2011. *The Freedman in the Roman World.* Cambridge: Cambridge University Press.

Nasrallah, Laura S. 2014a. "1 Corinthians." Pages 427–72 in *Fortress Commentary on the Bible: The New Testament.* Edited by Margaret Aymer, Cynthia Briggs Kittredge, and David A. Sánchez. Minneapolis: Fortress.

———. 2014b. "'You Were Bought with a Price': Freedpersons and Things in 1 Corinthians." Pages 54–73 in *Corinth in Contrast: Studies in Inequality.* Edited by Steven J. Friesen, Sarah A. James, and Daniel N. Showalter. Leiden: Brill.

Petersen, Lauren Hackworth. 2006. *The Freedman in Roman Art and Art History.* Cambridge: Cambridge University Press.

Puar, Jasbir K. 2005. "Queer Times, Queer Assemblages." *SocT* 23:121–39.

———. 2007. *Terrorist Assemblages: Homonationalism in Queer Times.* NW. Durham: Duke University Press.

Quigley, Jennifer A. 2018. "Divine Accounting: Theo-economic Rhetoric in the Letter to the Philippians." Th.D. diss., Harvard University.

Rivera, Mayra Rivera. 2014. "A Labyrinth of Incarnations: The Social Materiality of Bodies." *JESWTR* 22:187–98.

Schmithals, Walter. 1973. "Die Korintherbriefe als Briefsammlung." *ZNW* 64:263–88.

Schüssler Fiorenza, Elisabeth. 2009. "Slave Wo/men and Freedom: Some Methodological Reflections." Pages 123–46 in *Postcolonial Interventions: Essays in Honor of R. S. Sugirtharajah.* Edited by Tat-siong Benny Liew. Sheffield: Sheffield Phoenix Press.

Shaner, Katherine A. 2018. *Enslaved Leadership in Early Christianity.* New York: Oxford University Press.

Shaw, Brent D. 1998. "'A Wolf by the Ears': M. I. Finley's *Ancient Slavery and Modern Ideology* in Historical Context." Pages 3–74 in *Ancient Slavery and Modern Ideology.* By Moses I. Finley. Edited by Brent D. Shaw. Exp. ed. Princeton: Markus Wiener.

Slane, Kathleen Warner. 2000. "East-West Trade in Fine Wares and Commodities: The View from Corinth." *RCRFA* 36:299–312.

Spawforth, Antony. 1996. "Roman Corinth: The Formation of a Colonial Elite." Pages 167–82 in *Roman Onomastics in the Greek East: Social and Political Aspects: Proceedings of the International Colloquium Organized by the Finnish Institute and the Centre for Greek and Roman Antiquity, Athens, 7–9 September 1993.* Edited by A. D. Rizakis. Athens: Kentron Hellēnikēs kai Rōmaikēs Archaiotētos, Ethnikon Hidryma Ereunōn.

Theissen, Gerd. 1982. *The Social Setting of Pauline Christianity.* Edited and translated by John H. Schütz. Philadelphia: Fortress.

Thiselton, Anthony C. 2000. *The First Epistle to the Corinthians: A Commentary on the Greek Text.* NIGTC. Grand Rapids: Eerdmans.

Watson, Alan. 1987. *Roman Slave Law.* Baltimore: Johns Hopkins University Press.

Weiss, Johannes. 1910. *Der erste Korintherbrief.* Göttingen: Vandenhoeck & Ruprecht.

Wills, Lawrence M. 1997. *The Quest of the Historical Gospel: Mark, John and the Origins of the Gospel Genre.* London: Routledge.

Dionysus, Disidentifications, and Wandering Pauline Epiphanies

Timothy Luckritz Marquis

José Esteban Muñoz prefaces his book, *Disidentifications: Queers of Color and the Performance of Politics*, with a discussion of the work of Jack Smith, multimedia artist and progenitor of American performance art, whose mission was to "destabilize the world of 'pasty normals' and help us imagine another time and place."[1] One of Smith's film projects, titled *Normal Love* (1963), cycles characters of ambiguous gender and sexuality through a semi-plotless sequence—characters including a drag mermaid, a werewolf, a diaphanous Adam-and-Eve-like couple frolicking on a pastoral swing set, all ending with a mermaid-themed, Bacchic dance party campily massacred by a shrouded figure wielding a child's water gun.[2] In these figures, Smith appropriates and adapts a number of cinematic and cultural tropes to create his vision of normal love.

At the beginning of the film, the mermaid character erects a votive altar to Dominican B-movie star Maria Montez and worships the diva; the actor playing the mermaid is credited as Mario Montez. In so figuring Maria Montez, Smith, a queer white man, envisages his queer imagescape with appeal to a Latina star whose movies often played upon the orientalizing fascination of white audiences. It is as if Smith, though in many ways different from Maria Montez, could see his situation in hers. Maria Montez's ethnic difference created a productive tension with the normative

My thanks to the editor of this volume and the SBL Press editors for their helpful and generous comments.

1. 1999, ix. The following relies on the discussion in the preface to Muñoz 1999 and on information in Wyma 2012. *Pasty normal* is Smith's phrase.

2. A version of the film project can be found online at http://www.ubu.com/film/smith-jack_normal.html.

aesthetic paradigms into which she was inserted. Similarly, Smith's films performed his specific location in relation to New York, the United States, the entertainment industry, and normative understandings of sexuality. His work, in ambiguous and multiple ways, re-forms each of these intersecting dynamics. Smith and his company may be queer (and thus abject by society's standards of normal), they may be poor New York artists patching together their DIY cinematic visions, but they are stars nonetheless, to the extent that their performances undercut notions of both stardom and normalness. And, for Muñoz (1999, x), Smith becomes a paradigm for "the worldmaking power of disidentificatory performances."

This essay follows, with Muñoz and some other writers as traveling partners, a disidentificatory Bacchic scene less obvious than Smith's—that is, 2 Corinthians, viewing Paul's writing as a style of performance that makes room for new ways of being. In so following Dionysus, Paul, Smith, and Muñoz, I contend that future study of Paul's letters and communities should pay more attention to productive moments of misrecognition in Pauline interpretation—from his first communities' reception of his message and mission to our own attempts to map his rhetoric—since such moments are, in most new social movements, the ones that join to build a previously unseen community. Specifically, I trace, in the essay's first section, Paul's literary march in a triumphal procession as evoking images of Dionysus, most explicitly found in 2 Cor 2:14–17 but recurring throughout the letter fragment preserved in 2 Cor 1–9. In acknowledging how he walks in the paths of Dionysus, Paul addresses and reframes his seemingly deviant apostolic lifestyle. In this vein, I move on in the next section to join paths with Muñoz and other theorists and propose a reading of Paul's Dionysian procession as an oblique engagement of his own celibacy understood as foreign, suspicious, and abject, a disidentification with Dionysus that provides space both for his inchoate vision of apostleship as well as for communal- and self-fashioning among his communities, even in and through their disidentifications with him. Such a reading follows Paul's rhetoric in the letter and in the Corinthian correspondence as a whole—a rhetoric that pursues a wandering path marked by a series of traveling figures. By disidentifying with these figures, Paul creates a space for freedom in and through his ethnic and sexual identity—in particular, his avowed celibacy, which I treat in the third section. This space, however, functions also as a space for performative and disidentificatory response among members of his community in Corinth, a space, I finally propose, that is delineated by borders of illegibility, one that is created by the tension of disidentification. In identifying with difference, Paul (perhaps involuntarily, or perhaps in a way that problematizes volition itself) creates a situation in which his followers authorize their own difference, both from cultural norms and from the more legible aspects of Paul's apostolic example.

In following the wandering paths of Paul's disidentification with Dionysus and the reception of this disidentification in Corinth, then, I also hope to remain aware of my own interpretive paths (and those of New Testament scholarship circles I professionally inhabit), disidentifying with both Paul and his audience in Corinth in order to avoid centering Paul the Apostle and, through him, my own position as a pasty-normal biblical scholar. For while Paul was, on the one hand, in some ways ethnically and sexually nonnormative within his context and, on the other, differently nonnormative in relation to others in his communities (for example, women and enslaved individuals), the white, straight, cis-male gaze of the majority of Pauline studies continues to reconstruct an apostle firmly in control of himself and of a system of ideas that are intentional and, as system, thought to be intelligible to the careful critic. In response, a reading that assumes disidentification with Paul and his communities creates not a system but a space for decentered subject formation among readers, yielding the ethical promise of possible futures.

Dionysus as Pauline Traveling Partner

Paul's evocation of Dionysus occurs in a passage that rhetorically interrupts the beginning of his letter in 2 Cor 1–9.[3] After expressing his regret and tears over his ruptured relationship with the Corinthians and his anguished search across the Europe-Asia continental divide to find Titus and news of the community (2:1–13), he suddenly thanks God for strange blessings: "But thanks be to God who always leads us in triumph in Christ" (2:14).[4] The oddity of the image stems from the multiple valences of what it meant to be led in triumph. I put forth that his ancient audience, because

---

3. Much of the direct interpretation here summarizes my argument in Luckritz Marquis 2013, esp. ch. 3. I follow here one of the common compositional theories for 2 Corinthians, positing that 2 Cor 1–9 (excluding 6:14–7:1 as a non-Pauline interpolation) is a fragment of the latest extant letter, with 2 Cor 10–13 preserving a fragment of an earlier letter, mentioned in 2 Cor 2:3–4.

4. Unless otherwise indicated, all translations are my own.

of Paul's person and lifestyle, would have immediately imagined Dionysus, thought of by ancient writers as the triumphant god, foreign, effeminate, and licentious, returning from Asia to Europe.

The resonance makes sense for at least three reasons. First, Paul's activity would have called to mind wandering Bacchic preachers mentioned throughout ancient literature. Paul, like the preachers of Dionysus, was ethnically Eastern—specifically, Judean.[5] In general, ancient Greek and Roman writers often stereotypically conflated Eastern ethnicities. As early as the classical Athenian period, writers posited as nearly identical the worship of Dionysus, for example, who was often portrayed as foreign or from the East, and that of the Phrygian goddess Cybele or Magna Mater. Euripides's *Bacchae* contains the clearest and perhaps best-known examples of such stereotyped conflation. Later, in the early years of the Roman Empire, Strabo used Pindar's *Hymn to Dionysus* to describe styles of worship directed toward Dionysus, Orpheus, and Cybele as similarly Eastern or Asiatic (10.3.10–18).

Other authors included Judean devotions to the God worshiped at Jerusalem as another example of this stock type. In his *Table Talk*, Plutarch understands the Judean God in light of Dionysus, since both are harvest deities (*Quaest. conv.* 4.6). Jewish texts themselves portray Judean devotions in light of common Eastern features, or at least in ways that broader readership would have understood as Eastern or Asian. Both Jdt 15:12 and 2 Macc 12:7 depict Judean worship with *thyrsoi* (common Bacchic cultic objects) and percussive music (see also Strabo, *Geogr.* 10.3.15–16, on Asiatic percussion), largely seen as characterizing Eastern devotions. Furthermore, 2 Macc 6:7–8 claims that Antiochus IV Epiphanes instituted Bacchic sacrifices in Jerusalem, while 3 Macc 2:29 recounts that Ptolemy IV Philopater forced Alexandrian Judeans to brand themselves as worshipers of Dionysus. In attempting to understand Judean devotions, Greeks and Romans conflated Judaism with Bacchic rites, since both were understood as vaguely Eastern.

---

5. I assume the basic approaches of a growing number of scholars who—since the emergence of the so-called new perspective on Paul—have pushed even beyond the works of Stendahl, Sanders, and Dunn (for example) to interpret Paul firmly within the categories of Jewishness—that is, viewing Paul simply as Jewish/Judean (though to situate Paul within the broad matrix of Judean traditions and societies is, of course, less than simple). See, for just a few examples, Gaston 1987 and Eisenbaum 2009, and, more recently, Thiessen 2016 and Wendt's contextual reading of Paul in Wendt 2016, ch. 4.

Second, as just another preacher of a deity deemed Eastern, Paul also proclaimed a foreign god who promised eternal life and looming victory or destruction depending on his reception. In so doing, Paul specifically avails himself of a long tradition of civically sponsored Bacchic processions. Greek cities incorporated Dionysus into their municipal cults in parades cast as epiphanies of the god. As Paul Brooks Duff (1991) has explained in relation to 2 Cor 2:14–17, Paul in part calls to mind processions in which the righteous were summoned to approach the revelatory spectacle while the iniquitous were warned to make way. Such processions enacted revelation that produced a radical social division.

Third, Paul's complex deployment of the triumph metaphor plays upon royal appropriations of Dionysus, traced through Alexander's successors (the Ptolemies in Egypt and various Antigonid generals in Greece) to the several monomaniacal generals of the late Roman Republic such as C. Marius and Pompey Magnus (Livy, *Hist. Rom.* 33.53 and 8.2). Marc Antony more than anyone identified himself as the New Dionysus (see Plutarch, *Vit. Ant.* 24.4.2–6 and an Athenian inscription of 38 or 37 BCE calling him "new Dionysus" [*IG* 2² 1043.22–23]) before the victorious Augustus put a brief end to the string of Bacchic rulers, identifying with Apollo and declaring himself "eternally triumphant." Paul, by referring to his God as "always triumphing," may be evoking this Augustan notion (see Aus 2005, 8–9). Paul's wandering Judean body contained the promise of a foreign yet cosmic king.

In the triumph image, Paul parades himself as a prisoner without a captor, a reveler without a procession, though he insists that the god (God) is really there, invisible, orchestrating his movements and lifestyle. Indeed, after this four-verse glimpse of Paul as triumphal captive, Paul continues the letter with a series of other traveling images: the divine letter carrier (in the mold of Moses; 2 Cor 3), the Socratic philosopher facing death as a final journey (5:1–9), the ambassador of God offering reconciliation to the gentiles (5:19 and following), and the collector of offerings to the God of Judea, monetary offerings depicted as seeds sown in fertile soil (2 Cor 7–9). This cycle of images, evoking known tropes but deployed in strange contexts, makes the letter a textual parade, a low-fi procession not unlike Smith's nonlinear avant-garde projects treated by Muñoz. Paul may resemble—may in fact *be*—an impoverished, foreign proclaimer of a foreign god, but he asserts that he is also not, that he is more.

For Paul, however, the reframing of his travel not as abject wandering but as imperial triumph, and the subsequent marshaling of alternate images for his apostleship, does not sufficiently manage his Dionysian location. Thus Paul immediately and directly (2:17) addresses traditional suspicions about Eastern preachers: "For we are not like the many who huckster [*kapēleuontes*] the message of God." In general, ancient depictions of Eastern cultic practitioners warned that they preyed on the gullible to take their money. From Plato's castigation of "beggars and sorcerers" in the *Republic* (364b–365a) to the con artist devotees to Magna Mater in Apuleius's *Metamorphoses* (books 8–9), Greek and Roman writings evince the suspicion with which a foreign proclaimer would have been received. As Heidi Wendt (2016) has recently emphasized, Paul should be understood as one of these foreign "freelance religious experts" and thus as susceptible to the same expectations as other para-institutional practitioners. As such, Paul's activity in Corinth was, in fact, received with accusations of fraudulence. While Paul rejected financial support from his Corinthian community, the pairing of this refusal with his urgings to contribute to the collection for the Jerusalem assembly struck at least some in Corinth as a long con. (See occurrences of the words *pleonekteō*, "defraud," and *pleonexia*, "greed," at 2 Cor 2:11; 7:2; 9:5; 12:17, 18.) Thus we notice that Corinthian suspicions of Paul (as he reflects them in the letters preserved in 2 Corinthians) resonate with standard ancient castigations of Eastern preachers. Furthermore, the movement of Paul's image—raising the specter of God as triumphing (an image associated, in myth and politics, with Dionysus) to the more generic image of the huckstering preacher reinforces a more speculative reading of Paul's triumph figure as a method of traveling specifically with Dionysus in the hopes of taking him to different places.

At this point, New Testament scholars might ask: Did Paul really *choose* to portray himself as Dionysus? Is it possible to imagine a Christian apostle who would call upon a so-called pagan god in order to explain himself, a divine figure better explained (at least within traditional scholarship and the theologies that variously inform it) within Paul's worldview by the logic of demonology? Besides, Paul never explicitly mentions Dionysus. In reading the god in 2 Corinthians, we read something that is quite literally not there. And if, in indicating those accusations among Paul's community and his opponents that resonate with Dionysian stereotypes, we posit that Paul was forced to confront Dionysus, we are left with an apostle who, rather than positively (and positivistically) defining and defending his apostleship, undertakes a decidedly more reactive and even negative modality toward his image. (As Wendt [2016] shows, such attempts to assert distinctiveness in the face of the stock Eastern-preacher type would all the more typify Paul as just such a practitioner.) That Paul finds himself as Dionysus—that Paul does not choose Dionysus but instead Dionysus chooses Paul—forces a shift in how I imagine Paul's way of being and acting. More than this, such an observation alters my questions, my field, and my location as a scholar insofar as I am no longer studying Paul as an ideological and social actor whom I construe with a fairly simple theory of volition. Rather, I am confronted with a social field of Pauline discourse outlined by numerous and intersecting ancient discursive paths. Paul's (dis)identification with various traveling figures is less intentional than it is a response to interpellation. Stretching himself between triumphing and huckstering, Paul does not engage so much in self-construction. Rather, he locates himself on an existing spectrum of expectations and attempts to nudge himself toward one pole and away from another. Because he is a preacher of an Eastern god, the only way to distinguish and authenticate himself is to take Dionysus, God, and the baggage they come with in new directions. As such, Paul cannot present himself as *not* Dionysian, as *not* Eastern; rather, he must present himself as Eastern in new ways. Certainly, Paul denies outright certain aspersions associated with Eastern preachers. But, on the whole, the letter performatively presents Paul's lifestyle in ways that more subtly reform expectations. Paul's cycling of alternate images for his apostleship creates a rhetorical logic by which no one image is adequate to indicate his leadership role.

Disidentification and Pauline Interpretation

I find recourse to disidentification so illuminating in this cycle of surprising and ultimately inadequate images. For Muñoz (1999, 12), attention to disidentification "pave[s] the way to an understanding of a 'disidentificatory subject' who tactically and simultaneously works on, with, and against a cultural form." Before Muñoz's important work drawing attention to disidentification as a crucial strategy for world-building among queer individuals of color, other poststructuralist, feminist, and Marxist theorists had explored the constructivist nature of disidentification. In dialogue with Slavoj Žižek in her essay "Arguing with the Real," for example, Judith Butler asks:

What are the possibilities of politicizing *dis*identification, this experience of *misrecognition*, this uneasy sense of standing under a sign to which one does and does not belong? And how are we to interpret this disidentification produced by and through the very signifier that holds out the promise of solidarity?... It may be that the affirmation of that slippage, that failure of identification is itself the point of departure for a more democratizing affirmation of internal difference. (1993, 219, emphasis original)[6]

Butler offers that a politics based on subversive performativity works in part on a logic of disidentification—that the failure of language to encompass life, to regulate it under interpellative norms, offers possibility for its transformation. Indeed, as she asserts earlier in *Bodies That Matter*:

it may be precisely through practices which underscore disidentification with those regulatory norms by which sexual difference is materialized that both feminist and queer politics are mobilized. Such collective disidentifications can facilitate a reconceptualization of which bodies matter, and which bodies are yet to emerge as critical matters of concern. (1993, 4)

Butler's emphasis on the collective context of disidentification is crucial here, in both its potential for "factionalization" and "solidarity." Insofar as nonmajoritarian (like all) subject positions are constructed through performance, such performances require audiences, both among the communities they are making "matter" and among the majoritarian world of pasty normals, enthralled by the normalizing ideology that forecloses recognition and survival for abject individuals.

Muñoz builds on Butler's analysis and similarly emphasizes performance and spectatorship in his deployment of disidentification in queer subject/community formation. Simultaneously, Muñoz also inscribes disidentification in his interpretive prescriptions for scholars who would analyze such a politics and aesthetic:

I refer to disidentification as a hermeneutic, as a process of production, and a mode of performance. Disidentification can be understood as a way of shuffling back and forth between reception and production. For the critic, disidentification is the hermeneutical performance of decoding mass, high, or any other cultural field from the perspective of a

---

6. Butler here dialogues with Žižek 1989 and Berlant 1988.

minority subject who is disempowered in such a representational hierarchy. (1999, 25)

This language of traveling "between reception and production" links to a number of aspects of the present project. Such complicity between actor and observer(s) is as crucial for understanding disidentification among minoritized subjects today as it is helpful for understanding the growth of the Pauline communities. First, as I just posited, Paul as foreigner presents a fragmented apostle who not only is always under construction but is always already produced by forces beyond his own control. Paul receives his identity as an Eastern preacher as much as he produces it. Second, Paul's performance of apostleship could only occur in communal, public contexts—both the context of the broader world and its ethnic/gender/sexual expectations and the context of the community he was struggling to build up and maintain as unified despite the vicissitudes of recognition and misrecognition among his followers. That Paul is concerned about mutual recognition is belied by repeated use of the verb *epiginōskō* in 2 Cor 1:13–14. Third, disidentification as a reading strategy implicates the interpreter in the same sort of movement between (re)construction of Paul's ideology (what is traditionally called his theology) and *de*construction of the norms the interpreter brings to Paul, accomplished by the reception of contextual difference in relation to the interpreter's expectations and the novel picture of Paul that interpretation might produce. I return to disidentification as hermeneutic at the end of this essay.

Paul's procession of evocative yet inadequate apostolic signifiers before his community at least reveals something about the productive falsity of cultural idols. This "worldmaking negation" constitutes, for Paul and his communities, the epiphany of a new politics, a new type of triumph, over and against (but also somehow through) dominant suspicions and imperial norms. At the same time, Paul's discourse not only aims at delineating—at times negatively—his understanding of apostleship but, as Muñoz would assert, producing a world. And Paul's worldmaking occurs community by community. Insofar as 1 Corinthians responds to factionalism at Corinth, and insofar as 2 Corinthians responds to a split between the community and Paul himself, Paul's disidentificatory efforts should be read as part of a semiotic and performative contestation over the new world Paul and his followers are jointly bringing into being. We can more clearly see this contestation and how it materializes new identities by paying attention to another discourse engaged by Paul: his own sexuality and that of his community.

Pauline Celibacy, Disavowal, and Interpretive Failure

Paul's references to his own sexuality are scarce, save for his commending of his singleness and celibacy in 1 Cor 7 and 9. Here Paul casts his celibacy as moralistic self-mastery, eschatological readiness, and distinctive mission strategy. Yet what if Paul were also addressing suspicions over his sexual lifestyle in connection to his appearance as a foreign preacher?[7] Ancient texts frequently ascribe sexual immorality to foreigners and especially to preachers of Eastern gods. Think here of the seemingly paradoxical though well-known ancient stereotype of eunuchs as perverts (see Hester 2005). So, too, with the plot of Euripides's *Bacchae*: in lines 434–519, Dionysus appears before the Theban king Pentheus in the guise of one of his own preachers—poor, foreign, cryptic, and effeminate. In this suspicious package hides a power unaccounted for by Pentheus's normative sense of societal order. The preachers of Magna Mater in Apuleius's *Metamorphoses* also stand as an illustrative case in point; Apuleius pairs lasciviousness and gender violation with financial fraudulence in order to frame these foreign antagonists.

Like other Eastern preachers, Paul's foreignness and his unique sexual teachings may have compounded his problems in Corinth. A common reconstruction of the dispute identifies the individual mentioned in 2 Cor 2:5–11 (described by Paul as being pained) with the person who had a sexual relationship with his stepmother mentioned in 1 Cor 5:1–2. Paul's sexual teachings and lifestyle, however, may have left him open to suspicions that were broader than the accusation and punishment of one individual. In an ancient context, celibacy was often seen as a deviant lifestyle. Greek and Roman writers highlighted the dangerous effects of avoidance of sex and procreation (Roetzel 2000). In an age of high infant mortality, at least a few writers even framed not having children as akin to

---

7. Within the context of the letter, Paul does not raise the issue of celibacy on his own. Rather, some in Corinth (perhaps some among those he calls "the strong") inquire as to whether "it is well for a man not to touch a woman" (1 Cor 7:1). For the strong, I generally rely on something like the argument in Theissen 1975 that defines the quasi-party among Paul's Corinthian followers according to their relative socioeconomic superiority to the rest of the community; this group is the main rhetorical target of Paul's arguments in 1 Corinthians. One must further note that the question seems to come from men. For the question of how Paul's disidentification of his sexuality might have played with the women among the strong—that is, among the "Corinthian women prophets"—see below.

murder. A particularly clear example is Cassius Dio's account of Augustus's speech to senatorial Roman men resisting his marriage legislation (*Hist. Rom.* 56.4). In such an environment, Paul's celibacy challenges not only normative, procreative morality but also, in its eschatological outlook, the imperial logic of procreation and the management of populations— indeed, imperial time itself.

To understand more fully the dialogic way in which Paul's teaching contributed to the formation of Paul's persona and Pauline discourse, we should note that we first encounter Paul's teaching on celibacy because some in Corinth (perhaps some among those he calls "the strong") inquire as to whether "it is well for a man not to touch a woman" (1 Cor 7:1). The issue may well have been a cause for disagreement that Paul addresses with a nuanced clarification. On the whole, Paul's management of his sexual teachings is an intricate affair. Tat-siong Benny Liew, in his article "Redressing Bodies at Corinth" (2011), argues that Paul in 1 Corinthians simultaneously tackles apprehensions about his ethnicity. Liew deploys the category of race while avoiding and displacing concomitant stereotypes concerning the effeminacy and perversion of the ethnic other (among whom Paul is interpellated). We can build, I think, upon Liew's important points by focusing more intently on Paul's positive addressing of his own celibacy. Thus while Liew perceptively shows how Paul projects his own sexual anxiety onto women and those he views as sexually immoral, we can also read Paul's discussions of celibacy not just as an outbidding with regard to Greco-Roman norms of self-mastery or political pressure to pro- create but as a way of tackling any suspicions about his sexual lifestyle.

Indeed, as Liew outlines, it is hard to imagine Corinthian objections to Paul's lifestyle as omitting sexual stereotyping, both because of what we know about reactions to Eastern cultic practitioners and because of his explicit advocacy of celibacy in the Corinthian correspondence. Paul may be read here as repressing any sexual dimensions of the conflict with this community. Yet we may wish to build upon this repression hypothesis to speak of how Paul portrays his wandering lifestyle with a similarly wan- dering rhetoric that, as described above, cycles a series of traveling figures before the strong in Corinth. Paul asserts his legitimacy and freedom by resisting their attempts to pin him down with conventional terms, par- ticularly with regard to ethnicity or gender/sexuality. Here we might again follow Muñoz, who frames disidentification as a type of migration. Muñoz productively compares his conceptualization to the category of hybridity as used among postcolonial theorists as two helpful ways of addressing the divided agency of multiply minoritized subjects (in Muñoz's study, focusing on queers of color): "These hybridized identificatory positions are always in transit, shuttling between different identity vectors" (1999, 32). This cycling is due to the productive nature of the negative aspects of identification, the ways in which identifications fail, the ways in which what is said leaves an unsaid excess to be taken up by those who receive what is said in order to build the future. Subjects in transit eventually take leave of certain positions, either out of tactical reasoning or from being pulled or pushed out by others. With Paul and the Corinthians, we are dealing with both rhetorical/performative strategy and the productive use of some relatively unintentional communicative failures.

Wandering as Pauline Hermeneutic

In understanding Paul's disavowal of and disidentification with Diony-sian aspects of his life as a matter of physical and semantic wandering, I also join interpretive paths found in the recent work of Sarah Jane Cerve-nak, *Wandering: Philosophical Performances of Racial and Sexual Freedom* (2014). Cervenak explores works of art, literature, and performance from minoritized racial and sexual subject positions as reinscribing Enlighten-ment epistemologies of wandering and freedom as a strategy of producing freedom for those subject positions. Cervenak interprets depictions of wandering and travel, as well as rhetorical and conceptual wanderings figuratively considered, as philosophical acts rearranging existing epis-temologies through the acts' illegibility. From the furtive and evasive movements of escape in American abolitionist-era narratives of enslaved individuals to the performances of racially and sexually minoritized artists refusing to be straightened out, wandering as a philosophical act resists capture within hegemonic discourses and traces an ideological space of freedom for oppressed subjectivities. One way in which Cervenak explains this illegibility of wandering—and here she borrows from Fred Moten—is as "revelatory" or religious—that is, illegible with respect to Enlighten-ment rationality (see Cervenak 2014, 60, citing Moten 2004, 274). Here we can recall the religious overtones of Smith's *Normal Love*, where his appropriation of B-movie star Maria Montez is figured as worship. On the whole, numerous depictions in the film play off myth and ritualization, including Bacchanalia itself in the concluding events. For Muñoz (like Butler), disidentification points toward what cannot be accounted for, what cannot be, and thus what cannot be said, within a hegemonic regime of meaning. For Cervenak, wandering reveals new paths hidden from normative thoroughfares. Paul's wandering mission addresses the majority of his communities, who are neither wise, nor powerful, nor noble, so that God might choose what is not instead of what is (1 Cor 1:26–29).

With Cervenak and Muñoz, we can paradoxically read the illegible aspects of Paul's epiphanic and wandering rhetoric in 2 Cor 1–9.[8] A frustration of interpreting the letter has been to detect the referents of the many images that parade through it. On the contrary, perhaps we should view it as fruitful to read this letter—and indeed, the Corinthian correspondence as a whole—as a history of what Paul *fails* to tell Corinth. Since disidentification draws attention to difference, Paul's wandering rhetoric can be read not simply as indicating concrete situations or cultural figures but also as negatively indicating a yet-to-be-recognized future. Paul's traveling apostleship is a matter of walking in faith and not sight (2 Cor 5:7), valid because it indicates a future glory, one within the self and in a heavenly utopia, one Paul has seen but "whether in the body or out of the body, I do not know" (12:2–3). Paul's mission strives to bring bodies into recognition and being to the extent that they as of yet lack both. We can interpret 2 Cor 1–9 as bringing this strategy to a macrorhetorical expression in his odd series of wandering metaphors. As such, we need to take Muñoz seriously when he says that disidentifications constitute "world-making *negations*" and take into account the productive ways in which Paul's figures fail to communicate—out of a wandering style of rhetoric, a refusal to communicate, a disavowal, or a failure on Paul's part to take into account the semantic excesses of his own disidentifications.

Interpreters traditionally view Paul's project in 2 Corinthians as successful, as his turn westward in Romans, sponsored in large part by the activities of Phoebe of Cenchreae, speak to his regaining of Corinthian support (Rom 16:1–2). Any notion of Pauline success, however, once again raises the question of the mode of legibility by which we consider his letters and lifestyle. What it means for Paul's disidentificatory and illegible wandering to be successful is part and parcel, I argue, to contemporary questions of social change and communal formation. Illegibility is, of course, a relative concept, and it thus brings up the question of who is doing the reading. Paul, if illegible, would be primarily so not for us but

---

8. Cervenak (2014, 148–49) positively compares her project to that of Muñoz's (2009) construction of queer futurity.

for the Corinthians—or, to be more specific, the group in Corinth he calls the strong. In such a case, do we read Paul before the strong as if Dionysus before Pentheus? Or do we remind ourselves, first, that the strong were largely gentiles best understood as members of nations conquered under Rome (to borrow from Davina Lopez's 2010 argument) and, second, that many were women (for example, Chloe, and perhaps Phoebe) with their own claims to authority in Corinth, women onto whom Paul (following Liew 2011) may be displacing notions of sexual excess and disorder? In the face of the epiphanic displays of the spirit performed by these Corinthian women prophets (see Wire 1990), is Paul trying to cast the Corinthian women as his Bacchae and, figuratively, trying to get them in line behind him?[9] After all, the Corinthian correspondence explicitly raises the issue of identifying with Paul under the guise of imitation. As Joseph Marchal has noted, Paul's call to the Corinthians (including the women prophets) to imitate him (1 Cor 4:16, 11:1) leads to the odd position (especially for Paul) whereby the women take on the masculine role of prophets. Like Muñoz, Marchal (2014, 110) points to the productive nature of such ostensibly "bad attachments." Indeed, we can read the women prophets as disidentifying with Paul even before his call to imitation in 1 Corinthians, leading us perhaps to paraphrase Paul as asserting that "they imitate me, but not *that* way!" While disidentification can be a tactical way of redirecting received stereotypes—thus while Paul accepts he *is* a preacher of a foreign deity, he shifts the terms of that identification—it can also involve marginalized subjects grasping for seemingly unlikely muses. Like the white American Jack Smith evoking Maria Montez, the gentile women prophets act in the spirit of a Judean wanderer's example, creating a subject position that is both unintended and revelatory.

As a negative mode of subject construction that works by pointing away from the subject, disidentification acts similarly to and may be interpretively hard to distinguish from disavowal. Both disidentification and disavowal tend to escape the agency of a speaker or performer and leave an open space for imagination and interpretation. Thus when reading the unsaid and illegible in Paul's letters, we are delineating our own space of possibility, a zone of freedom. Paul's celibacy, whether reframed through disidentification with Dionysus or disavowed in the face of ethnic ste-

---

9. On Pauline women and reception more broadly, see Johnson-DeBaufre and Nasrallah 2011.

reotypes, leaves future room for new gender and sexual possibilities. So even if one of Paul's aims in writing Corinth is to control local women leaders—indeed, even as his disavowal of sexual aspersions and his projection of them onto some of his followers reinscribes a hierarchy within his community by creating a notion of abject sexual subjects—his disidentificatory negotiations still result in a semantic gap allowing members of his Corinthian community to receive his teachings and respond. Thus Paul's creation of his own apostolic space also opened space for his community in ways he did not expect.[10]

Even as Paul disavows, displaces, or represses the sexualized aspects of his mission (with all the unethical effects of this repression), his disavowal simultaneously allows space for some of the strong in turn to disidentify with Paul, drawing out the ethical possibilities he did not fulfill in himself. I think reading 2 Corinthians this way is something other than redeeming Paul or worshiping him as the great apostle; it is perhaps more akin to worshiping him like a matinee idol, a performer who awakens in us something he did not even see in himself.

As we try to follow Paul and the strong and their attempts to follow each other, we realize that we also are attempting to draw ever finer and more precise, legible borders around their ideological territories. We are, to risk being trite, wandering ourselves. In producing knowledge about the spheres and qualities of Pauline illegibility, we might decenter ourselves, might follow the spirit of Paul's injunction in 1 Cor 1:26–27 to consider ourselves insofar as we are not wise, powerful, or noble, insofar as we are illegible to pasty normals (even if we are pasty normal)—that is, insofar as we direct our attention to the crooked paths traced by the abject epiphanies emerging between Paul and his community in Corinth.

Works Cited

Aus, Roger David. 2005. *Imagery of Triumph and Rebellion in 2 Corinthians 2:14–17 and Elsewhere in the Epistle: An Example of the Combination of Greco-Roman and Judaic Traditions in the Apostle Paul.* Studies in Judaism. Lanham, MD: University Press of America.

---

10. Here I think of Muñoz's (2009, 83–96) discussion of the intersection between the early work of and biographical anecdotes concerning Amiri Baraka, in terms of his exploration and disavowal of homoeroticism, as leaving space for LGBT advocacy in the later decades.

Berlant, Lauren. 1988. "The Female Complaint." *SocT* 19–20:237–59.

Butler, Judith. 1993. *Bodies That Matter: On the Discursive Limits of "Sex."* New York: Routledge.

Cervenak, Sarah Jane. 2014. *Wandering: Philosophical Performances of Racial and Sexual Freedom.* Durham: Duke University Press.

Duff, Paul Brooks. 1991. "Metaphor, Motif, and Meaning: The Rhetorical Strategy behind the Image 'Led in Triumph' in 2 Corinthians 2:14." *CBQ* 53:79–92.

Eisenbaum, Pamela. 2009. *Paul Was Not a Christian: The Original Message of a Misunderstood Apostle.* New York: HarperOne.

Gaston, Lloyd. 1987. *Paul and the Torah.* Vancouver: University of British Columbia Press.

Hester, J. David. 2005. "Eunuchs and the Postgender Jesus: Matthew 19.12 and Transgressive Sexualities." *JSNT* 28:13–40.

Johnson-DeBaufre, Melanie, and Laura S. Nasrallah. 2011. "Beyond the Heroic Paul: Toward a Feminist and Decolonizing Approach to the Letters of Paul." Pages 161–74 in *The Colonized Apostle: Paul through Postcolonial Eyes.* Edited by Christopher D. Stanley. PCC. Minneapolis: Fortress.

Liew, Tat-siong Benny. 2011. "Redressing Bodies in Corinth: Racial/Ethnic Politics and Religious Difference in the Context of Empire." Pages 127–45 in *The Colonized Apostle: Paul through Postcolonial Eyes.* Edited by Christopher D. Stanley. PCC. Minneapolis: Fortress.

Lopez, Davina C. 2010. *Apostle to the Conquered: Reimagining Paul's Mission.* PCC. Minneapolis: Fortress.

Luckritz Marquis, Timothy. 2013. *Transient Apostle: Paul, Travel, and the Rhetoric of Empire.* Syn. New Haven: Yale University Press.

Marchal Joseph A. 2014. "Female Masculinity in Corinth? Bodily Citations and the Drag of History." *Neot* 48:93–113.

Moten, Fred. 2004. "Knowledge of Freedom." *CR* 4:269–310.

Muñoz, José Esteban. 1999. *Disidentifications: Queers of Color and the Performance of Politics.* CSA. Minneapolis: University of Minnesota Press.

———. 2009. *Cruising Utopia: The Then and There of Queer Futurity.* Sexual Cultures. New York: New York University Press.

Roetzel, Calvin. 2000. "Sex and the Single God: Celibacy as Sexual Deviancy in the Roman Period." Pages 231–48 in *Text and Artifact in the Religions of Mediterranean Antiquity: Essays in Honor of Peter Richardson.* Edited by Stephen G. Wilson and Michel Desjardins. Waterloo,

ON: Canadian Corporation for Studies in Religion/Wilfrid Laurier Press.

Theissen, Gerd. 1975. "Die Starken und Schwachen in Korinth: Soziologische Analyse eines theologischen Streits." *EvT* 35:155–72.

Thiessen, Matthew. 2016. *Paul and the Gentile Problem*. Oxford: Oxford University Press.

Wendt, Heidi. 2016. *At the Temple Gates: The Religion of Freelance Experts in the Roman Empire*. Oxford: Oxford University Press.

Wire, Antoinette Clark. 1990. *The Corinthian Women Prophets: A Reconstruction through Paul's Rhetoric*. Minneapolis: Fortress.

Wyma, Chloe. 2012. "Jack Smith's Unfinished Opus, 'Normal Love,' Revels in Delirious Genderqueer Pageantry at MoMA PS1." Blouin Art Info. https://tinyurl.com/SBL0699a.

Žižek, Slavoj. 1989. *The Sublime Object of Ideology*. London: Verso.

Bottoming Out: Rethinking the Reception of Receptivity

Joseph A. Marchal

When arguing over the relevance of Paul's letters, it often proves useful to stress the difference between the ancient world and the one in which we live. In debates about gender and sexuality, classical articulations of the Greco-Roman ethos of penetration and domination help interpreters of these letters put this matter of historical difference in stark terms. As a result, it becomes apparent that many arguments in the letters reinscribe this ethos, treating females as possessions belonging to their males (Rom 1:26; 7:2–3; 1 Cor 9:5; 11:3; 14:35; 2 Cor 11:2; Gal 4:22–5:1; cf. 1 Thess 4:4), giving instructions for males to acquire their own vessels to avoid sexual trouble (1 Thess 4:4; but cf. 1 Cor 7:2, 36), casting (free) males as in charge of when to make sexual use of females and possibly also enslaved people (1 Thess 4:4; 1 Cor 6:15–17; 7:1, 26–27, 36–38; 9:5; Phlm 11–14), and depicting (free) males as condemned particularly by their own receptivity (Rom 1:27; cf. Rom 7:5; 8:6–8; 1 Cor 7:9, 36; 10:8; Gal 4:12). In many other places, Paul reflects a general anxiety about passivity, weakness, and receptivity.[1]

An encounter with this difference from the ancient and biblical past can be instructive. It also, however, ignores that penetration and, or *as*, domination are not the whole story. These associations reflect the reigning sociopolitical order and the perspective of those at the pyramidal apex of power, but they fail to ask about those closer to the bottom of this kyriarchal order: the receptive "objects," those feminized as female,

---

1. A likely incomplete (if still contested) list of such passages would include Rom 4:19–20; 5:3–8; 6:15–7:25; 8:1–17; 14:1–4; 15:1–6; 1 Cor 1:25–2:5; 4:8–21; 7:8–9, 36–38; 8:7–13; 9:22; 11:2–16, 30–32; 12:22–26; 15:24–28, 53–58; 2 Cor 1:3–11, 23–2:5; 4:8–12; 6:4–10; 9:3–5; 10:8–11; 11:5–7, 19–30; 12:5–10; 13:3–4; Gal 4:3–7, 12–14; 6:8; Phil 1:12–17; 4:11–14; and 1 Thess 2:1–2.

enslaved, youthful, nonelite, and/or foreign.[2] A set of queer interventions can help biblical interpreters rethink how we have received receptivity and those cast as receptive in the first and twenty-first centuries; I do not propose identical sets of subcultures in the ancient assemblies that received these letters but instead suggest more porous relations to the past. With the help of theorists such as Ann Cvetkovich (2003), Darieck Scott (2010), Elizabeth Freeman (2010), and Carla Freccero (2006), ancient stereotypes of those toward the bottom might start to look more slippery than stark, raising the possibility that ancient people used sexual practices (and their intersecting evaluations) in ways that elite males could not have entirely anticipated. Queerly, we should remain receptive to that possibility.

Dissonance and Domination: Penetration and/as Activity

People often turn to Paul's letters for information about the "biblical stance" on sexual matters, especially same-sex erotic contact. When asked about clobber passages like Rom 1 or the vice list in 1 Cor 6:9–11, I respond (like many other biblical scholars, I imagine) by dutifully trying to place these texts in their ancient contexts, often stressing the difference between then and now.[3] One blunt strategy introduces these arguments in terms of the predominant protocol of penetration in the ancient Greco-Roman context. Most audiences are scandalized, outraged, or at the least surprised by this ethos, focused upon free, elite, imperial males, but relatively indifferent about the objects of their penetration, beyond the objects' lower sociopolitical status: their feminization as female, enslaved, youthful, nonelite, and/or foreign. Reciting excerpts from scholars like David Halperin (1990) or Holt Parker (1997) often does the trick.

Halperin (1990, 29) stresses that ancient Greeks saw "sex not as a collective enterprise in which two or more persons jointly engage but rather as an action performed by one person upon another." Sex is not done *with* someone else, but *to* someone else: "Sex possesses this

---

2. Elisabeth Schüssler Fiorenza created the term *kyriarchy* to describe the intersecting and mutually influencing pyramidal structures of domination. See, for example, the discussion in Schüssler Fiorenza 2001, 1, 118–24, 211.

3. For an introductory example of this tendency, see Marchal 2012. For historical contextualization of these passages, see Brooten 1996 and Martin 1995, 1996.

valence, apparently, because it is conceived to center essentially on, and to define itself around, an asymmetrical gesture, that of the penetration of the body of one person by the body—and, specifically, by the phallus—of another" (30). Parker (1997, 47) concurs with this view, stressing that "the ancient world, both Greek and Roman, did not base its classification on gender, but on a completely different axis, that of active versus passive." This axis creates a set of categories and organizes behaviors accordingly: "The Romans divided sexual categories for people and acts on the axis of 'active' and 'passive.' Active has, in their scheme, a single precise meaning. The one normative action is the penetration of a bodily orifice by a penis" (48). Parker then delineates the three different sets of vocabulary used for the three different orifices that could be penetrated (48–49). Either male or female could be penetrated, and this ancient protocol was indifferent about the object of this activity when it reflected and reinforced wider sociopolitical dynamics. "Sexual 'activity,' moreover, is thematized as domination: the relation between the 'active' and the 'passive' sexual partner is thought of as the same kind of relation as that obtaining between social superior and social inferior" (Halperin 1990, 30). This relation might look like it maps onto more recent dualistic norms of gender: "The active is necessarily and essentially male: penetrating with one's penis. To be passive, therefore, is to play the part of a woman" (Parker 1997, 50). But notice that Parker stresses that the receptive person is not always a woman, but one who plays a part or fulfills a role like the woman's. The relevant sociopolitical order, then, is not just patriarchal but more multifaceted and reflected in who are acceptable receptacles: "The proper targets of his sexual desire include, specifically, women, boys, foreigners, and slaves—all of them persons who do not enjoy the same legal and political rights and privileges that he does" (Halperin 1990, 30). Because this order lacks values like reciprocity or mutuality and organizes people in ways besides modern sexual orientations, Halperin pointedly recommends "not to speak of it as a sexuality at all but to describe it, rather, as a more generalized ethos of penetration and domination, a socio-sexual discourse structured by the presence or absence of its central term: the phallus" (34–35).

This ethos of penetration and domination, then, can be used to contextualize difficult or controversial passages in Paul's letters. When Paul alludes to intercourse that could be seen as natural or unnatural in Rom 1:26–27, the point of reference is this protocol and the wider order it reflects.[4] Bernadette Brooten demonstrates: "If we read Rom 1:26f in light of a broad variety of ancient sources on sexuality and gender roles, 'natural' intercourse means penetration of a subordinate person by a dominant one" (1996, 241). Indeed, it is not just the terminology of *nature* that reflects this dominant ethos; the Greek word commonly translated as "intercourse," *chrēsis* (1:26, 27), more closely means "use." As Brooten highlights, "a man 'uses' or 'makes use of' a woman or a boy" (245). A sexual act "according to nature" requires that a superior makes use of another, inferior body as a receptacle of their penetration. In the letter to Philemon, a similar set of terms is employed to pun upon the bodily vulnerability of the enslaved Onesimus: once "useless" (*achrēston*), but now "useful" or "good for use" (*euchrēston*, Phlm 11) (see the discussion in Marchal 2011b). Even texts that appear heteronormative, like Paul's admonition for a man to "take a wife for himself" (1 Thess 4:4), reflect the predominant protocol. Following the work of Jennifer A. Glancy (2006, 49–70), the male audience member is instructed to "obtain his own vessel" (*skeuos*), a starkly objectifying way to characterize the human receptacle in such asymmetrical systems. This vessel would be one way free males characterize a wife or an enslaved person as "morally neutral outlets for their sexual urges" (60). Indeed, each of these passages refers to potentially receptive parties, but only in the course of commenting upon or addressing their sociopolitical superiors.[5] The importance of acquiring a vessel in 1 Thessalonians is for a free adult male to avoid offending a "brother" (4:6), the source of the offense likely stemming from the use of someone who properly belongs to another community member, not himself. Similarly, in Philemon, Paul is careful in negotiating for the consent of the slave owner (v. 14) rather than the enslaved Onesimus. Even those females leaving behind so-called natural use in Romans are described (in only a brief clause) as "*their* females" (1:26), possessions of a "them" who are not properly masculine because they lack better control over their inferiors.

---

4. Brooten (1996, 1–2), for instance, opens her landmark study of female homoeroticism by highlighting how fundamental the active/passive hierarchy is for the Roman imperial period.

5. The use of two sexually receptive figures, Hagar and Sarah, in an allegory (in Gal 4:21–5:1) functions in a similar fashion: not to address these females, or people like them, but to encourage audience members to identify with the free son of just one of these women, as the free and legitimate heir of Abraham.

If audiences today are scandalized, outraged, or surprised by the ancient ethos of penetration and domination, they become distressed by the consonance of Paul's letters with this ethos. Not only do these letters make for a bad fit with present-day "family values," but the values they promulgate horrify, offend, disturb, and disgust.[6] Encountering this historical difference disrupts expectations in potentially productive ways. This strategy could interrupt the tendency to assume that we already know what biblical texts say. Indeed, such contextualization could be seen as an important precondition for opening up what biblical interpretations and interpreters can do. Yet an emphasis on this difference can have other, equally unexpected effects, particularly around the meaning of receptivity.

Receiving Receptivity, Again

Curiously, an investment in the explanatory power of this ethos of penetration and domination could provide a kind of stabilizing comfort. Once you know this context, you can easily plug it into a reading of these texts. When providing this context as a teacher or a visiting lecturer, I give you the solution, the answer, to the problem of these texts.[7] After the outrage or the upset, there is some relief, through a distancing resolution. You know that the texts belong to a distant and distinct ethical and political system, one riven by a series of intersecting asymmetries. Scholars like Halperin, then, become icons of alterity, suggesting that we might even jettison the term *sexuality* when describing the penetrating people and practices of the ancient Mediterranean world.[8]

This insistence on the modernity of sexuality could be helpful, but we would also be wise to attend to a series of studies by Denise Kimber Buell (2009, 180–81, 188; 2010, 325; 2014, 41) that trace how an emphasis on

---

6. This dissonance is one of the main points of Dale B. Martin's essay, "Familiar Idolatry and the Christian Case against Marriage," reprinted in Martin 2006, 103–24, 224–28. One rather important and convincing description of these imperial family values can be found in D'Angelo 2003. For my own attempt to extend reflections on these dynamics through a consideration of (imperial) sexual exceptionalism, see Marchal 2015.

7. Eve Kosofsky Sedgwick (1997) describes a similar kind of foreclosing comfort, confidence, or certitude about the mechanism for deriving meaning (albeit toward different ends in literary studies).

8. For further reflections on the relevance and pitfalls of emphasizing either alterity or continuity for considering biblical texts, see Marchal 2011a.

the modernity of race protects scholars from asking haunting questions about our relationship to the past (and the past's lingering effects upon and afterlives among us). What do we miss not only if we neglect the ways that gender and sexuality are kyriarchically intertwined with race, ethnicity, and religion but also if we remain exclusively focused upon the difference of other times (and places)?

Still, the ancient system I have described so far does not particularly attend to matters of mutuality, or consent, or pleasure; it classifies activities and people in ways quite unlike modern sexual orientations. That was then, this is now. Are we not so glad that we are not like them? That is a remarkably common reaction, for instance, to the grid Parker evokes to stress this difference, where active = penetrating = dominant = masculine and passive = penetrated = subordinate = feminine. To learn these relationships and begin applying them might be disorienting at first, but such equations also have a seductive simplicity to them. In her reconsiderations of receptivity, Cvetkovich (2003, 61) puzzles over the potential flattening effects of such constructions, noting: "It is peculiar that scholarship designed to suggest the variability of social meanings attached to sexual acts should have the unintentional effect of leaving the impression that penetration signifies domination and feminization, if not universally, then remarkably extensively." In spite of the effort to stress the difference between now and then, here and there, some scholarship runs the risk of falsely stabilizing the practice and significance of a variety of sexual acts.[9] Indeed, as the specifically personal and criminal history of Parker's own online activities indicate, there is still considerable—even horrifying— variability and possible continuities between current practices and ancient asymmetrical systems (see Scullin 2016).[10]

---

9. For another critique of Halperin or any who take an approach that presumes the self-evidence or clarity of "homosexuality as we conceive of it today," see Sedgwick 1990, 44–48.

10. Like several other biblical scholars, I only heard about Parker's arrest on child pornography charges more than a year after his conviction, and after the more subterranean conversations within classics (and after I first drafted this essay). For now, I believe I will continue to cite Parker, and this essay in particular, because (1) as my present essay indicates, other classics scholars (like Deborah Kamen and Sarah Levin-Richardson) have long esteemed and responded to his formulations, to situate their work requires at least some reference to Parker; (2) this essay narrates an actual historical scholarly practice of mine (the way I have used Parker and Halperin to clarify biblical texts for all sorts of audiences); and (3) these citations can be further

Cvetkovich turns to lesbian/queer sexual subcultures as resources for recasting the passive, abject side of this seemingly stable sociosexual grid by reimagining and rearranging the relations of receptivity to pathology and trauma. In doing so, Cvetkovich draws upon and differentiates her aims from those of Halperin and queer theorist Leo Bersani. Bersani celebrates the radical potential of gay (male) sex, and most especially anal receptivity, particularly for the ways it can counter the romanticization of sex. The value of anal receptivity is in its potential to produce a psychic experience of "self-shattering," highlighting the "strong appeal of powerlessness, or the loss of control," not just of passivity "but rather of a more radical disintegration and humiliation of the self" (Bersani 1987, 117). This theory of receptivity might just be leaning into the equation receptivity = passivity = subordination = femininity (or feminization), though. Cvetkovich cautions that "the fact that men like to get fucked only seems counterintuitive (or 'queer') if it is assumed that everyone really wants to be 'masculine' and on top or that the trauma of penetration must necessarily be negative" (2003, 63). To Cvetkovich, Bersani is important for linking trauma to sexuality but potentially forecloses in advance the variety of ways these might link.

Butch-femme roles and practices can begin to displace or complicate some of these assumed linkages, even when discussing penetration, since these practices expand penetrating body parts or objects beyond a penis (or penis substitute), the member so often assumed to be essential in both ancient and modern considerations of sexual practices. This persistent phallocentric focus indicates the impoverished state of terminologies that fail to consider how femmes play receptive roles without reducing them to modes of passivity or stigmatization. Cvetkovich (2003, 57–58) articulates how femme receptivity is not a null position but reflects the femme's desire; her role is not passive, but it involves moving under and in responsive interaction to and with the touch of the butch. This might be described, for example, as a give and take, but taking can be used for both femme receptivity and butch touch/penetration (64).

Cvetkovich (2003, 56) argues that this kind of penetrating touch can operate as "a significant vehicle for working through traumatic histo-

---

opportunities to discuss the politics of our scholarship, by naming rather than evading activities like Parker's. For further reflections, see Scullin 2016. I provide further reflections on other ways in which trauma can be linked to sexual practices in the remainder of this essay.

ries," as femme can be a type of labor in negotiating and acknowledging vulnerability. In a homophobic world, and an environment that enacts violence against women and/as sexual minorities, admitting and opening oneself to desire and accompanying touches are risky practices (65). In such practices, a femme is the subject of focus rather than the phallus; while she receives a body part, she receives attention. In doing so, butch-femme practices do not disavow the hierarchy that structures top-bottom or insertive-receptive pleasures, but they aim to depathologize, while acknowledging the traumatic element of penetration. Thus Cvetkovich is interested in "a sex positivity that can embrace negativity, including trauma" (63), the ways that vulnerability and passivity can be rethought. In contrast to Bersani's conception of receptivity, "the femme does not see penetration or violation of bodily boundaries to be a crisis of subjectivity, although she may experience it as a risky vulnerability" (80). Cvetkovich labors to archive kinds of receptivity that embrace and rework negativity, without simply repeating a foreclosed logic of penetration as domination and without trying to ignore it or pretend that it can simply be bypassed or overcome.

Similar dynamics are foregrounded in queer work on racialization and abjection. The risks, pleasures, and even necessities of grappling with traumatic and debasing histories run through Scott's daring work.[11] Scott (2010, 5) considers the value or *use* of something besides black pride or power by postulating that "blackness is constituted by a history of abjection, and *is* itself a form of abjection." Blackness is not only produced by this traumatic past; for Scott, it is crucial to "grapple with that apparently inescapable *aspect* of blackness" (5). The history of slavery (and its racialization) provides a different set of referents for the pleasure of the bottom, connecting the sexual and the political:

> I use *bottom* to signify the nadir of a hierarchy (a political position possibly abject) and as a sexual position: the one involving coercion and historical and present realities of conquest, enslavement, domination, cruelty, torture, and so on, the other involving sexualized or erotic consent/play which references the elements of the former. (28; see also 164)

---

11. For further reflections on the indignities, insults, desires, and disidentifications at the intersections of black and queer, see Reid-Pharr 2001; Stockton 2006; and Holland 2012.

Scott is interested in rethinking present-day relations to the historical silences surrounding the sexual exploitation of enslaved males: "What is unspeakable here is the sexual or erotic pleasure of the human being in extreme conditions of coercion and nonconsent" (155).[12] Yet this is precisely the coerced, humiliated, abjected subject about whom Scott seeks to speak.

Thus Scott does speak (or write) about black (power) bottoms, showing how gay male fantasies "draw on those histories, even if only by rough analogy" (154). In doing so, Scott stresses the relations enforced between the sexual bottom and the political bottom. To my own (admitted) surprise, Scott suggests another rough analogy: between the social and economic power organized through the sexual coercion of the enslaved and the ancient Greek protocols for sex between superior and inferior described by Halperin (159)! Both sexual-political formations present obstacles for comprehending the sensations, and possibly the pleasures, of such bottoms. Those past pleasures might be unspeakable, even unnameable, but the sexual-political analogy between different times and the present-day reference to this history indicate possibilities for reimagining pleasure and power in abjection:

> *Bottoming* thus becomes a metaphor and a model for one of the black powers we are seeking in abjection: among its many inflections of meaning, it evokes the willed enactment of powerlessness that encodes a power of its own, in which pain or discomfort are put to multifarious uses. (165)

Thus, unlike Halperin, Scott reconfigures the potential impacts of receptivity and imagines multiple uses for bottoming—both the silenced roles of those on the sexual-political bottom of slave societies and those for whom this history is still summoned, who receive this history as a legacy of racialization.[13]

Cvetkovich and Scott begin to complicate the stabilizing comforts of the supposed hard difference of the penetration paradigm by tracing

---

12. Here Scott initially follows, then departs from Spillers 1987.

13. Scott (2010, 265) highlights that these impacts are not exclusively connected to black masculinity, applying (differently and differentially) to black women as well, even as his project mostly focuses on masculinity, given how fiercely those particular impacts have been resisted. For a wider range of uses for racialized abjection and/as sexual receptivity, see Fisher 1996; Sharpe 2010; and Musser 2014.

some of the varying practice and significance of receptivity. They provide routes for negotiating rather than denying or evading trauma, stressing trauma's relation to sexual desires and practices. They reflect on the desires and pleasures of receptivity, of bottoming, as its own kind of activity, even power. As a result, they shift the focus away from the phallus, or the presumed possessors of it, even as they reconsider penetrative activities along interlocking gender, sexual, economic, and racial trajectories.

Scott and Cvetkovich also suggest different relations to the past, because these pasts are not yet past, resonating with other queer approaches to historiography. Freccero (2006, 102), for instance, has emphasized a queer spectrality that generates a "penetrative reciprocity" between us and our history. Building upon Cvetkovich and Freccero, Freeman (2010, 109) wonders about the potential for a "bottomy historiography" that similarly prizes porosity and receptivity. Each of these suggests thinning the boundaries between the present and past. It is time to get back, then.

From the Bottom, on to Our Back(ground)

Rethinking receptive practices and inquiring about those receptive parties in the ancient ethos of penetration and domination are not entirely new tasks.[14] Shortly after Halperin argued against using terms like sexuality or homosexuality, Amy Richlin (1993) pointedly titled her case for a Roman passive homosexual subculture "Not before Homosexuality"! Richlin's earlier work (1983) had cleared the ground for adapting the arguments Halperin made for Roman materials by delineating the aggressively violent and insertive system embodied by the figure of Priapus, but she also hoped that it would be "possible to historicize homosexuality without losing it as a concept" (Richlin 1993, 528). Even then, Richlin had to concede that this concept was only "partly adequate" for *cinaedi*, those males cast as preferring to be penetrated (530). Many of the (elite free Roman male) texts she considers refer to the passive—or receptive—party, often in the form of caricature, but Richlin wonders whether there might be a real referent, whose "characteristics were accurately reported and formed part of a self-presentation used for sexual signals and group cohesion" (542–43).[15]

---

14. For an important alternative consideration of prophecy and (im)proper receptivity to spiritual powers, see Buell 2014, 41.

15. Richlin (1993, 543), in part, proceeds by analogy with the difficulties of doing women's history: "No one would deny that Juvenal 6 had a real referent—women; why

Still, this referent appears to be less a homosexual and more a stereotyped deviant, as she admits in closing: "Marilyn Skinner suggested to me that a better title for this article would be 'Not Before Queers'; the current title is provocative rather than exact" (572; see also 530).

Richlin's main argument has not convinced many, but I find something provocative—even queer—about her efforts.[16] Skinner (1997, especially 5–6) did as well, particularly in framing the approach to these practices as a collage of multiple sexualities, a complication of any debates about a more monolithic—even totalizing—paradigm, as the protocol of penetration is sometimes imagined. As Brooten (1996, 49) explains it, "This focus on penetration as the principal sexual image led to a simplistic view of female erotic behavior," a view her landmark work interrogates and then addresses by surveying a range of ancient materials on female homoeroticism.

One obvious complication to consider is the rhetoricity of all sources for this ancient background. Anthony Corbeill, for instance, highlights how the *cinaedus* is apparently marked by external signs of effeminacy. These signs are then used in invective, but their "efficacy requires at least some degree of correlation" (1997, 115) between the charges and the parties targeted. Corbeill is convinced that the vigor of the invective indicates the likelihood of a specific category of person: "The rhetorical power of the invective would seem to depend on the theoretical possibility that these people existed as a category of human beings" (117). Like Brooten and Corbeill, Pamela Gordon (1997) wonders about the ostensibly masculinized activities of the *tribas*. Though subject to a comparable hostility as the *cinaedus*, this case is even more difficult, given the scarcity of materials. Nevertheless, Gordon notes that "portrayals of mannish lesbians may sometimes be inspired by actual women who adopt traditionally 'masculine' garb or behavior" (287). If so, then their practice may correspond, but not exactly, to how they are depicted as monsters or fools in ancient Roman texts. Reading through the rhetoric of these texts indicates that

---

should the referent for Juvenal 2 be less real? Juvenal's caricatures of women do tell us some things about real women; maybe his caricatures of *cinaedi* can be useful, too."

16. Rabun Taylor (1997) explicitly builds upon Richlin's suggestions about a subculture, in idiosyncratic and mostly unconvincing fashion, while John R. Clarke (2005) sees only cautious hints of such a subculture. For one brief treatment of the doubts concerning the utility of thinking of *cinaedi* as a subculture, see Williams 2010, 239–45.

we might, with Gordon, read these females as gender rebels instead (297–98). These figures are not exactly homosexual, but they could be queer to the interlocking gender, sexual, embodied, and ethnoracial hierarchies of their settings.[17]

Certainly, the ways rhetoric and history connect are not simple, yet for the ancient arguments about these figures to work, an audience would need, first, to accept that such people and practices are possible and, second, to recognize these accusations and characterizations. The rhetorical efficacy of these depictions thus must connect in some way with types of behavior audiences know or can imagine. After all, if a claim is entirely implausible, it undermines the person making the claim. The claim may not entirely correspond with already-accepted ideas, but it must resonate with them in some way.

Parker (1997, 60–63) helpfully illuminates this shifting relationship between rhetoric and history. *Cinaedus*, for instance, functioned in ancient texts as a stereotype. Although recognizable as a type (or, better, an antitype), there is insufficient evidence to determine whether this presented a mode for self-identification or the basis of a subculture. Since, however, the roles prescribed by types and antitypes likely do affect behavior, Parker suggests that the antitype "might have been deployed for individual self-fashioning" (62). In short, certain people might not have been *those people* exactly, in that they did not precisely correspond to the type (stereotype, antitype, or otherwise).[18] But it does not seem entirely implausible that there were people like *those people*, people who possessed qualities or practiced activities that appear in these types, or even people who mobilized the type in ways one could not entirely anticipate.

Indeed, there are accounts of elite males using these typologies to play with the presumed virtue of always being the hypermasculine "impenetrable penetrators" (Walters 1997, 30). Poets, for instance, would often deploy a feminized persona of a male "enslaved to love," even if they ultimately reinforced gendered hierarchies (see Skinner 1997, 17–19). Maud Gleason (1995, 74–76, 134–35, 161–62) notes several instances in which

---

17. The ethnoracially foreign aspect of these stereotyped figures is stressed by the use of Greek terms for them. See especially Hallett 1989.

18. Skinner (1997, 24) also concludes that these caricatures may contain traces of such people and that these practices "were perhaps more complicated, and actual sexualities more supple, than the mass of prescriptive and polemic documents would indicate."

adopting an effeminate persona, or the bodily comportment associated with femininity, could potentially appeal to audiences. Such a strategy may not have been particularly subversive, given the social class of the aristocratic males who competed with each other via both hypermasculine and (slightly) effeminizing performances: "There was something manly, after all, about taking risks—even the risk of being called effeminate. And there may also have been a temptation to appropriate characteristics of 'the other' as a way of gaining power from outside the traditionally acceptable sources" (162). Following Gleason, Corbeill (2004, 134–37) imagines just such a scenario behind the accounts of the rise of Julius Caesar. Caesar's bodily comportment is marked by the signs of effeminacy, particularly in his clothing and hair, but also in the rumors of his sexual receptivity. Yet if masculinity was firmly associated with the elite, then these practices could reflect some intentional positioning:

> the ways in which popular politicians appealed directly to the assembled people—through self-consciously untraditional dress, gestures, and speaking styles.... By not avoiding behavior specifically marked in his society as feminine, Caesar could be perceived as transgressing normal modes of male, aristocratic behavior. (137)

Even Caesar, then, could be (in)famously feminine, at least occasionally. There is at least some space for practices that depart from predominant equations of femininity (or feminization) with receptivity, passivity, and sociopolitical subordination.

Though these practices still seem to shore up the authority of those operating at the top rather than toward the bottom of Roman imperial protocols for penetration and domination, material culture offers evidence that the space for departures from or negotiations of these protocols is not limited to the tops. Visual culture, for instance, raises the likelihood that many more could encounter, recognize, and negotiate images of sexual practices (see Clarke 1998, 2003; Lopez 2012). Artifacts like the Leiden gemstone and the Warren Cup depict a male penetrating another male with a certain degree of mutuality, particularly because both male figures appear to be similar in age and status (Clarke 1998, 38–42, 61–90).[19] John

---

19. The Leiden gem depicts the bottom, or receptive participant, in two ways that would be atypical for textual sources (beyond the similarity in age/status): his own penis is erect, stimulated with excitement or pleasure, and his head is turned back to

R. Clarke posits that the creators of such objects "delighted in upsetting the norms of proper sexual relations by showing behavior that broke the codes set by the elite" (2; see also 239, 276–79). Both the gemstone and cup would have been expensive, but figures featured on more affordable and widely distributed Arretine pottery reflect similar scenes of both male-male and male-female acts. Clarke is particularly interested in the "signs of subjectivity in the penetrated partner" (116) in both types of sexual scene: the beauty and dignity of receptive female figures and the relative tenderness and romance of male-male scenes that focus more on the kiss than the anal insertion. Clarke commendably wonders what many different types of viewers would see, think, and feel when they encountered these objects in the ancient world, raising several possibilities for identifying with the figure who is typically assumed to be subordinate, inferior, and thus debased.

The sexual graffiti that survive from the Roman imperial period are even more intriguing than these (other) objects. Examples from Pompeii, for instance, indicate that enslaved or lower-status females could write and certainly read graffiti, including ones that reflected a negotiated subjectivity, even agency, for females and receptive males.[20] In a series of articles (with and without Deborah Kamen), Sarah Levin-Richardson has proposed that such graffiti nuance the predominant views of the protocols of penetration and domination. Females (Levin-Richardson 2013; Kamen and Levin-Richardson 2015a) and receptive males (Kamen and Levin-Richardson 2015b) are not only the subjects of the sexual verbs in this graffiti, but they often select more active verbs to describe sex acts. For example, when describing fellatio, these graffiti more often cast the presumably passive participants as subjects of the verb *fellare* ("to suck cock") than in terms more clearly aligned with the presumably "active" perspective as in the verb *irrumare* ("to mouth fuck").

In reconsidering these roles and practices, Kamen and Levin-Richardson argue that *activity* should refer to more than penetrative or insertive acts and include the ways these participants desire, move their body in,

---

gaze tenderly at the insertive participant (Clarke 1998, 38, 40). Side A of the Warren Cup features the receptive partner as physically on top of his top, holding a strap suspended from above while lowering his buttocks onto the insertive participant's penis (Clarke 1998, 64; see plate 1 just past page 142).

20. On other haunting possibilities for agency, particularly among subordinated groups, consider also Buell 2014, 33–34.

and/or perform a sexual practice (2015a, 236; 2015b, 455). They also contrast their categorization from Parker's (1997, 49) grid, since "in grouping together all penetrated individuals under the label 'passive,' this model obscures the potential agency of some of these individuals" (Kamen and Levin-Richardson 2015b, 455). A male could be penetrated anally or orally, but Kamen and Levin-Richardson insist that "an important distinction was made by the Romans between males who were conceptualized as agents in their own penetration (*fellatores, cinaedi,* and *pathici*), and those who were not (*irrumati, pedicati,* and *fututi*)" (455). All of these would have likely been objects of scorn, but not all of them were depicted as unwilling, inactive victims of a violent act (450–51).

Females could also be depicted as playing an active role while being penetrated (Levin-Richardson 2013, 333; Kamen and Levin-Richardson 2015a, 245), as *fellatrices* or *fututrices*. Indeed, the graffiti in Pompeii play a unique role in discerning the active female, indicated by nouns with the -*trix* ending, as they provide the only surviving instances of *fututrix* ("fucker" [feminine]) as a title (Levin-Richardson 2013, 333). With Parker (1997, 56), Kamen and Levin-Richardson note the ambivalences and contradictions around proper female comportment (2015a, 235–36, 248): elite Roman imperial males want cool, calm, and controllable wives, but complain if she is not passionate or responsive. Thus while *tribades* are the well-known antitype because they are cast as actively penetrating, usurping what is imagined to be the exclusively male role, females who actively participated, moved during, and/or desired to be the receptive participant in vaginal or oral intercourse (*fututrices* and *fellatrices*, respectively) "are both disparaged and highly sought after" (Kamen and Levin-Richardson 2015a, 248).

Graffiti thus highlight the opportunities and difficulties in this more complicated scene that distinguished forms of activity or even agency from an exclusive association with penetration. Levin-Richardson (2015) has also demonstrated that a range of marginalized practices and people were described by first-century residents of Pompeii as *calos*, the Latin transliteration for the Greek term for "beautiful." While previously it was

used to hail the beauty of respectable citizen boys, at Pompeii, the word *calos* was associated with individuals and places on the margins of society: with prostitutes, tavern-boys, and actors; and with gates, taverns, inns, and whorehouses. That is, Pompeians found the word appropriate to describe those who willingly put themselves on display for the public—the *infames* of Roman society, whose position provoked desire and disparagement. (280)

Graffiti was one practice that could mark a slightly different way of evaluating people and practices that were typically debased, a set of recognitions that these could be problematic *and* desirable.

Levin-Richardson (2013, 334–41) imagines the graffiti as not simply expressing the view of their creators but also providing opportunities for passers-by to read, appropriate, or redirect the colorful and direct exclamation. Kamen and Levin-Richardson (2015a, 250) argue that these materials signal "the agency that subordinated groups (like women and slaves) could exercise within the constraints of Roman society." These possibilities are striking, but I still think some caution is warranted. One could be an enthusiastic interpreter, for instance, of the Warren Cup, but it is only side A of this silver cup that subverts expectations about sexual asymmetry. Side B reflects the more common pose, since it features an enslaved male as the receptive participant (Clarke 1998, 86). Many of the Greek names that appear in the sexual graffiti of Pompeii indicate their likely slave status, and they may have been enslaved prostitutes (Levin-Richardson 2013, 335). Brooten (1996, 73–113) also strikes an ambivalent note in her examination of erotic spells, petitioned by females and aimed at their female objects of desire. The formulaic language of these spells reflects the enslavement, constraint, and domination of ancient asymmetries, yet they may just create a space for countercultural uses of such scripts (102, 105).[21] These remains indicate the potential traces of sexual subjectivity, even as they reflect sociopolitical inequities.

Receiving the Bottoms in Pauline Letters

In laying the ancient Roman imperial back on top of more recent queer bottoms, I have aimed to soften up the (imagined) divides between the past and present, replacing hard difference with something more porous and uncertain.[22] Such juxtapositions are likely to make many recipients

---

21. Brooten, with Hazelton (2010), has continued reconsidering the impacts of slavery on the forms that sexual ethics take, in antiquity and beyond.

22. For a potentially overlapping exploration, in search of a more capacious and variable set of potentials for ancient sex beside and within practices of penetration, see also Kotrosits 2018.

of these traditions uncomfortable. But we should linger longer with such discomfort when we recognize that the receptive parties are referenced in, but not exactly addressed by, these letters, as I suggested in the instances of 1 Thessalonians, Philemon, and Romans (among others). Going back and forth in time and space, rubbing these against one another, can hopefully generate some pleasurable and even necessary friction for recipients now by trying to focus on and reimagine those who were engaged in their own back and forth with Paul. Paul's letters contain arguments and ideas, figures and types closer to the predominant protocol of penetration and domination. Yet penetration and, or *as*, domination is not the whole story, even if that equation reflects the social order or at least the perspective of those at the pyramidal apex of power. There is more to this picture, and more than the perspective that Paul repeats and projects through these epistles.

Cvetkovich and Scott stress the contaminated history of and in sexual practices, insisting that we account for these, in antiquity and otherwise. Bottoming, as one mode of receptivity, correlates to embodied vulnerability and sociopolitical subordination, but not only. Sexual touching, including penetration, reflects trauma, but not only. As one can see now for both the past and the present, penetration coincides with coercion and exploitation, but not only. The then is distinctive from now, but not only. The past is not yet past, so it resonates, haunts, and repeats, with a difference. The hope is that people's pain and discomfort can have more uses than just continued exploitation and subjection. Desires and pleasures mix in with discomfort and pain, suggesting alternative relations between debasement and power. As Buell (2009, especially 167–68) has stressed for our racialized heritages, haunting can provide one way to connect past and present, without erasing specificity or surrendering in despair to seemingly immovable stabilities.

When Paul advocates for (free) males to acquire their own vessels (1 Thess 4:4), negotiates with them over the fate of (other) useful enslaved bodies (in Phlm 11–14), or casts condemned females and males in terms of excess and receptivity (in Rom 1:26–27), he repeats types and antitypes from the penetrative paradigm. For Paul's arguments to make sense, they would need to connect with the kinds of practices and people that the audiences know. Yet Paul underscores that his positions are not (already) the absolute and accepted given. His arguments reflect the distinct possibility that some people used aspects of these types and antitypes differently than expected and prescribed (by Paul and others). As we have seen, stories

about seemingly deviant rhetorical performances and the graphic renego-
tiations in graffiti both signal that departures from these prescribed orders
held some appeal for at least some in the larger Roman imperial context.

Sliding these against the figures in Paul's letters reopens our receptive relations with those cast as receptacles. The wives and/or enslaved
depicted as vessels in Thessalonica become visible to us in new ways,
beyond the brief allusions that make them so elusive to later recipients.[23]
They could be both disparaged and desired. After all, the letter recommends that (free) males should seek them (1 Thess 4:4), indicating not
only their desirability but also the possibility that they were not already
cooperating with the kyriarchal demands of the males who claim them
as their own.[24] Paul exhorts these (free) males to take possession of these
(potentially) receptive people, as if they have not already, and it is these
(free) males who appear to need these other Thessalonians, not vice versa.
The concern in this passage is that these (free) males lack sufficient self-
control and would cause offense (4:3–6); they could become effeminately
receptive to their passions. But those cast in the (potentially) receptive role
are not treated as especially problematic, as already out of control or in
need of discipline to prevent offense. They could be enacting their bottom
roles in ways that depart from ancient typologies.

A similar dynamic could be at work in Paul's appeal to the owner
of the (formerly) enslaved Onesimus. In the ambient sociosexual background, enslaved people are treated as useful receptacles for keeping (free)
males out of sexual trouble—not treading on other's property or making
use of someone who is supposed to be treated as equivalent in status. Paul
appears to be punning upon Onesimus's utility at a couple of points in the
letter: when he is described as once "useless" but now "good for use" (Phlm
11), and later when Paul requests a benefit from the owner-user using a
wordplay on Onesimus's name (using the rare optative verb, *onaimēn*,
"may I have this benefit"; Phlm 20). The letter looks like a delicate balanc-
ing act between Paul and the owner-user, but also between an enslaved
person and these males negotiating over his fate. Paul wants to arrange
their relations just so, reflecting the ways in which Onesimus is both disparaged and desired, eminently usable and "beloved" (Phlm 16).

---

23. On the difficulties of looking for these (ostensibly) elusive—even invisible—
members of the Thessalonian community, see Johnson-DeBaufre 2010.

24. On the queer potentials of female assembly members withdrawing from sex
(with males), in the case of Corinth, see Marchal 2018.

However, it is crucial not to falsely idealize the situation of these people cast as receptacles in letters like 1 Thessalonians and Philemon (and beyond). One cannot evade the ways in which these arguments resonate with an ethos of penetration and domination; they also disclose, however, if only slightly, that this ethos is not the only game in town. These letters index the coincidence of coercion and embodied pleasures. These are certainly fraught and risky contexts for those imagined as receptacles, to say the least.[25] It would be accurate to identify the operation of this ethos as not just perpetuating kyriarchal benefits for those toward the top but also generating various traumas for the many more toward the bottom.

Instead of focusing on the phallus, let us get down with the bottoms, become more receptive to those cast as receptive. They would have needed to negotiate these dynamics, but not everything about their lives was determined by them. Paul may appeal to (free) males to acquire their own vessels; he may even get those males to agree or secure the consent of Onesimus's owner. But that does not mean that those receptive parties, only glancingly referenced, would have cooperated with whatever arrangements Paul is seeking, even if it looked like acquiescence to their (supposed) sociopolitical superiors.

Ancient rhetorical performances and broader material culture present alternative, or at least additional, perspectives on sexual practices and their evaluations.[26] Not surprisingly, then, Paul's letters *as letters* reflect and reinforce the penetration paradigm prioritized in classical texts and that the audiences might be receiving them in contexts determined by (other) aspects of the material culture, including the pottery and graffiti that expand and complicate the picture of practices. There were many different hearers of these letters, and what they heard, thought, saw, and felt likely went beyond simple assent to or dissent from their arguments, even if they recognized them as a powerful perspective (or the perspective of the powerful). Compared to these letters, graffiti might have been more accessible to read and recite, more available for writing and speaking back, and better for circulating other approaches to surviving the everyday traumas of their kyriarchal circumstances. Those subjected to the treatment advocated in

---

25. For the difficulties the enslaved and—or as—sex-working Corinthians would have had in navigating the kinds of sexual ethics advocated in Pauline letters (especially 1 Corinthians), see Glancy 2006, 63–70.

26. For additional ways material culture can complicate our pictures of enslaved people, see Shaner 2018.

these letters might know that they are debased (in the eyes of the elites) but also prize others—or themselves—as enslaved people, prostitutes, tavern boys, and other infamous figures, as penetrated and participants, as survivors and subjects of various kinds of attention, as beautiful and desired (and not only by elite users). Their circumstances could have provided a kind of "agency that subordinated groups (like women and slaves) could exercise within the constraints of Roman society" (Kamen and Levin-Richardson 2015a, 250), in an elusive echo of Judith Butler's (2004, 15; see also 1) descriptions of gender and sexuality "as an improvisational possibility within a field of constraints." Onesimus and the so-called Thessalonian vessels may have shared knowing looks with their associates over their washing of Arretine ware or under colorful wall paintings; they may have etched their own jokes and exclamations on walls now long lost to the circumstances that instead lovingly preserved and praised texts like the invective of Juvenal and the epistles of Paul.

Thus we are haunted by a past of what else was spoken but made unspoken by the layers of texts and traditions we have received, with all of their "seething absences and muted presences" (A. Gordon 1997, 21; see also Buell 2010, 337). This is a history of exploitation and abjection with only rough analogies but persistent afterlives, often evaded but still summoned by and for those subject to the lingering trauma of its legacies. This pain, discomfort, and mourning still present unanticipated possibilities, possibilities that could be called queer. Indeed, as Freccero (2006, 77) reminds us regarding the clichéd "specter of homosexuality," these signs have long been anxiously assembled together as "the sense of a not-quite-visible contaminating near-presence that is also an anxious, often paranoid projection." Perhaps it is no wonder that I and others cannot quite let go of the figures obscured in these letters, most especially when they are targeted in texts like the oft-cited first chapter of Romans. The females condemned through their "unnatural use" (1:26) were and are anxiety producing, particularly when imagined as reflecting female-female erotic practices. Even trying to imagine these practices evokes an anxious response. If one situates this argument in the predominant protocol of penetration, then these females are *tribades*; their activities must compulsively correspond to the logics of penetration. Sex is phallocentric and penetrative, so one active female must somehow be inserting something phallic-like. These are gender transgressors, and one distancing technique might be to insist that this system of categorization and the objects of this system are nothing like the lesbians you and I all know.

Yet we also now know that sexual touching involves penetration, but not only. The varieties of sexual attention and embodied movement in butch-femme relations encourage us not to flatten the possibilities of the female-female contact fleetingly referenced in this letter. Even the label *tribas* trips up a user trying to reinforce the centrality of the phallus, since it refers to rubbing and friction, a potentially pleasurable and painful touch different from penetration or insertion (Hallett 1989; Brooten 1996). As Brooten (1996, 5–7, 43–44, 66–70, 131–32) has noted, although many texts try to phallicize these terms, both *tribas* and *frictrix* refer to rubbing practices and may just gesture beyond notions of active penetration and passive reception in instances when both females participants are called *tribades* and *fricatrices*. Is this what these females in the Roman assembly did? Oh, maybe they are like (some of) us after all! Indeed, these terms persist for longer than those used to describe male homoerotic practices, indicating that there might be fewer turning points, fewer ruptures, and more continuities in (often oppressive, stereotyped, and condemnatory) depictions of female homoeroticism (see Brooten 1996, 17–18, 23–24).

Nonetheless, in recognizing that we are haunted by this barely glimpsed presence, our contact with figures of the biblical past instead involves "the return of the object demanding to be a person of its own" (Cheng 2001, 200; also cited by Freccero 2006, 101).[27] Thus Freccero highlights that haunting involves a melancholic dwelling between identity and alterity:

> in order to enable the melancholic object-other to emerge and to demand from "within" the self, there must be identification, if not identity, between the subject and object. And yet, at the same time, for that object to demand, to become (a ghost), somehow to materialize, it must have a subjectivity of its own; it must, therefore, be other/different. (2006, 101)

This intrasubjectivity is a key aspect of Freccero's "penetrative reciprocity," being touched—even rubbed—by those marginalized in the text and the dominant sociosexual paradigm, and trying to reach back, toward these bottoms, in return.

The females and males of Rom 1:26–27 are like and unlike us. Our hauntingly semi-reciprocal relations urge us against flattening the pos-

---

27. For more reflections on unexplained alternatives and imperfect resemblances in the spectral presences of New Testament and early Christian studies, see Buell 2010, 331–38.

sibilities of sexual practices in their (and, in turn, our own) contexts. The females could be doing a variety of things with other females *or males* and be cast as beyond nature. Indeed, the same practices that bring disparagement are also sources of desire, even for elite males, who might actively seek female, or male, participants who are more than inert receptacles. What links the condemnation of "their females" and "males in males" (1:27) could be their refusal, however brief, of their prescribed asymmetrical roles. Certainly, an ancient condemnation of male-male erotic contact because they are too equivalent in status would both make good sense of this reference and trouble a modern presumption that homosexuality is the target of condemnation. The penetrative use of a superior, or just noninferior (or peer), is projected as an outrage in many elite Roman imperial texts, but some of the material remains signal the appeal of penetrative touches between those of similar age and status. The argument about males "receiving in themselves the due penalty" (1:27) is both a pun upon bodily receptivity (consonant with the predominant paradigm) and a hint of a sociopolitical top's willed vulnerability. The latter would, admittedly, be a risky vulnerability, but it could still turn out to be a masculine risk.

Thus I am not necessarily arguing for the irrelevance or even the receding of the ethos of penetration and domination; rather, I am suggesting that its presence is traumatizing but not totalizing. The figures marginalized (and in some instanced condemned) in texts like Romans, 1 Thessalonians, and Philemon would be negotiating their vulnerabilities alongside and within the attractions and pleasures of the practices that structure them as susceptible to trauma. Alternatively, this negotiation might occur not because of the pleasures and attractions but quite simply because of the necessity for one seeking a sexual touch to grapple with its painful aspects, its history of abjection, but not only. The obscured figures that haunt these epistles and our receptions of them may be using the types and antitypes of a dominant ethos in unanticipated ways that cite—but are not completely determined by—the kyriarchal present and past.

I find myself able to imagine or be haunted by such figures in the letter to the Romans. This is not due so much to the "specter of homosexuality" that hangs over (modern) anxieties about this text's opening chapter but more because there are so many named figures clamoring at the back end (16:1–16) of this Pauline letter. Like many of the names that appear in the graffiti farther down the Italian peninsula in Pompeii, many of these names are also Greek, reflecting the likely enslaved (or freed) status of people active in the assembly community at Rome.[28] Herodion (16:11), Hermes (16:14), Julia (16:15), and Nereus (16:15) are named, as well as the enslaved people implied by the circumlocutions "those belonging to Aristobulus" (16:10) and "those belonging to Narcissus" (16:11), conditions of belonging that would have involved various forms of bodily vulnerability and receptivity. Like Onesimus above, there are other "beloved" enslaved (or freed) people, like Epaenetus (16:5), Ampliatus (16:8), and Persis (16:12), desirable—if still demeaned—people. Some are mentioned in pairs or groups, but one pair stands out to me: Tryphaena and Tryphosa (16:12).

Interpreters typically assume that male-female evangelizing pairs are partners in marriage and in mission (as with Prisca and Aquila in Rom 16:3–5 and Andronicus and Junia in 16:7), unless otherwise specified (as with Rufus and his mother in 16:13). Is it reasonable to infer that Tryphaena and Tryphosa are more than just "workers in the lord" (16:12) together? Mary Rose D'Angelo (1990) has considered precisely this question by closely examining them, and two other female-female pairs, in the context of recut funerary reliefs in the Augustan era. If these women were both freedwomen, they may have been *conlibertae*, "freed together," and bound together in this process (75, 83).[29] Their similar names could be a marker of the same owner-user. Indeed, D'Angelo (2000, 165–66) notes the voluptuous or luxurious connotation of their names (both derived from the same Greek verb, *tryphaō*) as a potential indicator of the sexual tasks they were given as slaves, possibly even as prostitutes. This Greek term is a popular one for describing effeminacy, the presumed condition and position of the receptive party in the ambient kyriarchal ethos. D'Angelo (1990, 83) wonders if their choice to stay together and work together after manumission was also a sexualized choice.

These (enslaved or manumitted) females remind me of those Pompeian prostitutes who talked back through the surviving graffiti. Tryphaena and Tryphosa survived, and here they appear, if ever so briefly, toward the back of the letter, out of the sexual and political bottom. They likely knew a range of traumas, but they were not just penetrated. They were among the many recipients of this letter, but it is Paul who pursues the approval of the assembly by naming so many of these figures, pursuing *their* approval. This specific set of greetings indicates that they are known, not just sur-

---

28. See the discussion in Lampe 2003, 171–83. For another analysis of this letter in relation to remains from Pompeii, see Oakes 2009.

29. See the discussion in Schüssler Fiorenza 1986, 428; and Lampe 2003, 179–80.

viving, but working (it), engaged in practices that exceed and haunt the epistolary imagination. And in looking around for sex, we cannot ignore slavery and its legacies. The lives of Tryphaena, Tryphosa, Onesimus, and other (formerly) enslaved and "beloved" people, named and unnamed, were shaped by embodied vulnerabilities and political subordination, but not only. The letters haunt precisely because they give sometimes only the slightest hints of both these traumas and the *not only*. In reaching back and around to them and their embodied practices of surviving, we think through what kinds of touch they worked in the Lord. Any rough analogies between them and us or between them and other ancient people cast as receptacles (in Rome or Pompeii, Thessalonica or Corinth) cannot help but reflect a melancholic wavering between identity and alterity.

To look to the bottom means rethinking our relations as users *and* recipients. It also entails feeling our way toward being recipients not of Paul's letters but of *their* letters—the ancient recipients of these epistles, named and unnamed, addressed or marginalized, anticipated or unanticipated. We are reading and hearing and passing along *their* mail. If we are receptive not merely to the authority of an empire or apostle, to the demands of a kyriarchal ethos, we cultivate, in the words of Freeman:

> a kind of bottomy historiography: the potential for queer time—even queer history—to be structured as an uneven transmission of receptivity rather than authority or custom, of a certainly enjoyably porous relation to unpredictable futures or to new configurations of the past. (2010, 109)

In getting down to and reaching around for those who bottom in and then out of penetration as domination, users of these traditions now may just receive a touch from the past that is not yet past.

Works Cited

Bersani, Leo. 1987. "Is the Rectum a Grave?" Pages 197–222 in *AIDS: Cultural Analysis/Cultural Activism*. Edited by Douglas Crimp. OB. Cambridge: MIT Press.

Brooten, Bernadette J. 1996. *Love between Women: Early Christian Responses to Female Homoeroticism*. CSSHS. Chicago: University of Chicago Press.

Brooten, Bernadette J., with Jacqueline L. Hazelton, eds. 2010. *Beyond Slavery: Overcoming Its Religious and Sexual Legacies*. BR/WT/SJ. New York: Palgrave Macmillan.

Buell, Denise Kimber. 2009. "God's Own People: Specters of Race, Ethnicity, and Gender in Early Christian Studies." Pages 159–90 in *Prejudice and Christian Beginnings: Investigating Race, Gender, and Ethnicity in Early Christian Studies*. Edited by Elisabeth Schüssler Fiorenza and Laura Nasrallah. Minneapolis: Fortress.

———. 2010. "Cyborg Memories: An Impure History of Jesus." *BibInt* 18:313–41.

———. 2014. "Hauntology Meets Posthumanism: Some Payoffs for Biblical Studies." Pages 29–56 in *The Bible and Posthumanism*. Edited by Jennifer L. Koosed. SemeiaSt 74. Atlanta: Society of Biblical Literature.

Butler, Judith. 2004. *Undoing Gender*. New York: Routledge.

Cheng, Anne Anlin. 2001. *The Melancholy of Race: Psychoanalysis, Assimilation, and Hidden Grief*. RAC. New York: Oxford University Press.

Clarke, John R. 1998. *Looking at Lovemaking: Constructions of Sexuality in Roman Art 100 B.C.–A.D. 250*. Berkeley: University of California Press.

———. 2003. *Art in the Lives of Ordinary Romans: Visual Representation and Non-elite Viewers in Italy, 100 B.C.–A.D. 315*. Berkeley: University of California Press.

———. 2005. "Representations of the *Cinaedus* in Roman Art: Evidence of 'Gay' Subculture?" *JH* 49:271–98.

Corbeill, Anthony. 1997. "Dining Deviants in Roman Political Invective." Pages 99–128 in *Roman Sexualities*. Edited by Judith P. Hallett and Marilyn B. Skinner. Princeton: Princeton University Press.

———. 2004. *Nature Embodied: Gesture in Ancient Rome*. Princeton: Princeton University Press.

Cvetkovich, Ann. 2003. *An Archive of Feelings: Trauma, Sexuality, and Lesbian Public Cultures*. SerQ. Durham: Duke University Press.

D'Angelo, Mary Rose. 1990. "Women Partners in the New Testament." *JFSR* 6.1:65–86.

———. 2000. "Tryphosa." Pages 165–66 in *Women in Scripture: A Dictionary of Named and Unnamed Women in the Hebrew Bible, the Apocrypha/Deuterocanonical Books, and the New Testament*. Edited by Carol Meyers, Toni Craven, and Ross S. Kraemer. Grand Rapids: Eerdmans.

———. 2003. "Early Christian Sexual Politics and Roman Imperial Family Values: Rereading Christ and Culture." Pages 23–48 in vol. 6 of *The

Papers of the Henry Luce III Fellows in Theology. Edited by Christopher I. Wilkins. Pittsburgh: Association of Theological Schools.

Fisher, Gary. 1996. *Gary in Your Pocket: Stories and Notebooks of Gary Fisher*. Edited by Eve Kosofsky Sedgwick. SerQ. Durham: Duke University Press.

Freccero, Carla. 2006. *Queer/Early/Modern*. SerQ. Durham: Duke University Press.

Freeman, Elizabeth. 2010. *Time Binds: Queer Temporalities, Queer Histories*. PM. Durham: Duke University Press.

Glancy, Jennifer A. 2006. *Slavery in Early Christianity*. Minneapolis: Fortress.

Gleason, Maud W. 1995. *Making Men: Sophists and Self-Presentation in Ancient Rome*. Princeton: Princeton University Press.

Gordon, Avery. 1997. *Ghostly Matters: Haunting and the Sociological Imagination*. Minneapolis: University of Minnesota Press.

Gordon, Pamela. 1997. "The Lover's Voice in *Heroides* 15: or, Why Is Sappho a Man?" Pages 274–91 in *Roman Sexualities*. Edited by Judith P. Hallett and Marilyn B. Skinner. Princeton: Princeton University Press.

Hallett, Judith P. 1989. "Female Homoeroticism and the Denial of Roman Reality in Latin Literature." *YJC* 3:209–27.

Halperin, David M. 1990. *One Hundred Years of Homosexuality: And Other Essays on Greek Love*. NAW. New York: Routledge.

Holland, Sharon Patricia. 2012. *The Erotic Life of Racism*. Durham: Duke University Press.

Johnson-DeBaufre, Melanie. 2010. "Gazing upon the Invisible: Archaeology, Historiography, and the Elusive Women of 1 Thessalonians." Pages 73–108 in *From Roman to Early Christian Thessalonikē: Studies in Religion and Archaeology*. Edited by Laura Nasrallah, Charalambos Bakirtzis, and Steven J. Friesen. HTS 64. Cambridge: Harvard University Press.

Kamen, Deborah, and Sarah Levin-Richardson. 2015a. "Lusty Ladies in the Roman Imaginary." Pages 231–52 in *Ancient Sex: New Essays*. Edited by Ruby Blondell and Kirk Ormand. CM/MI. Columbus: Ohio State University Press.

———. 2015b. "Revisiting Roman Sexuality: Agency and the Conceptualization of Penetrated Males." Pages 449–60 in *Sex in Antiquity: Exploring Gender and Sexuality in the Ancient World*. Edited by Mark Masterson, Nancy Sorkin Rabinowitz, and James Robson. RA. New York: Routledge.

Kotrosits, Maia. 2018. "Penetration and Its Discontents: Greco-Roman Sexuality, The Acts of Paul and Thecla, and Theorizing Eros Without the Wound." *Journal of the History of Sexuality* 27:343–66.

Lampe, Peter. 2003. *From Paul to Valentinus: Christians at Rome in the First Two Centuries*. Translated by Michael Steinhauser. Edited by Marshall D. Johnson. Minneapolis: Fortress.

Levin-Richardson, Sarah. 2013. "*Fututa sum hic*: Female Subjectivity and Agency in Pompeian Sexual Graffiti." *CJ* 108:319–45.

———. 2015. "*Calos* graffiti and *infames* at Pompeii." *ZPE* 195:274–82.

Lopez, Davina C. 2012. "Visual Perspectives: Imag(in)ing the Big Pauline Picture." Pages 93–116 in *Studying Paul's Letters: Contemporary Perspectives and Methods*. Edited by Joseph A. Marchal. Minneapolis: Fortress.

Marchal, Joseph A. 2011a. "'Making History' Queerly: Touches across Time through a Biblical Behind." *BibInt* 19:373–95.

———. 2011b. "The Usefulness of an Onesimus: The Sexual Use of Slaves and Paul's Letter to Philemon." *JBL* 130:749–70.

———. 2012. "Queer Approaches: Improper Relations with Pauline Letters." Pages 209–27 in *Studying Paul's Letters: Contemporary Perspectives and Methods*. Edited by Joseph A. Marchal. Minneapolis: Fortress.

———. 2015. "The Exceptional Proves Who Rules: Imperial Sexual Exceptionalism in and around Paul's Letters." *JECH* 5:87–115.

———. 2018. "How Soon Is (This Apocalypse) Now? Queer Velocities after a Corinthian Already and a Pauline Not Yet." Pages 45–67 in *Sexual Disorientations: Queer Temporalities, Affects, Theologies*. Edited by Kent L. Brintnall, Joseph A. Marchal, and Stephen D. Moore. TTC. New York: Fordham University Press.

Martin, Dale B. 1995. "Heterosexism and the Interpretation of Romans 1:18–32." *BibInt* 3:332–55.

———. 1996. "*Arsenokoitēs* and *Malakos*: Meanings and Consequences." Pages 117–36 in *Biblical Ethics and Homosexuality: Listening to Scriptures*. Edited by Robert L. Brawley. Louisville: Westminster John Knox.

———. 2006. *Sex and the Single Savior: Gender and Sexuality in Biblical Interpretation*. Louisville: Westminster John Knox.

Musser, Amber Jamilla. 2014. *Sensational Flesh: Race, Power, and Masochism*. Sexual Cultures. New York: New York University Press.

Oakes, Peter. 2009. *Reading Romans in Pompeii: Paul's Letter at Ground Level*. London: SPCK.

Parker, Holt N. 1997. "The Teratogenic Grid." Pages 47–65 in *Roman Sexualities*. Edited by Judith P. Hallett and Marilyn B. Skinner. Princeton: Princeton University Press.

Reid-Pharr, Robert F. 2001. *Black Gay Man: Essays*. With a foreword by Samuel R. Delaney. Sexual Cultures. New York: New York University Press.

Richlin, Amy. 1983. *The Garden of Priapus: Sexuality and Aggression in Roman Humor*. New Haven: Yale University Press.

———. 1993. "Not before Homosexuality: The Materiality of the Cinaedus and the Roman Law against Love between Men." *Journal of the History of Sexuality* 3:523–73.

Schüssler Fiorenza, Elisabeth. 1986. "Missionaries, Apostles, Coworkers: Romans 16 and the Reconstruction of Women's Early Christian History." *WW* 6:420–33.

———. 2001. *Wisdom Ways: Introducing Feminist Biblical Interpretation*. Maryknoll, NY: Orbis.

Scott, Darieck. 2010. *Extravagant Abjection: Blackness, Power, and Sexuality in the African American Literary Imagination*. Sexual Cultures. New York: New York University Press.

Scullin, Sarah. 2016. "Making a Monster." Eidolon. March 24. https://tinyurl.com/SBL0699g.

Sedgwick, Eve Kosofsky. 1990. *Epistemology of the Closet*. Berkeley: University of California Press.

———. 1997. "Paranoid Reading and Reparative Reading: or, You're So Paranoid, You Probably Think This Introduction Is about You." Pages 1–37 in *Novel Gazing: Queer Reading in Fiction*. Edited by Eve Kosofsky Sedgwick. SerQ. Durham: Duke University Press.

Shaner, Katherine A. 2018. *Enslaved Leadership in Early Christianity*. New York: Oxford University Press.

Sharpe, Christina. 2010. *Monstrous Intimacies: Making Post-Slavery Subjects*. PM. Durham: Duke University Press.

Skinner, Marilyn B. 1997. "Introduction: *Quod multo fit aliter in Graecia...*" Pages 3–25 in *Roman Sexualities*. Edited by Judith P. Hallett and Marilyn B. Skinner. Princeton: Princeton University Press.

Spillers, Hortense J. 1987. "Mama's Baby, Papa's Maybe: An American Grammar Book." *Diacritics* 17.2:65–81.

Stockton, Kathryn Bond. 2006. *Beautiful Bottom, Beautiful Shame: Where "Black" Meets "Queer."* SerQ. Durham: Duke University Press.

Taylor, Rabun. 1997. "Two Pathic Subcultures in Ancient Rome." *Journal of the History of Sexuality* 7:319–71.

Walters, Jonathan. 1997. "Invading the Roman Body: Manliness and Impenetrability in Roman Thought." Pages 29–43 in *Roman Sexualities.* Edited by Judith P. Hallett and Marilyn B. Skinner. Princeton: Princeton University Press.

Williams, Craig A. 2010. *Roman Homosexuality.* 2nd ed. Oxford: Oxford University Press.

Pauline Anthropology as System and the Problem of Romans 1

Benjamin H. Dunning

Theology is basically an incoherent art.... Decent theologies struggle for coherence, the coherence that sexual systems also struggle for. Yet, we may ask what is wrong with being incoherent theologically?
—Marcella Althaus-Reid, *Indecent Theology*

The system is impossible.
—Jacques Derrida, *A Taste for the Secret*

In the vexed and ongoing debates about Scripture, sexuality, and the apostle Paul, the sheer amount of scholarly commentary on Rom 1:18–32 stands out. Much important scholarship has explored the relevance of ancient gender ideology for the interpretation of this passage, taking up a historicizing impulse that poses sexuality in antiquity as a question to be probed rather than as a given to be assumed (see the magisterial work of Brooten 1996; also, as representative, Martin 1995, 2006; Moore 2001; Swancutt 2003, 2004, 2006). In this way, while often differing from one another on particular points of exegesis and/or questions of continuity with the present, scholars working in this vein nonetheless tend to eschew any interpretation of Rom 1:18–32 that claims to carry either transhistorical or enduring theological implications in a simple or straightforward way. More recently, others have given this discussion a queer turn (or, more precisely, multiple turns), building on the aforementioned work to offer self-consciously queer readings of both the passage and the scholarly discussion surrounding it (see Marchal 2011 and discussion below).[1]

---

1. See also Menéndez-Antuña 2015. For a queer reading of Rom 1:18–32 not engaged explicitly with queer theory, see Townsley 2011.

In this essay, I join this emerging queer conversation from a different angle—one that focuses less on historicizing the specific details of Rom 1, as has already been undertaken so ably by other scholars—and instead endeavor to situate the passage and draw out its implications within a larger Pauline anthropological system, with a focus specifically on the interplay of anthropology, typology, and sexual difference in the apostle's thought. I have elsewhere proposed a framework for queering Pauline theological anthropology by way of focusing on the troubled and, so I have argued, ultimately irresolvable place of sexual difference within the apostle's system (Dunning 2011, 2014). Building on this previous work, this essay undertakes the thought experiment of considering how we might read the larger arc of Rom 1:18–32 differently (that is to say, queerly) in light of the conundrums of gender that inevitably attend that anthropological system.[2]

To that end, I begin by invoking another scholarly reading of Rom 1, one that charts a different course than the analyses referenced above, insofar as it pays little to no attention to how ancient gender protocols might impact the interpretation of the passage: that of Richard B. Hays in his influential essay on homosexuality in *The Moral Vision of the New Testament*. Here I single out Hays not to privilege his work unduly with respect to the field of relevant scholarship or to constrain my own analysis artificially. Rather, among mainstream biblical scholars, Hays is exemplary insofar as his exegesis of Rom 1:18–32, more than any other I know, puts on full display the degree to which a certain set of heteronormative conclusions are predicated on the presumed coherence of an underlying Pauline anthropological system. His work can thus serve as an especially apposite conversation partner for probing the specific nexus of issues that I take up here.

Hays (1996, 389) argues that while Rom 1 does not treat same-sex erotic acts as especially reprehensible (and indeed considers "self-righteous judgment of homosexuality … just as sinful as the homosexual behavior itself"), it nonetheless positions "*all* homosexual activity as prima facie evidence of humanity's tragic confusion and alienation from God the Creator" (emphasis original). When turning to normative theological conclusions, he makes clear that contemporary Christian communities should

---

2. While my previous work on Pauline anthropology and its afterlives deals extensively with questions of gender and sexuality as well as potential implications for queer theology, none of it engages Rom 1:18–32—a passage whose significance for Christian theological anthropology seems indisputable.

support civil rights for gays and lesbians and accept them as members of the Christian church (while not endorsing their ordination when noncelibate or supporting same-sex unions). Yet the thrust of his stance remains straightforward and unambiguous:

> In view of our propensity for self-deception, I think it prudent and necessary to let the univocal testimony of Scripture and the Christian tradition order the life of the church on this painfully controversial matter. We must affirm that the New Testament tells us the truth about ourselves as sinners and as God's sexual creatures: marriage between man and woman is the normative form for human sexual fulfillment, and homosexuality is one among many tragic signs that we are a broken people, alienated from God's loving purpose. (399–400; see also 1994)

To build this case, Hays (1996, 383) gives Rom 1 pride of place, characterizing it as "the most crucial text for Christian ethics concerning homosexuality."

Both the details and the conclusions of Hays's position have been extensively critiqued, most notably by Dale B. Martin (2006, 29–31, 51–64; see also 1995), and there is no need to rehearse Martin's now-classic counterargument here. Rather, as already mentioned, what I focus on instead is not so much the exegetical specifics of Hays's analysis as the degree to which his entire position assumes in Paul an implicit anthropological *system*—one in which the terms of sexual difference (i.e., male, female) and their relationship to desire (i.e., heterosexual, homosexual) function in ways that are entirely stable, coherent, and self-evident. Even more fundamentally, what is not in question for Hays is the notion of what constitutes the human in the first place—and thus his analysis shows no interest in interrogating the operations of the specifically Pauline "anthropological machine" (to borrow a phrase from Giorgio Agamben [2004, 33–38]) that undergirds the apostle's reflections on embodied desire and sexual difference in Romans.

This essay therefore engages both Rom 1 itself and Hays's reading of the text by way of posing precisely this line of inquiry: How might the terms of this discussion shift if we were to treat the contours and limits of the category of "the human" as a question rather than a given?[3] What

---

3. Here the question as framed has a certain consonance with the increasing interest in posthumanism within biblical studies. See, as representative examples, Koosed 2014; Buell forthcoming.

happens if we approach Paul's anthropological intervention as exactly that—an *intervention* in a historical field, one that works in historically specific ways and generates its own inevitable aporias along the way? And what are the implications of attending to a broader Pauline anthropological framework (and the troubled place of sexual difference within that framework) for how we read Rom 1:18–32—and especially verses 26–27? My contention is that the anthropological coherence that Hays assumes simply does not hold—and that this breakdown, in turn, not only casts various exegetical details of the Romans text in a different light but also (and perhaps more importantly) necessitates a critical reappraisal of the project to offer confident and self-assured claims to sexual knowledge that the passage ostensibly undertakes.

Theoretical Considerations

Joseph Marchal has argued that biblical scholarship on Rom 1:18–32 and associated issues might stand to benefit considerably from a more robust engagement with queer theory. He rightly identifies two opposite approaches to ancient sexuality that he labels *altericist*, "stress[ing] past formations as different and as 'over' in a new present that disrupts any identification with that past," and *continuist*, "highlight[ing] how the present is preceded by, yet also proceeding out of a history, a response to the past through which subjects identify (and disidentify)" (2011, 373–74). Yet when it comes to the tortured topic of "the Bible and homosexuality," Marchal is unconvinced of the political efficacy of either strategy. He is especially dubious of what he calls the "historiographic trump" associated with the altericist approach, worrying that more often than not—and especially in the case of the Bible—playing this sort of trump card fails in the project of "securing a more livable present for those who do not conform (enough) to hegemonic norms" (390 n. 52). As he pithily sums up this approach, "Sodom is not about sodomy, Leviticus also bans cotton-poly blends, or Paul does not have 'our' conception of sexual orientation in mind" (390). "Yet, the biblical, in moments like this…, exceeds itself, its ancient conditions, and many altericist arguments, as it adaptively crosses time" (390). Or as he puts it earlier in the article, "The biblical still persists, if not proliferates, as its own kind of argument" (383).

Marchal's analysis confronts this altericist/continuist impasse by way of a turn to queer theory—and most especially the work of Eve Kosofksy Sedgwick and Judith Butler—in order to provide "a queer, gender-troubled response to the trouble of how to make history" with a text as troubling as Rom 1 (Marchal 2011, 386–87). And his ensuing reading of the Romans passage compellingly offers what he calls "a less appalling way" to situate this text historically by way of highlighting the coexistence of multiple and conflicting models for knowledge of the divine; the performative (as opposed to merely descriptive) dimensions of the text's assumptions about the temporal priority of "proper" worship and/or sexual practice; the striking and perhaps unexpected resonances between the characterization of the deity and the excessive passions of those that Paul condemns, in light of which new possibilities for identification and disidentification with the figures that the passage conjures might potentially emerge; and, finally, the sheer heterogeneity of the community to which Paul writes, aptly characterized as "a motley crew, an eccentric assemblage" (387, 393).[4] Marchal's conclusion is that "we need less of heroically adventurous and saintly subversive solitaries like Paul and more of oddly assembled and critically reflective collectivities like the assemblies, with and through whom one could find contingent connections in, as, and with history" (394). More generally, his analysis persuasively demonstrates that the interrelations of identity and difference that necessarily attend the interpretation of the Romans passage are indeed tangled and complex, and that we thus need finely tuned theoretical tools to elucidate them.

To that end (but moving in another direction than Marchal's study), I want to consider Rom 1 in light of Paul's larger anthropological framework and commitments, as mentioned above. This is not (I hope!) in the service of reinstating Paul's point of view as that of an authoritative hero or saintly subversive. Indeed, I see the analysis that follows as differently oriented but nonetheless consonant (both in terms of analytical moves and political or theological aims) with Marchal's call to decenter Paul himself from holding an unquestioned pride of place in contemporary readings of Romans. My aim, however, is to interrogate the gendered operations of the larger Pauline anthropological machine as they bear upon Rom 1 specifically—insofar as these operations both necessarily undergird any general conclusions about embodiment, desire, and sexual difference (that is, *anthropological* conclusions) that are drawn from the passage and simultaneously tend to be taken entirely for granted in discussions of this

---

4. In addition to Butler and Sedgwick, other queer studies interlocutors for this analysis include Dinshaw 1999; Fradenburg and Freccero 1996; and Muñoz 1999.

vexed passage as a prooftext with respect to issues of sexuality, ancient and modern—for example, Hays's reading.

Here I also begin, like Marchal, with theory. But rather than starting with one or more of the canonical thinkers associated with queer theory, I suggest that the Derridean mode of philosophical argument that undergirds some strands of queer and feminist thought in a poststructuralist vein might be developed and profitably mobilized to attend to Rom 1 in this broader view. To put a finer point on this claim: as is well known, many of the important texts in queer theory advance their arguments by way of engagement with one or more key philosophical interlocutors—more often than not thinkers in the twentieth-century Continental tradition. For example, Lee Edelman's *No Future: Queer Theory and the Death Drive* (2004) mobilizes vocabulary and concepts drawn from the French psychoanalyst Jacques Lacan; Jasbir K. Puar's *Terrorist Assemblages: Homonationalism in Queer Times* (2007), while engaging a broad range of contemporary critical theory, nonetheless accords a certain conceptual pride of place to the work of Gilles Deleuze and Félix Guattari; and José Esteban Muñoz's *Cruising Utopia: The Then and There of Queer Futurity* (2009) frames the utopian logic of the analysis in conversation with the Frankfurt School and, most especially, the philosopher Ernst Bloch.

In a similar vein, Judith Butler, in her foundational contributions to queer theory—most notably *Gender Trouble: Feminism and the Subversion of Identity* (1990) and *Bodies That Matter: On the Discursive Limits of "Sex"* (1993)—dives deeply into the work of twentieth-century Continental thinkers spanning a range of disciplines from philosophy to psychoanalysis to so-called French feminism. These include, among others, Michel Foucault, Luce Irigaray, Julia Kristeva, Jacques Lacan, Monique Wittig, and Slavoj Žižek. Out of this dazzlingly diverse (and admittedly incomplete) list, it might be tempting to identify Foucault's work as the central philosophical scaffolding that informs Butler's argument, especially in *Gender Trouble*. And indeed, Foucault shows up throughout much of Butler's oeuvre as a primary interlocutor.

But while acknowledging the importance of Foucault to Butler's thought, what I highlight here is the philosophical debt—often more deeply buried in footnotes—that Butler bears to another contemporary French thinker, Jacques Derrida. To this end, I begin not with *Gender Trouble* or *Bodies That Matter* but with a text that, while generally less studied, is no less crucial for queer theory: *Excitable Speech: A Politics of the Performative* (Butler 1997a). In the latter text, Butler expands on the philosophical underpinnings of her theory of performativity (and especially the complex relationship between language and the body), invoking Pierre Bourdieu for his insight into "how norms become embodied, suggesting that they craft and cultivate the *habitus* of the body, … a promising account of the way in which non-intentional and non-deliberate incorporation of norms take place" (142). But she also critiques Bourdieu for treating language as "*a static and closed system* whose utterances are functionally secured in advance by the 'social positions' to which they are mimetically related" (145, emphasis added).[5]

Butler's counterargument on this point turns to Derrida, and most especially his reading of J. L. Austin on the performativity of speech acts in "Signature Event Context" and related writings (see Derrida 1982, 1988). She notes, following Derrida, that conventional utterances can be resignified "based on the prior possibility that a formula can break with its originary context, assuming meanings and functions for which it was never intended" (Butler 1997a, 147). Iterability is central here: the repetition of an utterance in specific social contexts through time relies on a citational structure that invokes previous uses. In this way, the utterance becomes sedimented or weighted down with its prior history. Yet it also carries the possibility of breaking with that context and history, and therefore the potential (at least sometimes) for resignification, as in the case of a term such as *queer* (14).[6]

Thus, according to Butler (1997a, 147), "for Derrida, the force of the performative is derived precisely from its decontextualization, from its break with a prior context and its capacity to assume new contexts."[7] She

---

5. Butler (1997a, 141) contends, "Bourdieu argues that the 'force' of the performative is the effect of social power and social power is to be understood through established contexts of authority and their instruments of censorship"—that is to say, the "static and closed system" referenced above.

6. Elsewhere, Butler (see 1993, 223) expresses some hesitation about whether such revaluation is always possible or whether certain terms (such as racial slurs) can be so sedimented historically as to be effectively stuck with respect to a "constitutive history of injury."

7. Here Butler (1997a, 148) faults Derrida for according iterability as convention "a structural status that appears separable from any consideration of the social." Note, though, that Derrida (1982, 323) himself describes "convention" in "Signature Event Context" as a "very historically sedimented notion," even as he fails to follow up on or develop the implications of this point in any way. For a nuanced analysis of both Butler and Derrida on this point (and a cogent defense of Derrida), see Hollywood 2006.

then goes on—by way of an argument that both relies on and critiques Derrida's position—to extend this philosophical point about language and speech acts narrowly construed to a broader framework that encompasses embodied action:

> It is in this sense that the bodily *habitus* constitutes a tacit form of performativity, a citational chain lived and believed at the level of the body.... The body, however, is not simply the sedimentation of speech acts by which it has been constituted. If that constitution fails, a resistance meets interpellation at the moment it exerts its demand; then something exceeds the interpellation, and this excess is lived as the outside of intelligibility. (155)

While the intricacies of this theoretical position go beyond what I can do justice to here, the central payoff for my purposes is the following: what Butler's Derridean reading of the force of the performative (in both its linguistic and embodied dimensions) renders visible is that failure— that is, the possibility for the sign to go otherwise than intended—is an irreducible and, indeed, constitutive component of any system of signification.[8] Accordingly, the pretensions of any such system to closure, unassailable coherence, and total mastery of meaning are, strictly speaking, *impossible*. This is, for Butler, "precisely the political promise of the performative, one that positions the performative at the center of a politics of hegemony, one that offers an unanticipated political future for deconstructive thinking" (161).

Keeping in view this philosophical backdrop to a prominent line of argument in queer theory, I now look more closely at Derrida's understanding of how systems work. More specifically, my interest is in pivoting from Butler's specific point about the force of the performative to a broader consideration of the more general mechanisms whereby a system stakes a claim to an all-encompassing coherence. Following a brief exploration of this issue in Derrida—and because my interest in the Pauline text revolves around anthropological systems specifically—I turn next to a lesser-known French philosopher, Étienne Balibar, who has done much to advance what he calls philosophical anthropology, often

---

8. Compare the analysis of the term *queer* in relation to gender performativity and drag (as well as the subtle but important role of a generally Derridean mode of argument) in Butler 1993, 223–42.

taking a generally Derridean approach. (I should note that while Butler cites him only infrequently, she, too, finds points of philosophical consonance with Balibar's thought; see, e.g., Butler 1997a, 89; 2012, 16–17; Butler, Laclau, and Žižek 2000, 38.) Here my goal is not to claim either Derrida or Balibar for queer theory. Rather, my analysis seeks to bring the ideas of both thinkers into conversation with those of Butler and other theorists in the queer theoretical canon (and especially with questions that Butler poses about the constitution of the human as a category). My proposal is that this point of intersection between Continental philosophy and queer theory can prove useful for exploring the particular constellation of issues around Pauline anthropology and Rom 1 that I take up in the remainder of this essay.

I begin, then, with Derrida. As noted, the late French philosopher was famously interested in the operation of systems. But this focus on systems is not a move to reenshrine authorial intent, even in those cases where the system in question is largely textual. For as Derrida notes in a reading of Plato's *Phaedrus*,

> the system here is not, simply, that of the intentions of an author who goes by the name of Plato. The system is not primarily that of what someone *meant-to-say*…. These communications or corridors of meaning can sometimes be declared or clarified by Plato…. Then again, in other cases, Plato can *not* see the links, can leave them in the shadow or break them up. And yet these links go on working of themselves. (1981, 95–96, emphasis original)

How do these signifying operations function *of themselves* in ways that exceed—yet are never entirely unrelated to—the guiding hand of an author or a conscious, intentional design? Is it, Derrida asks with respect to Plato, "in spite of him? thanks to him? in *his* text? *outside* his text? but then where? between his text and the language? for what reader? at what moment?" (96, emphasis original). Derrida is adamant that these questions cannot be answered "in principle and in general" (96); they therefore necessitate the labor of deconstructive close reading in any particular case. But he is equally clear that the problem posed here cannot be refused—or that this refusal can only be maintained when predicated on an untenable and intellectually dishonest commitment to "[avoid] all recourse to the difference between conscious and unconscious, voluntary and involuntary," thereby committing oneself to "a very crude tool for dealing with relations in and to language" (96).

Within any such system and its attendant operations—both transparent and veiled, conscious and unconscious—Derrida is especially focused on those "things that can irritate the system and at the same time account for the subterranean region in which the system constitutes itself by repressing what makes it possible, which is not systematic" (Derrida and Ferraris 2001, 4–5). As he argues, at stake is "not a method for discovering that which resists the system" but rather the necessity of showing, by way of the close reading of texts, that the capacity to bring about the system *qua system* in the first place is predicated on "a certain dysfunction or 'disadjustment,' a certain incapacity to close the system" (4). The project then becomes "a question of showing that the system does not work, and that this dysfunction not only interrupts the system but itself accounts for the desire of the system, which draws its *élan* from this very disadjoinment, or disjunction" (4). So while deconstruction has sometimes been accused of undercutting or immobilizing any impulse to politics that might attend textual interpretation, Derrida maintains otherwise: "I have tried to emphasize the fact that deconstruction has nothing whatsoever to do with privatizing philosophy, letting it take shelter in literature; the gesture, the division, is completely different" (10). Indeed, I argue that there is an undeniable (if often only implicit) politics in view here, insofar as this methodological orientation does not seek to smooth over or integrate the aporia that throws the system into crisis—or, more precisely, that renders visible that the system was always already in crisis. Rather, it insists on intensifying and radicalizing the aporia's force. Accordingly, the mode of reading for which Derrida advocates is "an attempt to train the beam of analysis onto this disjointing link" (4), in such a way as to call to account any system's pretensions to totality—and, by extension, the violence that necessarily attends those pretensions.

More recently, Balibar has turned this generally Derridean orientation in an explicitly anthropological direction. He calls into question the notion that the differences marking embodied human subjects—for example, gender, sexuality, race, ableness—are simply a matter of *particularity*—and, by extension, identity politics. Rather, he avers, such differences traverse the domain of the human from beginning to end, each one "represent[ing] the universal" against all attempts to constitute any system of human belonging in terms of such familiar categories as those of "'normal persons,' 'civilized men,' 'responsible subjects,' and so on" (Balibar 2017, 282). In this way, those anthropological differences that make a difference function as something like outlaws or rebels, bearing the weight of "nothing less than the differential of subjectivity by means of which the universal becomes (or rather becomes anew) a political figure" (282)—that is, a site of permanent contestation and remaking. On Balibar's reading, then, any anthropological system that aspires to totality and coherence will of necessity constitute itself by way of an inevitable dispossession, one that produces "nonpersons" in the name of "quasi-transcendentals" purporting to speak on behalf of the universal—for example, "life, nature, the history of humanity as a species, or the general conditions of civilization" (276).[9] Here "difference" tends to function euphemistically for this brutal dispossession, with the ironic effect that, even when performatively resignified to new ends (such as demanding recognition and rights), an anthropological difference can languish as no more than "a slogan—one whose political modality remains inherently problematic" (276).

In response to this perennial anthropological difficulty, Balibar argues that "it is less important—at least immediately—to perform analyses that illustrate the *particularity* of certain 'typical' differences or exclusions ... than directly to *make heard* voices that utter contradiction" (281, emphasis original). What is the philosophical—not to mention political—work that these voices do? They keep any claim to totality or universality honest, insofar as they render visible those operations within—and constitutive of—any supposedly universal anthropological system that in fact amount to a disavowed (but nonetheless real) devolution into "a more or less accommodating hegemony" on the part of that system (282). Thus Balibar poses the pointed question:

> What happens ... when we take into account ... the fact that anthropological differences are not merely *added to the universal* in a contingent fashion, arbitrarily *limiting* it or *overturning* its signification, but rather *contradict and thereby actualize it*, placing it into a determinate relation with itself and opening one or many abysses at the very center of universality that also usher inhumanity back into the human? (300, emphasis original)

---

9. Here Balibar attends to a crucial anthropological concern—what Butler calls "the problem of the unrepresented within the field of representation" (Butler, Laclau, and Žižek 2000, 23)—that is more or less ignored by some of his philosophical contemporaries also interested in questions of subjectivity and universality—e.g., Alain Badiou and Slavoj Žižek. For my critique of the latter on this point, see Dunning 2014.

Here the inhuman at the heart of the human incarnates in a specifically anthropological register the Derridean disadjustment or disjointing link discussed above.

At this point, I draw some connections to the project of queer theory—itself no stranger to the critical work that aporias can perform. And indeed, while not in conversation with queer theory as a discipline per se, Balibar does posit, by way of a brisk reading of Freud, Lacan, and Butler, that the problems (and possibilities) that attend sex, gender, and sexuality render especially acute the ways in which "anthropological difference—the less localizable and less substantial it becomes, never allowing individuals to be 'classified' without remainder into 'pure' types—can never … be neutralized or avoided when it is a matter of understanding what it means for several subjects *to join together in the realization of the universal*" (297, emphasis original). That is to say, when viewed from a systematic perspective, the stubborn distinctions of sexual difference do not permit an easy resolution or assimilation, functioning instead to trouble from within the terms of any anthropological system (such as, I argue, the Pauline one examined below) that attempts to lay claim to—or simply assume without comment or argument—the stability of sexual subject positions within a putatively universal frame.

Balibar goes on to argue that "anthropological differences in their unstable multiplicity are the only site where subjects can exist who raise the question, without preset answer, what it means to regard—*or not regard*—other subjects … as human" (301, emphasis original). Here we might note resonances with Butler's (2004, 35) plea that "we encounter the difference that calls our grids of intelligibility into question without trying to foreclose the challenge that the difference delivers"—an ethical stance that requires learning "to live and to embrace the destruction and rearticulation of the human in the name of a more capacious and, finally, less violent world, not knowing in advance what precise form our humanness does and will take." The site that Balibar has in view is indeed one that might provoke precisely this sort of encounter. As such, it is not really *habitable* in a strict sense, due to both its fundamental instability and the discriminations that tend to structure it. Nor, Balibar contends, is it "*acceptable* or *tolerable*," but it is something else—"the site of astonishment, excitation, identification—or of rebellion" (Balibar 2017, 301, emphasis original), and thus a space of possibility that we might justifiably characterize as queer.

Pauline Anthropology and Sexual Difference

With the above reflections providing a methodological orientation for what follows, I now turn to the issue of Pauline anthropology. I begin with a brief summary of my own previous arguments in *Specters of Paul* (2011) and *Christ without Adam* (2014). These are arguments that do not themselves include any interpretation of or engagement with Rom 1:18–32 but provide the necessary theological and philosophical context for the reading I offer below.

In Rom 5:12–21 and 1 Cor 15, the apostle puts forward a typological framework that commits his anthropology to a specific notion of the human, poised between creation and eschaton.[10] Thus in Rom 5, the prototypical human being, Adam, does not stand on his own but instead is figured as "a type (*typos*) of the one who was to come" (5:14), thereby linking human beginnings to an envisioned eschatological end. Therefore, however we are to understand the composition and situation of human beings qua human in the present, it must be with reference to these two typological poles, as 1 Cor 15 makes clear:

> Thus it is written, "The first human [*ho prōtos anthrōpos*], Adam, became a living being"; the last Adam became a life-giving spirit.... The first human was from the earth, a human of dust; the second human is from heaven. As was the human of dust, so are those of the dust; and as is the human of heaven, so are those of heaven. Just as we have borne the image of the human of dust, we will also bear the image of the human of heaven. (15:45–49 NRSV, slightly modified)

Within this anthropological system, Adam and Christ hold paradigmatic pride of place. Yet insofar as the male bodies of these two figures function as stand-ins for the human tout court, the place of the feminine remains radically unclear. That is to say, the bodily difference of Eve poses an unresolved problem for the system—one that extends, by way of the typological logic in play, to anyone whose embodied subjectivity is not straightforwardly "represented" by the male bodies of Adam and Christ. Here, then, we might consider the figure of Eve, both ostensibly absent but hauntingly present, to be a kind of third anthropological term in the Pauline system (Dunning 2011, 8–13, 22–25), and as Derrida argues, "in the

---

10. All biblical translations are NRSV unless otherwise noted.

end everything we have said about the system comes down to a question of the 'third'" (Derrida and Ferraris 2001, 5). He notes that while a third term in any given system *can* function to mediate toward some sort of synthesis or ultimate reconciliation (as in certain forms of Hegelian dialectic), his interests lie more with a different sense or interpretation of the third, "that whose absolute heterogeneity resists all integration, participation and system, thus designating the place where the system does not close" (5). And it is in this sense, I argue, that Eve troubles the putative coherence of Pauline anthropology. Put most simply, Eve's difference does not fit in any straightforward or consistent way within the Adam-Christ frame—a problematic that historically has continued to rankle the Christian typological dream that, in Derrida's (1974, 297–98) words, "perfect representation should represent perfectly" (see also Dunning 2014, 98–104).

Turning specifically to Romans: this Pauline anthropological system is undeniably operative in the text. As it appears explicitly in Rom 5, the rhetorical emphasis is on the contrast between the figures of Adam and Christ:

> For if the many died through the one human's trespass, much more surely have the grace of God and the free gift in the grace of the one human, Jesus Christ [*tou henos anthrōpou Iēsou Christou*], abounded for the many.... If, because of the one human's trespass, death exercised dominion through that one, much more surely will those who receive the abundance of grace and the free gift of righteousness exercise dominion in life through the one human, Jesus Christ. (5:15, 17 NRSV, slightly modified)

While both these verses set Adam and Christ in a relationship of contradistinction, the implication for theological anthropology in the Pauline present is that human beings are not to be identified exclusively with either paradigmatic domain. Instead they inhabit an interval defined by some sort of complicated relationship to both. And while Christ followers may look forward to the eschatological resolution of being "united with him in a resurrection like his" (6:5), this in no way consigns the figure of Adam to typological irrelevance. Rather, the in-betweenness of the human situation, irreducibly defined in relation to both poles, is precisely the point.

Given the configuration of this specific anthropological machine, it is perhaps unsurprising that Romans never mentions Eve explicitly, thereby avoiding any direct encounter with the anthropological conundrums of embodied difference that, I have argued, she both represents and generates within the system's own terms. As I have suggested elsewhere

(Dunning 2014, 104–8), however, we may be able to glimpse the interplay of Eve's explicit absence and her shadowy presence in the anthropology underlying the conflicted reflections of Rom 7:7–25. As is well known, the identity of the "I" in this passage has been much debated, and it has been suggested that if Paul employs some sort of *prosopopoeia* or speech-in-character here, the character in question is not the biblical Adam (as many have argued, hearkening back to the typology of Rom 5 as evidence) but instead his counterpart Eve (Busch 2004). The most compelling evidence for this proposal, to my mind, is that if we read the agonized explanation of 7:11—"For sin, seizing an opportunity in the commandment, deceived me [*exēpatēsen me*]"—in light of the narrative drama of Gen 3, then we must reckon with the fact that the intertextual echo here invokes the words of Eve, not Adam: "The serpent deceived me [LXX: *ēpatēsen me*], and I ate" (Gen 3:13, my translation). I have argued, however, not that the "I" in Rom 7 should be definitively identified as Eve but rather that what we see in this enigmatic passage is an anthropologically crucial instance of textual indeterminacy.

I would thus maintain that the anthropological framework of the Adam-Christ typology as articulated in Rom 5 is operative in this chapter, insofar as the unnamed speaker—this "wretched *anthrōpos* that I am" (7:24)—situates the agonizing plight in question by way of future-oriented reference (*tis me rhysetai*) to Jesus Christ (7:24–25; see also 5:15), the typology's other paradigmatic *anthrōpos*. Thus the typological shadow of Adam hangs over the scene. And yet it has been argued correctly that the text's allusions to the Genesis creation narrative map more appropriately onto the character of Eve than that of Adam (Busch 2004, 13–16). Rather than try to resolve this ambiguity, I contend, our interpretations of Romans (and, by extension, Pauline anthropology) ought to embrace it. Not only in Rom 5, then, but also in Rom 7—and, by extension, throughout the anthropology of the letter as a whole—Eve's bodily particularity cannot be fully represented within the Adam-Christ frame. But neither can it be totally discarded or ignored (as the text itself enacts by way of the ambiguous positioning of the "I" and slippery allusions to the Genesis narrative in Rom 7). Instead, Eve's difference functions as a persistent disjointing link, an unavoidable remainder troubling the system's pretensions to anthropological coherence and totality—and in the process, pointing to the theological instability of *all* sexual subject positions, within the terms of a system that attempts (or at least assumes) precisely this stability.

Romans 1:18–32

But what about Rom 1:18–32? The passage does not make mention of any of these key typological figures—Adam, Christ, or Eve. Yet the degree to which this typology underwrites Pauline anthropology—and in so doing brings along with it the problems and questions of sexual difference that it inevitably engenders—has implications for the reading of Rom 1 that need to be explored more fully. To be clear, here I would want to distance myself from the position, espoused by Hays and others, that the passage evokes a narrative of creation and fall drawing on the opening chapters of Genesis. On this reading, as Hays (1996, 387–88) proffers it, "Paul is offering a *diagnosis* of the disordered human condition: he adduces the fact of widespread homosexual behavior as evidence that human beings are indeed in rebellion against their Creator" (emphasis original). Critiquing this position and its "inscription of homosexuality into 'fallen human nature,'" Martin (2006, 52) rightly notes that "Paul does not here mention Adam, Eve, Eden, the fall, or the universal bondage of humanity to sin."[11] He proposes instead that what is in view in the passage is an origin story about idolatry and polytheism—one that can be located among other stories found within Second Temple Jewish literature and that "served to highlight the fallenness not of Jewish culture or even of humanity in general, but of the Gentiles due to the corruption brought about by civilization" (53; see also Stowers 1994, 85–100). At stake here for Martin is the need to expose what he terms a "heterosexist" bias among scholars such as Hays (2006, 54)—that is to say, scholars who acknowledge the passage's "homiletical sting operation … using rhetoric characteristic of Jewish polemic against Gentile immorality" (rhetoric that works, Martin notes, only if we read the passage as a condemnation of gentiles specifically, prior to the censure of Jewish self-righteousness) and yet nonetheless subtly or not so subtly shift their readings in the direction of universalizing claims about the perversion, pollution, and fallenness of the general human condition, as figured most powerfully and graphically by "homosexuality" (Hays 1996, 389).

While I side with Martin and Stowers on this issue, settling the question definitively is immaterial to the point I make here. Rather than seeing an implied evocation of Gen 1–3 (or lack thereof) in the Rom 1 passage,

---

11. For a nuanced account of how so-called natural theology functions in the passage (and in the history of its interpretation), see Brooten 1996, 222–28.

I instead highlight the degree to which Hays's position relies uncritically on the assumption of a straightforward coherence to sexual subject positions—a coherence, I argue, that does not obtain within the typological terms of Pauline anthropology writ large. Thus my point is not that we ought to find the figures of Adam, Eve, or Christ somehow lurking within the interstices of Rom 1, but rather that we *do* find in the passage reference to women, men, nature, and structures of desire that are embodied (and therefore implicated in sexual difference) and that this complex of anthropological references cannot be understood in a way that isolates them entirely from the orienting terms or the irresolvable problems of the larger Pauline anthropological frame—nor can they be used in a similar manner to underwrite normative theological conclusions.

Accordingly, the infamous verses 26 and 27 maintain the following:

> On account of this, God gave them over to dishonorable passions. For their women [*thēleiai*] exchanged the natural use [*tēn physikēn chrēsin*] for that which is contrary to nature [*para physin*]. And in a similar way also, the men [*arsenes*], giving up the natural use of women, were inflamed in their passionate lust for one another. Men committed shameful conduct with men and received in themselves the recompense that was necessary for their error. (my translation)

Here much scholarly ink has been spilt on the precise inflection of "natural," "contrary to nature," and the counterpart phrase "according to nature" (*kata physin*), the last of which does not appear in the passage (but cf. Rom 11:21, 24). On Hays's reading, these categories ought to be read in light of their frequent use within Stoic moral philosophy as a means of reflecting on correct ways of living. He notes further that "the opposition between 'natural' and 'unnatural' is frequently used (in the absence of convenient Greek words for 'heterosexual' and 'homosexual') as a way of distinguishing between heterosexual and homosexual behavior" (1996, 387).

Martin's counterposition rightly identifies that at issue here is not simply an inconvenient absence of terms but a different and culturally specific conceptual apparatus for understanding sex acts and sexual desire. In the dominant ancient Roman model, same-sex eros was treated in terms of social hierarchy—that is, questions about gender and status (Moore 2001, 135–46). Thus for an elite Roman male to penetrate sexually a male of lower status (such as one of his slaves) was for the most part unproblematic (Harper 2013, 24–27). But for an elite male to submit willingly to penetration himself—or even worse, to *desire* to be penetrated—was considered contrary to nature (*para physin*) and indeed represented the depths of erotic monstrosity (see Marchal's chapter in this volume). Within this model, at least generally speaking, Roman thinkers tended to treat the desire that drives same-sex erotic acts not as a qualitatively different form of sexual desire but rather as an excessive manifestation of a single undifferentiated desire (the same one that propelled all erotic activity). So, Martin argues,

> According to [Greco-Roman moralists], some people, due to unrestrained sexual desire, grew bored with "basic" sexual activity and went cruising for new and untried pleasures.... Men were so enslaved to their lusts that they were eager to try activities out of the ordinary, such as sex with one another. The problem had to do not with a *disoriented* desire, but with *inordinate* desire. Degree of passion, rather than object choice, was the defining factor of desire. (2006, 56–57, emphasis original)

In light of this distinctively ancient sexual logic (set in stark contrast by Martin [2006, 57] to "modern heterosexist rhetoric," in which "homosexuality is unnatural in that it results from disoriented desire, wrong 'object choice' ... like a craving to eat excrement"), Hays's too-easy conflation of the *kata physin/para physin* opposition with heterosexual/homosexual behavior—the latter positioned in a line of simple and straightforward continuity with modern configurations—is a rhetorical sleight of hand predicated on a set of assumptions simply not borne out by the distinctive realities of ancient thought and practice with respect to sex.

The degree to which Paul himself remained implicated in these traditional modes of ancient thought rather than staking innovative ground (conceptually speaking) has been a matter of ongoing scholarly debate.[12] Here I simply note that I find the tendency on the part of some commentators to assume uncritically a kind of default complementarity—whereby gender hierarchy in an ancient Christian text such as Romans is likely absent unless explicitly marked otherwise—to be historically untenable (Dunning forthcoming). But for the purposes of this analysis, I maintain

---

12. As mentioned above, interpretations of Paul that see him as deeply enmeshed in Roman ways of thinking on these issues include Brooten 1996; Moore 2001; Swancutt 2003, 2004; Martin 2006. For alternative perspectives, see Watson 2002 and the more sophisticated (but still ultimately unconvincing) reading in Harper 2013, 93–99.

that the apostle's recourse to language of "natural use" and that which is "contrary to nature" is an appeal to a *system*; that is to say, it presupposes an underlying anthropological framework in which sexual subject positions are stable and coherent. This in turn allows the evaluation of specific sexed bodies and their intermingling with other bodies in terms of conformity (*tēn physikēn chrēsin*), or lack thereof (*para physin*), to the system's terms. Indeed, it is only by virtue of an assumed system (encompassing if not necessarily limited to the anthropological register) that this sort of argument from nature has any force.

Yet taking a page from Balibar and Butler, the inevitable and intractable realities of embodied human variation (that is, anthropological difference) mean that any such system's claim to totality will of necessity produce an excluded outside, thereby either "compelling nature to annul itself or to produce '*nonpersons*'" (Balibar 2017, 276, emphasis original; see also Butler 2009, 7–9). And this insight points most basically, I argue, to a certain intractable nonviability or failure to achieve closure at the heart of the Pauline anthropological system. Indeed, the force of Paul's arguments from "the natural" in Rom 1 implies a refusal of any possibility that nature might annul itself on terms internal to the system. But at the same time, the Romans passage offers *thēleiai* and *arsenes*, women and men, in a way that assumes the fully coherent anthropological legibility of both categories within the system—and then trades on that assumed legibility to condemn embodied actions and desires not in keeping with the totalizing vision of nature that the system outlines.

However, as the above analysis of Paul's broader theological anthropology has sought to show, it is precisely with respect to the legibility of sexually differentiated subject positions that the system in question fails to deliver the closure that it promises. Thus, I maintain, however much Paul might assume to the contrary, *women* is not an anthropologically untroubled category in Rom 1—and neither, by extension, is *men*. Indeed, insofar as Pauline anthropology articulates sexual subject positions typologically—that is, situated between creation and eschaton in terms of the paradigmatic bodies of Adam and Christ—the women of Rom 1 who exchange "the natural use" embody a kind of excess or remainder that the typological system can neither offer an account for nor fully neutralize or put to rest.

But this means that the crux of the issue (in typological terms) runs deeper than the unnatural exchanges narrated by the passage. More fundamentally, what is always already thrown into question by the system's

failures to resolve its own gendered aporias is the basic theological legibility of binary sexual difference, male and female. Given the resolutely
androcentric structure of Paul's Adam-Christ typology, it is consistently
the female rather than the male that emerges as the disjunction or problem
in typological terms. And in this way, the underlying anthropological logic
of Romans participates in what Martin (2006, 47) calls, in another context,
"the ancient horror of the feminine." That said, I am clear that while it may
be the bodily difference of Eve over which the machine stumbles, the result
is to render visible a crisis of coherence that obtains no less forcefully (and
arguably more so) with respect to male bodies and their (Pauline) pretensions to universality, totality, and mastery.

On this constitutively unstable anthropological foundation, then, that
the apostle casts *some* gendered bodies as erotic monsters in Rom 1:26–27.
Hays emphasizes that Paul's reasoning here does not proceed primarily
with an eye to bringing judgment on these particular sexual behaviors or
the people who indulge in them. Rather, he argues, the purpose is diagnos-
tic, "laying bare the truth about humankind's dishonorable 'exchange' of
the natural for the unnatural. According to Paul, homosexual relations …
represent a tragic distortion of the created order" (1996, 396). This emphasis on representation is key. That is to say, according to Hays's reading,
the bodily relations in question signify beyond themselves, functioning
as a salacious synecdoche for the situation of all human beings, not just
the ones discussed in 1:26–27. These verses, then, function much more
broadly as "a sign of human alienation from God's design" (397).

Yet this invocation of design serves as a pointed reminder that what we
are discussing here is the operation of a theological and anthropological
system. And for Hays, the hope that human beings have within the system
is to be found in the eschaton: "Neither the word of judgment against
homosexuality nor the hope of transformation to a new life should be read
apart from the eschatological framework of Romans" (393). The trajectory
of Romans itself also moves, at least on one level, in this direction: "And
not only the creation, but we ourselves, who have the first fruits of the
Spirit, groan inwardly while we wait for adoption, the redemption of our
bodies" (8:23). So, Hays argues, "The 'redemption of our bodies' remains
a future hope; final transformation of our fallen physical state awaits the
resurrection. Those who demand fulfillment now, as though it were a right
or a guarantee, are living in a state of adolescent illusion" (393). Here it
would seem that Hays imagines an eschatological moment in which the
state of monstrous alienation in which *all* are somehow implicated (by

way, to be sure, of the signifying function of *some*) yields to a renewed and transformed version of the normative sexual subject positions and roles that Rom 1 assumes. In this redemptive vision, "our culture's present swirling confusion about gender roles" (399) will find its final and categorical resolution—that is, forms of masculinity and femininity that are not only ideal, stable, and mutually exclusive but also actually able to be inhabited flawlessly and fully by embodied human subjects—at the resurrection, the latter pole of the Adam-Christ typological frame.

The remarkable condescension of these passages aside, however, I argue that Hays's turn to eschaton simply ends up sidestepping the forceful and intractable problems of gender, sexuality, and embodiment that it aspires to solve. The eschatological vision of Romans never dispenses with the anthropological logic of the Adam-Christ paradigm (see, e.g., 6:5, 8:29). And thus the text never actually resolves—or even attempts to resolve—the aporia of sexual difference that Eve's absent presence figures within the typological frame. By ignoring these questions, however, Hays's reading implicitly presumes such a resolution; indeed, it must do so in order to shore up stable binary sexual difference as an unquestionable part of the eschatological order of things. As such, Hays falls prey to the kind of magical thinking that queer theorist Lee Edelman (2004, 134) diagnoses (in a different context), in which "the future holds out the hope of a final undoing of the initiating fracture, the constitutive moment of division, by means of which the signifier is able to pronounce us into subjectivity." Yet even as the terms of the Pauline anthropological system push toward precisely this sort of closure, they also, I contend, fail to achieve it. What I have called the unavoidable remainders of embodied difference simply *remain*, thereby haunting the system in a way that cannot be magically resolved—not even by appeal to eschatological mystery (see 1 Cor 15:51)—insofar as it is the system itself, inclusive of the eschaton, that constitutes these bodily distinctives as remainders in the first place.

Accordingly, these considerations might allow (or perhaps even oblige?) us to read the erotic monsters of Rom 1:26–27 in a new light. As I show, Hays's reading assumes a closed circuit theological anthropology, and his attendant moralizing conclusions take this foundation for granted as that which is both unquestioned and unquestionable. My countercontentions are twofold. First, insofar as the Pauline text exceeds its own drive to anthropological closure, our engagement with it is never complete if we do not take into account that Derridean "dysfunction or 'disadjustment' ... [that] not only interrupts the system but itself accounts for the desire of the system" (Derrida and Ferraris 2001, 4). Second, there are vital anthropological possibilities—what Ward Blanton calls the "transformative rewiring of sexual identities" (forthcoming)—entailed in the conceptual space that a resolute attentiveness to this disadjustment opens up. This is an interpretive strategy on my part that runs decidedly against the grain of the apostle's intention in the passage at hand but that is, I argue, nonetheless necessitated by the anthropological conundrums that his system ineluctably generates.

In this way, to return to Balibar, monsters—the inhuman at the heart of the human—may signify otherwise. That is to say, they are not *only* the inevitable remainder that the anthropological system seeks to eliminate as "perversion, alienation, or simply alterity," but they are also figures of potential and possibility, the site of surprises, disruptions, and counteridentifications: "The monster carries onward, without assignable limit, … the possibility of a multiplicity of transformations," a vehicle for those contradictions "that breathe energy and movement"—and necessarily so—into any project of anthropological universality (2017, 301–2). Butler asks poignantly at what cost we articulate "a coherent identity position by producing, excluding, and repudiating a domain of abjected specters that threaten the arbitrarily closed domain of subject positions." She goes on to conclude that "perhaps only by risking the *incoherence* of identity is connection possible.… Only the decentered subject is available to desire" (1997b, 149, emphasis original). In this light—both with and against Paul—we might read the interrelation of sexual subject positions and desire in Rom 1:26–27 not as a problem to be solved (or that even could be solved, in this sense) but rather as a window into those necessary anthropological remainders whose decentering force attends *all* embodied desire—and indeed points to something fundamental about what such desire is and has to be within a Pauline typological frame, spanning creation to (a still-embodied) redemptive eschaton.

Conclusion

Elizabeth Freeman has questioned a certain deconstructive emphasis in queer theory, maintaining that " 'queer' cannot signal a purely deconstructive move or position of pure negativity." Her primary concern is that the move to deconstruction runs the risk of "evacuating the messiest thing about being queer: the actual meeting of bodies with other bodies and with objects" (2010, xxi). I think Freeman is right to articulate this concern.

And indeed, as I note elsewhere, a Derridean reading of the Adam-Christ typology does not of itself provide the resources for thinking about sexual difference or desire differently. Thus this mode of critical interrogation is first and foremost a project in "ground-clearing," opening the space for looking elsewhere and listening more carefully to other elements in the tradition (Dunning 2014, 113).

But is that all it is? Is ground-clearing all that can be done with this aspect of the apostle's theology in relation to contemporary gender and sexual politics? It is here, I maintain, that attention to Rom 1:26–27 proves pivotal. For these verses stubbornly foreground "the actual meeting of bodies with other bodies." Yet when situated within the larger framework of the Adam-Christ typology, they also render visible the degree to which a theologically coherent condemnation of such erotic conjoining proves impossible within a Pauline system that drives relentlessly toward anthropological closure even as it necessarily fails to resolve bodily difference without remainder. The result, I contend, is that the epistemological confidence on which the judgment of Rom 1:18–32 rests is called into question—or, more precisely, thrown into crisis—in a structurally necessary and thus ultimately irresolvable way. Here we might follow the psychoanalyst Adam Phillips (2012, 76–77) in his argument that "when it comes to sexuality, we don't get it. But this doesn't mean that we just haven't yet come up with the right way of knowing, the kind of knowing suited to our sexual natures. It means that when it comes to sex we are not going to get it."

In conclusion, then, my final point is about knowledge—and, more specifically, about the way in which the reading of Rom 1 offered here works to undermine the will to a definitive sexual knowledge (a will to knowledge that the passage not only participates in but is also frequently called upon to defend). Indeed, it is my contention that the above reading might support a kind of parallax shift (see Žižek 2006), wherein Pauline anthropology in its constructive dimensions appears not solely as a totalizing, if broken, machine driving toward an always-impossible coherence but also as a powerful, if still problematic, witness to the kind of thing sexuality is—one that will always inherently resist our attempts to secure it as an object of knowledge, to narrativize it, and to assign it fixed and stable meaning, theological or otherwise.

In a gloss on Freud, Phillips (2012, 79) submits that "when it comes to sexuality, we have to give up on knowing, or, rather, since we can't give up on it[,] … we have to ironize the knowing that we do about our sexuality (the stories we tell about our sexuality will always be unsettled and unsettling)." My contention is that refusing to treat Rom 1 as an isolated prooftext with respect to sexuality but instead situating it within a larger Pauline constellation of theological issues—that is, anthropology, typology, and sexual difference—produces an imperative not unlike the one offered by Phillips. This stands in stark contrast to a reading such as Hays's, which offers epistemologically self-assured conclusions that require (and indeed assume) sexual difference to be an entirely self-evident, stable, and coherent category within Paul's theological anthropology.

Hays (1996, 389) himself notes that an ironizing reversal is a key maneuver (i.e., "a homiletical sting operation") within the larger argument of which Rom 1:18–32 forms a part. Paul thus opens Rom 2 with a sarcastic appeal to the moralizing self-righteousness of his imagined gentile interlocutors: "We know that God's judgment on those who do such things is in accordance with truth" (2:2). In the immediate context, the note of irony falls on the "we know" (*oidamen*) in the sense that the "we" who proudly make this claim and accordingly offer judgment on others turn out to be similarly guilty (2:1–3). Yet following Phillips (and in light of the gendered aporias of Paul's anthropology that I have sought to chart in this essay), we might construe the imperative to ironize *oidamen* in a different light—that is to say, queerly, taking aim first and foremost not at the objects of judgment but rather at the claim to perspicuous knowledge and categorical certainty as they bear on bodies, desire, and difference within the Pauline anthropological machine.

Works Cited

Agamben, Giorgio. 2004. *The Open: Man and Animal.* Translated by Kevin Attell. MCA. Stanford: Stanford University Press.

Althaus-Reid, Marcella. 2000. *Indecent Theology: Theological Perversions in Sex, Gender and Politics.* New York: Routledge.

Balibar, Étienne. 2017. *Citizen Subject: Foundations for Philosophical Anthropology.* Translated by Steven Miller. New York: Fordham University Press.

Blanton, Ward. Forthcoming. *The Radical Paul: Interviews.* Minneapolis: Fortress.

Brooten, Bernadette J. 1996. *Love between Women: Early Christian Responses to Female Homoeroticism.* CSSHS. Chicago: University of Chicago Press.

Buell, Denise Kimber. Forthcoming. "Posthumanism." In *The Oxford Handbook of New Testament, Gender, and Sexuality*. Edited by Benjamin H. Dunning. Oxford: Oxford University Press.

Busch, Austin. 2004. "The Figure of Eve in Romans 7:5–25." *BibInt* 12:1–36.

Butler, Judith. 1990. *Gender Trouble: Feminism and the Subversion of Identity*. TG. New York: Routledge.

———. 1993. *Bodies That Matter: On the Discursive Limits of "Sex."* New York: Routledge.

———. 1997a. *Excitable Speech: A Politics of the Performative*. New York: Routledge.

———. 1997b. *The Psychic Life of Power: Theories in Subjection*. Stanford: Stanford University Press.

———. 2004. *Undoing Gender*. New York: Routledge.

———. 2009. *Frames of War: When Is Life Grievable?* London: Verso.

———. 2012. *Parting Ways: Jewishness and the Critique of Zionism*. New York: Columbia University Press.

Butler, Judith, Ernesto Laclau, and Slavoj Žižek. 2000. *Contingency, Hegemony, Universality: Contemporary Dialogues on the Left*. London: Verso.

Derrida, Jacques. 1974. *Of Grammatology*. Translated by Gayatri Chakravorty Spivak. Baltimore: Johns Hopkins University Press.

———. 1981. *Dissemination*. Translated by Barbara Johnson. Chicago: University of Chicago Press.

———. 1982. "Signature Event Context." Pages 307–30 in *Margins of Philosophy*. Translated by Alan Bass. Chicago: University of Chicago Press.

———. 1988. *Limited Inc*. Translated by Samuel Weber and Jeffrey Mehlman. Evanston, IL: Northwestern University Press.

Derrida, Jacques, and Maurizio Ferraris. 2001. *A Taste for the Secret*. Translated by Giacomo Donis. Cambridge: Polity.

Dinshaw, Carolyn. 1999. *Getting Medieval: Sexualities and Communities, Pre- and Postmodern*. SerQ. Durham: Duke University Press.

Dunning, Benjamin H. 2011. *Specters of Paul: Sexual Difference in Early Christian Thought*. Div. Philadelphia: University of Pennsylvania Press.

———. 2014. *Christ without Adam: Subjectivity and Sexual Difference in the Philosophers' Paul*. GTR. New York: Columbia University Press.

———. Forthcoming. "Same-Sex Relations." In *The Oxford Handbook of New Testament, Gender, and Sexuality*. Edited by Benjamin H. Dunning. Oxford: Oxford University Press.

Edelman, Lee. 2004. *No Future: Queer Theory and the Death Drive.* SerQ. Durham: Duke University Press.

Fradenburg, Louise, and Carla Freccero. 1996. "Introduction: Caxton, Foucault, and the Pleasures of History." Pages xiii–xxiv in *Premodern Sexualities.* Edited by Louise Fradenburg and Carla Freccero. New York: Routledge.

Freeman, Elizabeth. 2010. *Time Binds: Queer Temporalities, Queer Histories.* PM. Durham: Duke University Press.

Harper, Kyle. 2013. *From Shame to Sin: The Christian Transformation of Sexual Morality in Late Antiquity.* Cambridge: Harvard University Press.

Hays, Richard B. 1994. "Awaiting the Redemption of Our Bodies: The Witness of Scripture Concerning Homosexuality." Pages 3–17 in *Homosexuality in the Church: Both Sides of the Debate.* Edited by Jeffrey S. Siker. Louisville: Westminster John Knox.

———. 1996. "Homosexuality." Pages 379–406 in *The Moral Vision of the New Testament: Community, Cross, New Creation: A Contemporary Approach to New Testament Ethics.* San Francisco: HarperOne.

Hollywood, Amy. 2006. "Performativity, Citationality, Ritualization." Pages 252–75 in *Bodily Citations: Religion and Judith Butler.* Edited by Ellen T. Armour and Susan M. St. Ville. GTR. New York: Columbia University Press.

Koosed, Jennifer L., ed. 2014. *The Bible and Posthumanism.* SemeiaSt 74. Atlanta: Society of Biblical Literature.

Marchal, Joseph A. 2011. "'Making History' Queerly: Touches across Time through a Biblical Behind." *BibInt* 19:373–95.

Martin, Dale B. 1995. "Heterosexism and the Interpretation of Romans 1:18–32." *BibInt* 3:332–55.

———. 2006. *Sex and the Single Savior: Gender and Sexuality in Biblical Interpretation.* Louisville: Westminster John Knox.

Menéndez-Antuña, Luis. 2015. "Is There a Room for Queer Desires in the House of Biblical Scholarship? A Methodological Reflection on Queer Desires in the Context of Contemporary New Testament Studies." *BibInt* 23:399–427.

Moore, Stephen D. 2001. "Sex and the Single Apostle." Pages 133–72 in *God's Beauty Parlor and Other Queer Spaces in and around the Bible.* Contraversions. Stanford: Stanford University Press.

Muñoz, José Esteban. 1999. *Disidentifications: Queers of Color and the Performance of Politics.* CSA. Minneapolis: University of Minnesota Press.

————. 2009. *Cruising Utopia: The Then and There of Queer Futurity*. Sexual Cultures. New York: New York University Press.

Phillips, Adam. 2012. *Missing Out: In Praise of the Unlived Life*. New York: Picador.

Puar, Jasbir K. 2007. *Terrorist Assemblages: Homonationalism in Queer Times*. NW. Durham: Duke University Press.

Stowers, Stanley K. 1994. *A Rereading of Romans: Justice, Jews, and Gentiles*. New Haven: Yale University Press.

Swancutt, Diana M. 2003. "'The Disease of Effemination': The Charge of Effeminacy and the Verdict of God (Romans 1:18–2:16)." Pages 193–233 in *New Testament Masculinities*. Edited by Stephen D. Moore and Janice Capel Anderson. SemeiaSt 45. Atlanta: Society of Biblical Literature.

————. 2004. "Sexy Stoics and the Rereading of Romans 1.18–2.16." Pages 42–73 in *A Feminist Companion to Paul*. Edited by Amy-Jill Levine with Marianne Blinckenstaff. London: T&T Clark.

————. 2006. "Sexing the Pauline Body of Christ: Scriptural Sex in the Context of the American Christian Culture War." Pages 65–98 in *Toward a Theology of Eros: Transfiguring Passion at the Limits of Discipline*. Edited by Virginia Burrus and Catherine Keller. TTC. New York: Fordham University Press.

Townsley, Jeramy. 2011. "Paul, the Goddess Religions, and Queer Sects: Romans 1:23–28." *JBL* 130:707–28.

Watson, Francis. 2002. "Spaces Sacred and Profane: Stephen Moore, Sex, and the Bible." *JSNT* 25:109–17.

Žižek, Slavoj. 2006. *The Parallax View*. Cambridge: MIT Press.

Stranger in a Stranger World:
Queering Paul with Michel Faber's
The Book of Strange New Things

Jay Twomey

What is your *genre*: masculine, feminine, or science fiction?
—Brian Attebery, *Decoding Gender in Science Fiction*

Michel Faber's (2014) *The Book of Strange New Things* imagines, or allows readers to imagine, Paul in space, an interstellar apostle to alien gentiles. Set in the near future, this intriguing work of literary science fiction realism features a pastor named Peter who missionizes the inhabitants of a newly discovered world, called Oasis by its human settlers. He has been hired by a global corporation, known only by its unexplained acronym USIC, to minister to the local native population. Peter leaves Bea, his pregnant wife, back on earth, where all manner of disasters and disruptions are challenging life across the globe. Eventually, Peter discovers that the Oasans really need a medical miracle much more than they need Christ. In fact, because their inexplicably undeveloped immune system puts them at mortal risk any time they suffer even minor injuries, they are chiefly interested in the faith to learn and to replicate what they call "the technique of Jesus" the healer. Peter, who had probably come to see his mission in fairly grandiose terms, is crestfallen, traverses a long, dark night of the soul, and finally decides to go home to be with, and to help, Bea. Bea, however, has told him (in her last email) that she does not want him to return and that she is setting off on her own.

I discuss the novel in greater analytical detail in the following sections of this chapter. But a plot summary such as I have provided above is never merely objective, and I should point out here that concluding with Bea's story, as I have, is more apt than strictly accurate. The novel actually concludes with hope and love, Peter's hope and love for Bea and their marriage. Indeed, the last line of the book is from Matt 28:20; Peter, suddenly a christological husband, recalls Jesus's farewell statement, "I am with you always, even unto the end of the world," as he recommits himself to his wife before embarking, once again, for home (Faber 2014, 500). This parting is a tender moment. Peter is presented sympathetically throughout the novel as a flawed but genuinely caring character. There are other characters, too, however, and their stories help to queer his. Indeed, their stories, were they not taken up so obliquely and briefly, may ultimately be the more interesting.

This essay begins by setting Peter's Pauline citations, or rather the peculiar elision of one citation in particular (Gal 3:28), into conversation with New Testament scholarship on the implications of that verse for critical reflection on gender and sexuality. My primary interest in these sections of the essay is Peter's apprehension of the aliens themselves. Throughout, I allude to Peter's heteronormative blinders, in order to better approach, in my concluding section, what I consider Bea's and the Oasan Christians's own queer apocalypses.

Peter as Paul

The main character's name, Peter Leigh, owes more to Faber's youthful interests in science fiction and fantasy, specifically to Marvel comics (Peter Parker, Stan Lee), than to the New Testament (Faber 2014, 501). Still, *The Book of Strange New Things* is explicit in its evocations of Paul. For starters, and most obviously, the main character compares himself to Paul, not least because he is a missionary who writes letters. In fact, the epistolary element is an essential part of this novel. In addition, the novel presents a portrait of two communities, one human and the other alien. The main character, a Christian minister, somewhat itinerant, shuttles back and forth between these groups. He ministers exclusively to the Oasans, for that was, you might say, the calling for which he was called by USIC—but he finds himself frequently defending his work among the Oasans to the humans, who consider the native inhabitants of the planet to be almost unbearably alien, deriding their settlement as "Freaktown" (e.g., 118).[1] While this way

---

1. To avoid tedious repetition in my citations from Faber, I give the page number when it is clear that I could only be referring to his novel.

of framing a basic plot dynamic does not do much justice to the complexity of the Pauline story, I am, as you can guess, trying to suggest a parallel with that story by reading the Jews as humans and the gentiles as Oasans à la Acts. Another connection concerns how the emotional stability of both groups on the planet seems to align with the remarkable lack of conflict in both communities. Peter reflects frequently on the peacefully cooperative nature of the Oasan Christians, who call themselves Jesus Lovers, but the humans on their base are, likewise, fairly nonhierarchical and harmonious (if not terribly interesting, and certainly not radically democratic). We are not talking about the impulse toward democracy that several contemporary theorists and Bible scholars hope to recover from Paul's texts. Still, affect and community are part of the Pauline dimension of this novel, suggesting a Pauline fantasy of social organization founded on peaceful unity (as in 1 Cor 1:10; Phil 1:27). In addition, the novel is also partly apocalyptic, with a character even invoking the rapture (425).

More concretely, as he takes his earthly leave of his wife Bea, Peter quotes 2 Tim 4:5–6 to himself (20), for instance, this after musing that his was "the most important missionary calling since the Apostles had ventured forth to conquer Rome with the power of love" (17).[2] Even though he is traveling an incomprehensible distance, he is able to use a communication system a lot like email to correspond with Bea, and so, again, he thinks of Paul. In his initial message to her he jokes that he is writing his "First Epistle to the Joshuans," after Joshua, their cat. Then, more seriously: "Oh, I know we both have our misgivings about St. Paul and his slant on things," particularly "given his problems with females" (45). But he cites Paul's typical salutation and the narrative returns, albeit somewhat infrequently, to the Pauline corpus throughout.[3] Bea's reply to Peter's first letter

---

2. Peter quotes from the KJV and makes no distinction between authentic and pseudepigraphal Pauls.

3. Tit 1:15 (50); Col 4:5 (81); 1 Cor 15:54–5 (253); Rom 3:23 (292); Gal 6:2–5 (323); Phil 4:6 (363), as well as general references to letters like Ephesians (136). But Paul or Pauline texts are referenced indirectly in the novel too. For example, Peter replies to a complaint from Bea about the lack of local color in his messages by reminding her that Paul (along with Peter, James, and John) was similarly stingy with details: "If only Paul could have spent a few words on describing his prison. Speaking of which, my quarters here are driving me" crazy (324). And early on, Bea and Peter discuss how "spread[ing] the love of Christ" can "create people who don't *want* to do wrong," an echo perhaps of the "new creation" of 2 Cor 5:17 (13, emphasis original), not to mention Rom 7:14–25.

is a tender missive that acknowledges how "our old friend Saint Paul ... might not approve of how much I wish I could curl up in bed next to you right now." Humming right along with Peter's tune, though, she adds that there is still a lot of value in the Pauline epistles and concludes by citing Col 4:5 (81).

Peter is a fairly progressive Christian. His comments here on what bugs him about Paul are just one indication of this. He is suspicious of the possible colonial intentions of the corporation sponsoring his mission- ary activity. He offers at one point to teach his Oasan congregants about other religious traditions on earth (273). He gets in an argument toward the end with a rogue linguist who, sounding a bit like Žižek, accuses Peter of being "one of those decaffeinated Christians" because Peter says things like "I'm just trying to treat people the way Jesus might have treated them" and because he does not believe in a final judgment (424–25). And so on. Yet even as they distance themselves from Paul's sexual politics, both Peter and Bea cite some of the texts most responsible for their discomfort with Paul. Second Timothy, for example, represents the Pastor's patriarchal conservatism with its reference to "silly women, overwhelmed by their sins and swayed by all kinds of desires, who are always being instructed and can never arrive at a knowledge of the truth" (3:6–7 [NRSV]). Bea's encouraging allusion to Peter's work on Oasis as a bringing of wisdom emerges from the same context that has wives submitting to their husbands (Col 3:18). She *could* have had 1 Cor 7:7 in mind when referring to Paul's sexual puritanism—"I would that all men were even as I myself"—that is, celibate—but that verse is not invoked, nor is its broader, complicating context of sexual possibilities. Interesting in this regard is the fact that Bea discovers she is pregnant soon after Peter leaves. Presumably, the child was conceived when she forced herself upon him in the car on the way to the airport—a remarkably unsubmissive woman (5–9, 217).

Galatians 3:28 and Science Fiction Futures

Faber does not seem to have set out primarily to rewrite Paul's story, and so one should not and need not constantly seek direct New Testament parallels to think about the book's relevance for Pauline reception study. Nevertheless, the absence of Gal 3:28 (and specifically "no longer male and female") is a notable lacuna in Peter's citational Paulinism, one that becomes ever more peculiar as the story progresses. Some of science fic- tion's most interesting writers have taken full advantage of the opportunity to recast gender and sexuality in the creation, ex-nihilo, of extraterrestrial worlds.[4] This is somehow true of Faber as well, since the native inhabitants of Oasis do not appear to embrace anything akin to human ideas of gender. When the main character inquires about gender directly, his closest native interlocutor either does not understand him or prefers not to respond in any definitive ways: "Please forgive my stupidity," Peter asks, "but are you male or female?" When he gets no reply, he shifts focus:

> "Are you your brother's brother or your brother's sister?" … "For you, I will name me with the word brother," she said. "Because the word sister is very hard to speak." "But if you could say 'sister' more easily, is that what you would say?" … "I would say nothing." "In the story of Adam and Eve," he pressed on, "God created man and woman. Male and female. Two different kinds of people. Are there two different kinds here too?" "We are all different," she said. (181)[5]

As was true of Genly Ai in Ursula Le Guin's (1969) *The Left Hand of Darkness*, this human character spending time in an alien society cannot help but assign gender right and left. He considers the Oasan to whom he speaks in the above conversation to be a woman. When at the end of the novel, this same Oasan friend, Jesus Lover Five, tells Peter "I will remain always … your brother," it seems less like a corrective revelation than a choice between synonyms made, once again, merely for ease of pronunciation (475).[6] It does not help that when Peter starts learning the Oasan language, he realizes that they have no linguistic genders and do not use pronouns.

The neither/nors and no longers of gender in Gal 3:28 are both precedent and proleptic vision, past and future.[7] They are precedent insofar as Paul may here be citing a recent baptismal formula, albeit one he does not

---

4. For a comprehensive discussion of gender and sexuality in science fiction, see Attebery 2002 and Pearson, Hollinger, and Gordon 2010.

5. To capture the specific second-language difficulties the Oasans experience with *s* and *t* in their adopted English, Faber uses alien-seeming typographic characters, not replicated here.

6. Similarly, another character refers to his/her "mother" as a "very important man" (257). We never learn the characters' own names. Instead, they refer to themselves with numbers indicative of the order in which they were converted by the previous missionary (306).

7. While the NRSV translation, "no longer male and female," is more accurate, a number of translations follow the KJV's "neither male nor female."

fully endorse.[8] Or they are precedent in a way specific to Paul's own project of theological filiation, linking some idea of social undoing to a more distant past.[9] But they are also proleptic since, as many would have it, the binaries of 3:28 are undone in a future "in Christ." But again, the question is: which future? The coming kingdom, perhaps? Or a time even more distant than could be imagined from the perspective of a first-century Pauline eschaton? From the perspective of this project, it is interesting to see that whatever texts like Gal 3:28 are doing with gender has sometimes inspired a rhetoric of fantastic futurity or even science fiction in relevant scholarship. Brigitte Kahl (2000, 37) opens an article on this verse with the reflection that "feminist and liberation oriented readings rather commonly have treated the baptismal formula of Gal 3:26–28 as a kind of ET, a lovely lonely alien unhappily trapped in the hostile matter of a Pauline letter." Steven John Kraftchick, essaying a conversation between Pauline studies and transhumanism, suggests that

> because of his insistence that "in Christ" distinctions based on physical features or cultural constructions of gender, race, and station are rendered inconsequential (Rom 12–14; Gal 3:28), if and when the boundary between the organic human and the hybrid human/cyborg is sufficiently blurred so that one cannot be recognized from the other, Paul may very well argue that these transhumans be included in the redemptive community along with the rest of God's creation. (2015, 69)

George Aichele (2014), in one of his studies of Mark, troubles the tendency to always invest Mark's resurrection language with supernatural meaning. He claims that the phrase "like angels in heaven" (12:25) gestures beyond gender toward the fantastic, the posthuman.[10] Aichele also wonders if the "disturbing (*and neither male nor female?*) appearance" of the young man

---

8. At least he seems to signal his lack of commitment to the undoing of the gender binary when he drops it from 1 Cor 12:13 (cf. Col 3:11).

9. "In Christ" also refers to Abraham, if we read Gal 3:16 with 3:28. See Kahl 2000, 41.

10. The "posthuman" is "a potential for transformation or larval condition that is intrinsic to human beings and closely connected to the death of God and therefore the postmodern" (Aichele 2014, 3). For Phyllis Trible (1978, 15–23), the posthuman, so described, may be the image of God itself, even after the death of God, but it is also certainly the earthling called *ha-adam* from the second creation story, a "sexually undifferentiated … creature" (80).

of Mark 16:5–8 is what actually causes the women to flee Jesus's tomb (103, emphasis added). He then compares Mark to two science fiction films, *2001: A Space Odyssey* and *Close Encounters of the Third Kind*. In each film, he writes, instances of "alien encounter/human transformation … echo the remarkable, fantastic element in Mark's language, especially phrases such as 'rise from the dead' and 'angels in heaven' " (106).

Critical reflections on Gal 3:28 that do not evoke science fiction tropes still frequently sidle up to the future anterior for thinking "in Christ." Dale B. Martin's chapter on Gal 3:28 in his *Sex and the Single Savior* provides a brief overview of recent egalitarian readings of the verse.[11] Even conservative Christians tend to find some idea of equality in "neither male nor female," he writes.[12] But all the readings Martin surveys, from the conservative to the most progressive, fail to embrace the truly radical nature of the text. Galatians 3:28 is not about establishing equality between men and women, whatever that equality might mean; it is about the abolition of dimorphic sexuality itself.[13] We are all "masculifeminine or feminimascupersons";

---

11. He does so after discussing ancient readings according to which Paul was referring to the primal but still ultimately male androgyne or "one-sex" body (D. Martin 2006, 83). Martin, whose position on this question is followed by many contemporary interpreters, including me, argues that neither ancient readings nor, importantly, historical-critical findings, should limit contemporary understandings of a biblical text (88). An intriguing alternative approach, one that uses a historical lens to arrive at essentially the same conclusion, is that of Joseph A. Marchal (2010, 173), according to whom egalitarian and other queer readings of Gal 3:28 founder on Paul's own inescapably militant masculinity (see also Punt [2010, 154], for whom maleness in Galatians is "maintained and even radicalized"). Nevertheless, the historical reconstruction—always uncertain and creative—of the Galatian community itself suggests that they, not Paul, might be models for the recognition of complexity in matters of gender and sexuality. As a result, "Galatians can be just one example of how even Paul could not (and cannot still) tell people the exclusive meaning of their bodies" (Marchal 2010, 177).

12. But this equality is most often limited in the texts D. Martin (2006, 79–82) cites to an idealist understanding of baptism, or perhaps to specific church contexts, not to lived social reality more generally.

13. Or it should be, for feminist, queer, and other interpreters, regardless of how the verse may have worked in Paul's original context (D. Martin 2006, 88). Obviously, there have been plenty of engaging variations upon this theme, several preceding Martin's own work. (For example, Antoinette Clark Wire [1990, 184] reads Gal 3:28 as an indication that in Christ the normative power of gender and sexual difference is abolished; Elisabeth Schüssler Fiorenza [1997, 227] suggests, differently, that Paul is here proposing the irrelevance of "patriarchal marriage" in the Christian community;

"everyone must take the macho, made-up, cross-dressing basketball star or actor as the Christian role model" (89). But in claiming that "the force of the phrase ['neither male nor female' or 'no male and female'] should be to challenge heterosexuality itself and entire" (90), Martin suggests—uncontroversially enough—that the fluidity of gender and sexuality is inhibited, culturally and affectively, by a stable configuration of identity (male, female) and orientation (heterosexual). There is a sense that "in Christ," or the most robust possible queer reading of that phrase, therefore requires a future orientation, a hope: in Christ, gender and sexuality "may be [re]invented"; in Christ, "as yet unknowable ways of gendering human experience," ways "we cannot foresee" right now (89), may become possible.

Patricia Beattie Jung (2015, 186), writing about intersex interventions in New Testament interpretation, claims that Gal 3:28 allows for the belief that "in risen life we will be transformed into people of the apposite (as in appropriate, rather than opposite) sex.… Self-giving, mutual indwelling, and complementarity need not be structured along a polar axis." This futurity far outpaces Martin's own, replacing queer hopefulness in the (near-) present with a radically different temporality. But it is not, for all that, an outlier. Virginia Ramey Mollenkott's (2007, xii) important work *Omnigender* suggests, on the one hand, that Gal 3:28—"there *is* no longer male and female"—ought to be taken literally. But on the other hand, she also seems to feel that it would take a "futurist" to understand what the practical realities of that verse would look like (183), while worrying that its present is still a millennium away (193).[14]

Fear of a Queer Planet?

Why does Peter not think about what some take to be Paul's most democratizing, most liberating verse, in a literary context that is all but its

---

and Susan Craig [2000, 197–98], writing in the form of a poetic prayer, sees Christ's oneness, mirroring the "wholeness of your creation," as the message of Gal 3:28 for bisexual believers—"neither gay nor straight, both gay and straight. / We are One in our beings and One in you.") More recent readings take Martin's work in various new directions. Martin's piece is Benjamin H. Dunning's point of departure in *Specters of Paul* (2011), which tries to show that the essential incoherence of patristic treatments of Gal 3:28 also supports contemporary queer and feminist theology (e.g., 5).

14. In context, Mollenkott (2007, 166) is discussing not Gal 3:28 specifically but rather the "truly gender-fluid society" that would come about if "no longer male and female" were, as she puts it much earlier in the book, literalized.

narrative complement? Faber, who has written not one but two science fiction novels, both of which reflect interestingly upon gender, sexuality, and power, likely knows that the genre is often deployed precisely as a way of exploring such matters from queer and feminist perspectives.[15] Possibly, Faber wonders about, or indeed is dismissive of, the value of this kind of writing. Wendy Gay Pearson, writing about the feminist aims behind Le Guin's *Left Hand of Darkness*, claims that "demonstrating the viability of a successful, happy, and entirely non-heteronormative world seems quite queer to me."[16] Is Oasis not, then, queer? Faber should be sympathetic to queer impulses in science fiction. In a 2008 interview in *The Guardian*, he noted that his (now deceased) wife Eva "was gay before I met her so my whole circle of friends [early on] were lesbians.... There was a lot of anti-male feeling in my environment. I was like an honorary female" (Jordan 2008). But even if we were to take this remark as generously as possible, at least a few scholars have complained that his representations of women, sexuality, and cross-dressing in perhaps his most famous book, *The Crimson Petal and the White* (Faber 2002), are neither feminist nor queer (see Llewellyn 2012 as an example). What is more, it is never his aim in *The Book of Strange New Things* to introduce us to the ways the Oasans experience and understand their own sexualities. Perhaps a certain moderate conservatism colors his appreciation of the genre? If so, he would not be alone in this. The Hugo Awards for science fiction writing are being given, more and more frequently, to politically interesting works that problematize questions of gender or racial identity, and the more traditional (i.e., straight, white, male) readership of science fiction has been up in arms, going so far as to establish a group, The Sad Puppies, that votes as a block in efforts to bring specific, more heteronormative science fiction titles into

---

15. The other is *Under the Skin* (2000), loosely adapted for film by director Jonathan Glazer in 2013.

16. Pearson 2010a, 27. Of course, neither happiness nor success are, at least not without further complication, necessary criteria in our thinking about a science fiction text's queerness. See Ahmed 2010 and Halberstam 2011. Pearson's essay originally appeared in 1999. In a later piece, she criticizes *Left Hand of Darkness* for never really challenging heteronormativity. The hermaphroditic Gethenians are still heterosexual in their couplings and Genly Ai's eventual discomfort with human (hetero)sexuality—after having come to valorize both Gethenian physiology and their cultural practices around sex—merely reverses the pathologization of sexual bodies (Pearson 2010b, 78).

contention.[17] Even assuming that Faber is not similarly reactionary (and I do not think he is), that in fact he does want to use the genre to push the boundaries of gender and sexual identity, at least a little, the problem is that we can only ever understand the Oasans from Peter's limited perspective. True, he feels that when he is among the Oasans, "it was as though his sexual nature went into hibernation. He was male, and male equipment hung from his pelvis, but it was just there, irrelevant as an earlobe. Only when he returned to the USIC base did his sexuality revive" (Faber 2014, 349), suggesting that he may be accommodating his experience to the lived reality of Oasan embodiment, even if he is not consciously doing so. If that is the case, though, he just does not get it. When he shows his Oasan congregants a picture of his wedding and asks if they have an institution like marriage, Jesus Lover One replies, "We have marriage." But Peter cannot tell what this response means. Was it "a mildly amused retort? Exasperated? Weary? Simply informative?" (168). And then we find out that no, they do not have marriage after all—"The Oasans didn't celebrate marriage"—but they have sex ... even though their "pairings were private arrangements, so discreet as to be seldom alluded to" (265). Ultimately, thanks to Peter's blinders, the reader cannot tell if these pairings are not alluded to out of discretion or simply because of his confused assumptions about how procreation happens on this planet, or at least among these people. Peter is invited to a birth ceremony in the home of a non-Christian Oasan. Unfortunately, this is before he understands much of the language, and so his comprehension of what he is witnessing is extremely limited. He decides, nevertheless, that a woman is giving birth and that the child is male (267).

Just as the Pauline corpus flirts with genderlessness in Gal 3:28, only to insist upon normative gender roles elsewhere (e.g., 1 Cor 11:1–16, 14:34–35; the Pastoral Epistles), the minister in Faber's novel, whose liberalism is expressed specifically in opposition to limitations on women's agency and sexuality in Pauline texts, has some difficulty ministering to a Christian community without the markers of a tangibly gendered identity. This leads me to wonder, again, if there is a relationship between the absence of gender and the absence of any reference to Gal 3:28 in the novel. The planet on which our futuristic Pauline missionary finds an almost perfect

---

17. There are apparently two groups of Puppies, the Sad and the Rabid, reacting to a cultural shift. See Wallace 2015.

community of believers, who call themselves lovers, is at least nominally a kind of paradise, an interstellar oasis. And insofar as the neither/nors of Galatians are actually emblematic of Christian life in this heavenly otherworld, it would seem that a key barrier to egalitarian readings of 3:28 in earthly contexts—namely, that "in Christ" is perpetually elsewhere—has been eliminated. All it takes to experience oneness with Christ in the eschaton is faster-than-light travel! But as I mentioned earlier, the alien community in Christ is fatally flawed. Peter learns, quite late in the book, that the Oasans are primarily interested in the gospel, what they call "the technique of Jesus" (e.g., Faber 2014, 105), because their bodies cannot heal, meaning that even minor injuries can lead readily to death (443–45). And with this realization, a host of behaviors that Peter had witnessed throughout the novel become comprehensive retrospectively as instances of extreme precaution. The scales fall from his eyes: he is not so much a missionary as a magician, if not a potential doctor.[18]

Does this mean that the Oasans's genderlessness, which could provide the opportunity to think creatively about bodies that resist normative expectations, is also a pathology of some kind? Possibly, especially if the frailty of the Oasan body seems to expose some anxiety about desire. Contemporary queer perspectives on Paul do not expunge desire from the repurposing of Gal 3:28—far from it.[19] And yet, strangely, the purpose behind what one reviewer of the novel calls its "complex treatment of religion" (Charles 2014) may be to reject—as inhuman, as irreconcilably alien—the genderlessness implied by "no longer male and female." Faber may well be concerned that the unclearly gendered beings in the more progressive reaches of the science fiction cosmos represent the evacuation of desire and thus of some core element of humanity.[20] Stable, obvious,

---

18. And indeed, the human community on Oasis first began interacting with the local inhabitants by providing medicines in exchange for food.

19. Martin, for example, has considered Paul's rejection of desire in the context of a discussion of his difference from the Stoics. Ultimately, Martin writes, mostly in contrast to Martha Nussbaum's (2013) appropriation of some Stoic ideals in *The Therapy of Desire*, there is danger in embracing passionless self-sufficiency. And besides, he adds, he is just not interested in a faith commitment that has no place for desire (D. Martin 2006, 76).

20. The juvenile masculinity desired by the more conservative fans of science fiction is not the only motive for questioning the more feminist and queerer goals of some writers. Fredric Jameson (2007, 140), in *Archaeologies of the Future: The Desire Called Utopia and Other Science Fictions*, has lamented as "an unhappy outcome for

heterosexual desire is precisely what Peter rediscovers and reauthorizes at the end of *The Book of Strange New Things*. I noted early on that both the Oasans and the humans live within their own separate communities quite harmoniously. That is putting it benignly. From another perspective, most of the humans themselves are desireless "zombies" (Faber 2014, 423), as one apparently semi-insane human character puts it. The Oasans, "little fairies" (422), are even worse in this character's view: "creepy, insipid, dick-less, ass-licking little pastel-colored vermin" (428). Remarkably, Peter is not offended by this overtly homophobic tirade, even though he defends both the humans and the Oasans. But by this point in the novel his com-mitments are wavering, and soon enough he is heading home, having abandoned his mission, his ministry, his calling—even his cherished Bible (489). He marks his transition back to his once and future earthling identity by ditching the dishdasha, or "Islamic gown" as he calls it (the loose-fitting attire he had worn for comfort on this humid planet), for the more "conventional attire" of jeans and a T-shirt (441), not to mention gazing somewhat wantonly at a woman's breasts (459–62), before setting out to rescue his woman back on earth.

Yet there is definitely something queer about Peter. It may be that his penis becomes "irrelevant as an earlobe" and his sexuality goes "into hibernation" (249) when he has spent time among the Oasans. But he is also somewhat obsessively interested in understanding Oasan sexuality in ways that suggest, albeit quite vaguely, a kind of latent attraction. During his conversation with Jesus Lover Five about gender, noted earlier, he tries to peek at her genitals but can only see what he believes to be an anus (180)—although, knowing virtually nothing about the Oasan physiology,

---

the Utopian and SF genre itself [that its] lines of exploration and invention have now been rerouted and *deviated* along the lines of gender and sexuality, rather than those of class dynamics and the mode of production" (emphasis added). There is something akin here to the critiques of identity politics in work by queer Marxist theorists like James Penney (2014) and Holly M. Lewis (2017). But Jameson (2007, 277) can also valorize Le Guin's (1969) thought experiment with gender in *Left Hand of Darkness* as structurally similar to what he sees as the novel's "attempt to rethink Western history without capitalism." Far more generally, elements of Jameson's (2007, xii) introductory discussion of utopian science fiction resonate with the work of José Esteban Muñoz and others: "The Utopian form is itself a representational meditation on radical differ-ence, radical otherness, and on the systemic nature of the social totality, to the point where one cannot imagine any fundamental change in our social existence which has not first thrown off Utopian visions like so many sparks from a comet."

how can he be certain? Later, writing to Bea, he laments, without at all
recognizing his own pun, that he "still hasn't got to the bottom of their
sexes, yet" (338). His realization that the Oasans do not heal comes at the
book's end, after Jesus Lover Five has been seriously injured and taken to
the USIC infirmary. A doctor there actually assumes that she is a he, until
hearing otherwise from Peter (443) who, for his part, confesses to her that
"out of all your people … you're the one I care about the most" (473).
She touches his lips and his thigh as he apologizes (understandably, but
also somewhat pathetically) about his need to return to Earth. Then, as
he takes his leaves, she says, "I will remain always … your brother" (475).
These are but fragments of queer possibilities, yes, but taken together, they
evoke what Butler (e.g., 1990, 96–97) calls melancholic heterosexuality,
insofar as Peter's insistence upon the feminine pronoun and his need to
confirm its anatomical justification are both a disavowal of his interest in
this ambiguously sexed person and a not-quite recognition of the fantastical quality of his own body parts. Surely he is on the cusp of understanding
that his penis (like his earlobe) is no ontological guarantor of heteronor-
matively masculine desire. So too, and just as surely, he is quite close to
recognizing that his reversion to a traditional husbandliness may be an act
of bad faith. Throughout the novel, he reflects on the way his experience
of Oasis is changing him. For example, when he learns of Bea's pregnancy,
he is surprised that he feels nothing. Or more precisely, as he puts it, "it
was difficult, in his current circumstances, to grab hold of feelings and
brand them with a name" (222). "Other men," he continues, "would at such
a moment be able to picture themselves with their as-yet imaginary offspring, accompanying them through their anticipated lives. Not Peter, or
at least not any longer: "He could imagine such scenes only in the most
contrived and generic way, as if they were two-dimensional panels in a
comic book written and drawn by shameless hacks" (222). This disorienting distantiation from what he believes ought to be expected of him—in
this case, the protocols of a contemporary fatherly pride in reproduction
and its future (fantastical) entailments—is so profound that when he sheds
his gown in favor of what he considers more masculine attire at the novel's
end, it is nearly an instance of drag.

Freaktowns

Freaktown, that is, has started to make a freak of Peter. As artist and theorist Renate Lorenz (2012, 165) claims in the appendix to her *Queer Art:*

A Freak Theory, at freak shows of the nineteenth and early twentieth centuries, the audience members, or "dupes[,] are constantly being given the chance to understand or at least to guess that they are being deceived…, [and their] pleasure lies in the instability passing through them that contains the possibility that even their own bodies and their social positioning might be exposed to a similar destabilization." Peter lives, works, and comes to be at home in the midst of a performance of Christian being that engenders certain unexpected transformations of desire in him while challenging not just heteronormativity but human norms of embodiment altogether, "without … in turn producing a unified and recognizable category" (166).

Yet because of his hetero-Pauline melancholia, most evident in his disavowal of Gal 3:28, Faber's apostle himself is less clearly evocative of queerness than the members of the faith communities most essential to him, the Oasans and his wife Bea. We do not have much to work with since the novel is so entirely a book about Peter. Still, the Jesus Lovers and Bea are freakish, in Lorenz's sense, to the extent that they choose, queerly, to inhabit a distance from exclusionary identity investments or modes of embodiment—indeed, from any concretizable or fully comprehensible identity claims.[21] Throughout this essay I mostly refer to the Oasans generally, but Peter engages almost exclusively with the Jesus Lovers, who form their own separate community. Most Oasans presumably share physical features that are entirely illegible to him. But the Oasan Christians have likewise made themselves illegible to their non-Christian peers. At least a couple of them either mention or seem to suggest that their new religion has alienated them from loved ones (Faber 2014, 178, 341).[22] One non-Christian Oasan reportedly rejected the English language lessons offered by a previous human visitor, the crazy linguist mentioned above,

---

21. Aware of the violence inherent in the objectifying spectacle of historical freak shows, Lorenz (2012) nevertheless wants to generate, or perhaps recuperate (through her own archival aesthetics as well as her critical explorations of others' works), the term *freak*'s empowering possibilities for "denormalizing social practices" (27) and economies, for "putting-oneself-in-connection" by means of "queer embodiments" that are stubbornly resistant to specificity, stability, and consensus" (144). Despite its countercultural origins, the use of freak to describe Christians, as Jesus Freaks, is not necessarily empowering and, indeed, can often refer to Christians with conservative social and political perspectives. See Young 2015.

22. Perhaps another Pauline echo, especially if the troubles referred to in 1 Thess 1:6; 2:14; 3:3–4 can be linked to similar social stresses. See Ascough 2017, 42.

by asking, "Why should we speak a language made for other bodies?" (186). In essence, that is exactly what the Jesus Lovers are doing. In their communal life as a church, they are literally beyond the pale, outside the larger settlement's walls. But they have also adopted apparently unnatural discursive practices, becoming as a result strangely different in their bodies as well.

Bea similarly slips outside the bounds of even her own normative self-understanding. Over the course of the novel, her messages to Peter become more and more fraught, reflecting the increasingly dire state of the world back home. After the situation becomes horrifyingly untenable for her locally, Bea tells Peter that she is abandoning her faith—writing, simply but emphatically, "there is no God" (389)—and, what is more, leaving. She writes:

> This is the last message I'll be able to send you, I'm not going to be able to stay in this house. I will be living with other people, strangers. I don't know where exactly. We'll be moving around. I can't explain, just take it from me that it's best. Nothing here is as it was when you left. Things can change so fast. It's irresponsible of me to bring a baby into this rotten world but the alternative is killing it and I just don't have the courage to do that. I expect things will end badly anyway, and it will be much kinder on you not to be here to see it. If you love me, don't make me watch you suffer. (496)

Like 1 Cor 7:25–31, Bea's note stresses the anxieties of sexual relations in a time of eschatological crisis: "Those who marry will experience distress…, and I would spare you that.… For the present form of this world is passing away" (NRSV). Bea does not have Paul's hope, and Paul lacks the immediate, tangible evidence of Bea's end-time experience (tsunamis, volcanoes, economic collapse, roaming gangs, and more), but they intersect, regardless, at sex and apocalypse. Bea plans to embark upon a peripatetic life, crossing a strange social landscape in inexplicable relation to unknown others. Nevertheless, "it's best." Certainly, she expects the worst, even for herself and their child. But she neither wants nor needs a husband in this changed reality. Peter replies almost instantly that, "safe or unsafe, happy or unhappy, my place is by your side" (496). Yet it is late, too late; she is already gone.

There is no reason to think that Bea's new life will involve different sexual arrangements or gender identities (on the other hand, why not?). But clearly she chooses radical new relationships in contexts and for reasons

Peter is ill-equipped to accept. Like the Oasans, who marry and yet do not, Bea is and yet is not his wife any longer: "Things can change so fast." Maybe the apocalyptic reveal suggests that on Earth as it is on Oasis, there is no reality that is not already otherwise.[23] The alien otherness of gender ambiguity, its vast distance and difference from earth-bound heterosexuality, is one of the most striking things about this novel. Faber's title is what the Oasans call the Bible, but it could just as easily refer to the (or some of the) cultural meaning(s) of embodiment on their planet: to be no longer male and female is apparently a strange new thing from Peter's perspective. But surely one could slip dimensions in a moment of confusion. Or, stepping off the ship that shuttles humans to and from Oasis and forgetting, in one's interstellar disorientation, which planet one is standing on, one could see Oasis's strangeness as the everyday reality of *this* world. As Teresa J. Hornsby (2016) writes in *Transgender, Intersex, and Biblical Interpretation*, a volume she coauthored with Deryn Guest:

> even if we know nothing else about gender, its construct, and its ubiquitous presence, we can *look around* and *know* that it is simply not true that there are only two opposing genders. Just as Paul writes in Rom 1:20: "Ever since the creation of the world his eternal power and divine nature, invisible though they are, have been understood and seen through the things he has made." (16, emphasis original)

There is no need to cast a New Testament–inflected, radical discussion of gender in extraordinary, futuristic—much less extraterrestrial—terms: "Clearly, materially, biblically," Hornsby continues, "nothing is either/or" (19). Bea's "strangers," as well as her "I don't know where" and "I can't explain," signal her sudden, if disorienting, validation of this fact.

It is interesting to imagine the possibilities for solidarity between the Jesus Lovers and Bea's new community.[24] Impossible distances separate

---

23. Mollenkott (2007, 44) suggests the use of *otherwise* to expand the horizons of inclusivity in representing any possible gender identity.

24. Lewis (2016, 259) begins *The Politics of Everybody: Feminism, Queer Theory, and Marxism at the Intersection* with a simple premise: solidarity need not be established on the basis of significant agreement between different groups or communities: "Solidarity is not a matter of pluralist, multicultural unity and harmony. The latter is not a vision of solidarity; it is a vision of the Kingdom of Heaven." All it takes is a "minimal connection between political actors," and she asserts that one such connection could be the desire, perhaps universal, to reject "pointless suffering" (11). If groups

them, and they are mostly unaware of each other. But they are bound by their recent conversions and the palpable certainty that the end really is nigh. Bea faces astonishing dangers, as do the Oasans. Meanwhile, whatever Peter might be doing to advance the faith, Bea writes caustically in a prior message, he is stuck up there on "Planet God" (Faber 2014, 409). Even if he were to return overnight, she writes, because of his obliviousness to her real concerns and his knee-jerk tendency to chastise her wavering faith (e.g., 404), he would still be on Planet God, emotionally, and "I'd be a trillion miles away from you, alone with you by my side" (409). Peter, we must remember, for all of his genuine feelings about his possible complicity in USIC's corporate, colonial endeavor, is also going to be extremely well-compensated for his efforts (30, 50). He even comes to understand how key he is to USIC's mission: the Oasans had threatened to withhold food from the human colonists unless USIC supplied them with a new missionary after the first one disappeared (121). This is because they believe that there is something essential to their survival to be gleaned from the technique of Jesus. In other words, he learns that from USIC's perspective, his function is pacification. But the only thought that occurs to him in the moment is that he regrets not knowing what leverage he had with the corporation when he signed up. By contrast, the Jesus Lovers and Bea (and her strangers) create new freakish assemblages in the interests of mutual support and survival, keenly feeling but nevertheless disregarding the ways that their choices put them at odds with others' and even their own prior social norms.

That is to say that Bea and her strangers, and the Oasan Jesus Lovers, these people beside Peter, resemble some of the figures and groups that we can, with queer care, discover interstitially in the Pauline epistles.[25] The women in Corinth, for instance, against whose innovations Paul sometimes rails, have most often been understood from Paul's own

---

queer and straight have historically made common cause in labor disputes (206–7), then maybe it is not so impossible to imagine an interstellar solidarity, however tenuous, between small organizations of Oasans and humans, especially if another thread tying them together is their shared oppression as it relates to USIC. The Oasans, as I have noted, labor for a USIC outpost that may be but the first stage of a large-scale occupation. According to one character, the same linguist mentioned above, the depredations on earth will soon be exploited by USIC as an opportunity to entice the ultra-wealthy of the world to safety on Oasis—for a price (Faber 2014, 425–26).

25. I am riffing on the title of a recent collection, *The People beside Paul: The Philippian Assembly and History from Below* (Marchal 2015).

(reconstructed) perspective. The history of that reconstruction, as Gillian Townsley (2017, 1–2) notes, reveals a vast "androcentric heteropatriarchal" scholarly enterprise that is still alive and well, especially in evangelical circles. But reading 1 Cor 11:2–16, for instance, in conversation with queer studies, and in particular with Monique Wittig's (1986) *The Lesbian Body*, allows Townsley (2017, 242) to construe the creative believers in Corinth as "rogue body parts in the Corinthian body, the body of Christ." This body, she argues, "undergoes dismemberment, fragmentation, and deconstruction" in its proliferation of differences, like "Wittig's lesbian body," but also—and thereby—it experiences "reconfiguration and transformation ... point[ing] to possibilities of being that extend beyond the normal" (243).[26] Like Townsley, who describes taking a queer studies approach to this Pauline text as in itself a queer endeavor, Joseph A. Marchal (2018) reads the Corinthian women prophets in the context of recent articulations of queer temporalities by Lee Edelman and José Esteban Muñoz, among others.[27] The women (and perhaps some men) in Corinth find themselves chastised by Paul for seizing the apocalyptic promise too quickly, taking it in novel but upsettingly unauthorized directions, challenging patriarchal paradigms of reproductive sexuality, embodiment, adornment, and social comportment—but, Marchal notes, all of this in ways that Paul really *ought* to recognize as cognate with his own gospel (53–55). A twenty-first-century interstellar Paul might even find himself flummoxed by the queerness of these ancient Corinthians, since they are "living in disjointed, out-of-sync ways, according to different life schedules or eccentric social and economic practices (including, but not limited to sexual ones)" (47–48).

To celebrate the circumstances that allow us to read Bea and the Jesus Lovers in queer terms proves difficult. Even if Faber consciously crafted these characters as foils to Peter, their prospects for thriving are disappointingly bleak. In fact, one could conclude that, according to the novel, it is only in dire crisis that these queer socialities can develop, that radical difference from the normal is a defensive maneuver, nothing more. But read in conjunction with the Pauline corpus, *The Book of Strange New*

---

26. For their part, some of the men in Corinth, Townsley (2017, 115) claims earlier, are "conceptual, theoretical lesbians."

27. Townsley (2017, 35) understands it as a queer endeavor precisely because it is "at odds with the normal, the legitimate, the dominant" in Pauline studies (quoting David Halperin's [1995, 62] definition of queer).

Things at least encourages us to imagine Paul's own possible infection by the queer alterities he encounters in his travels.[28]

Paul's eventual fluency with languages made for other bodies (even if, as Bea notes, he is something of a prude about how other bodies should enact desires) is a potential source of contagion. In Galatians, as elsewhere, "the works of the flesh" are pejoratively contrasted with "the fruit of the spirit" (5:16–22). In fact, flesh and spirit are precise opposites— or, rather, their desires are (5:17). The Galatians themselves are warned against reverting from their spiritual beginnings in his ministry to a more fleshly faith (3:3). Yet even as he maintains this clear binary throughout, Paul also reminds the Galatians that he was forced by flesh, his "infirmity," to bring the gospel to them (4:13), maybe even contrary to his wishes. What is more, he registers some awareness that both flesh and temptation (4:14) were factors in his original sojourn among them. Elsewhere, Paul even claims that his "thorn … in the flesh" is the only publically available proof that he has received "exceptional … revelations" (2 Cor 12:7), his divine stamp of approval. If what the flesh actually wants is to spread the good word, Paul's protests to the contrary notwithstanding, then might there be, in Galatians, an unavowed continuum linking fornication and faithfulness, licentiousness and generosity?[29]

---

28. See Lorenz (2012, 18), who uses the ideas of "contagion" and "infection" to describe art that "seeks to entangle the viewer as a participant in denormalizing practices."

29. Troy Martin argues against the fairly common association of Gal 4:13 with 2 Cor 12:7. In fact, in his view, the infirmity, literally "weakness of the flesh," is that of the Galatians themselves who, in their "pre-gospel condition" (drawing upon a parallel with Rom 5:5) required Pauline ministration (T. Martin 1999, 82–83). For their part, the Galatians resisted the temptation to despise Paul for his circumcision, in Martin's reading of 4:14. The essay is clearly an effort to harmonize Gal 4:13–14 with a traditional Christian theological understanding of Paul on flesh and spirit and in terms of the broader issues in the letter as a whole, despite the fact that Martin's argument forces him to ignore that the Galatians apparently accept circumcision and that Paul does not otherwise seem to be ironic at this point. But Martin's essay is nevertheless fascinating for the way it inadvertently hints at precisely the sort of approach I am gesturing toward here. For suddenly, at the end, Martin nearly obsesses over the circumcised "glans penis" as a sign (among gentiles) of arousal. He refers to "male sexual arousal," even "excessive sexual arousal," not once, but eight times in just a page and a half (88–89). It is as though Paul showed up among the Galatians one day seeking help for a terrible case of priapism, and they, eyeing his condition (4:15), were not tempted in the least to spurn his (evangelical) advances. Indeed, they "welcomed [him] as an

Other recent moments of Pauline reception also entertain interpretive possibilities of this sort. Gore Vidal's (1992) *Live from Golgotha* is nothing if not a queer romp through Acts and the epistles. Both Paul's relationship with Timothy and the thorn in his flesh evoke degrees of homoeroticism in Pier Paolo Pasolini's (2014, 42, 48) *Saint Paul. The Book of Strange New Things* may reimagine the desires and differences in the Pauline texts much more obliquely than do Pasolini's or Vidal's works. But like them, Faber's novel helps to make the apostle, as a figure of general cultural significance, intriguingly relevant to readers who may be searching for a more freakish Paul.

Works Cited

Ahmed, Sara. 2010. *The Promise of Happiness*. Durham: Duke University Press.

Aichele, George. 2014. *Tales of Posthumanity: The Bible and Contemporary Popular Culture*. BMW 65. Sheffield: Sheffield Phoenix Press.

Ascough, Richard S. 2017. *1 and 2 Thessalonians: Encountering the Christ Group at Thessalonike*. London: Bloomsbury T&T Clark.

Attebery, Brian. 2002. *Decoding Gender in Science Fiction*. New York: Routledge.

Butler, Judith. 1990. *Gender Trouble: Feminism and the Subversion of Identity*. TG. New York: Routledge.

Charles, Ron. 2014. Review of *The Book of Strange New Things*, by Michel Faber. *Washington* Post. November 25. https://tinyurl.com/SBL0699k.

Craig, Susan. 2000. "Untitled." Pages 197–98 in *Blessed Bi Spirit: Bisexual People of Faith*. Edited by Debra Kolodny. New York: Bloomsbury Academic.

Dunning, Benjamin H. 2011. *Specters of Paul: Sexual Difference in Early Christian Thought*. Div. Philadelphia: University of Pennsylvania Press.

Faber, Michel. 2000. *Under the Skin*. New York: Harcourt.

———. 2002. *The Crimson Petal and the White*. New York: Harcourt.

———. 2014. *The Book of Strange New Things: A Novel*. London: Hogarth.

Halberstam, Jack. 2011. *The Queer Art of Failure*. JHFCB. Durham: Duke University Press.

---

angel of God, as Jesus Christ" (4:14). See also Stephen D. Moore's (2001, 170–72) fantasy of God, Jesus, and Paul in a locker room ménage-à-trois.

Halperin, David M. 1995. *Saint Foucault: Towards a Gay Hagiography.* New York: Oxford University Press.

Hornsby, Teresa J., and Deryn Guest. 2016. *Transgender, Intersex, and Biblical Interpretation.* SemeiaSt 83. Atlanta: SBL Press.

Jameson, Fredric. 2007. *Archaeologies of the Future: The Desire Called Utopia and Other Science Fictions.* London: Verso.

Jordan, Justine. 2016. "Michel Faber: 'I Would Have Been a Different Writer without My Wife.'" Guardian. July 8. https://tinyurl.com/SBL0699m.

Jung, Patricia Beattie. 2015. "Intersex on Earth as It Is in Heaven." Pages 173–87 in *Intersex, Theology, and the Bible: Troubling Bodies in Church, Text, and Society.* Edited by Susannah Cornwall. New York: Palgrave Macmillan.

Kahl, Brigitte. 2000. "No Longer Male: Masculinity Struggles Behind Galatians 3:28?" *JSNT* 79:37–49.

Kraftchick, Steven John. 2015. "Bodies, Selves, and Human Identity: A Conversation between Transhumanism and the Apostle Paul." *ThTo* 72.1:47–69

Le Guin, Ursula K. 1969. *The Left Hand of Darkness.* New York: Ace.

Lewis, Holly M. 2015. *The Politics of Everybody: Feminism, Queer Theory, and Marxism at the Intersection.* London: Zed.

Llewellyn, Mark. 2012. "Authenticity, Authority, and the Author: The Sugared Voice of the Neo-Victorian Prostitute in *The Crimson Petal and the White.*" Pages 185–203 in *Cross-Gendered Literary Voices: Appropriating, Resisting, Embracing.* Edited by Rina Kim and Claire Westall. New York: Palgrave Macmillan.

Lorenz, Renate. 2012. *Queer Art: A Freak Theory.* Bielefeld: Transcript.

Marchal, Joseph A. 2010. "Bodies Bound for Circumcision and Baptism: An Intersex Critique and the Interpretation of Galatians." *ThS* 16.2:163–82.

——, ed. 2015. *The People beside Paul: The Philippian Assembly and History from Below.* ECL 17. Atlanta: SBL Press.

——. 2018. "How Soon Is (This Apocalypse) Now? Queer Velocities after a Corinthian Already and a Pauline Not Yet." Pages 45–67 in *Sexual Disorientations: Queer Temporalities, Affects, Theologies.* Edited by Kent L. Brintnall, Joseph A. Marchal, and Stephen D. Moore. TTC. New York: Fordham University Press.

Martin, Dale B. 2006. *Sex and the Single Savior: Gender and Sexuality in Biblical Interpretation.* Louisville: Westminster John Knox.

Martin, Troy. 1999. "Whose Flesh? What Temptation? (Galatians 4:13–14)." *JSNT* 74:65–91.

Mollenkott, Virginia Ramey. 2007. *Omnigender: A Trans-religious Approach.* Cleveland: Pilgrim.

Moore, Stephen D. 2001. *God's Beauty Parlor: And Other Queer Spaces in and around the Bible.* Contraversions. Stanford: Stanford University Press.

Nussbaum, Martha C. 2013. *The Therapy of Desire: Theory and Practice in Hellenistic Ethics.* Princeton: Princeton University Press.

Pasolini, Pier Paolo. 2014. *Saint Paul: A Screenplay.* Translated by Elizabeth A. Castelli. London: Verso.

Pearson, Wendy Gay. 2010a. "Alien Cryptographies: The View from Queer." Pages 14–38 in Pearson, Hollinger, and Gordon 2010.

———. 2010b. "Towards a Queer Genealogy of SF." Pages 72–100 in Pearson, Hollinger, and Gordon 2010.

Pearson, Wendy Gay, Veronica Hollinger, and Joan Gordon, eds. 2010. *Queer Universes: Sexualities in Science Fiction.* Liverpool: Liverpool University Press.

Penney, James. 2014. *After Queer Theory: The Limits of Sexual Politics.* London: Pluto Press.

Punt, Jeremy. 2010. "Power and Liminality, Sex and Gender, and Gal 3:28: A Postcolonial, Queer Reading of an Influential Text." *Neot* 44:140–66.

Schüssler Fiorenza, Elisabeth. 1997. "The Praxis of Coequal Discipleship." Pages 224–41 in *Paul and Empire: Religion and Power in Roman Imperial Society.* Edited by Richard A. Horsley. Harrisburg, PA: Trinity.

Townsley, Gillian. 2017. *"The Straight Mind" in Corinth: Queer Readings across 1 Corinthians 11:2–16.* SemeiaSt 88. Atlanta: SBL Press.

Trible, Phyllis. 1978. *God and the Rhetoric of Sexuality.* OBT. Philadelphia: Fortress.

Vidal, Gore. 1992. *Live from Golgotha.* New York: Random House.

Wallace, Amy. 2015. "Sci-Fi's Hugo Awards and the Battle for Pop Culture's Soul." *Wired,* 30 October. https://www.wired.com/2015/10/hugo-awards-controversy/.

Wire, Antoinette Clark. 1990. *The Corinthian Women Prophets: A Reconstruction through Paul's Rhetoric.* Eugene: Wipf & Stock.

Wittig, Monique. 1986. *The Lesbian Body.* Boston: Beacon.

Young, Shawn David. 2015. *Gray Sabbath: Jesus People USA, the Evangelical Left, and the Evolution of Christian Rock.* New York: Columbia University Press.

How Paul Became the Straight Word: Protestant Biblicism and the Twentieth-Century Invention of Biblical Heteronormativity

Heather R. White

When conservative Christians argue that their Bibles tell them that homosexuality is immoral, they are not wrong. Most contemporary Bibles—and especially the most popular versions—do quite clearly *say* that homosexuality is sinful. As evidence, we might take a look at the *Life Application Bible* (2011), a bestseller in the category called the study Bible. In its pages are everything a reader needs in order to make sense of the compendium of ancient texts that make up what Christians call the Old and New Testaments. There is also an index. Between *home* and *honesty* is the entry for homosexuality. Under the subheading "scripture forbids it," the entry lists Rom 1:26–27, 1 Cor 6:9, and 1 Tim 1:10. Readers who turn to these passages find not only the words of Scripture but also expanded commentary, which adds a pointed clarification: "the Bible specifically calls homosexual behavior a sin" (1572, 1916). There are, of course, Christians who reject this antihomosexual interpretation. They call these same passages the "clobber texts" for the way they are used to demean gay men and lesbians (Goss and West 2000, 79). But little evidence of a debate appears in the pages of the *Life Application Bible*. This Bible's user-friendly format guides readers unerringly toward a simple, uncontested truth, and it offers engaging moments to reflect, at every step, on what this truth means personally. Readers are left with little question: God has a fulfilling plan for your life. That plan is heterosexuality.

This essay traces how an ancient truth of antihomosexual condemnation came to be implanted in American Bibles and lodged—in particular—in the

Sections of this essay are reprinted with permission from White 2015.

epistles of the apostle Paul. The Pauline texts of Romans and 1 Corinthians are the most frequently cited prooftexts for biblical condemnation of homosexuality. The same-sex meanings of these passages are often not perceived as interpretations; they are imputed to the text and its historical context as the timeless, original meaning. Viewed historically, however, there are many things that are puzzlingly new about this plain biblical speech. The newer Bibles' sharply cast antihomosexual tradition is at best an ambiguous shadow in older Bibles. The seventeenth-century King James translation offers no such clearly articulated set of prohibitions directed at same-sex behavior. The older Bibles are missing not only the modern pedagogical apparatus of indices and expository notes; they also lack the foundational wording and cross-referenced textual tradition. Even more confounding, the sodomites of the King James Version are puzzlingly out of place: they appear in the Old Testament books of the Deuteronomistic History. These archaic pages not only lack Paul's didactic antihomosexual writings; they also speak of a jarringly different sodomitical past.

Paradoxically, it was Protestants' faith in the Bible's timelessness and enduring relevance that served as a key mechanism for these textual changes. As Brian Malley explains in his ethnographic study of Protestant biblicism, a key aim of Protestant Bible reading is to "establish transitivity between the text and beliefs." On its own terms, the practice of anchoring beliefs in the Bible is a guard against the vagaries of cultural change. But in practice, as Malley (2004, 19) observes, "the interpretive tradition mobilizes hermeneutic imaginations anew." Protestant biblicism thus does in practice precisely what it opposes in theory: it generates new meanings for biblical texts. The tradition and the past—"what the Bible *said*"—are continuously reinvented through the current encounter with "what the Bible *says*." Over the course of the twentieth century, these practices of Protestant biblicism have generated much more than new interpretations. They also had a material influence on the formatting and content of the burgeoning consumer market of mass-produced Bibles. Thus as American Protestants turned to their Bibles for timeless truths, they unwittingly effected a twinned sexual and textual transformation. Their quest for timeless meaning facilitated the reshaping of a King James Sodom tradition into a twentieth-century antihomosexuality tradition, and it authorized and naturalized new sexual paradigms by locating them—via the Bible—in the ancient past.

Twentieth-century English-language Bible translations and interpretive commentaries, that is, exhibit the increasing influence of modern medical constructions of a sexual binary—a distinct and opposing relationship between heterosexuality and homosexuality (Katz 1997). Historians of sexuality show how these medical constructions of the sexual binary shaped institutions of law and policy to form what historian Margot Canaday (2009) calls "the straight state." This essay traces the making of what we might call "the straight Word." Looking at American Bibles shows that religion has played an active part in these developments in sexuality, as practices of Christian interpretation molded new interpretive traditions into seemingly unchanging Scriptures. This essay illustrates these changes by working through the texts and associated commentaries for three major translation projects: the seventeenth-century translation of the King James Version (KJV), the mid-twentieth-century Revised Standard Version (RSV), and the 1978 translation of the New International Version (NIV). This history of Christians changing Bibles shows how Paul became the modern authority for a new doctrine of Christian heteronormativity, and it also shows how Protestant Bible-reading practices helped to authorize and naturalize twentieth-century innovations in sexuality.

The Homo/Hetero-Sexual Binary

Scholarship on the history of sexuality presents as axiomatic a view of bodies, pleasures, and relationships as socially and historically contingent. A famous passage from Foucault's *History of Sexuality* serves as exhibit A for this scholarly approach:

> Sodomy was a category of forbidden acts; their perpetrator was nothing more than the juridical subject of them. The nineteenth-century homosexual became a personage, a past, a case history, and a childhood.... The sodomite had been a temporary aberration; the homosexual was now a species. (1990, 43)

Here Foucault gives a descriptive account of the nineteenth-century emergence of sexology, a specialized subfield of psychology and psychiatry that he identifies as the metaphorical inventors of this "personage" of the homosexual. These new doctors generated a medical lexicon for human sexuality with the stated aim of replacing moralizing approaches to "forbidden acts" with scientific inquiries into causes and possible cures (White 2015, 21).

This famous passage from Foucault is often cited as evidence for a historical shift "from act to identity" (Jagose 1996, 10). The explanation goes like this: earlier taboos against sodomy condemned same-sex *behavior*, which modern medicine reconfigured as an interior *condition*. The medical categorization helped to unwittingly lay the foundation for politicized gay identity. The medical invention of the homosexual, that is, marked a shift away from a conception of sodomy as voluntary act to a new notion of homosexuality as durable identity.

Broader work in the history of sexuality, however, shows that the changes brought by the late nineteenth-century medical framework were not merely a shift from act to identity. The medical approach to sexuality also offered new ways of classifying and evaluating behavior. Over time, this process worked to normalize previously "unnatural" and "sodomitical" activity between men and women by mapping it onto a new interpretive grid. Thus a practice such as oral sex became normal as it came to be defined by the participants' genders rather than the act itself (Halley 1993). These changes also placed new scrutiny on formerly innocent expressions of same-sex affection. The terms homosexual and heterosexual appeared first in medical textbooks and gradually percolated outward as the therapeutic paradigm and its grounding in health and wellness entered mainstream awareness. In the decade after World War II, popularly dubbed the Age of Psychology, everyday Americans imbibed new ideas about heterosexual normalcy and homosexual perversion through popular reading. Lifestyle magazines gave advice about gender-appropriate sex education, and newspapers reported on purges of perceived sex deviates from federal employment. The pervasive message about sexual health was that it was vitally important—key to personal and social happiness—and also frighteningly fragile. Heterosexuality needed defending from the subtle invasion of homosexual perversion (Muravchik 2011; White 2015).

The contagion aspects of this medical framework for sexuality was challenged in later decades, but these challenges also inadvertently stabilized and naturalized the hetero/homo binary. In the 1970s, gay activists successfully challenged the disease classification and helped to establish homosexuality as a neutral aspect of human personality rather than a perverted version of heterosexuality that needed to be treated and cured. These interventions helped to right the lopsidedness of the sexual binary, producing a parallel framework for gay and straight as neutral and inborn sexual orientations (Bayer 1981). At the same time, these efforts also had the paradoxical effect of naturalizing heterosexuality. Heterosexual and homosexual came to embody more than stated sexual identity; they operated as descriptive terms for broadly classifying human social and erotic behavior. The modern sexual system thus not only constructed sexuality as an interior attribute of the self, but it also provided new typologies for classifying extrinsic social behavior.

The classificatory typologies of the modern sexual system are perhaps the most durably embedded parts of this system of knowledge, because they seem to operate descriptively rather than ideologically. Queer theorist David Halperin (2000) examines how these descriptive indicators have been used to find same-sex sexuality in history. Halperin's focus is on behavior and its perceived meaning; he investigates the broad range of historical and contextual meanings for attributes often perceived to signify homosexuality. Halperin argues that many seemingly gay characteristics have at many points in history marked typical—even aspirational—qualities of manliness. Halperin deploys the past as a queering mechanism: the strangeness of history helps to dissolve the fictive unity of modern sexual identities and reveal the "incoherence at the core of the modern notion of homosexuality" (90–91).

This essay adopts a version of Halperin's method, using Bible translations (and accompanying commentaries) as the queering device to dissolve the fictive unity of modern biblical heteronormativity. Whereas Halperin investigated the premodern cultural signification of ostensibly homosexual behavior, this essay searches for the earlier interpretive histories of Scripture and commentary about homosexuality. This body of outdated and seemingly irrelevant biblical commentary, especially as it appears in tertiary reference tools, has been largely overlooked in the contemporary scholarly discussion about the historical meaning of 1 Cor 6:9 and Rom 1:26–27, the go-to passages on homosexuality. Most biblical scholarship on these passages bypasses historical interpretation—and especially the interpretation directed at everyday Christians. The focus of this literature is instead the original languages and ancient historical contexts. While this approach may uncover new knowledge about ancient contexts, a direct dive into the primary sources also risks the beguiling mirror of a desired past. There is nothing more seductive—or more Protestant—than this desire for unmediated access to the text's so-called original meaning. An inquiry into the history of interpretation helps to mediate against this false sense of textual intimacy.

First, a caution: old Bible dictionaries are like outdated time machines. Each one of these contraptions promises to transport the reader into the mind and context of the historical author. Exploring these alternative pasts in sequence, however, jarringly unsettles their respective claims to timelessness. Each disparate past was generated in its time by an author convinced his insight gave us access to the true original. The discordant originals help to make visible the naturalizing operations of Protestant biblicism.

Other Sodomites

The first time machine: a Bible dictionary from 1929. *Homosexuality* is nowhere to be found in this reference work. The first Bible dictionary entries for this medical neologism did not appear until the 1960s (Baab 1962, 639). What do appear are entries for *Sodom* and, under that, *sodomite*. Definitions acknowledge a link between these terms: the former is a city referenced in various passages throughout the Old and New Testaments, most famously in Gen 19, which recounts the city's destruction by God as punishment for the sin of its denizens. Those denizens are the eponym for later namesakes: "sodomites" were guilty of "a loathsome vice" that "owes its name to their behavior" (Eiselen, Lewis, and Downey 1929, 232). Circling tautologically through city, sin, and denizens—these entries defined each term in reference to the others. A cross-listed biblical passage—Ezek 16—promised substance: this sin of Sodom, committed by sodomites, and thus bearing their name, is "defined as arrogant prosperity and callousness" (724). Another widely used early twentieth-century reference elaborated that *sodomite* was an English word translated from the Hebrew *keddeshim*, which designated persons guilty of "not ordinary immorality but *religious prostitution*, i.e., immorality practiced in the worship of a deity and in the immediate precincts of a temple" (Selbie 1902). Cross-listed passages point the reader to five Old Testament passages that reference these sodomites: one in Deuteronomy, three in 1 Kings, and one in 2 Kings. Similar definitions prevailed in other popular Bible reference materials (Barnes 1900; Orr 1915; Davis 1917).[1]

---

1. Deut 23:17: "There shall be no whore of the daughters of Israel, nor a sodomite of the sons of Israel." 1 Kgs 14:24: "And there were also sodomites in the land: *and* they did according to all the abominations of the nations which the LORD cast out before the children of Israel." 1 Kgs 15:12: "And he took away the sodomites out of the land, and removed all the idols that his fathers had made." 1 Kgs 22:46: "And the remnant of the sodomites, which remained in the days of his father Asa, he took out of the land." 2 Kgs 23:7: "And he brake down the houses of the sodomites, that *were* by the house of

First, we must notice the absences. The so-called clobber passages are not there. Not one of the Bible dictionary entries on sodomites points readers to a passage in the Pauline epistles or even in the New Testament. Homosexuality—or same-sex sexuality—is at best hinted at as a "loathsome vice," but other parts of the definition directly name other meanings— namely, arrogant prosperity or religious prostitution. The latter definition distanced sodomy from ordinary sexual immorality. Sodomy, in these definitions, was a perverse ritual practice.

The Bible translation to which these reference tools referred was the KJV. For American Protestants, as for the rest of the English-speaking Protestant world, this Bible was no mere translation. The KJV stood unrivaled for more than four centuries as *the* Bible (Noll 2011; Marks 2012). Published in 1611, the KJV was a product of the English Reformation, and this context gave rise to particular visions of Sodom.

Historian Harry G. Cocks (2017, 158) shows how the Reformers read the story of Sodom as a sacred history of the Reformation fight against the "Whoredom and Uncleanness" of Roman Catholicism. In this theological polemic, the biblical sodomites were perverse papists, and the city of Sodom was the Roman Church. Homoeroticism was a component part of these biblical and theological narratives, but same-sex perversion was only one thread in a nest of bodily perversions signified by Sodom, which also encompassed fornication, adultery, prostitution, gender inversion, and subhuman monstrosity. These forms of sexual, gender, and bodily deviance further tangled with religious difference. Roman Catholicism was at the center of this thicket, as the paradigmatic prototype of the illicit heathenism found in false religion (133–60).

American Protestants, as inheritors of the Reformation legacy and its English Bible, also narrated their encounters with religious and bodily difference through the biblical story of Sodom. This pairing of Sodom and perverse idolatry was an interpretive tradition that continued to hold

---

the LORD, where the women wove hangings for the grove." (A sixth passage, Job 36:14, contains the same original Hebrew word, but the KJV renders it "the unclean": "They die in youth, and their life *is* among the unclean.") None of these five passages appear in contemporary Bible dictionary references to homosexuality, and later translations substitute "cult prostitutes" (or a similar phrase) for "sodomites" in these verses. Several contemporary scholars challenge the sexualized meaning of the word as an interpretive gloss and argue that the English rendering should simply be "holy man." For a history of interpretation, see Budin 2008 and Lings 2013.

power through the early twentieth century. Indeed, the Bible dictionaries and commentaries cited at the beginning of this essay section appeared in writing by Protestant domestic missionaries in the 1920s. Herbert Welsh, an Episcopalian missionary to Pueblo nations of the American southwest, referenced definitions of sodomy as an immoral pagan rite in order to argue—speciously—that Pueblo dance ceremonies "resembled this ancient religion practiced by the people of Sodom and Gomorrah" (quoted in Wenger 2009, 218–19). Welsh was no wacky outlier: quite a number of religion scholars viewed the so-called primitive religion of pre-Israelite cultures as naturally similar to non-Western spiritual practice. The entry for *sodomy* in James Hasting's widely used *Encyclopedia of Religion and Ethics* was written by such a scholar: George Aaron Barton, professor of Semitic languages and history of religion at the University of Pennsylvania and seminal thinker in the field of Oriental studies (Speiser and Albright 1942). Barton surmised that biblical sodomites were practitioners of religiously based sex rituals, comparable to the reported "indecencies" practiced within Saivite sects of Hinduism and in the coming-of-age rituals of Australian aboriginal people (Barton 1921, 673). These interpretations of the biblical Sodom located sodomitical perversion on the bodies of religious and racialized Others.

These exotic constructions of sodomy tended to exempt from scrutiny the homoerotic affections of those within the Protestant fold— particularly when these believers were white Europeans. Historians' investigations of seventeenth-century sodomy discourses underscore this distancing effect: the associations of sodomy with a broader social disorder had the effect of removing everyday homoerotic affection from the fearsome condemnations of sodomitical sin (Herrup 1999; Bray 2006). Historians of sexuality in the United States also argue that other dynamics of nineteenth- and early twentieth-century American Protestantism contributed to a lack of concern about homoerotic behavior. Protestant practice focused on various worrisome aspects of relationships between women and men, which included not only attention to the marriage but also the more concerning task of preventing temptation between women and men. Same-sex friendships and single-sex institutions, in contrast, provided safe havens from sexual danger. In practice, these social and religious configurations meant that institutions like the Young Men's and Young Women's Christian Associations, with American branches founded in 1851 and 1858 respectively, provided surprising latitude to homoerotic relationships between women and between men

(Gustav-Wrathall 1998; Chauncey 1985). Historian Kathi Kern (2018, 18), examining the amorous same-sex friendships of one YWCA leader, argued that religion in this context offered "vocabularies of spiritual intimacy, religiously affiliated homosocial spaces, intimate rituals, and powerful theological concepts that transcended stigmas of deviance." For those within the spiritual fold, these religious spaces could nurture relationships of same-sex desire not in spite of theological commitments but because of them.

Homosexuality Comes Home to Roost

By the 1940s, as new frameworks of sexual health began to circulate in the American vernacular, same-sex love could no longer claim unexamined innocence. In 1946, for the first time, Christians could open a Bible and find a reference to homosexuality in its pages. This Bible was the New Testament of the RSV; the complete translation with the Old Testament came out in 1952. The American Standard Bible Committee, the group of biblical scholars that labored over this translation, began their work in the late 1930s. As Protestant liberals educated in elite intuitions, they were likely well acquainted with the fields of psychology and psychotherapy. In many ways, the RSV translation was the product of liberal Protestant commitments to glean insight from new historical and scientific research as a resource for Christian revelation. The RSV was advertised as the "first modern Bible"; it promised to match the "timeless beauty" of the KJV but with "more accurate and easier to read prose" (RSV advertisement 1952; Thuesen 1999). The new direct reference to homosexuality dovetailed with the translators' mission to replace the KJV's vague anachronisms with modern, accessible wording.

The Bible passage was 1 Cor 6:9, where homosexuals were now listed among the sinners barred from the kingdom of God. This change streamlined into one figure what the KJV listed in two words: "effeminates" and "abusers of self with mankind." The new wording received little notice, but various authors discussed how the new translation challenged previous assumptions about what kinds of sins were being addressed by the KJV's vague wording. One local pastor reminisced about a favorite sermon that expanded on the figure of the "effeminates" in 1 Cor 6:9. The minister understood the term as an obvious reference to "the soft, the pliable, those who take the easy road." The sermon's message was a challenge to undertake the difficult path of faith. This minister reported "his amazement and chagrin" when he read the same passage in the RSV and discovered that "effeminate" was translated "homosexuals" (Jones 1956, 77). The point of this anecdote was to warn other ministers to use updated reference tools in their sermon preparation. The outdated source for this sermon may well have been the 1929 *Abington Bible Commentary*, which expanded on the apostle Paul's concerns about "self indulgence of appetite and speech" (Eiselen 1929, 1178). This earlier understanding of effeminacy was not the only nonhomosexual interpretation of the sinners named in this passage. Another widely shared assumption about the reference to "abusers of self with mankind" was that it prohibited masturbation ("self-abuse") or any other kind of nonprocreative "spilling of seed," such as the use of birth control (Fletcher 1960, 118; Northcote 1906, 34). The RSV's unambiguous reference to "homosexuals" in this passage foreclosed these earlier interpretations with the simple insertion of a new word.

The new wording of 1 Cor 6:9 was only one part of a broader reconfiguration, which shuffled the KJV-based Sodom tradition into a new interpretive tradition that focused on homosexuality as a distinct category of deviance. These changes are exhibited with particular clarity in the twelve-volume *The Interpreter's Bible: The Holy Scriptures in the King James and Revised Standard Versions*, published by the theologically moderate Abingdon Press. Careful perusal of these twelve hefty volumes promised to open up timeless truths that transcended the time-bound translations of the KJV and RSV. This magisterial reference tool, in sum, built an accessible door for modern-day Bible readers to glean timeless truth from ancient texts. Even the editors marveled: this new commentary, the introduction promised, offered a "veritable 'open sesame'" to the world of the Bible (Buttrick 1951, xvii). This paradox of ancient truth and modern relevance also suffused the volume's newly frank discussion of homosexuality. The direct speech about homosexuality was a first for Bible reference tools. As the scholarly authors addressed it, this modern innovation was truth always present in the original texts.

The primary textual anchors for this new antihomosexual Bible tradition were in 1 Cor 6:9 and Rom 1, with Old Testament support found in Leviticus and in the Gen 19 story of Sodom. The *Interpreter's Bible* explained the same-sex meaning of these passages with language that evoked psychoanalysis. Commentary on Rom 1:26–28 explained that homosexuality was a "manifestation" of "the root cause of both the sin and corruption in idolatry," phrasing that followed disease diagnosis of homosexuality as the behavioral manifestation of a deeply rooted pathology (1954, 401–3). The biblical commentary also stressed the contagious aspects of this sexual pathology: those who "refuse to give God any place in their thoughts," this same commentator warned, might also be abandoned to corrupt desires (471).

The entry of new homosexual meanings into these Bible verses took place alongside the sodomite's exit. In five Old Testament passages where the KJV spoke of "sodomites," the RSV now named "cult prostitutes." The change in term offered what translators and commentators alike saw as not an innovation but a clarification. Biblical scholarship widely insisted that the term sodomites in the passage was misleading and inaccurate. While mid-twentieth-century scholars continued to interpret these as references to sex acts linked to pagan rituals, most of the biblical scholarship theorized that these practices were part of an ancient fertility cult, in which sexual intercourse was linked to the deities' power over the propagation of life (Brooms 1941). This interpretation would seem to necessarily exclude homosexuality. As one scholar pointedly argued, "homosexual coitus would be meaningless in the ritual of a fertility cult" (Bailey 1955, 53). These textual changes, as mere translations, made no claim to innovation. But they were shaped by a new common sense: heterosexuals could not possibly be sodomites.

The new homosexuality tradition was thus centered on a different set of passages than the earlier Sodom tradition. The Old Testament sodomites and their pagan idolatry were now replaced by a new therapeutic orthodoxy that focused on the New Testament. At the center of this antihomosexuality tradition were Rom 1 and 1 Cor 6:9. This shift introduced a new interiority to the sin of Sodom. Whereas earlier interpretations emphasized the foreignness of the biblical sodomites, the therapeutic turn of the mid-twentieth-century located homosexuality—at least potentially—within everyday Christianity. Biblical scholar Dale B. Martin has discussed this shift toward interiority as a peculiarly modern understanding of Rom 1: "What for Paul functioned as a sign of the boundary separating idolatrous civilization from monotheistic faith," Martin (2006, 64) writes, became "a symptom par excellence of what is wrong with 'all of us.'" Whereas sodomites were distant enemies of the faith, homosexual perversion threatened Christianity from within.

The RSV and accompanying commentaries, through the labors of mid-twentieth-century Bible scholars, generated a new antihomosexual biblical literalism. The interpretive strategies of historical criticism embedded a distantly modern interpretive tradition into the text as a faithful replication of original meaning. This process also effectively disappeared the earlier perceptions of these passages as erroneous translations or inaccurate interpretations. These interpretive changes pared down the capacious forms of deviance signified by the figures of "sodomites," "effeminates," and "abusers of self with mankind" and retrofitted these figures into a modern therapeutic framework as simple anachronisms for homosexuality. Thus a neologism that was not even a century old—and that had only recently appeared in theological commentaries—fit so smoothly into the grooves of older biblical prohibitions that it seemed as if it had been there all along.

The Antigay Tradition

This new tradition also influenced Protestant conservatives. There was, however, nothing inevitable about this influence; conservative Protestants initially resisted both the RSV and the therapeutic paradigm for sexuality. It was not until the mid-1970s that conservative Protestants began to write and reflect at length on the biblical teaching about homosexuality. Evangelical and conservative Protestants worked to adopt and adapt the therapeutic views of sexuality first circulated by their liberal counterparts into a framework that eschewed their liberal counterparts' deliberate adaptations of secular forms of knowledge. What conservatives embraced as biblical (rather than secular) truth, however, had been effectively christened by a previous generation of Protestant liberals. The Bible's plain word on homosexuality proceeded from a newly implanted therapeutic tongue.

Conservative attachment to biblical authority was key to a process of authorizing change in the supposedly bedrock text. Critical to the process of consolidating a new orthodoxy was the 1978 publication of the NIV. This Bible translation was the evangelical answer to the liberal RSV, and it quickly surpassed the KJV as America's bestselling Bible. The RSV was the first Bible to use the term *homosexuals* in the plain text—in a New Testament passage in 1 Corinthians. The RSV also excised some sodomites from the plain text as well. The KJV has several Old Testament passages that referenced "sodomites" as ancient pagan idolaters. The new translation changed them to "cult prostitutes." These changes tracked along a therapeutic logic, which narrowed the meanings of sodomy to homosexual behavior and thus sloughed off the previously attached meanings of idolatry. When the evangelical translators made their own choices for the NIV, they challenged a number of the RSV precedents, but they adopted this particular set of textual interpretations. In these translation changes, evangelicals belatedly followed liberals' modern therapeutic paradigm by reconfiguring an older sodomy tradition into an emergent homosexuality tradition. Thus the NIV translation worked to ratify and authorize a new antihomosexual tradition. Translators did not only change the Bible's meanings; they changed the wording to make plain newly understood meanings. The debate over whether a modern notion of a sexual orientation should moderate the Bible's plain prohibitions against homosexual acts obscured the more fundamental changes in modern Bibles. The seemingly plain tradition of homosexual prohibition was itself a product of earlier interpretive changes that through the process of translation became embedded into the words of the text.

The direct impetus to explicitly stake out this orthodoxy was not a secular movement for gay rights but the heterodox interpretations within the ranks of conservative Protestants. Leading conservatives were concerned about pro-gay Christian teachings that were gaining influence through the 1970s. The United Fellowship of Metropolitan Community Churches, a gay-welcoming fellowship, voiced a thoroughly biblicist message of gay acceptance (Perry 1972). At the same time, a small but vocal movement for gay and lesbian acceptance also began to emerge within evangelical institutions (Gasaway 2014). This group included Ralph Blair, who led the organizing efforts for Evangelicals Concerned, the affinity group for gay evangelicals founded in 1975 (see Blair 1977). It also included Virginia Ramey Mollenkott and Letha Scanzoni's (1978) best-selling pro-gay treatise, *Is the Homosexual My Neighbor?* Both respected evangelical Christian authors, Scanzoni and Mollenkott made an argument that even critics acknowledged took biblical authority seriously. The first systematic writing by conservative Protestants on the biblical condemnation of homosexuality was a defensive response to previous pro-gay Christian arguments (Lindsell 1973; Bockmühl 1973; Kinlaw 1976; Lovelace 1978; Kirk 1978).

These developments were important because they showed the covert ways that the interpreted meanings of the Bible changed over time, even for conservatives who strongly insisted upon biblical authority. What conservatives defended as tradition was in many ways a reanimated version of liberal therapeutic orthodoxy, which underscored the binding meanings of the Bible's condemnation against homosexual acts. Antihomosexual conservatives hewed closely to what they saw as the plain evidence of biblical authority. Liberals emphasized historical-critical methods that cultivated a critical distance between the reader and the perceived meanings of Scripture. Through this deliberate attention to interpretation, liberals challenged and reinterpreted seemingly plain Bible prohibitions on the grounds that they should be seen not as time-less rules but as contextual practices. In contrast, those who professed an attachment to the plain or literal meanings of the Bible accused their opponents of arguing away plain meanings that conveyed the Bible's unchanging authority.

The late twentieth-century explosion of new Bible products also further expanded and cultivated readers' connections to those newly plain meanings. Conservative Protestant publishing companies offered an expanding array of what one religion scholar calls the "culturally relevant Bible" (Gutjahr 2008, 326). Glossy covers, attractive images, and magazine-like styles were important to the consumer packaging of new translations, paraphrase editions, and Bible study tools. They offered the Bible as a lifestyle product with to-the-minute wisdom for everyday choices. These Bible products illustrate a second important aspect to conservative Christian practices of literalism that were important to the practice of this new antigay tradition. In addition to avowed fidelity to biblical authority, the practice of literalism also conveyed a personal and affective relationship to the text and its divine author—the Bible not only speaks authoritatively; it speaks *to me* (Malley 2004). Indeed, the format of late twentieth-century Bible products actively cultivated this sense of closeness. Formats that elicited readers' personal engagement with the text also gave material meaning to the repeated injunction to "hide God's word in your heart." The Bible's meanings were not an external authority but an interiorized truth. The personal attachment to the Bible's meanings served as a mechanism for the production of a distinctive sexual self. When evangelicals spoke of the ways that biblical authority marked out a distinct practice of sexual behavior—sexual abstinence, heterosexuality, and marital fidelity—they were not speaking of a rote performance of external rules; they were referring, rather, to living out a deeply embedded sense of self. The political rhetoric of "defending moral values" might communicate to outsiders an adherence to external rules and authorities; for the born again, however, the affective personal life of faith was about remaining authentic to an interior truth.

Conclusion

This history of the straight Word is not only important for understanding Christianity, but it also helps to illuminate the durable equation of heteronormativity with religion writ large. In the late twentieth-century debates over homosexuality, sexual identity and biblical orthodoxy seemed to proceed from opposing sources of truth. Gay and lesbian identities are modern and secular; the Bible is ancient and religious. This patent truth stood as such, however, because of the ways that Americans of various faith traditions—and none at all—perceived the Bible's newly implanted antihomosexual tradition as an accurate map of the past. What "the Bible says" about sexuality has circulated well outside the fold of believing Christians. Indeed, many non-Christians would aver that Scripture *does* plainly forbid homosexuality. These nonbelievers might regard the Scriptural condemnation as a fact—even if the significance they take away from that fact is that religion is homophobic. Modern Bibles, that is, are often read and interpreted as neutral historical evidence about religion writ large, as if modern English translations can account for the long and variable past of a monolithic Judeo-Christian tradition. Such influence suggests a further reason for inquiring into the sexual history of modern Bibles. Not only have they been shaped by modern medical constructions of sexuality, but they have also reinforced and naturalized these new ways of thinking about sexuality by projecting them—via new translations and interpretations—into the ancient past. Moreover, because these modern Bibles have been signified generically as *the* Bible (rather than *a* Bible or a particular Protestant translation), these practices of translation and interpretation have also played an important role in constructing a religious past assumed to be shared, monolithic, and heteronormative.

This felt sense of the past, this essay suggests, is a specter of twentieth-century Protestant biblicism, which continues to pervade civil law and public discourse as the rhetorical touchstone for what historian Mark Noll (2011, 72) calls a "biblical civil religion." Indeed, Noll's observation about the nineteenth-century debates over biblical teachings about slavery seems to hold continued relevance for today's debates over sexuality. Not only did both sides "read the same Bible," Noll (1998, 43) argues, but "they also read the Bible *in the same way*." The Bible's plain meaning continues to haunt the supposedly religion-free zone of the secular. Nowhere is this ghost more pervasive than in the ideology of *sexularism*, a neologism coined by Joan Wallach Scott (2009, 1–2) to name "the elision of the secular and the sexually liberated—their assumed synonymity." Protestant biblicism, as a felt sense of the past, powerfully underpins all sides of public debates over sex.

Works Cited

Baab, O. J. 1962. "Homosexuality." Page 639 in vol. 2 of *The Interpreter's Dictionary of the Bible: An Illustrated Encyclopedia*. Edited by George Arthur Buttrick. 4 vols. New York: Abingdon.

Bailey, Derrick Sherwin. 1955. *Homosexuality and the Western Christian Tradition*. London: Longmans, Green.

Barnes, Charles Randall, ed. 1900. *Dictionary of the Bible: Biographical, Geographical, Historical, and Doctrinal*. New York: Eaton & Mains.

Barton, George Aaron. 1921. "Sodomy." Pages 672–74 in vol. 11 of *Encyclopedia of Religion and Ethics*. Edited by James Hastings. 12 vols. New York: Scribner.

Bayer, Ronald. 1981. *Homosexuality and American Psychiatry: The Politics of Diagnosis*. New York: Basic Books.

Blair, Ralph. 1977. *An Evangelical Look at Homosexuality*. New York: Homosexual Community Counseling Center.

Bockmühl, Klaus. 1973. "Homosexuality in Biblical Perspective." *Christianity Today* 17.10:12–18.

Bray, Alan. 2006. *The Friend*. Chicago: University of Chicago.

Brooms, Beatrice A. 1941. "Fertility Cult Functionaries in the Old Testament." *JBL* 60:227–53.

Budin, Stephanie Lynn. 2008. *The Myth of Sacred Prostitution in Antiquity*. New York: Cambridge University Press.

Buttrick, George Arthur, ed. 1951. *The Interpreter's Bible: The Holy Scriptures in the King James and Revised Standard Versions Romans*. Vol. 9. New York: Abingdon.

Canaday, Margot. 2009. *The Straight State: Sexuality and Citizenship in Twentieth-Century America*. PSMA. Princeton: Princeton University Press.

Chauncey, George. 1985. "Christian Brotherhood or Sexual Perversion? Homosexual Identities and the Construction of Sexual Boundaries in the World War One Era." *JSH* 19:189–211.

Cocks, Harry G. 2017. *Visions of Sodom: Religion, Homerotic Desire, and the End of the World in England, c. 1550–1850*. Chicago: University of Chicago Press.

Davis, John D. 1917. *A Dictionary of the Bible*. Philadelphia: Westminster.

Eiselen, Frederick Carl, Edwin Lewis, and David G. Downey, eds. 1929. *The Abingdon Bible Commentary*. New York: Abingdon.

Fletcher, Joseph F. 1960. *Morals and Medicine: The Moral Problems of The Patient's Right to Know the Truth, Contraception, Artificial Insemination, Sterilization, Euthanasia.* Boston: Beacon.

Foucault, Michel. 1990. *An Introduction.* Vol. 1 of *The History of Sexuality.* Translated by Robert Hurley. Repr. ed. New York: Vintage.

Gasaway, Brantley W. 2014. *Progressive Evangelicals and the Pursuit of Social Justice.* Chapel Hill: University of North Carolina Press.

Goss, Robert E., and Mona West, eds. 2000. *Take Back the Word: A Queer Reading of the Bible.* Cleveland: Pilgrim.

Gustav-Wrathall, John Donald. 1998. *Take the Young Stranger by the Hand: Same-Sex Relations and the YMCA.* CSSHS. Chicago: University of Chicago Press.

Gutjahr, Paul. 2008. "The Bible-zine *Revolve* and the Evolution of the Culturally Relevant Bible in America." Pages 326–48 in *Religion and the Culture of Print in Modern America.* Edited by Charles L. Cohen and Paul S. Boyer. PCHMA. Madison: University of Wisconsin Press.

Halley, Janet E. 1993. "Reasoning about Sodomy: Act and Identity in and after Bowers v. Hardwick." *VLR* 79:1721–80.

Halperin, David. 2000. "How to Do the History of Homosexuality." *GLQ* 6:87–124.

Herrup, Cynthia B. 1999. *A House in Gross Disorder: Sex, Law, and the Second Earl of Castlehaven.* New York: Oxford University Press.

Jagose, Annamarie. 1996. *Queer Theory: An Introduction.* New York: New York University Press.

Jones, Ilion Tingnal. 1956. *Principles and Practice of Preaching.* Nashville: Abingdon.

Katz, Jonathan Ned. 1997. "'Homosexual' and 'Heterosexual': Questioning the Terms." Pages 177–80 in *A Queer World: The Center for Lesbian and Gay Studies Reader.* Edited by Martin Duberman. New York: New York University Press.

Kern, Kathi. 2018. "Winnifred Wygal's Flock: Same-Sex Desire and Christian Faith in the 1920s." Pages 17–33 in *Devotions and Desires: Histories of Sexuality and Religion in the Twentieth-Century United States.* Edited by Gillian Frank, Bethany Moreton, and Heather R. White. Chapel Hill: University of North Carolina Press.

Kinlaw, Dennis. 1976. "A Biblical View of Homosexuality." Pages 104–16 in *The Secrets of Our Sexuality.* Edited by Gary Collins. Waco, TX: Word.

Kirk, Jerry R. 1978. *The Homosexual Crisis in the Mainline Church: A Presbyterian Minister Speaks Out*. London: Nelson.

Life Application Bible, New International Version. 2011. Personal size edition. Wheaton, IL: Tyndall; Zondervan.

Lindsell, Harold. 1973. "Homosexuals and the Church." *Christianity Today* 17.25:8–12.

Lings, K. Renato. 2013. *Love Lost in Translation: Homosexuality and the Bible*. Victoria, BC: Trafford.

Lovelace, Richard F. 1978. *Homosexuality and the Church*. London: Lamp.

Malley, Brian. 2004. *How the Bible Works: An Anthropological Study of Evangelical Biblicism*. Walnut Creek, CA: AltaMira.

Marks, Herbert. 2012. Preface to *The Old Testament*. Vol. 1 of *The English Bible King James Version*. Edited by Herbert Marks. New York: Norton.

Martin, Dale B. 2006. *Sex and the Single Savior: Gender and Sexuality in Biblical Interpretation*. Louisville: Westminster John Knox.

Mollenkott, Virginia Ramey, and Letha Scanzoni. 1978. *Is the Homosexual My Neighbor? Another Christian View*. San Francisco: Harper & Row.

Muravchik, Stephanie. 2011. *American Protestantism in the Age of Psychology*. New York: Cambridge University Press.

Noll, Mark. 1998. "The Bible and Slavery." Pages 43–73 in *Religion and the American Civil War*. Edited by Randall M. Miller, Harry S. Stout, and Charles Reagan Wilson. New York: Oxford University Press.

———. 2011. "The King James Version at 300 in America: 'The Most Democratic Book in the World.'" Pages 71–98 in *The King James Bible and the World It Made*. Edited by David Lyle Jeffrey. Waco, TX: Baylor University Press.

Northcote, Hugh. 1906. *Christianity and Sex Problems*. Philadelphia: Davis.

Orr, James, ed. 1915. *The International Standard Bible Encyclopaedia*. Chicago: Howard-Severance.

Perry, Troy. 1972. *The Lord Is My Shepherd and He Knows I'm Gay*. New York: Nash.

RSV advertisement. 1952. *Life Magazine*, October 6. Available online at https://tinyurl.com/SBL0699b/.

Scott, Joan W. 2009. "Sexularism." Ursula Hirschmann Annual Lecture on Gender and Europe at the European University Institute, Florence, Italy. https://tinyurl.com/SBL0699n.

Selbie, J. A. 1902. "Sodomite." Page 559 in *A Dictionary of the Bible: Pleroma-Zuzim*. Edited by James Hastings, Alexander Selbie, Andrew

Bruce Davidson, Samuel Rolles Driver, and Henry Barclay Swete. New York: Scribner.

Speiser, E. A. and W. F. Albright. 1942. "George Aaron Barton, 1859–1942." *BASOR* 87:1–5.

Thuesen, Peter. 1999. *In Discordance with the Scriptures: American Protestant Battles over Translating the Bible*. New York: Oxford University Press.

Wenger, Tisa. 2009. *We Have a Religion: The 1920s Pueblo Indian Dance Controversy and American Religious Freedom*. Chapel Hill: University of North Carolina Press.

White, Heather R. 2015. *Reforming Sodom: Protestants and the Rise of Gay Rights*. Chapel Hill: University of North Carolina Press.

Responses

Interpreting as Queer or Interpreting Queerly?

Lynn R. Huber

In the introduction to *Feeling Backwards*, Heather Love (2007) describes the desire of queer critics and readers to reach back into a past looking to find and maybe rescue forebears who we intuit as queer like us. Although these haints and haunted souls resist our advances, we find it hard to stop glancing backward. Love, however, finds something productive in these backward glances, since "tear-soaked accounts of same-sex desire compel readers in a way that brighter stories of liberation do not." Thus the queer affect is often despairing, melancholic, and even nostalgic, on account of "the historical 'impossibility' of same-sex desire" (3). This backward-looking queerness colors many of our attempts at engaging in queer biblical interpretation, as a number of the essays in this volume reveal. In the following, I engage a select number of these essays as a way of thinking more broadly about the contours of queer biblical interpretation.

In his essay, Tyler M. Schwaller foregrounds the queer practice of glancing back, as there exists "pleasure and power … in alliances forged across time with those who resist and exist beyond dominant ideals." In his own look back at Paul's writings, Schwaller connects enslavement with queerness.[1] The relationship between these categories commends itself, since the question of whether those enslaved in the first century were understood as full members of the *ekklēsiai* in Christ resonates with contemporary discussions about who deserves full inclusion within the Christian community.

---

1. In adopting the language of "the enslaved" rather than "slave," I follow the lead of Pauline scholars such as Katherine A. Shaner (2018, 123 n. 4). This shift in language points to the fact that oppressive structures construct the identity category of the *slave* and that it is not an identity inherent to an individual.

While he ultimately focuses his attention upon Paul as a queer subject, since Paul self-identifies as a slave, Schwaller begins by discussing the queer potential of the ancient enslaved individual more generally. In so doing, Schwaller converses with Jasbir K. Puar's 2005 essay "Queer Times, Queer Assemblages," adopting Puar's understanding of queerness as capable of both resisting and colluding in structures of domination. Puzzlingly, while the terrorist as queer assemblage provides the focal point of Puar's essay and her subsequent monograph *Terrorist Assemblages* (2007), this character remains unnamed as Schwaller applies Puar's insights to the enslaved. Seemingly, however, the terrorist is essential for understanding queerness as described by Puar here, especially as she associates queerness with complicity and collusion. While the queerness of the terrorist resides within her body as an assemblage of organic and nonorganic materials and as a site of both self-annihilation and self-preservation (Puar 2005, 128–29), it is seemingly the way the terrorist body is deployed by others that lends queerness its collusive potential. For it is the homonationalist practice of leveraging queerness to justify US military, and other invasive forms of international, intervention that serve as the focus of Puar's critique. Even though Schwaller mostly forgoes mention of homonationalism, attention to this seems helpful for understanding how Paul's self-designation as a slave deploys the potential queerness of being enslaved in a way that colludes with structures of domination.[2]

Schwaller's rich discussion of Paul's self-appellation as enslaved in 1 Corinthians reflects the struggle that characterizes much of queer biblical interpretation and historical investigation. We follow Schwaller through a process of asking "Is he?" or "Isn't he?" as we try to nail down Paul's queerness. Even though Paul's use of enslavement as a strategy for lowering himself (i.e., disassociating himself from the elite) suggests queerness, Schwaller ultimately seems to indicate that Paul's self-portrayal as the ideal slave—a slave who recognizes and accepts his role as one who brings in profits for others—points to queerness employed toward reinforcing the ideology of slavery. What may appear as a queer move on the surface complies with a variety of rhetorical strategies that employ "slavery" to maintain extant hierarchies. Paul employs queerness to "pro[p] up dominant material and discursive practices." And yet, Schwaller observes, Paul is unable to control how people read his performance. His slavery is

---

2. Schwaller does explain homonationalism in n. 30.

interpreted variously, as evidenced in Paul's defense of his violable body in 2 Cor 11:25–28. In other words, some read Paul's rhetoric queerly, despite his own intentions.

Throughout, Schwaller notes the importance of recognizing the material reality of enslavement in the ancient world, even though Paul's use is primarily metaphorical or rhetorical. Among other things, Schwaller encourages readers to think about how the enslaved within Paul's congregations might have heard and responded to Paul's teachings, including his call to flee from *porneia*. Given first-century protocols, participating in *porneia* might have been a fundamental aspect of an individual's enslavement.[3] This focus on materiality and the reality of enslavement in the ancient world prompts me to think about two related things. First, I am interested in how material objects, such as collars and fetters, contributed to the enslaved body as an assemblage and how this relates to queerness. For Puar, the terrorist embodies queerness as a pastiche of explosives, timing devices, and the organic matter of the body. Do we see Paul (or other New Testament and early Christian authors) ever using rhetoric that draws on these material aspects of enslavement?

Second, not only am I interested in how the ancient enslaved might hear and deploy Paul's self-description as a slave, but I am also curious as to how this rhetoric falls on the ears of contemporary queers who self-identify as slaves or submissives. Similarly, I wonder how the practices of modern BDSM communities might shed light upon appropriation of the enslaved identity. Can an exploration of how participants within BDSM communities negotiate power relationships help us understand how Paul attempts to negotiate power? As in the case of Paul, submissives are not literally enslaved and, in fact, consent to be dominated, controlled, hurt, and even humiliated by the dominant other. Can Paul's self-description as a "slave to all" be understood as his consent to be dominated and even abused by the Corinthian community? Furthermore, exploring Paul's use of enslavement imagery in relationship to BDSM provides an opportunity to think critically about how one identifies as slave or a submissive in historical contexts where the literal buying and selling of people occurs and is accepted as natural.[4]

---

3. The sexual element of enslavement is explored by Marchal 2011.

4. According to the International Labor Organization (https://tinyurl.com/SBL0699c), in 2016 there were approximately 40 million individuals enslaved around

Like Schwaller, Timothy Luckritz Marquis looks to the Corinthian correspondence for insights into queerness. Drawing upon José Esteban Muñoz's 1999 monograph, *Disidentifications: Queers of Color and the Performance of Politics*, Luckritz Marquis demonstrates that *disidentification* proves useful for understanding how Paul, as a minoritized subject, is always under construction. His identity is shaped by cultural forces that push him to be read in particular ways, as well as through his own disidentification or disassociation with these forces.

Among the cultural forces that shape Paul's identity, providing him with a range of identities with which to disidentify, are literary tropes about traveling Bacchic or Dionysian preachers. These representatives of a foreign or Eastern god (Dionysus was often associated with Asia Minor) were both depicted as triumphantly bringing their deity into the cities of the West and maligned as hucksters and frauds. Paul creates a space in relation to these depictions to craft his identity. It is not that Paul *chooses* the Dionysian tradition as a foil; rather, as Luckritz Marquis observes, "because he is a preacher of an Eastern god, the only way to distinguish and authenticate himself is to take Dionysus, God, and the baggage they come with in new directions. As such, Paul cannot present himself as *not* Dionysian, as *not* Eastern; rather he must present himself as Eastern in new ways." Among other strategies of disidentification, Paul highlights his difference from the Bacchic bunch, typically associated with drunkenness and sexual excess, by emphasizing his celibacy. One might argue that a life of celibacy implies Paul's queerness, given the political and social importance placed upon marriage and procreation within the Roman imperial period. It is interesting to note, however, that while Lucritz Marquis depicts Paul employing a queer method of world building, he never really outs Paul as a queer. But Paul's celibacy arguably does the work of queerness, as it is a form of resistance in the vein of Lee Edelman's (2007) vision of queer negativity.

Even though Paul uses a queer strategy for world building, Paul uses it here to underscore how different he is from some of the queerest cats in the empire.[5] Luckritz Marquis mentions that Dionysus is imagined as "effeminate and licentious," but he does not really connect this to queer-

---

the world. This includes those in forced labor and forced marriages. In other words, the tacit acceptance of slavery is not just a historical problem.

5. I am indebted to former research student Zachary Gianelle for insights into the queerness of the cult of Dionysus.

ness. In fact, the Bacchanalia, an annual festival to honor the god, was repressed in Rome during the second century BCE on account of its radical queerness. Not only was the event associated with sexual transgression and excess, but these practices, according to Roman history Livy, included violence and death (*Hist. Rom.* 39.8–9). While Livy's account of the cult likely exaggerated the participants' depravity, one cannot help but imagine the Bacchanalia as a precursor to the performances of queer artists who explore the boundaries between pain and sexuality, such as Ron Athey and Dominic Johnson. Given the queerness of Dionysus and his followers, what does it say that Paul, whom others may read as similar to this Eastern cult, disidentifies himself with the movement? Yes, Paul adopts another queer positionality vis-à-vis sexuality, but he appears to throw his queer sisters under the bus. Is Paul perhaps a self-hating queer? This makes me wonder about the value of focusing on Paul's use of disidentification as a specifically *queer* rhetorical strategy.

Both Schwaller and Luckritz Marquis emphasize the critical aspect of queerness as a form of resistance (and complicity for Schwaller, following Puar) and not as some thing, identity, way of being, or doing related to sex, sexuality, or gender. Even though I understand the movement away from connecting queerness to particular identities, as though individuals and communities had stable identities, I must confess that I personally like some sex and gender transgression in my queerness.

One of the things I find most interesting about Luckritz Marquis's essay is his aim to unsettle "the white, straight, cis-male gaze of the majority of Pauline studies [that] continues to reconstruct an apostle firmly in control of himself and of a system of ideas that are intentional and, as system, thought to be intelligible to the careful critic." This type of willingness to unsettle the field strikes me as one of the most important features of queer biblical interpretation and something we see only rarely.

One essay in this collection that really takes on the possibility of unsettling the conventions of straight biblical studies is Jay Twomey's essay, since Twomey invites another partner, the novelist Michel Faber, to join him in an interpretive *ménage à trois* with Paul. Exploring Faber's (2014) science fiction novel *The Book of Strange New Things*, Twomey looks to a future "Paul" as a means of looking back to find a queer or questioning Paul. Faber uses the model of Paul as an apostle to the gentiles to shape his portrayal of the character Peter's mission to the Oasans, the indigenous population of a far-away planet that a global corporation is considering—so it seems, at least—as a possible alternative to Earth, given the impacts of climate change and the disintegration of political and social structures.

The novel's conceit, sharing the gospel with the inhabitants of a new planet, raises a host of issues and questions, including the complicity of religion in colonizing projects and the *human* nature of religious belief. Among these issues Twomey focuses his attention on Faber's depiction of the protagonist, Peter, and Peter's embodiment of gender expectations and sexual desire. Specifically, Twomey highlights the subtle depiction of Peter's affection for one of the genderless Oasans, who goes by the name Jesus Lover Number 5. Peter tries, rather obliviously, to fit the Oasans into binary gender categories; Peter identifies Jesus Lover Number 5 as female, while another human assumes the Oasan is male. Since he has some unexplored and possibly romantic feelings for Jesus Lover Number 5, "she" must be female according to Peter's perspective. On account of this gendering, as Twomey explains, Peter becomes a locus for unsettling the assumption that heterosexuality and gender categories are natural. The irony here is that Faber manages this even while constructing Peter as about the straightest and most clearly cis-gendered, white man a person can imagine. The portrayal of Peter comes complete with a penchant for mansplaining and a lack of empathy for his wife and future mother of his child. Twomey's sympathetic reading almost makes Peter bearable.

Given the explicit connections that Faber draws between Peter and Paul, Twomey suggests, "*The Book of Strange New Things* at least encourages us to imagine [or to see more clearly?] Paul's own possible infection by the queer alterities he encounters in his travels." Even though Paul appears bound by the protocols of an ancient sexuality that operates upon a masculine/feminine binary, perhaps Paul's encounters with others to some extent unsettle this view. Paul's invocation of an early Christian baptismal formula in Gal 3:28, which claims that there is no longer "male and female, for you are all one in Christ Jesus" (NIV), suggests this possibility for Twomey. This is especially the case if the formula is read as Paul's description of the present rather than a future status. Given this, Twomey suggests that perhaps Paul, like his future counterpart, is queerer than he appears on the surface or, perhaps, that Paul is at least questioning. One possibility that Twomey does not fully explore is that Paul, confronted by differing embodiments of sex and gender (including the Corinthian women's prophetic tendencies), simply clings even more tightly to binary gendered expectations. I would argue that Paul's torturous reasoning in 1 Cor 11:2–16 points to the viability of this third option. And yet I still think that Twomey's suggestion that we imagine the possibility of Paul changing his views on gender and sexuality in light of experiences with others is important and provocative.

Twomey's use of science fiction to explore the contours of Paul's understanding of gender and sexuality offers an interesting contrast to readings that look primarily to the past as a way of queering Paul. In so doing, he evokes Muñoz's (2009) *Cruising Utopia: The Then and There of Queer Futurity*, in which Muñoz challenges the predominance of queer negativity in favor of the more constructive aspects of queerness. For Muñoz, queerness is a type of eschatological hopefulness. Queerness is the "not yet" that we imagine and live into, a little like how some might imagine Paul's eschatological vision. This is an eschatological vision of "belonging in difference," to use a phrase from Muñoz (2009, 20). Given Paul's eschatological vision, queer futurity seems like a productive area for thinking about how we might queer Paul.

Finally, Joseph A. Marchal grapples with the connection between past and present perspectives on sexuality. In so doing, Marchal offers a valuable discussion of what has become a canonical assumption in discussions of ancient sexuality—namely, David Halperin's insight that ancient sexual practices should not be equated with modern understandings of sexual identity, particularly hetero- and homosexual identity. As Halperin succinctly states, "Sexuality is not a somatic fact; it is a cultural effect. Sexuality, then, does have a history—though ... not a very long one" (1989, 257). Marchal recognizes the earlier work of scholars such as Amy Richlin and Bernadette Brooten who have troubled this mandate by examining what they understand as particular ancient sexual identities, *cinaedi* (males who like being penetrated) and lesbians respectively. Marchal builds upon these insights by suggesting the possibility that modern scholars flatten the complexity of ancient experiences and perspectives because of the boundary drawn by Halperin and others.

Marchal suggests that modern scholars overemphasize the perspectives of elite males about what constitutes appropriate and even desirable sexual practices in the ancient context. In other words, we buy into and privilege what Halperin (1990, 34–35) described as "an ethos of penetration and domination." Just as Twomey uses the lens of Faber's novel to rethink Paul, so Marchal leverages theorizing about contemporary queer experiences and ways of being to rethink how we participate in this ethos. Drawing upon the insights of Ann Cvetkovich (2003), Marchal encourages us to question the sexual mathematics that scholars use to understand ancient sex—namely, that penetration equals activity/ strength/the masculine and that receptivity equals passivity/weakness/ the feminine. Then each item separated by the slash would be a single word. Contemporary examples that challenge these binary equations are the power bottom and power femme; as Marchal notes, however, ancient material artifacts, including the raunchy graffiti of Pompeii's *tabernae*, already defied the strict understanding of ancient sexuality that scholars are wont to erect.

By challenging the boundary between the past and the present, Marchal's essay raises the question of why scholars offer queer readings of Pauline and, for that matter, biblical texts. Marchal seemingly wants scholars to think about queering our own relationship to the sources we engage. Quoting Elizabeth Freeman (2010, 109), Marchal argues,

> To look to the bottom means rethinking our relations as users *and* recipients. It also entails feeling our way toward being recipients, not of Paul's letters, but of *their* letters—the ancient recipients of these epistles, named and unnamed, addressed or marginalized, anticipated or unanticipated. We are reading and hearing and passing along *their* mail. If we are receptive not merely to the authority of an empire or apostle, to the demands of a kyriarchal ethos, we cultivate, in the words of Freeman: "a kind of bottomy historiography." (2010, 109)

Interpreters should not just use and penetrate the past; we should allow ourselves to "receive a touch from the past," as the boundary between past and present is more porous than we might think. In light of this, I wonder about the role of scholarly identity in queer readings of Paul and biblical interpretation more generally. Are we reading *as* queers and/or *in search of* queers? Maybe we are reading *in service to* queers?

The idea that scholars might allow themselves to be receptive to the past, to be touched and possibly haunted by its ghosts, raises a question regarding our use of sources. In challenging the boundary between past ideas about sexual practices and contemporary interpretation, Marchal draws upon Holt N. Parker's influential 1997 essay "The Teratogenic Grid." This essay, only one among Parker's multiple publications, proves useful for understanding how power relations defined what constituted socially acceptable sexual practices in the ancient world. The effectiveness of this piece is due mainly, in my estimation, to the author's unambiguous presentation of sexual acts and his construction of an actual grid that describes specific sex acts by naming which appendages are inserted into which orifices in order to describe what constituted acceptable sex. For example, "There is the *vir*, the normal/active/male, who has open to him three possible sexual activities: to fuck someone in the vagina, the anus, or the mouth" (49). The lack of circumlocution aids understanding. However—and this is a big however—the directness with which Parker addresses past sexual acts takes on another valence when read through the lens of the author's admission to and arrest for collecting and trading child pornography.[6] Court documents related to his arrest, conviction, and imprisonment reveal that Parker had an email address, "daddy.cruel@ yahoo.com," that even pointed to his own position on the teratogenic grid. Likewise, these documents reveal that Parker employed the same direct language that characterizes his essay on the teratogenic grid in some of his illegal online conversations.

The resonance between Parker's academic work on the sexual practices characterized as monstrous (*terastios*) and his private life are striking and startling. Parker, one might argue, was unusually receptive to the practices and perspectives of the past even while highlighting historical distance and difference. Perhaps that is why scholars of Paul are, as Marchal notes, quick to underscore how different things were when Paul wrote his missives.[7] In other words, we draw strict boundaries so that we do not receive parts of the past, as a way of ensuring that we do not re-create, normalize, or justify past oppressions and injustices. At least in the case of Parker, however, an arguably extreme case, those boundaries were not sufficient. The case, moreover, raises the question of how scholars, especially those who identify as queer and feminist, express commitments to ethical sexual practices and frameworks—such as consent, mutuality, and being sex positive—in their work: Do we avoid the work of those who operate with practices and frameworks that diverge from our own, use their writings conditionally with appropriate explanatory footnotes, or approach the work as something disconnected from the scholar?

---

6. I first became aware of the charges against Parker in the summer of 2017, when I read Scullin 2016. There are a number of online articles about the case against Parker. See, for example, Grasha 2017. For a link to the FBI complaint against Parker, see "University of Cincinnati Professor Arrested" 2016.

7. I am not faulting Marchal for using Parker. Personally, while I am not ambivalent about Parker's admitted crimes, I am ambivalent about using his work. My conflicting feelings here align with those of other scholars, whom Scullin (2016) quotes anonymously in her online essay about this case.

The main question that these essays (which constitute only a few of the thoughtful contributions to this important volume) raise for me is: What constitutes the queer biblical interpreter? To return to Puar, I wonder if we might imagine the queer biblical interpreter as an assemblage. The queerness of this interpreter does not reside within a gay/lesbian/bi/trans/intersex/asexual/gender fluid/aromantic/asexual/et cetera identity; rather, this queerness emerges out of the interpreter's willingness to move nimbly and nonlinearly across time and location, to embrace difference in terms of affect and aesthetics, and to transgress canons and interpretive conventions as a way of creating space for difference, especially difference in terms of sex, gender, sexuality, and desire. All of the authors discussed here do this skillfully. Of course, as I note with Schwaller's essay, the queer assemblage envisioned by Puar is the terrorist. The terrorist is disruptive and dangerous, which prompts us to ask whether our scholarship is or even can be dangerous. Do the words, ideas, and images we offer disrupt the bodies encountering them? Do they disrupt to the extent that we risk the scholarly self, risk implosion? Do we embrace the opening up of space for queer futures other than our own?

Works Cited

Cvetkovich, Ann. 2003. *An Archive of Feelings: Trauma, Sexuality, and Lesbian Public Cultures*. SerQ. Durham: Duke University Press.

Edelman, Lee. 2007. "Ever After: History, Negativity, and the Social." *SAQ* 106:469–76.

Faber, Michel. 2014. *The Book of Strange New Things: A Novel*. London: Hogarth.

Freeman, Elizabeth. 2010. *Time Binds: Queer Temporalities, Queer Histories*. PM. Durham: Duke University Press.

Grasha, Kevin. 2017. "Ex-UC Professor Admits Child Porn 'Addiction.'" Cincinnati.com, January 26. https://tinyurl.com/SBL0699v.

Halperin, David M. 1989. "Is There a History of Sexuality?" *HistTh* 28.3:257–74.

———. 1990. *One Hundred Years of Homosexuality: And Other Essays on Greek Love*. NAW. New York: Routledge.

Love, Heather. 2007. *Feeling Backward: Loss and the Politics of Queer History*. Cambridge: Harvard University Press.

Marchal, Joseph A. 2011. "The Usefulness of an Onesimus: The Sexual Use of Slaves and Paul's Letter to Philemon." *JBL* 130:749–70.

Muñoz, José Esteban. 1999. *Disidentifications: Queers of Color and the Performance of Politics*. CSA. Minneapolis: University of Minnesota Press.

——. 2009. *Cruising Utopia: The Then and There of Queer Futurity*. Sexual Cultures. New York: New York University Press.

Parker, Holt N. 1997. "The Teratogenic Grid." Pages 47–65 in *Roman Sexualities*. Edited by Judith P. Hallett and Marilyn B. Skinner. Princeton: Princeton University Press.

Puar, Jasbir K. 2005. "Queer Times, Queer Assemblages." *SocT* 23:121–39.

——. 2007. *Terrorist Assemblages: Homonationalism in Queer Times*. NW. Durham: Duke University Press.

Scullin, Sarah. 2016. "Making a Monster." Eidolon, March 24. https://tinyurl.com/https-tinyurl-com-SBL0699e/.

Shaner, Katherine A. 2018. *Enslaved Leadership in Early Christianity*. New York: Oxford University Press.

"University of Cincinnati Professor Arrested on Child Pornography Charges." 2016. WKRC. March 15. https://tinyurl.com/SBL0699d/.

Getting to the Bottom of Paul's Letters, or Getting Real with Biblical Studies?

Tat-siong Benny Liew

Just as *queer* has been turned from a derogatory term into one of self-identification, the tendency to present queer as an undesirably grotesque and outlaw figure becomes, in this wonderful collection of essays, a positive and productive entry point to interrogate Paul's letters. For me, the variety of images—such as children (Guy), slaves (Schwaller), animals (Hartman), monsters (Nicolet), and freaks (Twomey)—used in these essays to emphasize, scrutinize, and utilize the idea of the queer can all fall under the category of the "inhuman," as arguably pointed out most clearly in Benjamin H. Dunning's essay (see also Runions 2014, 179–212). While the inclusion of children as an inhuman category may strike some sentimental readers of the twenty-first century as inappropriate, we must note that children in ancient Greco-Roman traditions are often understood as sharing a similar nature with animals; as a result, they are often depicted as accompanied by and playing with animals (Dasen 2011, 311). Xenophon felt completely comfortable, for instance, calling a child a "cute puppy" (*Cyr.* 1.4.4). In fact, Plato recommends swaddling or massaging a child in the first two years of his or her life because a child in those early years is comparable to wax and needs to be properly molded or made into a human (*Leg.* 7.789e); without such swaddling, a child would keep on walking on all fours like an animal (Dasen 2011, 302).

In any case, the inhuman is threatening because it is not simply nonhuman. As Slavoj Žižek (2005, 159–60) suggests, the inhuman is "monstrous" because "although it negates what we understand as humanity, is inherent to being human." In other words, the inhuman remains internal to humanity rather than external to it, despite being marked by a terrifying lack and/or excess; as such, the inhuman threatens human identity and boundary. If the inhuman's combination of familiarity and unfamiliarity to the human evokes what Sigmund Freud (1955, 219–52) calls "the uncanny," the term *inhuman* itself calls to mind what Jacques Lacan (2008, 51–86) does with *la chose* or *das Ding*—in English, "the Thing" (see also Nasrallah 2014). According to Lacan, the Thing represents an intrusion of the Real, which exceeds and threatens the Symbolic order (namely, law and language) that organizes and gives us a coherent but really fashioned and fantastical reality (see Chang 2012, 8–9).

The reality under threat in this anthology is primarily what Paul's letters seek to construct and impose on various Christ-following assemblies regarding gender and sexuality. The queer as inhuman and the queering of the inhuman expose not only Paul's illusion of control but also the contradictions and excesses of his own vision. As their constant and consistent employment of the term *assembly* (or the Greek *ekklēsia*) shows, contributors to this anthology generally assume Elisabeth Schüssler Fiorenza's (1987) position and read Paul's letters within rhetorical situations where Paul's audience might or might not have been persuaded to agree with Paul's viewpoints. In ways similar to what Schüssler Fiorenza suggests about their counterparts in the first century, Paul's readers in this anthology end up rejecting or disidentifying with his attempt to create a united community that is based on conformity. Mikhail Bakhtin (1984) has also theorized about the polyphonic, multivocal, or heteroglossic dynamics *within* any discourse, so discourses are inevitably dialogical. These essays therefore emphasize, in Midori E. Hartman's words, "the radical possibility of the *ekklēsia*'s interpretation of the Christ message." This radical possibility is emphasized, for example, in response to Paul's self-identification as a slave and Paul's self-presentation through a textual parade, including that of a Dionysian procession, in his correspondences with the Corinthians, as Tyler M. Schwaller and Timothy Luckritz Marquis argue, respectively. Paul might have tried to exert pressure and control on various assemblies, but he could not guarantee how his letters would be received or how his words would be interpreted. In various ways, then, the essays in this collection query and queer hegemonic forms and inhuman forces of community and belonging, especially when it comes to matters regarding gender and sexuality. As Ann Laura Stoler has argued,

> To study the intimate is not to turn away from structures of dominance.... Foucault's "biopolitics" ... provides not an abstract model but one analytical tool for asking grounded questions about whose bodies and selves

were made vulnerable, when, why, and how—and whose were not.... It reminds us how central the emotional economy of sexual access, parenting, and domestic arrangements have been to colonial politics. (2006, 13–14, emphasis original)

Paul's castigation of gentile sexual practice, as mentioned by several contributors—especially Lindsey Guy, Midori E. Hartman, and James N. Hoke—reveals how the presence of what Paul sees as sexual deviance may ironically be tied to the boundary-crossing logic of Paul's mission to the gentiles. As Hoke puts it, "The Thessalonian Christ followers live among and, indeed, are from these [supposedly deviant] *ethnē*." Given Paul's mission of going out and bringing in the nations, it should not be surprising that certain alien practices, including sexual ones, might be found in the assemblies he founded or helped form. Perhaps Paul scapegoated certain sex acts and sexual dissidents so these early Christ-following assemblies would gain recognition from or inclusion in the empire, as Hoke suggests. Alternatively, perhaps Paul was simultaneously fascinated and terrified by the nations. Destabilizing existing boundaries inevitably blurs together the interior with the exterior, thus creating what Lacan (2008, 171) calls *extimité*, or "extimate," with the external, exotic, or estranged actually becoming internal, intimate, and innate. We see similar dynamics in the ways that imperialistic expansions have resulted in the presence of immigrant communities and various foreign practices within the homelands and heartlands of empires. Paul's rhetoric may then be read as his attempt, in ways typical of colonizers, to cover over the alterity that he himself introduces by blaming others. Paul sought to reestablish a boundary by removing a sense of belonging from some who had already been incorporated into the orbit of his gospel. While Paul welcomed the nations to become part of Christ-following assemblies *as* the nations (i.e., without the need for circumcision), Paul did expect them, as a result of this affiliation, to live different lives as "ex-*ethnē*," to use Hartman's terminology. Paul's attempt to create and maintain a coherent community with homogeneous practices betrays, therefore, the fact that his gospel is not as free, democratic, or open to all as it seems. We do know from other noncanonical writings that early Christ-following assemblies might have had vastly diverse understandings and practices, as many of the contributors to this volume, following Schüssler Fiorenza, assume. The Gospel of Mary, for example, suggests that what one does with one's body is never sinful; what is sinful is mistaking one's physical body for one's true self (see King 2003).

Did some of the assemblies to which Paul wrote interpret his gospel of freedom in similar ways? If so, is it conceivable that Paul's opposition to and aggression against certain queer understandings and practices might actually be caused by his jealousy or envy of the *greater* freedom being enjoyed by these Christ followers? I cannot help but wonder about these questions given the connections with Lacan that I mentioned above.

To be fair, several contributors do see Paul himself as being subversive in some ways. In addition to focusing on different letters by Paul, they also bring different emphases. While both Hoke and Hartman fault Paul for ending up privileging Roman norms to keep the assemblies from getting any queerer, Timothy Luckritz Marquis and Jay Twomey seem more inclined to emphasize the openings that Paul's rhetoric provides for further queer variations in the future without highlighting Paul's desire to rein in the assemblies. Having said that, there are certainly more than sufficient overlaps and crossings among the various essays to make this a delightfully coherent collection. For instance, several authors (Guy, Hoke, and Schwaller) underscore the economic context or dynamics in their reading of Paul's letters. Hartman's emphasis on animality is echoed by Schwaller's point that slaves in Paul's time were "akin to animals" and were hence threats to "ideal humanity," while both Schwaller and Hoke refer to Jasbir K. Puar's work in order to caution that queerness can become complicit with dominant and oppressive discourse. The implication of Paul's rhetoric about growth and maturity on children, as Guy discusses in the case of 1 Corinthians, is, as Valérie Nicolet shows, also found in Gal 4:1, 6–7, though Nicolet does not develop her reading of those verses in the direction that Guy does.

The anthology is also well planned, with articles focusing on different letters from Paul, such as Romans (Dunning, Marchal), 1 Corinthians (Guy, Hartman, Schwaller), 2 Corinthians (Luckritz Marquis, Schwaller), Galatians (Nicolet, Twomey), 1 Thessalonians (Hoke, Marchal), and Philemon (Marchal). Readers will no doubt observe that only one of Paul's seven authentic letters—Philippians—is missing in this lineup. Despite that lacuna, this collection of essays gives me plenty to consider and reconsider.

The inhuman figure in many of these essays points to the failure to normalize in the subjectivation process that has long been explored by Michel Foucault (1988–1990). I appreciate how authors in this anthology discuss this failure through the inhuman for the purposes of pleasure rather than for purposes of protest (see Chang 2012). They do not put the inhuman in the position of Freud's woman, who is forever trapped within a longing for something she lacks by going after all kinds of substitutes (see Chow 1994, 129). In other words, they celebrate the queer as inhuman or the inhuman as queer. By not making arguments that the inhuman is actually human, they refuse to reinforce the exclusion of whoever or whatever that does not fit the human norm. Hoke's essay on homonationalism helpfully points out how tempting and easy it is for sociopolitical dissidents, even sexually deviant dissidents, to (re)make themselves into "subjects worthy of rehabilitation" (Puar 2007, 38). Writing about Paul's emphasis that the Thessalonians become sexually exceptional and respectable in the eyes of the larger society and hence critiquing Paul's Romanormativity in 1 Thessalonians, Hoke's statement about "sexual exceptionalism" is true and readily transferrable to the problem of (re)fortifying the human as norm: "Being exceptionally sexually moral produces bodies that are sexually immoral exceptions." Or, in the telling words of Nancy Armstrong,

> To insist on being "subjects" as opposed to "objects" is to assume that we must have certain powers…; these powers make "us" human. According to the logic governing such thinking as it was formulated…, only certain kinds of subjects are really subjects; to be human, anyone must be one of "us." (1990, 33)

Instead of assuming that humans are the only acceptable and real subjects, contributors to this anthology embrace the inhuman—often through a creative mixing of queer, animal, affect, and postcolonial studies—as a powerful counterhegemonic trope. Nicolet, for instance, refers to Susan Stryker's (1994) performance of "transgender rage" and proposes that "monsters are angelic, even prophetic, figures requiring, even demanding greater attention…. Thus, monsters have the potential to question this desire for an ideal body." Confronted with the inhuman, readers are asked to imagine and reconstruct some form of queerness at the heart of many early Christ-following assemblies despite or perhaps even because of Paul's letters. As Nicolet argues in light of Paul's own criticism of circumcised, female, and enslaved bodies in Galatians, this queerness is actually found in Paul's own body (which Paul presents as maternal, disgusting, and stigmatized) as well as in the Galatian assembly's baptized, re-created, and hybrid body (which Paul sees as embodying Christ in drag and as united in one despite differences in ethnicity, status, and gender). Or, as Hartman notes, Paul's use of ritualistic language and the plural *pornoi* in 1 Cor 5 to warn against *porneia* shows that this problem "can never be completely excised." This is especially so and quintessentially queer, adds Schwaller, if one takes into consideration slaves who belonged to the assemblies, including Paul's self-identification as "a slave to all" in 1 Cor 9, given how bodies of slaves were readily available for sexual uses by their masters. The same can be said of Twomey's reading of Gal 3:28 as an "abolition of dimorphic sexuality," Dunning's reading of Rom 1 to underline Eve's haunting presence in Paul's anthropological system that supposedly centers on a male Adam and a male Christ, Guy's reading of a Christ-following assembly as a family in drag because Paul's ascetic emphasis in 1 Corinthians actually denies the logic of family, and Luckritz Marquis's reading of Paul's words in 2 Cor 1–9 in light of Dionysus's foreign, suspicious, and deviant associations. Is Paul, as Julia Kristeva's (1982) theory of abjection proposes, trying to disavow and flush out what is a part of his gospel and his assemblies by projecting the queer or the inhuman onto some external or externalized others? Both Paul and the assemblies to which he wrote come across as more queer, complicated, and multifarious—and hence, to me, more real—in this anthology.

The desire to, in Luckritz Marquis's words, "decenter" and "disidentify with" Paul takes an even queerer turn in Joseph A. Marchal's essay. Seeking to rethink how the so-called passive partner in sexual acts during Paul's time might have agency for both pleasure and power, Marchal ambitiously proposes a "more porous" relation between two sets of seemingly binary opposites: on the one hand, active penetration and passive reception, and on the other, Paul's texts from the past and queer questions of the present. In fact, the anthology's emphasis on how different Christ-following assemblies might have variously interpreted Paul's gospel and responded to Paul's letters in general, and Marchal's attempt to reconsider "the bottom" in particular, brings out something that biblical scholars, especially those who are more historically inclined, do not generally (want to?) talk about—namely, the importance of imagination and the concern with the present in our work.

Hayden White (1973, 1987), of course, pointed out decades ago that while people working with the past like to think that they are working with the real past, they must rely on an often-implicit framework to imagine and organize that past in and through a narrative. Heather R. White's essay in this volume certainly shows how an implicit heteronormative framework was at work in modern English translations of the Bible. In addition to talking about how our work about the past involves our active manipulation rather than merely passive collection of data, Michel de

Certeau (1986, 1988; see also Nasrallah 2015) points to our dependence on the modern and mighty computer, and hence our own embeddedness in the present. This is further evidenced in this anthology by the pervasive references to cutting-edge queer scholarship (especially the work of Jasbir K. Puar, Judith Butler, Judith Halberstam, and José Esteban Muñoz), to—albeit to a lesser extent—current works in the classics (particularly by Hoke, Luckritz Marquis, and Marchal), and, in a single but spectacular case (by Twomey), to a 2014 science fiction novel that seems to literalize the title of Judith Halberstam's (2005) influential book, *In a Queer Time and Place*. Today's readers will and do bring their questions and their contemporary resources to their reading of Paul's letters. If John Ellis (1974, 44) is correct in defining literature as texts "that are used by society in such a way that the text is not taken as specifically relevant to the immediate context of its origin," then biblical literature like Paul's can hardly be confined to its original or "immediate context"—even those letters are by definition occasional. As J. Albert Harrill (2000, 175) has suggested, "Contemporary moral debate can and does shape broad and influential trends in biblical criticism." If this anthology, as I mentioned earlier, emphasizes the failure of the subjectivation process, it confronts us with not only the failure to normalize sexual subjects (by Paul and others) but arguably also (as Luckritz Marquis discusses more explicitly) the failure to engender a monolithic tradition of "real" biblical scholars who identify with Paul and read Paul's letters in a certain way. Today's assembly of biblical scholars is as diverse as a first-century Christ-following assembly being assumed in this anthology; their biblical scholarship involves different understandings and different practices, including even queer ones that others may deem as perhaps not inhuman but certainly incorrect. Despite the rigid "regime of truth and error" (Foucault 2003, 164) that many of these contributors went through in their formal education within the discipline of biblical studies, they came up with this collection of counterreadings, counterstories that are, in my view, similar to de Certeau's (1986) pluralized "heterologies." These readings of Paul's letters do not sharply separate the past from the present by inscribing or imprisoning the (minoritized) other, whether that is Paul or an assembly of early Christ followers to whom Paul wrote, in the past; they are committed to know these (minoritized) others without domesticating them or suggesting that they can be fully known (see Buchanan 1996). Instead, they work with the present and the past to open up real questions, questions of which we will never be able to get to the bottom but through which there can be real academic and political effects.

Works Cited

Armstrong, Nancy. 1990. "The Occidental Alice." *dif* 2:3–40.

Bakhtin, Mikhail. 1984. *Problems of Dostoevsky's Poetics*. Edited and translated by Caryl Emerson. Minneapolis: University of Minnesota Press.

Buchanan, Ian. 1996. "What Is Heterology?" *NBf* 77:483–93.

Certeau, Michel de. 1986. *Heterologies: Discourse on the Other*. Translated by Brian Massumi. Minneapolis: University of Minnesota Press.

———. 1988. *The Writing of History*. Translated by Tom Conley. New York: Columbia University Press.

Chang, Juliana. 2012. *Inhuman Citizenship: Traumatic Enjoyment and Asian American Literature*. Minnesota: University of Minnesota Press.

Chow, Rey. 1994. "Where Have All the Natives Gone?" Pages 125–51 in *Displacements: Cultural Identities in Question*. Edited by Angelika Bammer. Bloomington: Indiana University Press.

Dasen, Véronique. 2011. "Childbirth and Infancy in Greek and Roman Antiquity." Pages 291–314 in *A Companion to Families in the Greek and Roman Worlds*. Edited by Beryl Rawson. Malden, MA: Wiley-Blackwell.

Ellis, John. 1974. *The Theory of Literary Criticism: A Logical Analysis*. Berkeley: University of California Press.

Foucault, Michel. 1988–1990. *History of Sexuality*. 3 vols. Translated by Robert Hurley. Repr. ed. New York: Vintage.

———. 2003. *Society Must Be Defended: Lectures at the College de France 1975–76*. Edited by Mauro Bertani and Alessandro Fontana. Translated by David Macey. New York: Picador.

Freud, Sigmund. 1955. *An Infantile Neurosis and other Works*. Vol. 17 of *The Standard Edition of the Complete Psychological Works of Sigmund Freud*. Translated by James Strachey. London: Hogarth.

Halberstam, Judith. 2005. *In a Queer Time and Place: Transgender Bodies, Subcultural Lives*. Sexual Cultures. New York: New York University Press.

Harrill, J. Albert. 2000. "The Use of the New Testament in the American Slave Controversy: A Case History in the Hermeneutical Tension between Biblical Criticism and Christian Moral Debate." *RelAmer* 10:149–86.

King, Karen L. 2003. *The Gospel of Mary of Magdala: Jesus and the First Woman Apostle*. Santa Rosa, CA: Polebridge.

Kristeva, Julia. 1982. *Powers of Horror: An Essay on Abjection*. New York: Columbia University Press.

Lacan, Jacques. 2008. *The Ethics of Psychoanalysis, 1959–1960: The Seminar of Jacques Lacan Book VII*. Edited by Jacques-Alain Miller. Translated by Dennis Porter. New York: Routledge.

Nasrallah, Laura S. 2014. "'You Were Bought with a Price': Freedpersons and Things in 1 Corinthians." Pages 54–73 in *Corinth in Contrast: Studies in Inequality*. Edited by Steven J. Friesen, Sarah A. James, and Daniel N. Schowalter. Leiden: Brill.

———. 2015. "Out of Love for Paul: History and Fiction and the Afterlife of the Apostle Paul." Pages 73–96 in *Early Christian and Jewish Narrative: The Role of Religion in Shaping Narrative Form*. Edited by Ilaria Ramelli and Judith Perkins. Tübingen: Mohr Siebeck.

Puar, Jasbir K. 2007. *Terrorist Assemblages: Homonationalism in Queer Times*. NW. Durham: Duke University Press.

Runions, Erin. 2014. *The Babylon Complex: Theopolitical Fantasies of War, Sex, and Sovereignty*. New York: Fordham University Press.

Schüssler Fiorenza, Elisabeth. 1987. "Rhetorical Situation and Historical Reconstruction in 1 Corinthians." *NTS* 33:386–403.

Stoler, Ann Laura. 2006. "Intimidations of Empire: Predicaments of the Tactile and Unseen." Pages 1–22 in *Haunted by Empire: Geographies of Intimacy in North American History*. Edited by Ann Laura Stoler. Durham: Duke University Press.

Stryker, Susan. 1994. "My Words to Victor Frankenstein above the Village of Chamounix: Performing Transgender Rage." *GLQ* 1:237–54.

White, Hayden. 1973. *Metahistory: The Historical Imagination in Nineteenth-Century Europe*. Baltimore: Johns Hopkins University Press.

———. 1987. *The Content of the Form: Narrative Discourse and Historical Representation*. Baltimore: Johns Hopkins University Press.

Žižek, Slavoj. 2005. "Neighbors and Other Monsters: A Plea for Ethical Violence." Pages 135–90 in *The Neighbor: Three Inquiries in Political Theology*. By Slavoj Žižek, Eric L. Santner, and Kenneth Reinhard. Chicago: University of Chicago Press.

Survival and the Nonetheless

Will Stockton

1.

I take, one sentence at a time, one of the passages in Eve Kosofsky Sedgwick's essay "Queer and Now" to which I—a former disciple of Christ *cum* queer atheist literary scholar—attach:

> I think that for many of us in childhood the ability to attach intently to a few cultural objects, objects of high or popular culture or both, objects whose meaning seemed mysterious, excessive, or oblique in relation to the codes most readily available to us, became a prime source of survival (1993, 3).

A few of my childhood's high culture objects: Shakespeare plays, Thomas Hardy novels, and Beethoven sonatas. A few of my childhood's pop culture objects: Michael Jackson, the Rocky film series, and the epistles of Paul, especially their more athletic passages such as 2 Tim 4:7: "I have fought the good fight, I have finished the race, I have kept the faith."[1]

I did not know until six or seven years ago that Paul most likely did not write 2 Timothy, or 1 Timothy for that matter. I learned about the deutero-Pauline epistles on Wikipedia. Would my youthful attachment to Christ's spiritual athlete have grown or diminished had I been a better student of ancient history, early Christianity, Pauline theology, and Greek?

---

1. All biblical translations are from the NIV.

2.

Paul (the real one) wrote to the Corinthians: "When I was a child, I talked like a child, I thought like a child, I reasoned like a child. When I became a man, I put the ways of childhood behind me" (1 Cor 13:11). When I became an adult, I put away my faith in Christ. I did not, however, lose my attachment to certain objects of Christian faith. In their adult form, queer children often retain their fascination with those objects whose meaning seemed mysterious, excessive, oblique. Our relationship to these objects may take on new dimensions: embarrassment or, perhaps, scholarly mastery. But we do not so easily let go of those objects that helped us survive.

3.

For evangelical Christians like my former self, the apostle Paul is both high *and* pop culture. High because his epistles come from on high and represent the height of wisdom. They are the height of *all* culture. There is no knowledge more rarified—and, paradoxically, more widely available—than knowledge of salvation in Jesus Christ.

Paul is pop culture, too, because Christianity is, and has long been, popular. Evangelical Christians often position themselves against a monolith they call "the culture," but the truth remains that evangelicals have profoundly shaped contemporary culture, or cultures, especially in the West, and especially in the United States. Contemporary pop culture Paul is not quite the apostle found in the pages of these essays. Pop culture Paul does not worry over the lingering traces of ethnic monstrosity among the converts (Nicolet). He does not disidentify with Dionysus—unwittingly, perhaps, inviting his readers *not* to follow his example (Luckritz Marquis). He does not identify as a slave in order to queer, even if only to also normalize, the body of Christ (Schwaller). Pop culture Paul brings to all nations the simple message of love: compassion, sacrifice, and martyrdom, always, if only implicitly, heterosexual.

4.

As a child, I wanted to be a boxer, sort of. That athletic investment was, and remains, weak. The boxing in the Rocky movies interested me less than the running. Rocky in Converse high tops and gray sweat suits jogging through early-morning Philadelphia streets; in shorts and a tank-top on the beaches of LA; in jeans, boots, and a fur-lined leather coat on a Siberian mountain.

Little about the Rocky films is oblique in relation to the codes of American sports narrative. More mysterious to my childhood self: my fascination with Sylvester Stallone's striding musculature.

5.

Sedgwick (1993, 3) continues: "We needed for there to be sites where the meanings didn't line up tidily with one another, and we learned to invest those sites with fascination and love." The Paul who claimed authorship of 2 Timothy probably was not the real Paul. The meanings of the former do not always line up with the latter. But that imposter Paul invested his imitation with as much fascination and love as I did my reading of all the Pauline epistles. The real Paul wrote, too, about running and fighting; see 1 Cor 9:24: "Do you not know that in a race all the runners run, but only one gets the prize? Run in such a way as to get the prize." See also Phil 3:14: "I press on toward the goal to win the prize for which God has called me heavenward in Jesus Christ."

I am no natural runner. In sixth grade at The Heiskell School, a Christian elementary school in the wealthy Buckhead suburb of Atlanta, Georgia, my PE teacher, Mr. Lewis, a short, boxy man with a thin beard, told me I ran like a girl. He meant that I let my arms swing around. I needed to hold them tight to my side. "I do not run like someone running aimlessly," Paul says. "I do not fight like I am beating the air" (1 Cor 9:26).

6.

One last sentence from Sedgwick (1993, 3): "This [childhood investment] can't help coloring the adult relation to cultural texts and objects; in fact, it's almost hard for me to imagine another way of coming to care enough about literature to give a lifetime to it." Objects of the apostle Paul's childhood fascination include the law, flesh, and gentiles. We can deduce as much from the literature.

7.

Religiously speaking, those "sites where the meanings didn't line up tidily" (Sedgwick 1993, 3) interest two kinds of people: apologists and skeptics.

The former sees their interpretive task as one of cleanup—of alignment *nonetheless*. Benjamin H. Dunning quotes Marcella Althaus-Reid (2000, 24) in the epigraph of his essay on the anthropological (dis)order of Rom 1: "Decent theologies struggle for coherence, the coherence that sexual systems also struggle for."

Several years ago, Hank, a campus youth minister with whom I worked out, asked me to have coffee with him. For thoroughly suspicious reasons, Hank wanted to talk about my work on Shakespeare and Reformation-era marriage theologies. During our conversation, I mentioned that the Paul who only begrudgingly endorses marriage as preferable to burning in 1 Cor 7:9 seemed to me a different Paul than the one who, in Eph 5, enthusiastically likens the relationship between a husband and a wife to that between Christ and the Church. "They're two sides of the same coin," Hank told me. "No," I replied, with no small amount of academic brattiness, "I think they're two different coins."

But I am a skeptic, which is to say, I am no less fascinated by and in love with those sites where meanings do not tidily line up than Hank. Absent a fascination with Paul, there is no way I could have written a book about that particular site, about the differences between the Pauls presented as Paul and all the forms of sexual relationality this impossibly singular Paul is supposed to endorse, prohibit, reluctantly accept, and fear (Stockton 2017).

8.

I did not learn how to run until college, when I took up the sport to distract myself from sexual immorality—from Paul's *porneia*, mostly gay.

9.

At the risk of being quotationally excessive, there is a far more famous passage from Sedgwick's "Queer and Now" that is also worth repeating, if only because it helps tie the disparate pieces of this essay together (my childhood crush on Sylvester Stallone, my afternoon coffee dalliance with an evangelical who showed an outsized interest in my esoteric literature scholarship). I refer to Sedgwick's (1993, 8) definition (or antidefinition) of queerness as "the open mesh of possibilities, gaps, overlaps, dissonances and resonances, lapses and excesses of meaning when the constituent elements of anyone's gender, of anyone's sexuality, aren't made (or *can't be* made), to signify monolithically." What possibilities of gender, of sexuality, was I performing, embodying, and signifying as I ran floppy-armed around the Heiskell School gymnasium? What possibilities was I running from when I finally took up long-distance running—telling myself I was imitating the apostle Paul, for whom physical and spiritual fitness were so intimately linked?

10.

What forms of erotic activity, of desire, is Paul condemning when he orders the Corinthians to flee sexual immorality? He gives one example: a man living with his father's woman (1 Cor 5:1). But his concerns about *porneia* do not reduce to this one incident of incest, and he is not exactly forthcoming with more specifics. *Porneia* has a strategic ambiguity about it; Paul wants it held in reserve, to be deployed whenever he comes across something, anything, that violates his strange combination of Romanormative (Hoke) and apocalyptic sensibilities.

I fooled around with a boy for the first time in seventh grade. That boy is now a man who runs his own ministry. We took off our clothes and took turns laying on top of one another. I reminded him that God is omnipresent. He watches us from the corner of the room. He will be displeased. My friend, always more mature than me, countered: "No, He won't." He meant, I think, that there would be no penetration, no kissing, no sucking, barely even a laying on of hands.

11.

A rainy Monday night in early April of 2018, I went with a friend to an early evening showing of Andrew Hyatt's *Paul, Apostle of Christ* (2018). The film had been out for several weeks. In Anderson, South Carolina, however, the AmStar theater was half full. I would have gone alone; my fascination with such films is so intense. My friend, also named Will, came with me only because I promised to buy his ticket and because he, like me, is a former evangelical with a lingering appetite for objects of Christian pop culture.

The plot of the film is almost entirely apocryphal. It is 67 CE, and half of Rome has burned to the ground. Nero blames the Christians and throws them to the lions. He lights the streets with the burning bodies of believers. He imprisons and sentences their leader Paul to death. Meanwhile, a secret community of Christians, led by Priscilla and Aquila, struggle with the question of whether to remain in Rome or flee to safety. They want word from Paul. They await his wisdom.

The film's title notwithstanding, *Paul, Apostle of Christ* focuses equally on Luke, who uses his government connections to visit Paul in prison. The physician finds the beleaguered apostle at once haunted by the ghosts of his past—the Christians whom he used to persecute—and at peace with his coming execution. At one point in the film, Luke confesses his desire to fight the Romans, to avenge the savagery visited upon the believers in Christ. But paraphrasing 1 Cor 13:4–8 (love is patient, kind, etc.), Paul stills him with the message of love.

Paul, Apostle of Christ stays far away from the actual apostle's anxieties about sex and gender, relations between Jew and gentile, or the church's relationship to the Roman Empire. We do not see this Paul counsel singleness and celibacy or tell women to stay silent in church. Nor does this Paul explain what he meant in Gal 3:28, when he wrote (or perhaps quoted), "There is neither Jew nor Gentile, neither slave nor free, nor is there male and female, for you are all one in Christ Jesus." Near the film's end, this Paul does smuggle out a letter, presumably the first of two, to Timothy, which diligent readers of the Bible will know reminds the young pastor of the reasons for the law ("not for the righteous but for lawbreakers and rebels…, for the sexually immoral, for those practicing homosexuality" [1 Tim 1:9–10]) and which takes the time, too, to dilate on female attire and sexual hierarchy (1 Tim 2:9–15). These are peculiar issues for Paul to contemplate while awaiting execution as Christians supply the city's Roman candles. But the film is not interested in the letter's content—only its smuggling, the act of secret, forbidden communication.

Halfway through the film, Will leaned over his Vanilla Coke (a relic of childhood: "I used to have one every morning on the way to school") to whisper that the handsome, bearded Luke (Jim Caviezel) must have been Paul's "thorn in [the] flesh" (2 Cor 12:7). I laughed. Jim Caviezel is a handsome man. That is why Mel Gibson had him whipped and beaten and hung on a cross. But the queer erotics of *Paul, Apostle of Christ* are less sadomasochist than those of *Passion of the Christ* (2004). The queer erotics of *Paul, Apostle of Christ* are procreative, textually productive. Under the sunlight pouring in from a hole in the roof of the prison cell (a ham-fisted representation of the inspirational light of God), physician and single apostle sit back to back, Paul telling Luke the story of his journeys and Luke writing what will become the book of Acts. Brothers in Christ. Queer collaborators. Somewhere in there, maybe, Paul's gloss on his thorny desire, that prick in his flesh.

12.

Will and I laughed a lot throughout *Paul, Apostle of Christ*. The man behind us cried.

I imagine this man thought Will and me irreverent at best, blasphemous at worst. I felt for him, though, and tried to keep my laughter down.

13.

Reading queerly can entail many different strategies. With the cross-disciplinary growth of queer studies over the past several decades, queer reading methods have only become more expansive. At its most rudimentary, however, reading queerly can mean, as Sedgwick writes, "to smuggle queer representation in where it must be smuggled" (1993, 3). Sometimes this smuggling equates with gay spotting: finding the hidden homosexual. Think, for instance, of John Shelby Spong's (1992, 117) somewhat infamous suggestion that "Paul was a homosexual person," whose repression of his own desire, his identity, produced his antagonism toward sex and the body. More often, queer reading, especially of texts produced in the distant past, entails a mixture of imagination, projection, and restraint—a desire to correspond coupled with a consciousness of the historicity of sex and sexuality identity.

14.

What bounds queer interpretation? What constitutes a persuasive or good queer reading? These questions might sound suspicious, at least to queer ears. If, pace Sedgwick, queerness is recalcitrant to definition, why should a queer hermeneutic be any less so? In practice, however—and I mean the practice sketched out in these chapters—one answer to the first question seems to be something like history itself. And one answer to the second question seems to be something like the reading's production of a rich opacity.

History introduces us to alterity, to new forms of difference, denaturalizing contemporary ideologies of sex and gender, revealing their contingency, the condition of their production. In queer terms, history here is not a monolith, or a cold set of irrefutable facts, but an open mesh of possibilities, gaps, overlaps, and excesses of meaning. Reading Paul queerly means reading Paul historically and reading for those moments in Paul's epistles when the "constituent elements of anyone's gender, of anyone's sexuality, aren't made (or *can't be* made) to signify monolithically" (Sedgwick 1993, 3)—not within our own contemporary sex/gender system, which is hardly monolithic and quite wobbly, but in the Greco-Roman one, which good historicizing shows is also wobbly.

15.

The question of method seems to have played out somewhat differently in biblical studies than in my home field of Renaissance studies. Among queer early modernists, historicizing is sometimes suspect as normalizing, antagonistic to queerness; to historicize might mean to straighten out, to correct, in ways eerily suggestive of ex-gay therapy. The so-called unhistorical turn in queer Renaissance studies has urged us, instead, to forms of presentism, such that queerness resides not so much in the text's original conditions of production as in its many transformed and reimagined afterlives, its resonances with queer communities now (see Goldberg and Menon 2005; Traub 2013). One reason queer reading works differently in biblical studies, I imagine, is simply that the texts are far more ancient and, at the risk of undermining my own work, culturally important. No one cites Shakespeare in condemnation of gay, lesbian, or trans people. They cite Paul.

Under these conditions, historicizing is a tool of present queer survival.

16.

Yet as Heather R. White notes in the opening sentence of her chapter, "when conservative Christians argue that their Bibles tell them that homosexuality is immoral, they are not wrong." Their Bibles tell them as much via reductive, anachronistic translations (like "homosexuality" in the NIV's 1 Tim 1:10) and topical indexes that cross-reference passages that previous readers did not think to align. The Bible says that homosexuality is wrong because the Bible is a historically accretive text, one whose ostensibly manifest content has transformed alongside ideologies of sex and gender. By tracking changes in what "the Bible says," White peels back the ostensibly manifest content of homosexual condemnation to reveal, instead, sites of difference, conflict, and contestation, which are often intelligible only in terms of ancient concerns.

Today's gays are not temple prostitutes, however many of us may have hooked up at church camp.

But it is also true that by "homosexuality," conservative Christians mean *some* of the things the Bible, in ancient and modern contexts, condemned as sexual immorality: men getting fucked in the ass or sucking dick, and women fucking, with hands or tongues or clitorises, other women. In Rom 1, most scholars agree, Paul condemns these acts without naming them, coding them as unnatural in relation to the natural distinction between active/masculine and passive/feminine. These people who commit these acts by no means exhaust the modern category of the homosexual. Their etiologies are actually completely different: Paul's queers have been given over by God to their lust because of their sin of idolatry, whereas homosexuality results from some complex confluence of genetic, environmental, historical, and discursive factors. But today's homosexuals *do* many of the same things with their bodies that Paul's queers do.

One strain in antihomophobic biblical scholarship has worked to historicize our way out of condemnation, to take the so-called clobber passages and so carefully contextualize them that they do not—could not—refer to us. Hence the real relief offered to me and other gay Christians by books like Daniel A. Helminiak's (1994) *What the Bible Really Says about Homosexuality*. I purchased Helminiak's book my freshman year of college, impressed and reassured by the PhD following the author's name on the cover. I needed—wanted—expert guidance; my survival as a Christian and a human being were at stake.

For Helminiak, the Bible does not say anything about homosexuality, because homosexuality—as a sexuality, a sexual identity—did not exist in the ancient world. The Bible is always talking about something other than what we talk about when we talk about homosexuality. *What the Bible Really Says about Homosexuality* offered me survival through the study of history, yes. But in its confident prose, this slim volume of queer Christian apologetics also inspired a new unease. Disassociation with biblical condemnation could not be that easy. It could not be the case that homosexuality and the sexualities of the ancient world *simply* do not line up—that Paul, the pseudo-Pauls, and the authors of Genesis, Leviticus, and Deuteronomy were not talking about anything I had done or wanted to do with my body.

Historical difference is not that monolithic. The relationship between my body, ancient history, and the Bible is an open mesh of possibilities.

17.

Another strain of antihomophobic biblical criticism, exemplified in these chapters, questions whether Paul's thought should be so determinative, in the first place, of Christian sexual morality and practice. The contentious bodies in this book are the bodies that argue with Paul—the bodies that contest his prescriptions: Corinthians practicing *porneia* (Hartman) and senselessly prophesying (Guy), Onesimus and the Thessalonian vessels sharing "knowing looks with their associates over their washing of Arretine ware or under colorful wall paintings" (Marchal), even Michel Faber's Peter, a Pauline evangelist who rejects the apostle's misogyny but still struggles to adapt a progressive Christian sexual ethics to an alien race (Twomey).

18.

Thesis: In its evangelical and fundamentalist forms, if not also its many other forms, Christianity has survived by adapting to, not resisting, the evolution of modern sexual ideologies.

19.

One final quote, this time from Paul, via Luke: "I consider my life worth nothing to me; my only aim is to finish the race and complete the task the Lord Jesus has given me—the task of testifying to the good news of God's grace" (Acts 20:24).

Paul, Apostle of Christ concludes with Paul laying his head on the chopping block and the executioner raising his sword. Paul and Luke have talked about how to end their book on the history of the early church. Luke rejects any mention of Paul's death. The history began with the ascension of Christ in Jerusalem (Acts 1) and should end with Paul "proclaim[ing] the kingdom of God" in Rome (Acts 28:31). If Acts is a training montage for future apostles, Paul should finish the race alive, preaching "with all boldness and without hinderance" (Acts 28:31).

It is not a good argument. I am not even sure I understand it. The film makes a flimsy effort to explain why Acts does not end with what the film nonetheless presents as the last historical act of the apostle. But I like the argument because it admits that some imagination is required to produce Christian history. Desire shapes the story around and through the facts of the historical record. (And how factual is Acts to begin with?) Desire for coherence creates a univocal Paul, sorts the authentic from the apocryphal, smoothes out the differences in the gospel accounts of Jesus's life, and plots out the end of days. But desire can also create a history more or less monolithic, more or less open to possibility.

For the sobbing man behind Will and me, *Paul, Apostle of Christ* forged an unimpeachable episode in the history of Christian persecution. At least, I assume so; this man's tears testify to his belief in the martyrdom of Paul the apostle, the inspired rightness of all of Paul's teachings, and the accurate recording of Paul's life by his friend Luke. His tears might further testify to his belief in the ongoing persecution of the church in contemporary secular (atheist, feminist, gay and lesbian, anti-Christian and pro-Islamic) culture. As for Will and myself, we preferred a queerer history; our laughter testified to the "holiness" of the film's history, the erotic possibilities it opened despite itself.

Neither reading, evangelical or queer, hews closer to fact, however much both offer themselves as sources of survival.

Works Cited

Althaus-Reid, Marcella. 2000. *Indecent Theology: Theological Perversions in Sex, Gender and Politics.* New York: Routledge.

Goldberg, Jonathan, and Madhavi Menon. 2005. "Queering History." *PMLA* 120:1608–17.

Helminiak, Daniel A. 1994. *What the Bible Really Says about Homosexuality.* Tajique, NM: Alamo Square.

Sedgwick, Eve Kosofsky. 1993. *Tendencies.* SerQ. Durham: Duke University Press.

Spong, John Shelby. 1992. *Rescuing the Bible from Fundamentalism: A Bishop Rethinks the Meaning of Scripture.* New York: HarperOne.

Stockton, Will. 2017. *Members of His Body: Shakespeare, Paul, and a Theology of Nonmonogamy.* New York: Fordham University Press.

Traub, Valerie. 2013. "The New Unhistoricism in Queer Studies." *PMLA* 128:21–39.

Contributors

Benjamin H. Dunning is Professor in the Department of Theology at Fordham University with affiliated appointments in Comparative Literature and Women, Gender, and Sexuality Studies. He is the author of *Specters of Paul: Sexual Difference in Early Christian Thought* (2011) and *Christ without Adam: Subjectivity and Sexual Difference in the Philosophers' Paul* (2014) and the editor of the forthcoming *Oxford Handbook of Gender and Sexuality in the New Testament*. He currently chairs the Board of Directors for Fordham University Press and serves as an associate editor for the *Journal of Early Christian Studies*.

Lindsey Guy is a PhD candidate in New Testament and early Christianity at Drew University. Her current research on Revelation engages queer theory and cultural studies in order to illuminate the text's political uses of satire. Guy is an instructor at William Paterson University in New Jersey.

Midori E. Hartman received her PhD in Historical Studies in the area of Christianity in late antiquity from Drew Theological School. Her research interests include the relationship between citizenship and slavery in antiquity, as well as rhetoric, as it intersects with issues of gender, ethnicity, and animality in ancient Christian literature. She is also currently the Web Director for the nonprofit organization Feminist Studies in Religion, Inc.

James N. Hoke is Visiting Assistant Professor of Religion at Luther College. Hoke's research reconstructs conversations within the earliest assemblies of Christ followers and shows how they manifest and contribute to contemporary queer, feminist, and affect theories. Hoke is currently working on a new (first) book, which uses feminist and queer theories of assemblage to think with the wo/men around Paul's Letter to the Romans.

Lynn R. Huber is Professor of Religious Studies at Elon University. Her research focuses on the book of Revelation, including feminist and queer readings of the text. She is the author of *Thinking and Seeing with Women in Revelation* (2011) and has recently explored the queering of Revelation in Keith Haring and William S. Burroughs's 1988 collaboration "Apocalypse" as part of a special forthcoming issue of *CrossCurrents*.

Tat-siong Benny Liew is Class of 1956 Professor in New Testament Studies at College of the Holy Cross. He is the author of *Politics of Parousia* (1999) and *What Is Asian American Biblical Hermeneutics?* (2008). He also edited the *Semeia* issue on "The Bible in Asian America" (with Gale A. Yee, 2002), *Postcolonial Interventions* (2009), *They Were All Together in One Place?* (with Randall C. Bailey and Fernando F. Segovia, 2009), *Reading Ideologies* (2011), *Psychoanalytical Mediations between Marxist and Postcolonial Readings of the Bible* (with Erin Runions, 2016), *Present and Future of Biblical Studies* (2018), and *Colonialism and the Bible* (with Fernando F. Segovia, 2018). Liew is also the executive editor of Brill's *Biblical Interpretation* and the series editor of T&T Clark's Study Guides to the New Testament.

Timothy Luckritz Marquis is Instructional Designer at the ALT Lab at Virginia Commonwealth University. He has served as a tenured faculty member at Moravian Theological Seminary and an instructor at the University of North Carolina at Greensboro. After receiving his PhD in religious studies from Yale University in 2008, he published *The Transient Apostle: Paul, Travel, and the Rhetoric of Empire* (2013). He writes on and researches ancient itinerancy, communication, sexuality, ethnicity, and political theology, as well as contemporary issues of mobility, education, and social formation in digital and real-life spaces.

Joseph A. Marchal is Associate Professor of Religious Studies and affiliate faculty in Women's and Gender Studies at Ball State University. Marchal is the author and editor of several works, most recently *The People beside Paul: The Philippian Assembly and History from Below* (2015), *Philippians: Historical Problems, Hierarchical Visions, Hysterical Anxieties* (2017), and *Sexual Disorientations: Queer Temporalities, Affects, Theologies* (with Kent L. Brintnall and Stephen D. Moore, 2018). Marchal has also completed a separate solo-authored project that queerly rethinks our contact with figures, besides Paul, within these letters, titled *Appalling Bodies: Queer Figures before and after Paul's Letters* (2019).

Valérie Nicolet is maître de conférences at the Institut protestant de théologie (faculté de Paris), where she teaches New Testament and ancient Greek. In her research, she focuses on the Pauline letters. She is currently working on the rhetorical construction of the law in Galatians. Her scholarship highlights interdisciplinary approaches, most prominently philosophy and, recently, queer theory. She has published a book on the construction of the self in Romans, *Constructing the Self: Thinking with Paul and Michel Foucault* (2012).

Tyler M. Schwaller is Assistant Professor of Religious Studies and Ackerman/Hurdle Chaplaincy Chair at Wesleyan College. His research focuses on slavery in the Roman Empire; women, gender, and sexuality in early Christianity; feminist and queer theory; and the ethics of biblical interpretation. Schwaller has contributed to *Democratizing Biblical Studies* (2009) and is working on his first book, an examination of how slavery language in the letters of Paul is entangled with the material-discursive conditions of Roman enslavement and contains traces of enslaved life.

Will Stockton is Professor of English at Clemson University. His publications include *Members of His Body: Shakespeare, Paul, and a Theology of Nonmonogamy* (2017) and *Jesus Freak* (with D. Gilson, 2018).

Jay Twomey is Associate Professor of English at the University of Cincinnati. He is the author of *The Pastoral Epistles through the Centuries* (2009) and *2 Corinthians: Crisis and Conflict* (2013) and the coeditor of *Borges and the Bible* (2015).

Heather R. White is Visiting Assistant Professor at the University of Puget Sound, with a joint appointment in the Department of Religion and the Program in Gender and Queer Studies. White is a specialist in American religious history and the author of *Reforming Sodom: Protestants and the Rise of Gay Rights* (2015). White has also coedited (with Gillian Frank and Bethany Moreton) the anthology *Devotions and Desires: Histories of Sexuality and Religion in the Twentieth-Century United States* (2018).

Ancient Sources Index

Modern Authors Index

CPSIA information can be obtained
at www.ICGtesting.com
Printed in the USA
BVHW081210020519
547130BV00001B/1/P